FOR HUMANITY'S SAKE
THE BILDUNGSROMAN IN RUSSIAN CULTURE

For Humanity's Sake is the first study in English to trace the genealogy of the classic Russian novel, from Pushkin to Tolstoy to Dostoevsky. Lina Steiner demonstrates how these writers' shared concern for individual and national education played a major role in forging a Russian cultural identity.

For Humanity's Sake highlights the role of the critic Apollon Grigor'ev, who was first to formulate the difference between Western European and Russian conceptions of national education or Bildung – which he attributed to Russia's special sociopolitical conditions, geographic breadth, and cultural heterogeneity. Steiner also shows how Grigor'ev's cultural vision served as the catalyst for the creative explosion that produced Russia's most famous novels of the 1860s and 1870s.

Positing the classic Russian novel as an inheritor of the Enlightenment's key values – including humanity, self-perfection, and cross-cultural communication – *For Humanity's Sake* offers a unique view of Russian intellectual history and literature.

LINA STEINER is an academic advisor attached to the Chair of Theoretical Philosophy at the Institute for Philosophy at Rheinische Friedrich-Wilhelms-Universität Bonn.

LINA STEINER

For Humanity's Sake

The Bildungsroman in Russian Culture

UNIVERSITY OF TORONTO PRESS
Toronto Buffalo London

© University of Toronto Press 2011
Toronto Buffalo London
utorontopress.com

Reprinted in paperback 2021

ISBN 978-1-4426-4343-7 (cloth)
ISBN 978-1-4875-4182-8 (paper)

Library and Archives Canada Cataloguing in Publication

Title: For humanity's sake : the Bildungsroman in Russian culture / Lina Steiner.
Other titles: Bildungsroman in Russian culture
Names: Steiner, Lina, 1973– author.
Description: Paperback reprint. Originally published 2011. | Includes bibliographical references and index.
Identifiers: Canadiana 20210126167 | ISBN 9781487541828 (softcover)
Subjects: LCSH: Russian fiction – 19th century – History and criticism. | LCSH: National characteristics, Russian, in literature.
Classification: LCC PG3098.3 .S84 2021 | DDC 891.73/309 – dc23

University of Toronto Press acknowledges the financial assistance to its publishing program of the Canada Council for the Arts and the Ontario Arts Council, an agency of the Government of Ontario.

To the memory of my grandparents

Contents

Acknowledgments ix

Introduction 3

Part I: Culture (*Obrazovanie, Bildung*) and the Bildungsroman on Russian Soil

1 Russian Literature from the National Awakening of the 1800s to the Rise of *Pochvennichestvo* in the 1850s 17

2 Apollon Grigor'ev's Theory of Russian Culture 29

3 Yurii Lotman's Idea of the 'Semiosphere' 38

4 The Semiospheric Novel and the Broadening of Cultural Self-Consciousness 49

Part II: Nineteenth-Century Russian Novels of Emergence

5 Pushkin's Quest for National Culture: *The Captain's Daughter* as a Russian Bildungsroman 57

6 Educating Russia, Building Humanity: Tolstoy's *War and Peace* 91

7 Dostoevsky on Individual Reform and National
  Reconciliation: *The Adolescent*   135

Conclusion   174

Appendix: The Russian Texts   181

Notes   189

Bibliography   239

Index   265

Acknowledgments

My debts of gratitude are many, and it is a pleasure to acknowledge the largest of them here. I have always been fortunate in my teachers. My high school teacher of Russian and world literature, Galina Borisovna Khmyrova, shielded my young mind from the chaos and bitterness of the post-Soviet debacle by turning my attention to the rich world of poetry, novels, and drama, from Sophocles' *Antigone* to Mayakovsky's *Misteriia-Buff*. I was equally fortunate at Moscow University and at Yale, where I first understood the meaning of true scholarship. My mentors, including my dissertation advisors Peter Brooks and Michael Holquist, as well as Vladimir Alexandrov, Katerina Clark, Paul Fry, and Caryl Emerson, who graciously agreed to serve as an outside member of my dissertation committee, presented me with examples of intellectual excellence that continue to inspire – and I hope will forever inspire – my work.

This book on the Russian Bildungsroman is not a revised version of my dissertation, but a new work that I conceived and wrote at the University of Chicago, where I greatly profited from frequent conversations with the members of my department, including Robert Bird, the late Anna Lisa Crone, Victor Friedman, Lenore Grenoble, Daria Khitrova, Bożena Shallcross, and Malynne Sternstein, as well as a number of remarkable scholars across the Humanities division, including James Chandler, Sheila Fitzpatrick, Michael Forster, Paul Friedrich, the late Richard Hellie, Boris Maslov, Itzhak Melamed, Françoise Meltzer, David Nirenberg, Thomas Pavel, Joshua Scodel, Neta Stahl, Justin Steinberg, Yuri Tsivian, and David Wellbery.

The project that finally evolved owes much to many other individuals and institutions. Thus I am especially grateful to the Franke Institute for the Humanities for affording me the time to work on this manuscript, and to the fellows at the Franke in 2006–7 and the interim director, Françoise Meltzer, for their thoughtful comments on my work.

I want to express my heartfelt gratitude to Martha Roth, the Dean of Humanities at Chicago, and to Mr Harve A. Ferill, for generous funds that made possible the publication of this book.

Many colleagues and friends read and commented on different chapters at various stages of their creation: my thanks go to Vladimir Alexandrov, David Bethea, Robert Bird, Caryl Emerson, Michael Forster, Kate Holland, Ilya Kliger, Renate Lachmann, Alexander Martin, Boris Maslov, Irina Paperno, Nina Perlina, Galin Tihanov, William Mills Todd III, and Ilya Vinitsky. I am also thankful to Roger Garthman, who patiently proofread several parts of my manuscript.

I am deeply grateful to Donna Orwin, Anne Lounsbery, and one more anonymous reader of my manuscript for the University of Toronto Press. Their comments improved and enriched by book immeasurably. I am thankful to my editors Richard Ratzlaff and Barbara Porter for the exceptional care and professionalism with which they worked on this project. Last but not least, I wish to recognize my family. My mother, Tamara Rusanova, an expert performer of Vienna classics and Romantic composers, has always been one of the greatest influences on my personal *Bildung*. I also warmly thank my brother Nikolai Roussanov and my sister-in-law, Jessica Jacobs Roussanov, for their love and continual encouragement, as well as my nephew Peter, whose arrival in this world in September 2006 has made this book so much more meaningful to me.

FOR HUMANITY'S SAKE

Introduction

Russian literature emerged as a distinct voice and presence on the international cultural scene only in the second half of the nineteenth century. Up until then, most Europeans knew little about Russia, besides the fact – widely publicized by Voltaire, Diderot, and Rousseau – that since the early eighteenth century the Russian upper class had borrowed Europe's scientific and technological achievements and imitated its customs and manners. While Russia's ambitious rulers, beginning with Peter I and Catherine II, made Russia a political force to be taken seriously by European governments, most cultivated Europeans continued to regard the Russian Empire as a massive prison-house for serfs where culture had reached only a narrow fraction of the upper class. As Astolphe de Custine put it in his bestselling account of Russia in 1839, 'La Russie est policée; Dieu sait quand elle sera civilisée.'[1]

Yet Russia's image in the West was about to change, as important writers like Prosper Mérimée began to translate and popularize the literary works of Pushkin, Gogol, and Turgenev.[2] First in French, then in English, German, and other European languages, Russian literature was soon being disseminated widely throughout Western Europe and North America. On the brink of the First World War, as European culture experienced one of its deepest crises, the 'Russian point of view' – a phrase Virginia Woolf used as the title for one of her many essays on Russian literature – became a crucial point of reference for artists and intellectuals across the Western hemisphere.[3] If up until then Russia and Eastern Europe still presented themselves to the Western imagination as rather remote and exotic, the modernists grew increasingly aware of their proximity to their eastern neighbours as well as of their shared cultural inheritance. In the minds of thinkers like Walter Benjamin or

André Gide, Russia stood out as a realm of exciting experimentation, a bolder and more dynamic culture than its Western European counterpart.

Most recently, as part of the post-Soviet re-evaluation of Russian history, a number of scholars have persuasively argued that Russia and its successor the Soviet Union were intellectually connected to the Western Enlightenment and represented another variant of modernity.[4] This insight points toward the extent to which Russia's cultural and intellectual history since the era of Peter I has been intertwined with that of Europe. The Russian novel, which began to emerge as early as the mid-eighteenth century and reached full-blown maturity in the mid-nineteenth century, was one of the main media through which the ideas of the European Enlightenment were absorbed by Russian thinkers. Indeed, as has been often remarked, the Russian novel, especially in the nineteenth century, served not only as literature in the narrow sense (i.e., belles-lettres), but also as the medium of enculturation and social critique.[5] As this book will argue, the novel also played a fundamental role in shaping a sense of cultural and national identity in nineteenth-century Russia.

These are by no means altogether new claims. Generations of intellectual historians and literary scholars have explored numerous intersections between the European Enlightenment and Russian literature and culture.[6] This rich body of work has been of enormous help to me as I embarked on the project of analysing the relationship between the emergence of 'Russianness' as a cultural category in the period following the Napoleonic Wars and the accelerated development of the novelistic genre in the same period. My project began to take shape as a coherent story after I established direct links between the ideas of Johann-Gottfried Herder (1744–1803) and several Russian thinkers who were inspired by Herder's approach to 'culture' – a notion which he designates by various terms, including *Bildung, Kultur,* or *Nation.* Among these terms, *Bildung* eventually became the most recognized one, as it was placed in broad circulation throughout Europe by Herder's follower Wilhelm von Humboldt (1767–1835). As V.V. Vinogradov remarks, the Russian term *obrazovanie* was coined by analogy with this German term.[7] Bearing in mind the history of the British reception of the concept of *Bildung* from Matthew Arnold (1822–88) and John Stuart Mill (1806–73) to Raymond Williams (1921–88), throughout my study I either use the terms *Bildung* and *obrazovanie* or translate them into English as 'culture.'[8]

How did Herder become such a crucial influence on the development of nineteenth-century Russian identity? Sympathetically disposed toward Eastern Europe as a whole and toward Catherine II's Empire in particular, Herder devised a new conception of culture that answered the needs of rising, unevenly developed nations like Russia. Already in Herder's *Journal of 1769* (*Journal meiner Reise im Jahr 1769*),[9] which describes the 'grand tour' that took him from Riga to Paris, we find an intense polemic with Rousseau and the key figures of the French Enlightenment.[10] While Herder takes issue with Rousseau's idealization of the state of nature and his vision of society as based on a contract among fully mature citizens, he also diverges from Voltaire's theory of a unified human civilization geared toward progress. As he travels through Eastern Europe, Herder meditates on the destiny of the emerging Russian Empire, as it encompassed ever more peoples and tongues. He expressly disagrees with Rousseau's harsh judgment of Peter the Great. As Rousseau argued in *On the Social Contract*, 'the Russians will never be truly civilized because they were civilized too early.'[11] According to Rousseau, Peter the Great was limited to 'the genius of imitation,' lacking true genius of the kind that 'creates something out of nothing.' Peter, according to Rousseau, tried to cultivate his backward county 'by making Germans and Englishmen, whereas it was necessary to begin by making Russians.'[12] Rousseau's damning judgment of the Russian Tsar who 'prevented his subjects from ever becoming what they could be by convincing them that they were what they are not' was, of course, a thinly veiled attack on Rousseau's philosophical rival Voltaire, who had glorified Peter the Great and played the role of doyen to Catherine II's Enlightenment.[13]

As a German philosopher living and working under the Russian Crown in the peripheral town of Riga, Herder intervenes in this debate, putting a positive slant on the Russians' tendency to imitate the French, the Germans, and the English. Let a young nation learn from different 'tutors,' says Herder.[14] Another age will come, he adds, alluding to the rule of Catherine II, and the job of educating Russia left unfinished by Peter the Great will be completed. Herder's approval of Russia's cultural politics and especially his glorification of Peter I and Catherine II sound idealistic to those who know the human cost at which the westernization of Russia was attained by Peter and his successors. To be fair to Herder, however, we must understand that as much as he might have admired Catherine II, royal apologetics are not his primary concern. Rather, he is groping for a new conception of history and culture, one that would take into account the plurality of human languages and cultural organisms. The intersection of Slavic, German, native Baltic, and Jewish cultures in Riga must have inspired Herder to embark on the ambitious project of redefining culture as an evolution that does not follow a single straightforward trajectory, but involves a vacillation between different cultural points of view – the claim put forward in Herder's *Ideas for the Philosophy of History of Humanity* (1784–91) and *Letters on the Advancement of Humanity* (1793–7), for instance.

Herder's influence on German thinkers such as Goethe, Hegel, and Schelling is well documented, but his reception in Russia has received scant attention.[15] Nikolai Mikhailovich Karamzin (1766–1826) was one of the first to bear an imprint of Herder's influence. During his own European tour Karamzin met with Herder in Weimar, leaving a detailed account of this visit in his *Letters of a Russian Traveler* (1791–1801).[16] Later in his career Karamzin translated several essays and excerpts from Herder's larger works and published them in his journal *Messenger of Europe* (*Vestnik Evropy*, 1802–3). Karamzin's understanding of cultural development as first of all the development of language and literary culture is indebted to Herder, who argued that culture and knowledge developed along with human language.[17] Karamzin's mature political vision of Russia as both an independent nation state and a dialogic partner to Europe, whose special historical mission is to introduce Asia to Europe and Europe to Asia, is also imprinted with Herder's pluralistic vision of world culture.[18]

Russia was not excluded from the rise of Romantic nationalism across Europe at the time of Napoleonic Wars. Throughout the 1820s and 1840s Russian intellectuals continued to dwell on the problem of national identity, while the government busied itself with strengthening its hold on the rapidly developing public sphere by modernizing its ideological mechanisms – a process which resulted in the emergence, in the 1830s, of the so-called official nationality doctrine. Divided into the 'official' and the unofficial and often anti-official (with many shades in between), the Russian public sphere during the reign of Nicholas I (1825–56) presents a very complex picture. In order to examine in greater detail this crucial period in Russian cultural history before moving onto the literary analyses proper, my book is divided into two parts.

Part 1, 'Culture (*Obrazovanie, Bildung*) and the Bildungsroman on Russian Soil,' traces an important line in Russian intellectual and literary history that has so far remained almost unexplored by intellectual and cultural historians. It begins with Herder, whose observation that cultural evolution is stimulated by collision with other cultures found a sympathetic reception in Russia, influencing a number of scholars, intellectuals, and writers. I highlight the contributions of two critics and cultural theorists whose ideas appear to be particularly consonant with Herder's: Apollon Grigor'ev (1822–64) and Yurii Lotman (1922–93). This is not merely a case of 'elective affinity,' since both Russian scholars knew Herder's work. Lotman was also well acquainted with Grigor'ev's criticism. Both Grigor'ev and Lotman saw themselves as inheritors of European thought as well as representatives of the organically Russian cultural tradition. Both of them understood that the intersection of Western and Russian world views, mores, and value systems unhinged the mechanisms of traditional culture, with its stable hierarchical system of norms and values, pushing Russia toward modernity.

So far Grigor'ev has been best known as a creator of the school of 'organic criticism,' a champion of Russian national theatre (especially of the playwright A.N. Ostrovsky, 1823–86), and a poet with democratic sentiments who strongly influenced Russian modernists. My study emphasizes Grigor'ev's affinity with Herder, whose work he knew and whom he occasionally mentions by name. Grigor'ev was strongly influenced by Herder's theory that human cultures and languages are plural, and therefore each culture, just like an individual human being, can grow and accrue new knowledge through contacts with different cultural and linguistic communities. Echoing Herder's *Journal of 1769*, Grigor'ev suggests that Russia's unique geographic location between Europe and Asia, North and South, encourages the development of what he calls a 'broad' cultural consciousness.

Borrowing from Grigor'ev, F.M. Dostoevsky would later claim, in his famous speech at the opening of Pushkin's memorial in Moscow (1880), that Russian culture is endowed with a special propensity for sympathy, which he calls 'universal responsiveness' (*vsemirnaia otzyvchivost'*).[19] Refracted through the lens of Dostoevsky's eschatological vision of world history, in which Russia was to play a messianic role, Grigor'ev's ideas received new and potentially dangerous connotations in the 'Pushkin speech.'

Grigor'ev was a very important figure for Dostoevsky, helping him find his place in the literary world of the 1860s and recognize himself as heir to the tradition, inaugurated by Karamzin and Pushkin, destined to take Russian literature and culture beyond the age of the

Great Reforms. Therefore it is not always easy to draw a clear line between Dostoevsky's ideas and Grigor'ev's. As I will argue, however, it is in Dostoevsky's novels, rather than in his journalistic and public interventions, that we should look for his most interesting and valuable responses to Grigor'ev's ideas. Here Dostoevsky found a way to explore the 'breadth' of the Russian soul without succumbing to overt didacticism. When reading Dostoevsky's novels alongside Grigor'ev's criticism we come to realize that one of Dostoevsky's major goals throughout his maturity was to create an authentically Russian Bildungsroman, at the centre of which he wanted to place a hero who attains self-consciousness by reconciling himself to his dual patrimony, Russian and European.

Dostoevsky's attempt to transpose the Bildungsroman onto the Russian soil was not unique. As Franco Moretti suggests, the European Bildungsroman was arguably the leading genre of Western modernity, capturing the specifically modern experience of coming of age that involved a broadening of intellectual and psychological horizons.[20] A growing awareness of European culture not merely as a neighbouring culture but also part of its own legacy since the reign of Peter the Great motivated many Russian authors to create their own version of the genre. Pushkin's turn to the novel in the 1830s was already symptomatic of this tendency, which rapidly increased toward the 1850s and 1860s, along with the rise of capitalism, industrialization, and the eventual liberalization of society. If this book were to encompass the entire history of the Bildungsroman in Russia, it would have to include, in addition to chapters on Pushkin, Tolstoy, and Dostoevsky, those focused on a number of other writers, such as Karamzin, Lermontov, Gogol, Herzen, Goncharov, and others. I had to resist the temptation of offering a synoptic account in order to accomplish what I see as the main task of this book: to describe how several generations of Russian thinkers experienced their coming of age at a time of dramatic political and social upheavals, when, thanks to ever-intensifying contacts with the West, traditional cultural norms were no longer as binding as they had been a couple of generations ago, allowing for almost unprecedented psychological, social, and cultural dynamism.

Expanding the theoretical base for my analyses of the Russian Bildungsroman beyond Grigor'ev, I turn to the twentieth-century literary scholar, semiotician, and philosopher Yurii Lotman. Lotman was trained in Leningrad as a scholar of eighteenth-century Russian literature and spent the rest of his career at the University of Tartu in Estonia, which he transformed into one of the leading intellectual centres of the day. As the leader of the Moscow-Tartu school of semiotics, Lotman continually expanded his horizons beyond literature, making forays into cybernetics, philosophy, and the history of science, though he never gave up philological research. Lotman's semiotics shed light on his literary analyses and vice versa. Lotman's studies of Pushkin's novels *Eugene Onegin* and *The Captain's Daughter* are especially consonant with his culturological theory. Upon closer examination, Lotman's idea about Pushkin's unique propensity for irony (or Pyrrhonian scepticism), which Lotman sees as the quintessential characteristic of Pushkin's *Eugene Onegin* as well as the 'formula of the Russian novel' as a whole,[21] recalls Grigor'ev's famous characterization of Pushkin as the symbol of Russian culture's openness toward other cultures. Like Grigor'ev, Lotman envisioned culture as a perpetually evolving or expanding organic entity, rather than as a mechanistic system of normative constraints. What encourages this perpetual evolution is continual exposure to new information.

However, Lotman goes further than Grigor'ev in arguing that a cultivated mind should never reach the point of 'maturity' understood as stasis, but must constantly push the boundaries of knowledge and be constantly engaged in negotiating various points of view.[22] Lotman's take on irony recalls the more sceptical side of Herder as represented in works like *This Too a Philosophy of History for the Formation of* Humanity (1774).[23] A number of factors can be adduced to explain this affinity. As I have already noted, Lotman, whose first dissertation (*kandidatskaia*) was focused on the political prose of Karamzin and Radishchev, was well acquainted with Herder's work, despite only citing him occasionally.

Lotman's work in the 1970s and 1980s was also influenced by Bakhtin's theory of the novel as an inherently unstable dialogic form of discourse. Their projects converged insofar as both of them saw the increasing heterogeneity of language and consciousness as a sign of modernity. For both thinkers, nineteenth-century Russian literature, with its intense self-awareness as a hybrid of the traditional Russian culture and European ideas, was a particularly poignant example of a radical cultural shift – indeed, a revolution. And yet, both of them infused their works with a humanistic pathos reminiscent of the age of Enlightenment. For example, in Lotman's televised lectures on Russian culture and various interviews in the 1980s he frequently uses the world *gumannost'* (humanity), which he understood not as a natural gift, but as a result of a broadened cultural sensibility.[24]

In part 2 I bring the theoretical conceptions outlined in part 1 face to face with concrete literary works, rooted in their cultural and historic contexts. I test the idea that human cultural awareness accrues through exposure to otherness and translation or negotiation of different views through an analysis of the works by Pushkin, Tolstoy, and Dostoevsky. I focus on these particular authors because all three were deeply engaged in the question of Russian cultural identity and saw themselves as national educators. The novels that I examine most closely – Pushkin's *The Captain's Daughter* (1836), Tolstoy's *War and Peace* (1869), and Dostoevsky's *The Adolescent* (1874–5) – reflect the intellectual and psychological challenges that their authors encountered as they tried to envision a modern Russian apprenticeship.

Pushkin's historical novel *The Captain's Daughter* is set at the time of the Pugachev uprising (1773–5), which shook Catherine II's empire, testing the limits of her 'enlightened absolutism.' For a long time, however, this novel remained eclipsed by Pushkin's earlier work, especially his novel in verse *Eugene Onegin*, until Apollon Grigor'ev and his follower and fellow 'native soil' critic Nikolai Strakhov began to draw attention to it. They saw it as one of Pushkin's finest literary achievements. Since then *The Captain's Daughter* has been widely recognized as one of the pivotal examples of Pushkin's historic imagination. Both Georg Lukács in *The Historical Novel* and Lotman in 'The Ideological Structure of *The Captain's Daughter*' emphasize the dialectical structure of this story, represented by the confrontation between the world of the peasant rebels led by Pugachev and that of the imperial culture of Catherine II and the gentry.

In recent scholarship both Lukács's and Lotman's readings have met with a lot of criticism. Scholars have noted that these approaches overestimate the role of 'Walter-Scottian' historicism in Pushkin's world view. In chapter 1 of part 2 I revisit these debates in order to show that Pushkin's view of the dialectic of enlightenment was in fact different from that of Scott and French Romantic historians. The latter believed that there existed an objective force underlying history that could prevail over the will of individual characters. In Pushkin's text, however, chance and chaos gain full sway. At the same time, Pushkin did believe in self-perfection. A follower of the Karamzinian ethic of personal improvement, Pushkin was convinced that society could be gradually improved through the efforts of enlightened individuals. In *The Captain's Daughter* he described the maturation of a model Russian nobleman, Grinev, in whom he sees, *pace* Karamzin, a hereditary member of Russia's cultivated elite. His moral duty is to impart his knowledge and culture to others.

Grinev's self-development does not follow the kind of straightforward trajectory that one might expect from a story of an aristocratic hero's *entrée dans le monde*. Instead, it involves a radical expansion of the hero's horizon that could not have occurred had he stayed at home or been sent to complete his education in Petersburg instead of in the frontier region of the Urals. Thanks to his father's decision to inflict true hardship on his son, Grinev encounters Pugachev and witnesses the civil war that nearly destroyed Catherine II's Empire. In this respect both Grigor'ev's insight into *The Captain's Daughter* as a text that conveys Pushkin's desire for greater cultural breadth and Lotman's analysis of the 'ideological structure' of Pushkin's novel[25] as revealing a dialectical struggle between two socially opposed forces, the peasants and rebels on one side and the nobility on the other, are extremely helpful. They allow us to appreciate the difference between Grinev, who is exposed to Russia's heterogeneous sociocultural reality, and the preceding Russian 'developing heroes,' such as Pushkin's misanthropic Onegin or the solipsistic hero of Karamzin's *The Knight of Our Time* (which, as scholars agree, can be viewed as the first unfinished Russian Bildungsroman).[26]

In the 1860s Tolstoy also joined the debate on Russian culture, seeking a viable role for himself and members of his class, the gentry, in the changing atmosphere of the post–Great Reforms era. As I argue in chapter 2 of part 2, Tolstoy, who first began educating his own peasants in Iasnaia Poliana in the late 1840s, was keenly aware of the vast gap that separated the educated elite from the people. How could one even begin bridging this enormous gap? Moreover, how could one hope to envision some kind of uniform 'Russian' identity?

From this angle we can view Tolstoy's *War and Peace* as a multi-plot *Bildungsroman*, consisting of several different paradigms of personal maturation. This structural complexity resulted from Tolstoy's polyphonic vision of history and identity, which he refused to reduce to a uniform pattern along the lines of Goethe's *Wilhelm Meister's Apprenticeship* or Scott's *Waverley*. In dialogue with these European apprenticeship narratives, Tolstoy's offers us a series of examples of individual self-formation.

Among the heroes of *War and Peace*, Pierre Bezukhov – an illegitimate son of the old count Bezukhov and a mother who is never mentioned in the novel and is probably a serf – comes closest to a Western-style Bildungsroman protagonist insofar as his social position makes him capable of playing the role of a 'middling' hero or a go-between for the aristocracy and the people. To some extent, particularly during the war, Pierre does play this role. However, by the end of the novel Pierre does not represent a 'typical' citizen of a fledgling national community. In this respect, it is significant that Pierre's liberal vision of Russia (symbolized by the secret society or *Tugendbund* he organizes at the end of the novel) clashes with the traditional patriarchal gentry vision represented by Nikolai Rostov, another leading hero of *War and Peace*. At the same time, Pierre's enlightened idea of liberal brotherhood is also at odds with the ethic of humility and love represented by the peasant-soldier Platon Karataev, whom Pierre meets and befriends in the camp for Russian prisoners of war during the war of 1812. Tolstoy's work ultimately drives home to us the idea that there can be multiple conceptions of happiness within a country as large and uneven as Russia. Tolstoy's insight into the plurality of human organic communities and their respective images of happiness led him to rebel against contemporary historiography, which stressed the idea of Zeitgeist.

But Tolstoy does not actually give up his teleological view of the human being – only *his* vision of *Bildung* is aimed not at successful socialization (as Moretti would have it), but at self-transcendence and spiritual freedom. Tolstoy presents us with a powerful narrative of spiritual *Bildung* by narrating the death of Prince Andrei. This character's gradual 'awakening from life' is juxtaposed to the story of Pierre's discovery of life and happiness, demonstrating Tolstoy's need for a metaphysical narrative that would justify human experience from the standpoint of immortality.

My final chapter is centred on Dostoevsky's first and only completed Bildungsroman, *The Adolescent*. I chose to focus on this lesser known work, because in my opinion it holds the key to the entire final phase of Dostoevsky's career, when he began to see himself as a leading national cultural authority on par with Karamzin, Pushkin, and Tolstoy. Dostoevsky's turn to the genre of the Bildungsroman in the 1870s was deeply rooted in his interest in education and cultural formation. I read Dostoevsky's turn to the Bildungsroman against the background of *pochvennichestvo*, which held that cultural and linguistic 'breadth' was the only certain basis for the budding nation. Dostoevsky's personal connections to Grigor'ev and Nikolai Strakhov provide a historical validation for such an approach.

Like Tolstoy's Pierre Bezukhov, the protagonist of *The Adolescent* is an illegitimate son of a nobleman father and a peasant mother. His self-consciousness is greatly affected by his encounter with his legal father, a saintly peasant named Makar Dolgorukii – a figure arguably modelled on Tolstoy's Platon Karataev. Arkadii's personality is emblematic of the rising Russian middle class. His task (as suggested by his first name, which means 'happy') is to attain happiness. In order to do this, he must come to terms with his dual patrimony and reconcile his own conflicting psychological tendencies. Through the course of the novel Arkadii evolves from a disgruntled young man with an 'underground' psychology into one who is more self-confident and balanced. He even appears to be capable of 'polyphonic' thinking (to use Bakhtin's famous term) and of 'active love' (to use Dostoevsky's own term). Arkadii becomes Dostoevsky's model hero, serving as a representative member of his emerging national community.

The novels discussed in my study are all part of a continuous conversation on national identity and culture taking place among Russian writers and intellectuals since the turn of the nineteenth century. Yet, in keeping with the Latin proverb *Habent sua fata libelli* [Books have their own fates], these works have had rather different fates in history and criticism. Pushkin's first and only finished prose novel, *The Captain's Daughter*, still remains eclipsed by his novel in verse, *Eugene Onegin*, in the eyes of the reading public. Tolstoy's *War and Peace*, on the other hand, has been translated into all major European and non-European languages and celebrated as one of the finest examples of Russian literary prose. The destiny of Dostoevsky's penultimate novel has been similar to that of the *Captain's Daughter* in the sense that it has had a more modest reception than the other four of the 'five great' novels of Dostoevsky's maturity.

In stressing the intellectual and artistic importance of these particular works and re-establishing the historical connections between them, one of my main goals is to enrich our understanding of one of the most dynamic periods in Russian intellectual and literary history. The period I discuss in this book also deserves special attention because it marked one of the turning points in modern Western literary history. From this point on a 'peripheral' literature came to be recognized as indispensable to further development of the Western mind. The process of cultural exchange between 'centres' and 'peripheries' that began in the eighteenth and nineteenth centuries is gaining greater and greater intensity in the contemporary world as a result of the information technology boom. It makes the problem of properly interpreting foreign literary texts, as opposed to assimilating them under one's own norms, ever more vital.[27]

PART I

Culture (*Obrazovanie, Bildung*) and the Bildungsroman on Russian Soil

1 Russian Literature from the National Awakening of the 1800s to the Rise of *Pochvennichestvo* in the 1850s

To get a better sense of Apollon Grigor'ev's originality as a thinker, we need to approach his ideas against the broader horizon of Russian intellectual history, which received a powerful impetus from Russia's encounter with Europe during the Napoleonic Wars. As is generally assumed by historians, the rise of national self-consciousness in Russia corresponded with the military campaigns of 1805, 1812, and 1813–14. The first decade of the nineteenth century was also marked by the development of the liberal public sphere, an event in which Nikolai Karamzin played a key role. His journal, *Messenger of Europe* (*Vestnik Evropy*), which appeared in 1802–3, became a genuine 'window to the West' for Russian readers.[1] After Alexander I relaxed the repressive cultural policies of his father, Paul I, a number of journals, as well as numerous literary 'societies' and salons, sprang up in St Petersburg, Moscow, and provincial urban centres.[2] The educational reform of 1804 brought about the creation of new universities in St Petersburg, Dorpat (Tartu), Khar'kov, and Kazan'. These were modelled after the most progressive university in Europe, the University of Berlin, founded by Wilhelm von Humboldt.[3] Masonic lodges, which had been outlawed by Paul I, were reopened and attracted new members.[4]

The new ideology of cultural nationalism, with its new vocabulary (created by thinkers like Johann Gottlieb Fichte) and its new sense of the organic connection between the rulers and the ruled, migrated from Germany to Russia and attained critical mass during the campaign of 1812. It was observed by a witness as informed and sharp-eyed as Mme de Staël, who travelled to Russia in 1812 seeking protection from Napoleon's persecution. She recorded with admiration the rise of public opinion and the awakening of patriotic spirit among virtually every class of Russian society.[5] Among the Russian intelligentsia, too, the War of 1812 (or as the Russians still call it, 'The Patriotic War' or 'War for the Fatherland' [*Otechestvennaia voina*]) came to be seen as the war of national liberation.

Several recent studies have revisited the so-called Myth of 1812 to analyse its ideological function, firstly in creating a national compact in the summer and autumn of 1812, during the most intense period of the anti-French campaign that took Alexander's war and made it a Russian war, and secondly in legitimating Russian nationalism throughout the rest of the nineteenth century.[6] For example, Alexander Martin's monograph uncovers the origins of the myth of the 'people's war,' which emerged during the summer and autumn of 1812 as a result of collaboration between nationalistically minded intellectuals from several political factions at the court of Alexander I.[7] In spite of any ideological differences that came between them, the Russian intellectual elite, including Karamzin, Alexander Shishkov (1754–1841) (the leader of the conservative literary society Beseda liubitelei russkogo slova and subsequent Minister of Enlightenment, who earned this post over Karamzin), and writer and conservative political theorist Sergei Glinka (1776–1847), all collaborated in weaving an image of Russia's war against the Napoleonic Empire as a holy war, attributing to it a global historical, or even apocalyptic, magnitude.[8]

The essence of the myth that gradually spread across Petersburg salons during the years of the Napoleonic Wars, when the parallel between the apocalypse and Russia's struggle against Napoleon (representing the Antichrist) arose and gained momentum, is familiar to readers of Lev Tolstoy's *War and Peace*. This myth is an idea that marks the novel's character Pierre Bezukhov, steeped in Masonic secret science and enthused by the anti-Napoleonic propaganda unleashed across Moscow in 1812 on the eve of the French occupation by General Governor Count Fyodor Rostopchin (1763–1826). It is at this point that Pierre contemplates the assassination of Napoleon. Although Pierre is, of course, part of Tolstoy's fictional world, Pierre's state of mind during the war, so vividly imagined and conveyed by Tolstoy, reconstructs the general mood and public opinion recorded in the press of that era, as well as eyewitness accounts, which Tolstoy well knew.[9]

Alexander Martin argues that the intellectual roots of Russian nationalism are inextricably linked to early German Romantic philosophy of history. In particular, he claims that Johann Gottfried von Herder was a major influence on both Shishkov and Karamzin long before he influenced circles of Moscow intellectuals.[10] While Shishkov emphasized *nationhood* and Karamzin *statehood*, at root, both concepts seem to derive their inspiration from Herder's idea of *das Volk*, or an organic national community.[11] I would like to add, however, that while Karamzin shared Herder's understanding of nation as a historically evolving entity, Shishkov was quite unresponsive to this aspect of Herder's philosophy. He was indeed a true archaiser and his project for a language reform, unlike Karamzin's, was in the end consigned to the dustbin of history.[12]

At first, the government of Alexander I was surprised and suspicious as it watched nationalistic spirit quickly spread across different strata of the population, reaching even the peasants. Just as the Prussian court had earlier sought to tame German nationalism, Alexander's ministers associated Russian patriotism with the liberal and subversive ideas of the French Revolution. However, unable to arrest the progress of national self-consciousness, Alexander's government decided instead to co-opt it, beginning the policy that was eventually formulated by Count S.S. Uvarov into the 'official nationality doctrine' in 1833.[13] Thus, from a historical point of view, both the state-sponsored 'official' nationalism and the idea of Russianness as a stepping stone to 'universal responsiveness' and humanity (which eventually found its spokesman in Grigor'ev and his followers) originally sprang from the same source: the patriotic campaign of 1812.

The Russian 'Myth of 1812' envisioned a unified national community that cut across class or estate boundaries.[14] However, the romantic dream of nationhood encountered some major obstacles when it was tested by reality. Not only did this myth overlook the ethnic diversity of the vast imperial peripheries, but it also disregarded the estate and cultural disparities within the Russian core of the Empire. The persistence of serfdom until 1861 stood firmly in the way of creating a homogeneous civil society on par with other European nations. Raised and educated differently from other estates, the gentry remained culturally and psychologically cut off from the lower estates. This situation persisted well into the 1860s, 1870s, and beyond. As Dostoevsky puts it in *Winter Notes on Summer Impressions* (1863), an educated Russian of the post-Petrine age has not one but two fatherlands: Russia and Europe.[15] By 'educated' Dostoevsky meant a representative of 'cultivated' society. Even the war against France, which seemed to bind the population together, did not close the cultural gap between the city and country, and the gentry and peasants, which had existed since Peter the Great's time, when Westernization first touched the upper classes. Under Peter, while radical innovations were introduced into the system of state government, the military, social life, and the arts, the vast majority of the population – the peasantry – were left behind to toil under a complex serf system and, over time, came to be perceived as either a backwards, animalistic mass by the upper class, or as an archaic depository of authentic Russian cultural traditions by a certain faction of the intelligentsia.

The lack of a firm sense of national identity was recognized by the imperial administration in the wake of the Decembrist uprising of 1825, which signalled a profound conflict between the state and civil society. In response, the government of Nicholas I put into motion a number of educational reforms aimed at creating an officially approved and guided set of nationalistic sentiments for the upper class and the small urban middle class, thus building a bridge between the state and society. The government also sponsored a propaganda campaign spearheaded by Count S.S. Uvarov, Minister of Enlightenment since 1833, whose famous triadic concept, 'Orthodoxy, Autocracy, and Nationality' (*Pravoslavie, Samoderzhavie, Narodnost'*), survived as an imperial credo into the 1880s. Uvarov's doctrine was by no means a simple fabrication; rather it was deeply rooted in Karamzin's notion that the form of government best suited to the Russian state was autocracy, inasmuch as only such a strong authoritarian power could tame the disparate forces created by the country's wildly varying geopolitical conditions. Uvarov was also well schooled in German philosophy, and his focus on *narodnost'* clearly reflects a debt to Herder and his Romantic followers.[16]

However, as Andrei Zorin points out, despite Uvarov's learning and his rhetorical dexterity, his formula is open to the simple critique that it utterly failed to reflect contemporary reality.[17] Russian society in Uvarov's time was still divided into four estates separated by nearly impermeable boundaries and therefore was far from a nation state bound by a sense of common identity and equality before the law. As Zorin notes, because *narodnost'* was not embodied in any concrete social phenomenon, Uvarov defined it syllogistically, by connecting it to the two other components of his triadic formula, namely, 'orthodoxy' and 'autocracy.'[18]

We should not forget, however, that Uvarov did not originate the concept of *narodnost'*. In fact, it predated the epoch of 'official nationality.'[19] As Yurii Lotman has argued, the term *narodnost'* was first used by another Göttingen graduate, Andrei Turgenev, in a speech addressed to the Free Society of Friends (*Vol'noe druzheskoe ob'schestvo*).[20] With this view, *narodnost'* emerges as an organizing concept in the semiotic field of Russian cultural history paired not with Uvarov's 'autocracy' and 'orthodoxy,' but with the liberal notion of personality or individuality (*lichnost'*). Uvarov's task was to reconfigure the idea developed by the liberals and Decembrists with a new 'conservative spirit' (*okhranitel'nyi dukh*).[21]

The reign of Nicholas I from 1825 to 1856 is traditionally regarded as a reactionary period during which the historical clock was stopped or even set back to the time of Paul I. This opinion, expressed by Herzen in *My Past and Thoughts* and later supported by A.N. Pypin and some other historians, refers to Nicholas I's suppression of the Decembrist rebellion, the reinstitution of capital punishment (which had been officially abolished by Empress Elizabeth in 1741 and re-enacted only once during the eighteenth century to execute Emel'ian Pugachev and his principal henchmen in 1775), the refusal to reform the serf system within Russia, and the campaign of anti-radical (and essentially anti-Western) propaganda led by Uvarov. Outside of Russia, Nicholas earned a reputation as the 'gendarme of Europe,' whose military strength supported the status quo of the 'Holy Alliance.'[22] As attested by the Marquis de Custine's account of Russia in 1839, the country appeared to its Western observers as a vast prison-house.[23]

At the same time, it is important to recognize that Nicholas also learned the political lesson offered to him by the Decembrists, whose objective was to create either a constitutional monarchy or a constitutional republic. Nicholas I's actions in the first few years after his ascension to the throne suggest that he did listen carefully to the Decembrists during their trials and understood that their ideas, including narodnost', were in sync with 'spirit of the age' and could not be rejected wholesale. This realization prompted him to appoint the well-educated and intelligent Uvarov to the key post of Minister of the Enlightenment and with his help to launch cultural and educational reforms aimed at 'nationalizing' the Empire. Nicholas's advisors included a number of other talented and highly cultivated people, including the poet Vassilii Zhukovskii. As L.N. Kiseleva has recently argued, it was Zhukovskii who advised the Tsar to return Pushkin from exile and engage him in the campaign of building a Russian *Kultur-Nation*.[24] Along with Zhukovskii and Uvarov, Pushkin became one of those intellectuals whose opinion on the development of culture and education Nicholas I solicited upon his ascension. In response to this call, Pushkin wrote his memorandum 'On National Education' (*Zapiska o narodnom vospitanii*).[25]

The beginning of a new stage in Pushkin's career, when he (in his own words) 'made peace with the government' and embraced the role of Russia's enlightener or *Aufklärer* (left vacant by the death of Karamzin in 1826), should also be linked to Pushkin's acquaintance with several Moscow-based intellectual circles, including a Germanophile circle of the so-called Lovers of Wisdom (*Liubomudry*),[26] and a group that clustered around the influential historian Mikhail Pogodin (1800–75) and his journal the *Moscow Messenger* (*Moskovskii Vestnik*). After his return from exile in 1826, Pushkin settled in Moscow, which was once again becoming the country's major intellectual centre. There was still an aura of heroism surrounding Moscow in the wake of the great fire of 1812, and the city was coming to be seen as Russia's national centre, whereas Petersburg was being perceived as the capital of the earlier, Petrine period.[27] It is not surprising that Moscow's intellectual circles were receptive to the ideas of Herder, Humboldt, early German Romantics, and, somewhat later, of Schelling and Hegel. Although Pushkin found the *Liubomudry*'s penchant for abstract philosophizing somewhat annoying, he actively contributed to Pogodin's journal throughout 1827 and 1828.[28]

The questions debated in Moscow intellectual circles during this time could be formulated as follows: 'Is there a cultural path specific to Russia, a country whose unique geographic and historical positioning makes it so different from the rest of Europe?' and 'What form will the education of the Russian nation take?' These issues gained additional urgency after the scandal produced by the publication in 1836 of Pyotr (sometimes spelled as Petr) Iakovlevich Chaadaev's *First Philosophical Letter* (written in 1829), in which he bemoans the fact that Russia, due to its historical and geographic conditions, would never catch up with the West.[29] Having received Christianity from Constantinople rather than Rome, Russia remained cut off from the great process of civilization that transformed barbaric Europe into a culture.

The main idea of Chaadaev's text, which shocked contemporaries, including Pushkin, was that Russia's separation from Europe throughout the medieval period had so delayed the country's cultural formation that even Peter the Great's reforms were a hopeless attempt to stir this sleeping giant.[30] Russia had missed the age that Chaadaev describes as Europe's 'adolescence.' Chaadaev writes:

> Il est un temps, pour tous les peuples, d'agitation violente, d'inquiétude passionnée, d'activité sans motif réfléchi. Les hommes pour lors sont er-

rant dans le monde, de corps et d'esprit. C'est l'âge des grandes passions, des grandes emotions, des grandes enterprises des peuples. [...] Toutes les sociétés ont passé par ces périodes. Elles leur fournissent leurs reminiscences les plus vives, leur merveilleux, leur poésie, toutes leur idées les plus fortes et les plus fécondes. Ce sont les bases necessaries des société. Autrement, elles n'auraient rien dans leur mémoire à quoi s'attacher, à quoi s'affectionner; elles ne tiendraient qu'à la poussière de leur sol. Cette époque intéressante dans l'histoire des peuples, c'est l'adolescence des peuples; c'est le moment où leurs facultés se développent le plus puissamment, dont la mémoire fait la jouissance et la leçon de leur âge mûr. Nous autres, nous n'avons rien de tel. Une brutale barbarie d'abord, ensuite, une superstition grossière, puis une domination étrangère, féroce, avilissante, dont le pouvoir national a plus tard hérité l'esprit, voilà la triste histoire de notre jeunesse. Cet âge d'activité exubérante, du jeu exalté des forces morales des peuples, rien de semblable chez nous. L'époque de notre vie sociale qui répond à ce moment a été remplie par une existence terne et sombre, sans vigeur, sans énergie, que rien n'animait que la forfait, que rien n'adoucissait que la servitude. Point de souvenirs charmants, points d'images gracieuses dans la mémoire, point de puissantes instructions dans la tradition nationale. Parcourzez l'oeil tous les siécles que nous avons traversés, tout le sol que nous couvrons, vous ne trouverez pas un souvenir attachant, pas un monument venerable, qui vous parle des temps passés avec puissance, qui vous les retrace d'une manière vivante et pittoresque. Nou ne vivons que dans le présent le plus étroits, sans passé et sans avenir, au milieu d'un calme plat.[31]

In his analysis of Chaadaev's intellectual sources, Mikhail Gershenzon shows that they included German and French theological and spiritual literature and very little, if any, Russian philosophy, literature, or history. Gershenzon specifically singled out the German mystic Johann Heinrich Jung-Stilling, whose teachings were popular among the Russian aristocracy of the 1810s and whose works Chaadaev read carefully.[32] According to Gershenzon, Chaadaev adopted Jung-Stilling's Pietist method of self-examination, which he used in his private dairies and, to some extent, even in his *Philosophical Letters,* which were written in the form of private letters addressed to a lady acquaintance. When thinking about his country's historical predicament, Chaadaev, with his training by Jung-Stilling, came to the conclusion that the majority of Russians were utterly underdeveloped, dull, and even savage people because they were unaccustomed to reflection and self-criticism.[33]

The debate over the meaning and directions of Russian history, which Chaadaev helped to launch by publishing his *First Philosophical Letter*, has been amply discussed in scholarship.[34] One of the consequences of this debate is that it polarized Russian intellectuals, leading to a split by the 1840s into two camps: the Slavophiles and the Westernizers. Shortly after the publication of his *First Philosophical Letter*, though, Chaadaev himself, partly under the pressure of criticism and partly due to his own, not yet entirely developed system of thought, began to change or refine his position. Only a year later, in 1837, Chaadaev wrote 'The Apology of a Madman,' where he changed his pessimistic evaluation of post-Petrine Russia claiming that, thanks to Peter's reforms, Russia could escape from the long period of inferiority and begin a new era of Western development.[35] The subsequent *Philosophical Letters* (seven all together, which, except for the first, remained unpublished until 1935) argue that Russia's separation from Europe during the Middle Ages and Renaissance was not a fateful flaw but almost a blessing in disguise. According to Chaadaev's revised conception, Russia was destined to play a special role in world history. While not being part of the same historical movement as the rest of Europe, it was destined to find its own path of development.[36]

As Andrzej Walicki has pointed out, Chaadaev's provocative first *Philosophical Letter* was a key factor in polarizing the Russian *literati* of the 1830s.[37] Based in Moscow, the original Slavophile camp included the philosophers I.V. Kireevskii and A.S. Khomiakov, the writers S.T. and K.S. Aksakov, and several others. As Walicki points out, in their criticism of Hegelian universalism, the Slavophiles were sometimes very close to Herder. Walicki says:

> Like Herder, they attacked the hidden Europocentric premises of all conceptions of a unilinear, teleological development of history. However, they did not share Herder's tendency to create another universalism – universalism as a principle of plenitude, sanctifying cultural differences, explaining them as irreducible to each other but equally important for the elaboration of the all-embracing pluralist idea of mankind. The Slavophiles saw in this the danger of aesthetic relativism to which they were decidedly opposed. This is, perhaps, the reason why they were so strangely cold towards Herder, in spite of his high and deserved reputation among the western and southern Slavs. They were not satisfied with destroying the Europocentric universalism and replacing it with a pluralist universalism to which every nation could bring its unique and irreplaceable contribution. They wanted a type

of universalism which would ascribe universal value to their own, 'truly Christian' (i.e. 'truly Russian') principles. They rejected all kinds of cultural relativism because they believed in absolute truth and identified it with their own truth. Thus the Russian people, as the carrier of 'truly Christian' principles, became the only incarnation of a true universalism.[38]

The Slavophiles saw the scientific and industrial revolutions coming from West as a threat to the patriarchal organic community or *Gemeinschaft*, to use a term suggested by Ferdinand Toennies.[39] Hence the Slavophiles' animus against the West captured in Khomiakov's juxtaposition of the 'rotting West' with the still vital Russia.[40]

One of the pivotal figures in the circle of Westernizers who came to the fore in the mid-1840s was the historian T.N. Granovskii. A former student of Pogodin, Granovskii became a professor of European history at Moscow University and served as a magnet for the younger generation of intellectuals, including V.P. Botkin, N.V. Stankevich, and A.I. Herzen, whose Weltanschauung was being formed under the influence of Western philosophy and who rejected the Slavophiles' doctrine. Like the Slavophile camp, the Westernizers sprang from a friendly circle of young Moscow University students. They became consolidated into a sizeable political movement only after one of the most brilliant and energetic members of the original Moscow circle, the critic Vissarion Grigor'evich Belinskii (1811–48), moved to Petersburg in 1841 and became the editor of *The Contemporary*.[41] Belinskii's circle in Petersburg included I.F. Panaev, P.V. Annenkov, N.A. Nekrasov, and I.S. Turgenev. Like the Slavophiles, the Westernizers derived their ideology from German idealism, as well as from the work of left Hegelians who became particularly influential on Belinskii in the last decade of his life. Unlike the Slavophiles, however, they did not believe in Russia's exceptional place in history, but instead saw it as an underdeveloped country that ought to catch up with the industrialized West. After Belinskii's death and the failure of the revolution of 1848, the Westernizers began to change their political orientation from Utopian socialism to liberalism. By this time, however, a new intellectual movement emerged that positioned itself between Slavophiles and Westernizers, seeking to reconcile them. This new voice belonged to the 'native soil' movement led by the critic Apollon Grigor'ev and the publishers of the journal *Time*, Mikhail Dostoevsky (who acted as the official editor) and his brother Fyodor (who, as an ex-convict, was not allowed to publish a journal, although de facto he did).

While the history and main tenets of the Slavophiles' and Westernizers' doctrines have been thoroughly explored by Russian historians and literary scholars, the intellectual profile of Grigor'ev and the origins of the 'native soil' movement are comparatively less well known, especially in the West. One of the facts that has so far escaped scholars' attention is that Chaadaev's critique of Russian culture was not only instrumental in awakening the Slavophiles and Westernizers, but it also promoted a new way of thinking about national culture not as a fixed entity, a repository of certain given traits, but as an evolving, multifaceted ethos.

In this regard, the work and personality of Mikhail Pogodin deserve a special mention. Pogodin had a long and successful academic career. In 1828 he became an adjunct at the department of General History (*kafedra obschei istorii*) at Moscow University; in 1833 he was made professor of the same department. He is perhaps even better known to contemporary scholars as editor of the *Moscow Messenger* (*Moskovskii Vestnik*) and *The Muscovite* (*Moskvitianin*) and as an important public figure throughout the reigns of Nicholas I and Alexander II. Pogodin's life and career have been carefully documented by Nikolai Barsukov in a twenty-one-volume memoir. Acting as Pogodin's Boswell, Barsukov may not always be unbiased in his interpretation of the events and characters he describes.[42] Nonetheless, his book contains extremely valuable information about the historian who befriended Pushkin in the late 1820s, was instrumental in shaping Grigor'ev's career in the second half of the 1840s, and was highly respected by and probably influential on Tolstoy while he was at work on *War and Peace*.[43]

By the time Chaadaev published his *First Philosophical Letter*, Pogodin was already a well-established historian specializing in ancient or pre-Petrine Russia. He was a graduate of Moscow University, where he also defended his famous master's dissertation, 'On the Origins of Rus'' (1825). Pogodin's thesis sought to prove the existence of the Norman tribe of Varangians called Rus' on the basis of evidence found in Byzantine, Arabic, and Frankish chronicles. As Barsukov clarified, Pogodin was not equipped to conduct first-hand philological research. His thesis was based on the prodigious study of secondary sources by the German philologists Johann Thunmann, J.G. Stritter, V.F. Miller, and others, as well as on Karamzin's analyses of Russian chronicles. Throughout his life Pogodin considered himself a follower of Karamzin, to whom he dedicated his dissertation. He also became the first academic biographer of Karamzin.[44]

Pogodin's master's dissertation served as the foundation stone for his later scholarship. He made his name as a historian by advancing the theory of the Varangian rule in Russia by invitation (*'po prizyvu'*) rather than through conquest. During the reign of Nicholas I, Pogodin grew progressively more influential and more conservative, and his ideas acquired a more overtly exceptionalist tenor. He was one of the progenitors of the idea that the Russian national character was rooted in Russia's peaceful history, devoid of the religious wars and class struggle that characterized the European Middle Ages and the Renaissance.[45] Therefore, Russians were supposedly the only truly peace-loving people in Europe.

In the 1850s (during the Crimean War) Pogodin grew more and more conservative. During the Balkans crisis of 1875–6, which provoked the Russo-Turkish War (1877–8), he became one of the leaders of the Pan-Slavist movement. However, earlier, in the second half of the 1820s and through the 1830s, when Pogodin befriended Pushkin and the Lovers of Wisdom, he occupied an intellectual position, which was quite open-minded and progressive for his time. Pogodin argued that Russians were not a single ethnos. Rather, he saw Russia as a complex organism that had evolved over a long period of time out of several different ethnic and linguistic groups. 'What a Russia! How many worlds it contains!' (*'Chto za Rossiia! Skol'ko mirov v nei!'*) wrote Pogodin in his diary in 1829, emphasizing his belief that the Russian Empire ruled over one of the most culturally heterogeneous communities in recent history.[46]

As a public figure, Pogodin, throughout the 1820s and 1830s, advocated a closer intellectual dialogue between Russian and European literatures. In the mid-1820s he was received at the salon of Princess Zinaida Volkonskaia – the most brilliant Moscow intellectual centre of the day, where Johann Wolfgang von Goethe's idea of *Weltliteratur* was being promoted by the hostess herself, as well as by such poets and intimates of hers as V.A. Zhukovskii, D.V. Venevitinov, and other young intellectuals from the group known as the 'archival youths.'[47] Pogodin, who was by then well versed in German philosophy and science, appears to have shared the intellectual orientation of this circle, which revered Pushkin as the Russian 'genius' whose special mission was to win respect and admiration from Western as well as Russian audiences, thereby proving that a Russian poet could be heard and understood beyond his native land. Upon closer examination, it seems that the main rationale for the creation of the *Moscow Messenger* in 1826 was to create a forum for publicizing the latest Russian and European scientific and cultural ideas. Pushkin's participation certainly helped secure the high quality and visibility of Pogodin's venture. However, the literary section constituted only one among many sections of this genuinely 'multidisciplinary' organ, which also published works on philosophy, natural sciences (including geography, geology, and botany), historiography, ethnography, and archaeology. Essentially, the *Moscow Messenger* became the leading Russian forum for the advancement of *obrazovanie* or *obrazovannost'* (as Pogodin and his contemporaries often spelled the word they considered to be the Russian equivalent of the German term *Bildung*).

Pogodin's work as a historian, publicist, and editor helped to bring home to many contemporaries the idea that Russian history was a rich and still comparatively undeveloped field. Arguing against the Westernizers, Pogodin insisted that Russian history was in no way inferior to that of the West. On the contrary, it was a treasury containing many forgotten or still undiscovered cultural jewels. Consequently, the most urgent task confronting every Russian intellectual was to continue to expand his and his countrymen's knowledge of Russia and its geography, history, and culture.

2 Apollon Grigor'ev's Theory of Russian Culture

Many of his contemporaries, including F.M. Dostoevsky, saw Grigor'ev (1822–64) as one of the geniuses of the age. The son of Alexander Ivanovich Grigor'ev, a Moscow gentleman (*dvorianin*), and Tat'iana Andreevna, a daughter of one of the serfs belonging to the Grigor'evs, Apollon Grigor'ev was conceived before his parents were married. Therefore throughout his life Grigor'ev was officially registered not as a gentleman but as a member of the third estate – a biographical element that had profound and lasting significance for his self-consciousness and his intellectual position as a poet and critic. Griogr'ev spent his childhood in Zamoskvorech'e, an unfashionable part of the old capital populated mainly by merchants. He left a wonderful description of his childhood, youth, and several years of his young maturity in his unfinished autobiography, *My Literary and Moral Wanderings* (*Moi literaturnye i nravstvennye skital'chestva*), inspired in part by Goethe's *Wilhelm Meisters Wanderjahre* (parts of which Grigor'ev had actually translated into Russian), and in part by Herzen's *My Past and Thoughts*.[1] The first part of this work was published in 1862 in M.M. and F.M. Dostoevskys' journal *Time* (*Vremia*), and the second, unfinished part in 1864 in their journal *Epoch* (*Epokha*).

The house in which Grigor'ev was raised was a very pious one, and he remained respectful of the spirituality of the common Russian people throughout his life. At the same time, at Moscow University, where Grigor'ev studied law from 1838 to 1842, he came into contact with Western philosophy. In the 1830s and 1840s Moscow University once again became a leading university where many future scholars and intellectuals received their training (including M.Yu. Lermontov, A.I.

Herzen, N.P. Ogarev, N.M. Stankevich, V.G. Belinskii, M.A. Bakunin, E.N. Edel'son, and many others).

Like every Moscow student, Grigor'ev encountered Hegelianism early in his career. However, he gradually distanced himself from Hegelianism. His mature Weltanschauung was shaped under the influence of a most eclectic group of philosophers, including Herder, Goethe, Schelling, and early German Romantics, as well as such thinkers as Jakob Boehme, Franz von Baader, Thomas à Kempis, Jacques-Bénigne Bossuet, François Fénélon, Jean Baptiste Massillon, and Louis Bautin.[2] He was also, at least for a while, interested in freemasonry.[3]

Having graduated from Moscow University with a degree in jurisprudence in 1842, Grigor'ev did not want to practise law or serve as a government employee in any other department. 'The last Romantic,' as he called himself (with the 'soul of Dmitrii Karamazov,' as poet Alexander Blok once remarked), Grigor'ev suffered his first spiritual crisis in 1842. Some scholars believe that it was caused by Grigor'ev's recognition of the irreconcilable contradictions between Hegel's philosophy and Orthodox dogmatics.[4] Others blame it on Grigor'ev's unrequited love for Antonina Korsh.[5] In any case, the mid-1840s became the time of Grigor'ev's intense intellectual and moral 'wanderings,' as well as the period of high artistic creativity. He wrote a number of interesting novellas in prose as well as highly innovative poetry, which in the early twentieth century attracted the attention of Russian modernists.

Grigor'ev left Moscow for St Petersburg in 1844 with the hope of establishing himself in the capital as a poet, translator, and critic. His life in Petersburg was full of calamities and adventures. He continued to write both poetry and prose, some of which he published under the pseudonym A. Trismegistov. This pseudonym, an allusion to George Sand's novel *The Countess of Rudolstadt*, reveals Grigor'ev's sympathies with George Sandism and Utopian socialism. After the 1849 arrest of the members of the Petrashevskii circle in Petersburg, Mikhail Saltykov-Schedrin testified at the enquiry that Grigor'ev had frequented the group's Friday gatherings.[6] Whether because he was known to be the protégé of the politically 'reliable' Mikhail Pogodin or for some other reason, Grigor'ev escaped arrest. For a while he lived in Orenburg and then returned to his native Moscow, where his former professor Pogodin (who had taught him Russian history at Moscow University) accepted him, apparently with serious reservations, to join the editorial board of his journal *The Muscovite* (*Moskvitianin*) in 1845. Thus Grigor'ev became one of the 'young editors' of *The Muscovite*, helping to revive this journal and making it competitive with the most powerful Petersburg journals, such as *Library for Reading* (*Biblioteka dlia chteniia*) and *The Contemporary* (*Sovremennik*). Meanwhile, Grigor'ev's personal life remained miserable. An unhappy marriage to Lidiia Korsh and later a liaison with a former prostitute, who became Grigor'ev's common-law wife from 1859 to 1862, did not provide him with the kind of stability this overly sensitive person needed in order to have a long and productive career. Grigor'ev died at an untimely forty-two years of age from a stroke, probably brought on by his unstable life and alcoholism.

Notwithstanding his tragic life, Grigor'ev received recognition in his lifetime as a remarkable poet and a subtle thinker. His solid education and vast reading, which included philosophy, art criticism, literature, and the social sciences, made him one of the most brilliant young critics to move into the limelight after Belinskii's death in 1848. As we learn from one of Grigor'ev's letters to Pogodin (written from Italy, where Grigor'ev lived from October 1857 to August 1858 while serving as a tutor to the adolescent Prince Trubetskoi), contemporaries and Grigor'ev himself often compared him to the dead Belinskii and felt that he ought to replace him. Grigor'ev wrote:

> Turgenev has arrived and we spend entire nights together talking. I read to him what I wrote while abroad. He, putting his finger on the most painful of my personality drawbacks, the lack of systematicity in my thought, its unchecked flow, nonetheless said that 1) only I, at this particular point in time, write with force, that only I have the fullness of knowledge of a certain doctrine, which is not the Slavophile's doctrine, because mine does not advocate exceptionalism [...] 2) that for success I must *repeat over and over again*, like the late Vissarion [Belinskii], that I must limit myself, and that I must repeat again, again, and again without any qualms, 3) and that I have no place where I would repeat my thoughts over and over again, because I cannot join any of the existing movements because none of the existing movements will accept me, because I cannot make any concessions to any of them since I have my own, very strong and integral viewpoint.[7]

This letter was written on 10 March 1858. At this time, Grigor'ev was already a famous critic, but found himself isolated. His only stable professional connection had been with *Moskvitianin*, which he had left in 1857 to go to Italy. Living in Petersburg in 1859, Grigor'ev began to frequent the literary gatherings at A.P. Miliukov's, where he first met Nikolai Strakhov (1828–96), a young scientist and journalist who was a contributor to the *Journal of the Ministry of Public Enlightenment* (*Zhurnal Ministrerstva narodnogo prosvescheniia*).[8] Grigor'ev probably also encountered Mikhail and Fyodor Dostoevsky at Miliukov's. The Dostoevsky brothers and Strakhov, who soon began their collaboration as editors of the new journal *Time* (1861–3), adopted Grigor'ev as the intellectual leader of their budding movement. Throughout the rest of his career, Strakhov remained Grigor'ev's dedicated pupil and keeper of his flame. F.M. Dostoevsky also continued to draw on Grigor'ev's ideas through to the very end of his career. I will return to this topic in the final chapter of this book.

Grigor'ev left an important critical legacy, including a number of articles where he laid out the foundations of his 'organic' school of criticism, important works on A.N. Ostrovskii's dramas and on theatre in general, and a score of incisive literary reviews.[9] He systematized the entire body of Russian literature and criticism in order to show that this body of work represented a gradual historical unfolding of the national spirit, or *narodnost'*.[10] By calling his method 'organic,' he emphasized his distance from the the later Belinskii, a follower of Utopian socialism and materialism. Grigor'ev was also careful to stay away from the then-powerful utilitarian school, which advocated a mechanistic view of both nature and human life. Grigor'ev's method was unabashedly old-fashioned in its commitment to idealism. According to Grigor'ev, Russian culture had existed for centuries in a merely vegetative form (*rastitel'naia forma*) that was devoid of self-consciousness. Only thanks to Peter the Great's reforms, which brought Russians face to face with another culture and made them recognize their own cultural backwardness, did Russians slowly begin to acquire self-consciousness. Grigor'ev saw this process in rather dramatic terms:

> While this nature, with its rich primordial forces and its merciless common sense, lives its own life without confronting other living organisms, as was the case before Peter the Great's reforms, it can still blissfully believe in itself. [...] But suddenly this ancient type, this rich but still unconscious character is brought face to face with another, heretofore completely alien type of life – and this occurs not accidentally and not for a short while, but forever. [...] Primordial forces, once moved from their old place, rise like the ocean waves aroused by a storm; terrible spasms ensue. A bottomless abyss opens up. As soon as the old exclusive [national] type had crumbled, we discovered that we have sympathy for all kinds of different types, that is to say, that there exists an elemental basis for creating various ideals.[11]

Pushkin's art marks a decisive turning point for Grigor'ev: from this point on, the Russian soul, having gone through a stage of romantic self-negation and passionate longing for alien ideals, begins to regain a sense of balance. A mature ability to reconcile different, and even contradictory, intellectual and psychological tendencies is what makes *The Captain's Daughter* and *The Tales of the Late Ivan Petrovich Belkin* truly autonomous expressions of the Russian national character.[12] Here, Pushkin is no longer prey to various enchanting ideals, such as the Byronic hero. Instead, he is now a skilful master capable of wielding different forces (*stikhii*).

Grigor'ev's emphasis on Pushkin as the beginning of a qualitatively new stage in the history of Russian culture is to a large degree indebted to Belinskii's famous cycle of articles, '*Sochineniia Aleksandra Pushkina*.'[13] However, there is a considerable difference between Belinskii's and Grigor'ev's approaches to Pushkin, as was quickly noticed by contemporaries. Belinskii was famously cold toward the poet's prose works written after 1828, and, during the period of his fascination with George Sand, he bitterly criticized Pushkin's Tat'iana Larina for rejecting Onegin's passion and remaining in her loveless marriage. Alexander Druzhinin felt compelled to defend Pushkin's heroine, the undisputed icon of femininity in Russian literature, against Belinskii's overly tendentious critique.[14] It is to Grigor'ev's honour that without ever attacking Belinskii, he boldly states his own critical creed. According to Grigor'ev, Russia's literary genius – Pushkin serving here as the case in point – is open to different influences and is polyphonous and eclectic, reflecting the psychological 'breadth' of the Russian people. The idea of Russian artists' special 'breadth' was Grigor'ev's favourite, an idea that he wanted, as we learn from the above-mentioned letter to Pogodin, 'to repeat again and again.'

Grigor'ev's vision of Russian culture as one characterized by intrinsic heterogeneity, tolerance, and openness toward differences stands out among other, more narrowly partisan aesthetic and critical schools of nineteenth-century Russia. Grigor'ev's ideas played a crucial role in the emergence of the 'native soil' or *pochvennichestvo* movement in the 1860s. It has to be pointed out, however, that although this movement experienced a revival at the end of the nineteenth century and again in the twentieth century, these later versions of pochvennichestvo bore only a distant resemblance to Grigor'ev's original conception. While Grigor'ev's cultural philosophy foregrounded 'breadth,' that is, the desire to continue to expand one's own culture through dialogue with other cultures, later *pochvenniki*, such as Konstantin Leont'ev or

Konstantin Pobedonodtsev, often put the idea of 'native soil' to the service of militant nationalism with a strong dose of xenophobia, sentiments that were alien to Grigor'ev.

Only one twentieth-century cultural theorist shares considerable common ground with Grigor'ev: Yurii Lotman. Lotman's analyses of Pushkin's *Eugene Onegin* and *The Captain's Daughter* as texts formed on the crossroads of different cultures or semiotic 'codes' and, thus, models of what he calls the 'semiosphere,' are somewhat reminiscent of Grigor'ev's writings on Pushkin. This should not be especially surprising since Lotman was well acquainted with Grigor'ev's work. One of the contexts in which Grigor'ev must have emerged on Lotman's intellectual horizon was the poetry of Alexander Blok. The rhetorical shift that Blok, reared in the most elite cultural circles, accomplished in order to become a 'people's poet' was in some ways analogous to Pushkin's trajectory in the 1830s as analysed by Grigor'ev. Together with his wife, Zara Grigor'evna Mints, a prominent Blok scholar, Lotman studied Blok's transformation from a highbrow symbolist poet into one interested in popular culture, including the gypsy romances, some of which were in fact based on Grigor'ev's verses.[15] Indeed, Grigor'ev himself was a major force in transforming Russian lyric poetry, which originated in the aristocratic salons, into a more democratic medium. Therefore, both as a critic and as a poet, Grigor'ev was extremely influential on Blok and some other modernists.[16]

It is also noteworthy that one of Lotman's close personal friends and his first biographer, Boris Egorov, was the leading Soviet scholar of Grigor'ev and the editor of most Soviet editions of Grigor'ev's works.[17] Indeed, on closer scrutiny it becomes clear that the two critics had much in common as individuals. Both saw themselves as thinkers representing the cultural periphery. Grigor'ev, with his noble and peasant heritage, saw himself as a champion of middle-class and provincial Russian culture, whereas Lotman, as a Jew, could never hope to get appointed to a chair in Leningrad or Moscow but managed to transform the peripheral Tartu University into the leading intellectual centre of his age.[18] By dint of good fortune, these two thinkers were able to put their mark on Russian culture, known for its strong centripetal tendency and a rigid normativeness imposed from above, imprinting it with their vision of culture as a constant interplay between centre and periphery, and between different ideas and points of view.

Looking back still further into the history of ideas, we discover that the decentralizing impulse conveyed by Grigor'ev's and Lotman's criticism that I find consonant with the spirit of the Russian Bildungsroman has its background in the German culture of the *Aufklaerung* and, in particular, Herder, whose ideas played a seminal role in Grigor'ev's thinking, and who, upon closer examination, also appears quite congenial to Lotman, which is also not surprising given the latter's lifelong interest in Russian-German intellectual connections during the eighteenth and early nineteenth centuries.

Before going further, I want to focus briefly on Grigor'ev's debt to Herder, for he is ultimately the thinker whose ideas underlie Grigor'ev's culturological insights and also inspired Lotman to reconsider his earlier mechanistic-structuralist position and arrive at the idea of culture as a spiritual organism whose growth depends on dialogue with other cultures.[19]

Herder's understanding of culture, not as a set of rules or norms attained through schooling and maintained through habit, but rather as a lifelong process of *Bildung* that begins when a child first learns his mother tongue and native customs and continues throughout his life through exposure to other cultures and languages, was aimed polemically against French culture, with its emphasis on uniformity and normativity. Herder was also one of the most powerful defenders of the 'smaller' nations, such as the Latvians, the Slavs, and the Jews (whom he encountered during his years in Riga). Not surprisingly, Herder's aesthetics struck a sympathetic chord in the heart of a Russian critic who prided himself on being a denizen of Zamoskvorech'e, rather than a Petersburger, and a spokesman for the urban middle class and working people.[20]

In his early writings on aesthetics, Herder argued that poetry generates psychic energy capable of moving people more effectively than any physical force. Poetry has the power not only to communicate particular thoughts and images but also to elicit in people's minds a special creative capacity.[21] An 'elective affinity' sparks in the reader's soul when he or she encounters a work of art. A like-minded spirit comes to play a powerful role in both individual psychology and history. Grigor'ev's notion of 'current' (*veianie*), which he attributed to spiritual and psychic life and which he carefully distinguished from the realist idea of 'influence' (*vliianie*) borrowed from physics and mechanics, is in the same family of concepts as Herder's notion of 'force' (*Kraft*).[22]

Extrapolating from Herder and applying his ideas to the case of Russia, Grigor'ev argued that Russia's European apprenticeship (which lasted from the time of Peter the Great to Pushkin's age) had a painful, yet momentous significance for the future development of Russia because it broadened the Russian soul, or psyche, and made it responsive to various currents beyond its native milieu. While the period that Grigor'ev designated as 'romantic' was marked by a painful self-alienation, the arrival of the mature Pushkin and his prose works signalled the beginning of a new phase in Russian cultural history: the epoch of maturity.[23] From that point on, Russian culture found its own centre of gravity and its own personality, without, however, losing its propensity for sharing in and learning from the spiritual lives of other people.

In Grigor'ev's analysis, Pushkin, whose soul was able to sympathize with the Byronic hero Aleko and with the old Gypsy, with the raucous Pugachev and with the humble Belkin, becomes for Grigor'ev the epitome of Russia's spiritual strength and psychological breadth befitting a nation situated on the crossroads between East and West, North and South.[24] Dostoevsky echoed Grigor'ev when he spoke later about Pushkin's 'universal responsiveness' (*vsemirnaia otzyvchivost'*).[25] In Grigor'ev, however, the same idea does not carry the chauvinistic and eschatological connotations that it would carry for Dostoevsky. Rather, Grigor'ev's thesis bears a close resemblance to Herder's cosmopolitan vision of intercultural communication, based on the sympathetic encounter between different nations, in the *Letters on the Advancement of Humanity*.[26]

'Humanity' in this sense, though, is not defined by the Enlightenment idea of universal human rights.[27] In fact, both Grigor'ev and Herder were hostile to the idea that a universal principle could ever subsume culture or history. In this respect, it is noteworthy that Grigor'ev rejected Belinskii's reading of Russian literature as destined to synthesize all previous cultures and attain universal humanity, opting instead for the Herderian belief in the irreducibility of individual points of view. Grigor'ev's view (which I find more sophisticated) is never tempted by these messianic hopes. Grigor'ev argues, instead, that as a result of Russia's fortuitous geographical location between Europe and Asia, its culture developed a proclivity for sympathy as a cultural necessity. But given that cultural resource, Russia was uniquely equipped, in the Europe of Grigor'ev's time, to become a leader in the emerging humanistic dialogue among nations. What may seem like evidence of Russia's backwardness from the Western perspective – the lack of a homogeneous culture to which all could refer – was actually a secret advantage in Grigor'ev's view: Russia's special vitality emerged from the interaction of various cultural forces and would resist, as well, the homogenizing force of instrumental reason that was sweeping Europe.

Grigor'ev's philosophy cast a long shadow over Russian culture in the decades after his death in that he codified the Russian intellectuals' sense that their culture was a legatee of European civilization while also having its own inimitable face. In this connection, it is important to bear in mind that when, in the 1880s, Grigor'ev's self-appointed heir, Nikolai Strakhov, defined Russia's entire *Geistesgeschichte* in terms of 'struggle with Europe,' he added a crudely antagonistic connotation to the heretofore peaceful ideology of *pochvennichestvo*.[28] Grigor'ev himself carefully avoided binary oppositions, keeping his cultural nationalism from turning into a militant theory of national exclusivity.

3 Yurii Lotman's Idea of the 'Semiosphere'

Yurii Lotman spent most of his career as a professor of Russian literature at the University of Tartu, formerly the University of Dorpat, in Estonia. By coincidence, it was here that the German critic Karl Morgenstern presented his lecture on the Bildungsroman in 1819, which introduced into Russian cultural space the idea of the novel of apprenticeship as a symbolic form of modernity. In keeping with Humboldt's pedagogical theory, Morgenstern conceptualized *Bildung* as the cultivation of the enlightened individual personality within the favourable conditions of the peaceful post-Napoleonic age.[1] The supposed 'eternal peace' of the age of 'Holy Alliance' coincided with the epoch when the idea of *Bildung*, or cultivation, first crossed the border into Russian culture. The boundary between the Russian and German cultures was quite porous at the time, with the Baltic region serving as what Lotman would call a 'membrane' across which mutual translation and dialogue occurred most intensely. This is not to say that Lotman was consciously thinking of himself as the heir to Morgenstern, a professor of aesthetics at the German-speaking Russian Imperial University of Dorpat, even though both of them worked on the same campus. Unlike Morgenstern, who was a typical German intellectual of his age,[2] Lotman felt himself to be part of several intellectual schools and traditions. After writing his dissertation on Radischev and Karamzin, Lotman completed his training as a specialist in eighteenth-century literature. However, later in his career he extended his scholarship beyond this field. As a mature scholar, Lotman exploited his singularly broad horizon of interests and his immense erudition to range over subjects from Old Russian literature and medieval theology to modern scientific disciplines like cybernetics, quantum mechanics, and information theory.[3]

Lotman's connections with eighteenth-century culture are attested by the fact that, toward the end of his life, he publicly embraced the vocation of public educator or *Aufklaerer*. His lectures on Russian culture were recorded and televised throughout the former Soviet Union. Indeed, the imprint of the Enlightenment concern for intellectual rigour and culturally informed tolerance is easily discerned in every one of Lotman's texts. Here, indeed, he is a spiritual cousin to Morgenstern, who also believed that literature can play an active educational and humanitarian role in society. Lotman, like Morgenstern, also saw the novel as a quintessentially modern, Janus-faced genre with one face gazing inward toward the personality of the protagonist and one outward toward the audience it seeks to develop. At the same time, Lotman's theory of the novel implicitly offers a revision of the nineteenth-century idea of the Bildungsroman.[4] Informed by the new science of semiotics, Lotman's approach owes an intellectual debt to the German discourses on Bildung and the Bildungsroman of the eighteenth century. Yet we should not exaggerate the Enlightenment influence on his ideas. Most importantly, I want to point out that Lotman's cultural theory and his theory of the novel articulate themes from Russian intellectual and literary history, with their characteristic emphasis on cultural breadth, dynamism, and hybridization. The German national project, seeking a homogeneous Germanness, could not be more foreign from Lotman's project, which embraces the tradition extending from Grigor'ev's emphasis on Russia's exposure to Europe as a symptom of Russian spiritual maturation. A recent biography of Lotman written by his friend and colleague B.F. Egorov sheds new light on the significance of the twin issues of cultural identity and tolerance for differences that were so important to Lotman, a Jew from Leningrad who narrowly escaped assignment to a teaching position (*raspredelenie*) in a remote region of the Urals or Siberia. Lotman was lucky to find his position at the Soviet Empire's western periphery, where memories of Estonian independence, won in 1920 and maintained until the end of the Second World War, were still fresh. German was still the language of the educated elite in Estonia. Many of Lotman's colleagues were trilingual. And yet, when Lotman first came to Tartu in the early 1950s, Stalin's anti-cosmopolitanism campaign still weighed heavily in the atmosphere, making it dangerous to express the idea that, since each national culture and language carries its own 'world,' a complex hermeneutic is logically required to understand how translation occurs between different cultures.

How is translation possible? How is it enacted? In this connection, we might recall that the problem of translation was also a huge factor in the rise of structuralism during the 1950s and was taken up by such diverse figures as the American philosopher Willard Van Orman Quine and the French anthropologist Claude Levi-Strauss. This was partly the result of the cybernetic revolution after the Second World War. The question of coding was no longer an abstract, philosophical one, but, as Norbert Wiener, the son of Leo Wiener (one of Tolstoy's American translators) pointed out, it became a question of translation as the 'interpretation of language by ear and by brain.'[5]

Stalin's Russian chauvinism must have reminded Lotman, whose mind was well stocked with Russian history, of the 'official nationalisms' of Nicholas I and Alexander III. However, as soon as Khruschev's 'thaw' came along, Lotman began to formulate his new approach to Russian literature, one that took into account the inherent heterogeneity and diversity of Russian culture. Already in the 1962 essay 'The Ideological Structure of *The Captain's Daughter*' we can glimpse the idea that there is an inherent multiplicity of perspectives and approaches to the truth in any cultural sphere, which is the first indication of his future semiotic theory of culture.[6]

Lotman's turn to the theory of the novel and narratology (for which he is best known in the West) is codified in his *Structure of the Artistic Text* (*Struktura khudozhestvennogo teksta*) and his 1975 monograph on Pushkin's *Eugene Onegin*, based on an article published in 1966.[7] David Bethea, Amy Mandelker, and some other critics have already pointed out Lotman's connections with his older contemporary, Mikhail Bakhtin, and his notion of polyphonic discourse, which seems congenial to and yet in subtle ways different from Lotman's approach.[8] Like Bakhtin, Lotman sees dialogue as a sine qua non of any communication event that leads to an advance of consciousness. It is also generally assumed now that Lotman is indebted to the narrative theories of the Russian Formalists. His attempt to reconceive dialogism (which Bakhtin perceived in phenomenological, ethical, and aesthetic terms) as a narratological principle is linked to the influence of Viktor Shklovskii, Yurii Tynianov, and Vladimir Propp. Thus, where Bakhtin himself saw the polyphonic novel as a genre related to philosophical dialogue and the Menippean satire, or *satura*, Lotman instead views the novel in more traditional diegetic terms, as a story reflecting the movement across a space populated by different cultures and languages. This insight is expressed most poignantly in *The Structure of the Artistic Text*, where

Lotman introduces optical metaphors to discuss the narrative originality of Pushkin's *Eugene Onegin* as a story that takes multiple points of view as a structuring principle.[9] By moving from one point of view to another, Pushkin's narrator, and the reader along with him, broaden their horizons – their capacity to imagine possibilities – and grow inwardly though the accumulation of experiences.

I suggest that Lotman's emphasis on the novel's 'realistic irony,' the form's inherent capability to transcend the subjective point of view – a capacity that Lotman calls 'realistic irony' to differentiate it from the playful 'romantic irony' that Kierkegaard criticized with reference to Friedrich Schlegel – may be viewed not only, or perhaps even not necessarily, as a sign of Lotman's rapprochement with Bakhtin's dialogism.[10] As is well known, considerable differences remained between Bakhtin and Lotman. Bakhtin's notion of 'novelization' implied a strictly teleological view of human history with which Lotman disagreed.[11] My hypothesis is that Lotman's conception of 'realistic irony' harks back to Apollon Grigor'ev's conception of 'universal responsiveness' (*vsemirnaia otzyvchivost'*). This is not so surprising given that, as mentioned above, Grigor'ev was the main subject of Egorov's research and was constantly within Lotman's purview while Lotman was developing his semiotics. Remarkably, the Lotman-Egorov connection was a dialogue rather than simply a one-way street. While Egorov was mostly a traditional philologist, in the 1970s he also began to apply more innovative methods of analysis, apparently under Lotman's influence.[12]

I will offer another hypothesis: Lotman's interest in Pushkin during the 1960s and 1970s was at least in part inspired by Grigor'ev's famous thesis about Pushkin as the quintessence of modern Russia's cultural proteanism. According to Grigor'ev, whose humanistic rhetoric was shot through with implicit references to Herder and Goethe, Pushkin's novelistic phase constituted Russia's coming of age as a culture, the point at which Russia shed its defensiveness or hostility toward the inevitable European 'other.' This did not mean, however, that having entered into 'history,' Russian culture could stop developing. As I have argued above, Grigor'ev envisioned spiritual maturity as a continual intellectual growth that has no natural limit. This stage of true *Bildung*, as opposed to simple instinctual mimicry, begins once the individual Weltanschauung has been developed. Only then can one truly expand one's horizons and learn from others without mimicking them or compromising one's own self.

Lotman's conception of the 'multiperspectival' novel did not place this narrative under the sign of romantic dandyism, a sort of extension of Pushkin's Byronic moment, but interpreted it as a narrative that escaped the problem of the romantic self by postulating genuine spiritual growth or Bildung. To see what Lotman was up to here, we need to look at his theory of the novel in conjunction with his semiotic theory. From this vantage point, the 'multiperspectival' novel appears as a particularly salient moment in what Lotman calls the 'semiosphere,' the realm of human cultural activity that embraces all social strata, linguistic registers, and semiotic codes.[13] The term 'semiosphere' was coined as an analogy to the terms 'biosphere' and 'noosphere,' suggested by V.I. Vernadskii, a prominent twentieth-century geologist, geochemist, and philosopher who subscribed to the organicist conception of continuity between organic and inorganic, material and spiritual forces.[14] Thus, the earth is itself an evolutionary entity, according to Vernadskii, which has gone through several stages that can each be studied as a separate layer: 'geosphere,' 'biosphere,' and 'noosphere.' The last term, which stems from the Greek *nous*, represents the evolutionary stage connected with the advent of human intelligence. Lotman's 'semiosphere' likewise rests on evolutionary assumptions. He explicitly states that the realm of human intelligence and sign-making is dynamic and has found no material limit to its continuing expansion.[15]

However, as suggestive as his larger conceptions have proven to be, according to my hypothesis, Vernadskii was not the primary source of inspiration behind Lotman's turn to organicism. I believe that Grigor'ev's organic criticism, with its emphasis on culture as a dynamic entity that accrues through dialogic encounters with other cultures, ultimately stands behind Lotman's transformation from a more or less canonical *literaturoved* trained by G.A. Gukovsky and N.I. Mordovchenko into a semiotician and an original philosopher of culture. Grigor'ev's most important legacy is his anti-Belinskian (and anti-Hegelian) view of culture, not as a dialectic aimed at a certain rationally cognizable goal, but rather as a perpetual interplay of different 'forces' that constantly displace the cultural 'centre,' bringing 'peripheries' to the fore. Once Grigor'ev introduced these ideas into Russian cultural space, they proceeded to have their own, sometimes subterranean, existence, affecting thinkers even during the part of the Soviet period when a vulgar form of 'dialectical materialism' was de rigueur in academia. Reading Lotman and Grigor'ev side by side, we discover striking similarities between these thinkers in terms of spirit. Both of them were anti-dogmatic thinkers with a broad purview interested in the possibility of reconciling national identity with a genuine interest in foreign culture. We also discover overlaps in terms of language and terminology. Knowing Lotman's expertise in eighteenth-century culture and intellectual history, we can also assume that Grigor'ev's sources, including, first of all, Herder, were not unknown to Lotman (not that Herder could have been neglected in any case by a semiotician, given the Herderian background of modern linguistics, semiotics, and cultural theory).[16]

Uncovering Lotman's filiations with Grigor'ev and Herder can be useful in a number of ways. It throws into relief Lotman's originality as a thinker vis-à-vis such influential contemporary thinkers and schools as the Russian Formalists, Bakhtin, French structuralism, and especially Niklas Luhmann's influential 'systems-theoretical' method, which was in vogue at the time when Lotman was working out his own theory of the 'semiosphere.'[17] A brief comparison of Lotman's theory with Luhmann's might be helpful here as a way of drawing a contrast between organic and mechanistic visions of human social life, especially since the themes of these two thinkers are sometimes conflated. Against the background of Luhmann's post-humanist 'systems theory,' which provides an all-encompassing mechanistic explanation of society and cognition, Lotman's 'semiosphere' appears as one of the last great humanistic visions.[18] It is an open system endowed with more than the capacity for mere self-reproduction, as it can be traversed by qualitative transformations that are not the linear effect of some specific cause. The most dynamic layer of the 'semiosphere' is art, which allows humans to attain self-consciousness and mastery over their existence. By modelling their lives through art, human beings are able to look beyond the realm of mechanistic nature and attain freedom. The idea of the human being as an author of his own life was one of Lotman's favourite metaphors. Thus, he concludes 'The Phenomenon of Art,' one of the pivotal chapters in *Culture and Explosion*, with the following statement:

> Art is a means of acquiring knowledge and, above all, the knowledge of man. This position has been repeated so often that it has become trivial. However, what should we understand by the expression the 'knowledge of man'? The plots defined by this expression have one common feature: they place man into a situation of freedom and investigate his behavior in that situation. No real situation – from the most everyday to the most unexpected – can exhaust the entire sum of possibilities and, therefore, all

of the actions which serve to reveal the potentialities of man. The authentic essence of man cannot, in reality, be revealed. Art transports man into a world of freedom and thereby elaborates his possible behaviors. Thus, any work of art generates a kind of norm and then violates this norm and sets – at least within the realm of the free imagination – a new norm for all actions. The cyclical world of Plato destroying the unexpected in the behavior of man and introducing indisputable rules, itself destroys art.[19]

This statement is one of many in Lotman's oeuvre where art is celebrated as the realm of 'the free imagination,' which offers a way of transcending the realm of 'reason.'[20] It brings to mind the aesthetic theories of the Romantics and modernists, the interpretation of which was the object of many of Lotman's philological studies. But the reader without this background knowledge might also think that this bears a resemblance to Luhmann's theory of systems in the prominent role given to the 'autopoesis' of consciousness by both theorists. We must bear in mind, however, that Luhmann's 'autopoesis' is modelled on the neurobiological explanation of cognition as a self-producing mechanism offered by the Chilean biologist and cybernetician Humberto Maturana, whereas Lotman's theory is, at root, organicist and humanistic.[21] Indeed, as I will show, while the letter may seem Luhmannian, the spirit is Herder's. A profound belief in the universal human desire for understanding and friendship underlies Lotman's theory, setting it apart from the stochastic causal structure of Luhmann's.

Of course, Lotman does recognize the crucial role that contingency plays in communication.[22] In his essay 'On The Two Models of Communication,' the merely automatic information processing of the machine is distinguished from human communication as a productive event precisely by the fact that the latter is spurred by chance. The starting point of Lotman's analysis recalls a situation that Luhmann calls 'double contingency,' in which two (plus) persons and their respective 'codes' (a term that Lotman and his Tartu colleagues may have borrowed from Roland Barthes, whose fame had already reached them), each of which is unknown to the other, are placed side by side.[23] Neither party can predict the other's behaviour.[24] Their encounter resembles a card game in which the opponents try to keep their cards from being seen by each other, with the significant difference being that they are playing from different decks, with cards that are assessed at different values. Both Luhmann and Lotman agree that this process cannot be modelled as a simple transmission of information since 'information' is not a discrete, unchangeable entity.

It is not a 'thing.' Therefore, both scholars prefer the term 'communication' to 'information exchange' when describing the collision of two communicating 'systems' (to use Luhmann's language) or between two semiotic 'codes' (to use Lotman's term from the 1970s and early 1980s).[25]

In Luhmann's picture, as the two systems rub against each other, they create an illusion of understanding. This forms material for new information, which is thus discharged into informational space, but this activity only increases the quantity of human knowledge without introducing any qualitative changes into the structure of the human mind. The sender and receiver, in other words, are unchanged, except insofar as they have accumulated more information. Lotman's analysis of what he calls the 'I-I communication,' or 'autocommunication,' differs in very subtle ways from Luhmann's.[26] 'Autocommunication,' Lotman suggests, involves the feedback of information to oneself, leading to the restructuring of the semiotic subject, or, as we might say, to his or her *Bildung*. The sender is not only, in this picture, potentially changed externally by forming a relationship with the receiver, but the sender's internal sense of him/herself will also be changed in that relationship. The same feedback effect applies to the receiver.

Both Lotman's 'autocommunication' and Luhmann's 'autopoesis' involve the destruction of the habitual point of view. In this regard, both theories resemble the Formalist conception of 'defamiliarization,' or *ostranenie*, also aimed at shaking off routine ideas and perceptions and liberating creative energy. However, only Lotman insists that this shift in perspective leads to qualitative change within the communicative agent's personality. As Lotman explains, 'The communicative system "I-He" allows only the transmission of a certain constant amount of information, whereas the channel "I-I" allows for a qualitative transformation of this information. This transformation leads to the restructuring of the subject of communication, the original "I." '[27]

A necessary condition of this restructuring of the semiotic agent, or 'I,' is the fact that this 'I' is not simply confined to a particular 'code,' but is herself immersed in the milieu that Bakhtin would call polyphonic. In Luhmann's picture, dialogue occurs between two semiotic systems, whereas in Lotman's theory, there is always a third party involved, another 'code' or person in whom we can recognize Bakhtin's 'superaddressee':

> The mechanism of information translation in the channel 'I-I' can be described as follows: first we introduce a certain message in the natural

language. Then we introduce some secondary code, which can be a purely formal syntagmatic construction, which is either completely free from semantic meanings or aspiring to such freedom. A tension arises between the original message and the secondary code. As a result, the semantics of the original code acquire additional (relative) meanings by becoming associated with the syntagmatic construction of the secondary code.[28]

We can now briefly sum up the differences between Lotman's 'autocommunication' and Luhmannian 'autopoesis.' Luhmann's goal is to provide a model that would describe the increasing complexity of human intellectual life as a product of the completely immanent human capacity. There is no 'outsideness' in Luhmann and no opportunity for transcending the realm of sheer contingency. Consequently, there is no room for any kind of ethically meaningful freedom. Lotman, on the other hand, finds it necessary to add a dimension of inner growth, or *Bildung*, to 'autocommunication.'

Bearing in mind the influence of Bakhtin's idea of dialogue on Lotman, it is clear that Lotman's 'autocommunication' has a humanistic dimension that supervenes on contingency. There is a meaningful sense in which we can speak of choices made by the actors in the 'semiosphere.' The encounter between two mutually opaque, untranslatable codes, Lotman tells us, is a situation that cries out for responsible agents, and even heroes. In one of the chapters of *Culture and Explosion*, he offers a close reading of Blok's poem 'Khudozhnik' ('The Artist'), which illuminates his view of creativity by bringing into the picture Blok's own metapoetic description of it.[29] Lotman argues that the poet's search for the right word requires a leap outside of the semiotically structured reality into the realm of the noumenal, or what Kant called 'the thing itself.' It is a transcendental feat. According to Lotman, this creative leap produces a shock within the poet's soul that consists of stripping away the automatism that has grown up around the routine codes of her everyday, institutionally approved use. It also gives the poet an acute sensation of freedom, or of the possibilities inherent in the word, which we cannot obtain in our routinized daily lives, where words are subordinate to their instrumental uses. In this moment of suspension between different codes, the poet enjoys freedom.[30] But as soon as she makes up her mind and fixes her line by choosing a particular word, transforming pure potentiality into actuality, she abdicates her freedom and once again succumbs to inertia.[31]

Even a brief comparison of Lotman's system with Luhmann's is sufficient to throw into relief the humanistic presuppositions and aspirations behind the former. As is shown in my brief analysis of his 'autocommunication' model, Lotman endows 'defamiliarized' thinking with moral value, manifesting his latent commitment to the idea of 'action,' or *praxis* (which was banished by Luhmann as too 'metaphysical').[32]

This humanistic bent becomes more pronounced in Lotman's later work, as he works out the principles of the 'semiosphere.' Thus, for example, in his biography of Pushkin, Lotman elaborates on the idea of contingency, suggesting that Pushkin's genius manifested itself in life and art as a special improvisatory knack that allowed him to seize opportunities for creative thinking and transform them into action. Lotman takes Pushkin's duel as the prime example of how contingency can be transformed into one's self-chosen destiny, imparting dignity and deep meaningfulness to an otherwise tumultuous, unhappy, and chaos-ridden life.[33]

In this connection, one might well ask whether Lotman's elevation of self-conscious, goal-driven praxis was the effect of some compromise with the Soviet Marxist orthodoxy of his time. My own sense is that Lotman was quite sincere in his vindication of art as the realm of humanistic *Bildung*. Incidentally, Raymond Williams viewed creativity along similar lines as Lotman. Williams, too, was trying to reconcile his Marxist Utopianism with a rigorous scientific approach to meaning-making.[34]

Parallels between Lotman and Williams (whose socialism made him less of a persona non grata in the Soviet Union than some other Western sociologists, including Luhmann) have yet to be explored in any depth.[35] Here I will limit myself to noting just a few parallels, as well as some striking overlaps between these thinkers' ideas, in order to establish a context outside the Russian cultural sphere that will help us gain a perspective on the dynamics within that sphere. Both men were well aware that the task facing the contemporary cultural critic was to grasp the dynamics of cultural change in the age of media revolution and gradual democratization of life. One of the notable parallels between these thinkers is that they share an interest in recovering the legacy of conservative cultural thinkers – Karamzin and, covertly, the *pochvenniki* line in Russian cultural history in Lotman's case, and Burke, Coleridge, and Arnold in the case of Williams. In *Culture and Society*, Williams tells a story of how nineteenth-century radicals and conservatives, materialists and idealists, who are usually seen as separated by unbridgeable intellectual gaps, were, in fact, part of the same broad cultural stream and jointly possessed the same cultural inheritance.[36]

Lotman's critical retrieval of thinkers like Karamzin and those he influenced, including, first of all, the later Pushkin, proceeds along similar lines. Lotman's objective as a cultural historian is to uncover the dialogic construction of Russian culture via different media and across the spectrum of ideological positions. Thus, the history of modernity as told by both Williams and Lotman emerges as a story of gradual social revolution (which Williams calls 'long revolution'), gathering momentum in the epoch of the technological revolution, which produced and intensified exchanges between different people and points of view that had once been globally distant. The sphere of 'humanity' shaped through communication and interpretation continually expands throughout modernity.

4 The Semiospheric Novel and the Broadening of Cultural Self-Consciousness

I want to argue that Lotman's so-called formula of the Russian novel represents an updated version of Grigor'ev's conception of what Pushkin's prose meant to the subsequent Russian literary tradition, that is, that Russian culture would henceforth be self-consciously dependent on the presence of other cultures for its continual vitality and growth.[1] Sympathy (*sochuvstvie*, Herder's *Einfuehlung*) with otherness is, for Grigor'ev, the precondition for genuine *Bildung*. In this way, Grigor'ev abolishes the determination of *Bildung* by some set end or purpose (for example, Schaftesbury's 'virtuosity,' which influenced Wilhelm von Humboldt's idea of 'individuality') and takes it, instead, as a process that broadens and deepens the consciousness beyond the personality's immediate social milieu and innate instincts and tastes. The social determination implicit in the inevitable transformation of thought into language is trumped and transcended by the freeing power of dialogue. Elaborating on Grigor'ev's idea, Dostoevsky later spoke about the 'universal responsiveness' of Pushkin's muse, which he saw as a sine qua non of Russia's literary maturity.[2] We can recognize the imprint of these ideas in Lotman's writings on Pushkin, which also present him as the reformer who took the Russian novel out of its captivity by 'romantic' subjectivity and released it into a multiperspectival 'realistic' form.[3] I am setting 'romantic' and 'realistic' in quotation marks here to emphasize the fact that Lotman's use of these terms relies on a long-standing Russian critical tradition of juxtaposing these two artistic visions or methods. According to the Soviet critical orthodoxy, whose pillar was V.G. Belinskii, the inception of realism signalled the overcoming of the narrowly subjective romantic consciousness and a move toward a broader and more objective vision of reality. In his earlier works, Lotman follows this ideological pattern, which regarded realism as a more 'progressive' stage of consciousness, one that signals the reconciliation between the subject and object, and the individual and society.[4]

Grigor'ev, on the contrary, in calling himself 'the last Romantic,' implied that his artistic credo diverges from Belinskii's. Grigor'ev was unconvinced by the Hegelian synthesis of subject and object; he believed that a genuine 'breadth' of vision would not yield a peaceful reconciliation between the striving hero and the surrounding world such as was encoded in Goethe's *Wilhelm Meister's Apprenticeship* and his autobiography, *Dichtung und Wahrheit*. Thus it is telling that in Grigor'ev's own autobiography, *Moi literaturnye i nravstvnnye skital'chetsva*, he depicts the intellectual and spiritual expansion of his personality as an unsettling process that never yields any sense of holism. Like Dostoevsky's mature novels (which, as I will show in chapter 7, were intellectually indebted to Grigor'ev), Grigor'ev's autobiography is 'unfinalized,' lacking closure. This formal decision is in sync with Grigor'ev's view of culture and subjectivity, which he understood in pluralistic terms. For him, neither a national culture nor an individual subject could ever attain the kind of formal coherence and 'harmony' that became codified in the European Bildungsroman tradition from Goethe to Thomas Mann.[5] As I argued earlier, Grigor'ev's view stems from his perception of Russian reality, with its extreme diversity of cultural viewpoints and ideologies. However, it is also rooted in Herder's view of world culture, diverging from those of Herder's subsequent interpreters, including Goethe and Hegel, who hypothesized that the end of *Bildung* must occur in some moment of peaceful reconciliation and synthesis with, as Hegel put it, the Absolute Spirit.

For Lotman, to affirm Romanticism against realism would have been tantamount to breaking with the critical tradition in which he was trained. And yet, already in 'The Ideological Structure of *The Captain's Daughter*' Lotman wrestles with the problem of irreducible, unbridgeable cultural differences that cannot be overcome through *Aufhebung* ('sublation'). In *The Structure of Artistic Text*, Lotman continues to think through this problem by offering a compromise between Romanticism (with its subjectivism) and realism (viewed traditionally as the broadening of perspective beyond one's own subjectivity). 'Realist irony' is the bridging term, which Lotman defines as follows:

> [...] the sequence of semantic-stylistic breaks creates, not a focused but a scattered, multiple point of view, and it becomes the centre of a

supra-system which is perceived as the illusion of reality itself. For the realistic style, attempting to exceed the boundaries of subjectivism of semantic-stylistic 'points of view,' and to create an objective reality, there was great import in the specific interrelation of these multiple centers, these varied (adjacent or mutually superposed) structures. Each one does not replace the others, but correlates with them. As a result the text means not only what it means, but something else as well. The new meaning does not supplant the old, but correlates with it. As a result the artistic model reproduces a very important aspect of reality – the fact that there is no exhaustive, finite interpretation.[6]

If this definition still seems somewhat tenuous, it is because at this stage in his work, Lotman still lacked a full methodological and conceptual independence from the Soviet-era doctrines of realism and Romanticism. Yet here we can already see the seed of what later on would become his theory of the 'semiosphere.' The 'multiperspectival' novelistic text is a microcosm that models reality as envisioned pluralistically, that is, as a sphere populated by multiple semiotic agents and 'languages.' This diversity leads to the infinite proliferation of opinions and ideas.

But as the realm of human knowledge continues to expand, the capacity to relate different points of view to each other becomes more and more problematic. The problem of what the French philosopher Jean-François Lyotard calls the *différend* – the incommensurability of different ideologies and cultures, or 'modes of presenting the universe' (for instance, the tragic as opposed to the technical) – preoccupied Lotman, as well as many intellectuals whose careers spanned the Cold War, when the problem of incompatible ideologies incited violence across the globe and threatened to precipitate a nuclear war.[7]

In this connection, the topos of humanity (*chelovechnost'*), first mentioned in Lotman's 1962 essay on Pushkin's *The Captain's Daughter*, resurfaces with increasing frequency in his later work, especially his biographies of Pushkin and Karamzin.[8] He comes to think of texts not purely as literary creations but also as human documents through which their authors seek to make sense of lived experience. It is, of course, impossible for Lotman to return to the idea of authorship as a stable observation point. Still, the Barthesian scepticism about authorship gives way in the mature Lotman to the idea of the author as a responsible agent who has managed to find a *point d'appui* amid the flux of languages and ideas and, by so doing, to establish a channel through which different individuals and cultures can talk to each other.

Using the terminology of the 'semiosphere' essay, we could speak of the author as somebody who self-consciously decided to serve as the 'membrane' that accomplishes 'translation' between different semiotic fields and agents.[9]

In his final book, *Culture and Explosion* (*Kul'tura i vzryv*), Lotman unequivocally defines the novelistic genre as a vehicle of dialogue between the author and readers – a dialogue that does not result in a dialectical synthesis of different points of view but instead creates a medium where individuals can commune in their shared experience of empathy with fictional heroes: 'The novel [...] creates the space of the "third person." In linguistic terms, the latter is objective and external to the world of the reader and the author. Nevertheless, the space is simultaneously experienced by the author as something created by him, i.e. intimately colored, and by the reader as something personal. The third person is emotionally enriched by the aura of the first person.'[10]

In a gesture that Bakhtin would have probably dismissed as overtly didactic, Lotman aligns his theory of the novel with the traditional idea of the Bildungsroman as a text that gazes outward toward the community it tries to mould. But the spirit of this admonition is not quite the same idea as the nineteenth-century German vision of self-cultivation, where good moral sense was cultivated via aesthetic judgment or taste. For Lotman, however, *Bildung* is a process that structurally resists any kind of aesthetic closure. In this regard it differs from the Humboldtian approach to *Bildung* reiterated in Morgenstern's lecture on the Bildungsroman. The nineteenth-century idea aims at the cultivation of a 'beautiful soul' and should be seen in the context of the nineteenth-century fetishism of the supposedly ideal Greek soul. In juxtaposition to this stable ideal, Lotman proposes the idea of culture as a perpetual defamiliarization and 'explosion.' A cultivated mind, according to Lotman, is one that can cross multiple semiotic boundaries and that thrives on the challenge posed by translation and interpretation.

As Caryl Emerson has shown, *Culture and Explosion* is Lotman's most eloquent defence of the ethics of unfinalizability, made famous by Bakhtin's philosophy of art as prosaics.[11] The key idea of this work, which was not written but rather dictated, is summed up in the interview with one of the perestroika-era journals that is the epigraph to this chapter. It cogently states Lotman's credo as a Russian-Jewish intellectual whose successful academic career was, at least in part, due to his good luck, which brought him to the peripheral Estonian university where he could enjoy intellectual freedom and take advantage of the multicultural intellectual atmosphere. Lotman's optimistic vision of the 'semiosphere' as a realm of constant intellectual development and growth (rather than merely as an arena of culture wars) shows that he saw himself as a beneficiary of historical circumstances. This was a self-consciously chosen position on the part of an intellectual who preferred to be the master of his intellectual realm and not merely a subject to history, fate, or the norms established by others.

The critical approach I bring to the novels I will be discussing in this book is organized by the idea of *Bildung* and the theory of the multiperspectival novel that developed on Russian soil from the time of Grigor'ev to Lotman. These novels belong to a special type of Bildungsroman that I see as a specific pattern in Russian cultural life, one propelled into existence by the resistance to monological official discourse on national identity in nineteenth-century Russia. Therefore, despite their shared thematic focus on national identity, we will not find in these texts a uniform sense of what it means to be Russian. My task is to show that the animosity to any kind of fixed ideological or instrumental thinking, which Western scholars now associate with the work of the Russian literary theorists Bakhtin and Lotman, is, in fact, central to the nineteenth-century novelistic tradition. Thus, all three novels discussed in this study portray personal and national evolution or *Bildung* as a perpetual expansion of the horizon that forecloses on all attempts to bring about some kind of absolute, identifying closure, whether imposed by philistinism, by political oppression, or – as we shall see most clearly in the case of Tolstoy – by death (which, as Tolstoy would claim, actually opens an altogether new vista and offers us a new, brighter vision of life).

Although these works play into a specifically Russian experience of modernity as an increasing demand to face heteroglossia within an unevenly developed society, they have been received, especially by critics and novelists outside of Europe and North America, as an occasion for meditating on the problem of culture beyond the confines of normativity imposed by and supported through the political and pedagogical institutions of the nation state. In light of the intellectual tradition I am trying to uncover, the Russian imperial milieu can be seen as the prototype for Lotman's 'semiosphere,' which is itself a distant echo of Herder's ideal of *'Humanität'* (humanity) and of Goethe's *Weltliteratur*.

Consequently, the ideas of culture and acculturation, or *Bildung*, come to take on new meaning by being put into relation with the problem of mutual untranslatability and the non-synchronicity of different layers or strata of the 'semiosphere.' The works of Pushkin, Tolstoy, and Dostoevsky offer imaginative scenarios that flesh out these increasingly vital modern issues, raising our awareness and helping us find a language in which to debate them.

Part II

Nineteenth-Century Russian Novels of Emergence

5 Pushkin's Quest for National Culture: *The Captain's Daughter* as a Russian Bildungsroman

О сколько нам открытий чудных
Готовят просвещенья дух
И опыт, сын ошибок трудных,
И гений, парадоксов друг,
И случай, Бог изобретатель

Oh we have so many wondrous revelations
In store from the spirit of enlightenment
And experience, the son of arduous errors,
And genius, that friend of paradoxes,
And coincidence, God the inventor.[1]

Pushkin and the Enlightenment

Pushkin's attitude toward *prosvechshenie*, the Russian term for enlightenment as education (when the word begins with a small 'p') and for the Age of Enlightenment (when it starts with a capital 'P'), has always appeared as one of the more puzzling aspects of the writer's legacy.[2] Pushkin was undoubtedly one of the most cultivated persons of his age, and his writings display a firm grasp of contemporary European intellectual life as well as a very good command of the classics. As the writer grew more mature, he became interested in popular education, contributing fairy tales and books that could be read by the people. At the same time, Pushkin's journalistic writings also contain some deeply sceptical remarks about the virtues of the public sphere, which he saw as prone to conformism and vulgarity. Furthermore, Pushkin was well aware of the darker side of the eighteenth-century Enlightenment in the form in which it had been autocratically imposed upon Russia. In fact, he spent the last phase of his life studying eighteenth-century history and culture and working on a history of Peter the Great's reign, which he never finished.

The only completed historical work by Pushkin is his *History of Pugachev's Rebellion*.[3] It recounts one of the bloodier episodes in eighteenth-century Russian history: a civil war (1773–5) that shook the very foundations of Catherine II's 'enlightened autocracy' and resulted in the infliction of appallingly barbarous punishments on the rebels and the population that supported them.[4] This historical event also serves as the background for Pushkin's novel *The Captain's Daughter*, published in the fourth issue of Pushkin's journal, *The Contemporary* (1836). As I will argue, this novel, conceived alongside Pushkin's historical study but aimed at a younger and broader audience, represents one of the first novels of apprenticeship in Russian literature. At the same time, this work also offers a summary of Pushkin's reflections on the destinies of the Russian *prosvechshenie*.[5]

Published in a journal rather than as a separate volume, *The Captain's Daughter* was evidently addressed to the expanding circle of subscribers to the Russian 'thick journals,' whom Pushkin wanted to edify as much as entertain.[6] In the second half of the 1830s this audience was getting broader than it had been in Catherine or Alexander's time (when the public sphere first emerged), stretching beyond the cultural elite of the two capitals and including an increasing provincial readership.[7] It encompassed the nobility, the gentry, and members of other social strata, such as merchants, who had also become consumers of literature as it transformed from a product of the court to a product of commerce. Even as the social conditions of his readership were changing, however, Pushkin continued to see himself in terms of the old humanistic ideal of the poet-cum-sage advising the rulers and men or women of influence. He retained his eighteenth-century view that writers must be men of honour (*honnêtes hommes*), selflessly dedicated to cultivation, learning, and the pursuit of the truth. In this connection, I want to stress the enduring significance of William Mills Todd III's approach to Pushkin's *Eugene Onegin* as a literary work embedded in the cultural codes and norms of polite society. My own goal in this chapter is to demonstrate the continuity between Pushkin's formative years, when he was still steeped in the culture of the salon society, and his later phase as a public educator on the national scale who was interested in broadening his readership beyond the salon.[8]

In Pushkin's mind, the role of public intellectuals overlapped with that of Russian gentlemen (i.e., the middle and low gentry, many of whom belonged to old but impoverished families), to whom the guidance of public opinion was entrusted.[9] From the mid-1820s and to the end of his life in 1837 Pushkin was preoccupied with envisioning this new Russian cultural elite, somewhat analogous to what Coleridge described as 'clerisy' and what Goethe and Wilhelm von Humboldt tried to promote as the German cultural and pedagogical ideal.[10]

Like many of his fellow countrymen, Pushkin believed that Russia's destiny involved saying a new word or developing a unique cultural ethos, which would eventually come to eclipse the decaying old Europe. However, unlike the Slavophiles, Pushkin never denigrated the importance of the Western cultural canon. Nor did he reject the cultural legacy of the Petrine revolution, although he did criticize the roughness and expediency with which this revolution was carried out. Pushkin believed that the reforms could be more efficient if they were implemented gradually, via culture and education, instead of being simply superimposed from above upon an unprepared population.[11] Pushkin believed that his task as a national educator consisted in translating the vast body of knowledge and culture he had imbibed with his European education into a Russian vernacular, where it could be easily grasped and absorbed by as many readers as possible. Before turning to the text of *The Captain's Daughter*, which provides us with a concrete example of how Pushkin translated a complex and nuanced historical vision into a popular modern genre, I would like to pause briefly on Pushkin's intellectual background, in order to clarify how Pushkin's project of cultivating his readers related to the broader nineteenth-century Russian quest for enlightenment and national culture.

The poet received his education at the Imperial Lyceum in Tsarskoe Selo, which had been founded by Alexander I (ostensibly in order to educate the Tsar's younger brothers Nicholas and Mikhail together with young boys from other noble families).[12] It was a very progressive school by contemporary standards, its philosophy shaped by the architect of Alexander's projected liberal reforms M.M. Speranskii and by Alexander's former tutor La Harpe. Thus, the curriculum in this Lyceum was on a par with those of the best French and Swiss boarding schools of the time. The comparative advantage might well be said to rest with the program at the Lyceum, in that it incorporated the study of Russian language and literature into the standard curriculum of the classics, French and German languages and literatures, and the basic introduction to all sciences. It was at the Lyceum that Pushkin began writing poetry (at first in French). His legendary performance at the graduation from the Lyceum, where he recited his poem 'Recollections of Tsarskoe Selo' (*Vospomnianiia o Tsarskom Sele*) and received the enthusiastic approval of Russia's most celebrated eighteenth-century poet, Gavriil Derzhavin, was the beginning of Pushkin's fame as Russia's pre-eminent poetic genius.[13]

From 1818, when he left Tsarskoe Selo and settled in St Petersburg, to the mid-1820s, Pushkin identified with the Romantic conception of the poet-genius, impelled by his muse to pursue freedom and his artistic individuality.[14] Meanwhile, Pushkin also associated with dissenting Guards Officers (among whom were some of the future Decembrists) and the circle around P.Ia. Chaadaev (the future author of the *Philosophical Letters*).[15] Many of Pushkin's earlier poems are informed by the spirit of liberalism that he 'caught' from the conversations in these circles. The product of Pushkin's early introduction to radical thought, the ode 'Liberty,' prompted Alexander I to exile the young poet for five and a half years in the Crimea and Bessarabia, although the tsar later granted the poet leave to live on his father's estate in the Pskov region.[16]

Pushkin's ode praised the idea of universal 'Law' ordained by reason and called on the Tsar to follow laws rather than his whims. As Oleg Proskurin points out, these ideas were aligned with the views Alexander expressed in his own speeches during the more liberal phase of his reign. Therefore it was probably not the ode's ideological content, but rather the personal allusions to the Tsar that provoked Alexander's anger and caused Pushkin's exile.[17] Pushkin's dispatch to the south coincided with the end of the 'liberal' phase in Alexander I's reign. What followed was a period of reaction presided over by the reactionary favourite, A.A. Arakcheev (1769–1834). Still, the liberal impulse lived on in elite circles until it finally surfaced in the famous armed rebellion organized by a group of liberal-minded officers in Petersburg on 14 December 1825.

The Decembrists had no popular support and proved easy to put down. Put down, as well, was hope for socio-political reforms – the abolishment of serfdom, the introduction of constitutional rule, the broadening (or, in fact, creation) of the political sphere – which formed the core of the Decembrists' liberal agenda. Nicholas I, whose elevation to the throne had been threatened by the Decembrist coup d'état, henceforward cast himself in the role of the 'defender' of organic traditions and institutions. Eight years after the revolt, he elevated Pushkin's acquaintance and a former member of the literary society 'Arzamas,' Sergei Uvarov (1786–1855), to the post of the Minister of National Enlightenment [*Ministr Narodnogo Prosvescheniia*]. Uvarov devised the cultural policy of Nicholas I to which historians frequently refer as the 'Uvarov formula': 'Orthodoxy, Autocracy, Nationality.' This new ideological 'scenario' (to borrow Richard Wortman's term) lasted until the death of Nicholas I in 1856, weathering a revolt in Poland in 1831, the revolutions of 1848, the Crimean War (1853–6) and even the war with Turkey in 1877–8. It also outlived Pushkin. However, Uvarov's 'official nationality' was not the only form under which cultural nationalism developed in the mid-nineteenth century. In fact, there was apparently a period between the Decembrist revolt and Uvarov's rise to power when different nationalistic ideologies competed with each other. To shape a powerful ideological scenario for his regime, Nicholas apparently turned to a number of intellectuals, including Pushkin, whom he had summoned back from his exile in the Pskov region.[18] The Tsar asked the poet to express his views on national education, and Pushkin responded by writing 'The Memorandum on National Education' (*'Zapiska o narodnom vospitanii'*).[19]

This document, which failed to receive the Tsar's approval and was therefore not allowed to circulate during Nicholas I's reign, sheds light on Pushkin's thinking during his period of exile.[20] The 'recent events have revealed many sad truths,' Pushkin writes in an allusion to the Decembrist rebellion as a symptom of the twofold fissure existing, on the one hand, between the educated elite and the government, and, on the other hand, between the elite and the populace.[21] As Pushkin's 'Memorandum' implies, the Decembrists failed to understand their nation's innermost spiritual and historical tendencies – while the people failed to understand the conspirators. The first problem, according to Pushkin, was a result of the conspirators' insufficient and rather superficial education.[22] Pushkin proposed a reform of the educational system and bureaucracy that would strengthen the country's hereditary aristocracy or *dvorianstvo*. Interestingly, high on Pushkin's list of reforms was repealing the system of examinations for higher public officials (introduced by Peter the Great to force the nobles to receive formal training and to promote mobility for talented non-nobles). This insistence on limiting social mobility and curbing ambition anticipates Pushkin's reactions to the July Revolution of 1830 in France, in which he took the side of the legitimists and opposed the bourgeois government of

Count Polignac. Taken altogether, these thoughts, scattered throughout Pushkin's oeuvre during this period, indicate a drift away from his radical youth toward a more conservative reformist approach to social modernization.[23]

Another sign of Pushkin's changed political outlook is the tragedy *Boris Godunov*, which was written in Mikhailovskoe in 1824–5. Although it is set in the seventeenth-century Time of Troubles, the play also speaks to some vital contemporary issues. Thus, for example, Tsar Boris, who came to power by ordering the murder of the rightful heir Tsarevich Dimitrii, could remind contemporary readers of Alexander I, whose ascension to the throne was notoriously engineered by the assassins of his father Paul I – presumably with Alexander's tacit consent.[24] Boris's illegitimate ascent to autocratic power threatens the stability of the state. He ends up bringing suffering to himself, his family, and his subjects. His drama, like Macbeth's, is that of the usurper who depends on personal charisma, and when that is lacking, on brutal force, to maintain a power obtained through scheming and sheer chance.[25] The usurper also attempts to suppress the hereditary nobility, one spokesman for whom in Pushkin's play is Gavrila Pushkin, one of the poet's ancestors. In a famous monologue, he complains about the uncertainty of the nobles' existence under Tsar Boris, which impedes them from serving the state honourably and faithfully.[26] According to Pushkin (echoing Montesquieu, who, along with Burke, was a traditional reference point for Russian conservative liberals), the task of the hereditary nobility is to exhibit the ethos of honour and be ready to enact their selfless dedication to the sovereign as soon as the country is in danger.[27]

Although we will never know what Pushkin and Nicholas I said to each other in their famous meeting on 8 September 1826 in the Chudov monastery in Moscow, we do know, from a letter that Pushkin wrote to his friend and publisher P.Ia. Pletnev, that the Tsar took him 'into his service' (*'Tsar' vzial menia na sluzhbu'*).[28] What this meant in practice was exemption from regular censorship and the permission to work in all state archives. The Tsar granted Pushkin the post of the 'Historiographer of the Russian State,' left vacant after the death of N.M. Karamzin in 1826. There was a heavy symbolism in Pushkin's succeeding Karamzin's office. It was due to Karamzin's intervention that, back in 1820, Alexander I had not expelled Pushkin from the country or imprisoned him. In return for the Tsar's promise of a comparatively lenient internal exile, Karamzin had extracted Pushkin's pledge not to write political poetry for two years.[29] Of course, Pushkin also fully realized the value of Karamzin's historical work, which he used as the basis for *Boris Godunov*.

Pushkin not only succeeded Karamzin in the office of historiographer but also, in time, his intellectual legacy as a public enlightener. Indeed, from the time he composed *Boris Godunov* (1824–5) to the last days of his life, when he was busy preparing the next issue of his journal *The Contemporary* (*Sovremennik*), Pushkin was under the spell of Karamzin, whom he once compared to Columbus.[30] If the latter had discovered the New World, Karamzin's pioneering historical work had opened new vistas before his Russian readers, whose minds and sensibility had been (since the time of Peter the Great) shaped mainly by foreign cultural ideals and tastes. It was largely thanks to Karamzin that nineteenth-century Russians began to break free of this cultural dependence and think of themselves as members of a national community with a distinctive character deeply rooted in national history.[31]

In laying foundations for imagining Russia as a national community, *The History of the Russian State* also gave rise to some lasting controversies, including first of all Karamzin's emphasis on autocracy as Russia's organic form of government.[32] During the interregnum crisis of 1825 this aspect of Karamzin's historical-political doctrine seemed particularly topical. This, of course, ran counter to liberal thought, and certainly to the Decembrist ideology. The *History* was written to illustrate the idea that Russia's spiritual and cultural flourishing was dependent on its internal stability and strength in the international arena, which, in turn, was dependent on centralized power.[33] Thus, as Karamzin showed in the section of his *History* devoted to the Time of Troubles, the interruption of legitimate rule and the usurpation of power by opportunists like Boris Godunov brings the country to the brink of the civil war and makes it prey to foreign usurpers, like the Pseudo Dimitrius.[34]

Karamzin, who produced the most persuasive argument supporting Russian autocracy as the guarantor of national sovereignty, served as the iconic reference for various conservative factions of the post-Decembrist period, including Mikhail Pogodin's circle. How does Pushkin figure in this scene? I will argue that Pushkin was both sceptical about the messianic view of Russia (expounded by the emerging Slavophiles) and rather cautious about Western-style liberalism, because he doubted its applicability to Russia. In the post-1825 phase of his life Pushkin actively searched for a new ideological position and eventually found a stable point of view and a practical goal, which he pursued steadily over the last decade of his life. He found his new vocation in prose literature, believing that this medium would allow him to awaken in the expanding circle of his readers the desire for moral and cultural self-improvement.

Pushkin's hope that the government would recognize his efforts to build a viable cultural elite that would help improve the relationship between the highest and lowest strata of society and promote reforms (in the possibility of which Pushkin still believed) might have been suggested to him by the success of the educational reforms in Britain, which he followed by reading the *Edinburgh Review* and other journals. This would suggest that Pushkin's vision of Russian national education was congenial to the ideas of Burke, Coleridge, Lamb, J.S. Mill, and Carlyle – one of the groups of thinkers analysed by Raymond Williams in *Culture and Society*. This is not to say that Pushkin was single-mindedly committed to a rigid 'high' cultural standard. Rather, what he aspired to was a gradual opening up of the cultural sphere and its dissemination, via the press, to the fringes of the Empire and the bottom stratum of society. His notion of enlightenment envisioned a gradual democratization of culture and drawing new peoples into its orbit.

Pushkin looked back on the well-trusted didactic and sentimental techniques of the age of sensibility and saw how they could be revived to produce new Russian prose. In this connection, I fully agree with Vadim Vatsuro and Alexander Dolinin, who have argued that Pushkin's prose works, including not only *The Tales of the Late Ivan Petrovich Belkin* but also *The Captain's Daughter*, aim at regenerating rather than debunking the sentimentalist literary tradition transplanted to Russia by, first and foremost, Karamzin.[35] These works – and particularly Pushkin's last novel, which will concern me in this chapter – may seem 'anachronistic' in terms of their plotting, their didactically driven aestheticization of reality, and their sometimes overtly sentimental tone. This deliberate incorporation of stylistic cues from the age of sensibility might have contributed to the failure of *The Captain's Daughter* on the literary market, where it was beaten out by such fashionable works as Zagoskin's *Yurii Miloslavskii* or Bulgarin's *Ivan Vyzhigin*. Considering, however, that Pushkin's goal was not so much market success as cultural impact, the genesis of a genuine cultural elite rooted in a sense of Russian history and reality, his novel performed its task admirably.

The Captain's Daughter gradually found its admirers among the leading critics of the time. Apollon Grigor'ev, in particular, believed that in this work and in *The Tales of the Late Ivan Petrovich Belkin* Pushkin found the way out of the dangerous cul-de-sac of the 'superfluous man.' In creating the characters of Grinev, Captain Mironov, and Masha, Pushkin found, according to Grigor'ev, a new way to think about Russian identity and history. It is not surprising, then, that *The Captain's Daughter* inspired Russian writers of the next generation, including Lev Tolstoy and Fyodor Dostoevsky, to continue experimenting with the novelistic form as a vehicle of sentimental and spiritual education. I will return to this issue shortly, after providing a brief historical survey of Pushkin's literary connections in the late 1820s and early 1830s, which will help explain why and how he became interested in the history of Catherine II's reign and the events surrounding the Pugachev rebellion.

Pushkin in Moscow (1826–8) and the *Moscow Messenger*

Two days after meeting with the Emperor, on 10 September 1826, Pushkin gave a public reading of *Boris Godunov* in the home of the poet Venevitinov.[36] This reading became a sensation among the intellectuals of the old capital, and Pushkin was asked to read extracts from his tragedy again. The next reading, which took place on 12 October again at the Venevitinovs', one of the habitual meeting places of the intellectual circle known as the Lovers of Wisdom (*Liubomudry*),[37] attracted a new audience, which included not only the poet's intimates, but also some people whom he had never met, including historian Mikhail Pogodin.[38] At this time Pogodin was already a well-established historian and considered himself a follower of Karamzin. Pogodin, who had been close to the members of the Lovers of Wisdom circle, had heard about Pushkin and was eager to meet this legendary poet. Pogodin's rapture over *Boris Godunov* was immediately translated into an invitation to Pushkin to contribute to a new journal, which Pogodin planned to launch in the wake of Nicholas I's coronation. Pogodin's calculations proved successful. At first, Pushkin was quite eager to publish the works he had accumulated during exile and his new works in the *Moscow Messenger* (*Moskovskii Vestnik*), a name which inevitably called to mind the titles of Karamzin's journals, the *Messenger of Europe* (*Vestnik Evropy*) and *Moskovskii Zhurnal* (*Moscow Journal*). The first issue of Pogodin's journal opened with an extract from *Boris Godunov*: Pimen's monologue followed by his conversation with the monk Grigorii Otrep'ev. Thus Pogodin managed simultaneously to announce the birth of a new public organ dedicated to Russian history and culture, to celebrate Pushkin's return to literary and social life, and to pay tribute to the memory of the late Karamzin, from whom Pushkin borrowed the story of Boris Godunov and the impostor Grishka Otrep'ev.

Dominated by the members of the Lovers of Wisdom circle, the *Moscow Messenger* was conceived as the forum for the propaganda of *obrazovanie* or *Bildung*, understood along the lines of Wilhelm von Humboldt's pedagogical ideal.[39] Pushkin became the most renowned Russian author to be published in the *Moscow Messenger*, whereas Goethe was the most frequently published European author. Pushkin soon became annoyed with the Germanophile and overly 'theoretical' direction of the *Moscow Messenger*. In some of the issues nearly half of the contents consisted of translations from German.[40] Thus Pushkin's contributions became less frequent in 1828 until he stopped contributing altogether. However, Pushkin may have owed it to Pogodin for planting the idea for such a journal in his mind, and so the poet petitioned for and obtained the permission to start his own journal.[41]

The period during which Pushkin was close to Pogodin and the Moscow intellectuals was an important benchmark in the writer's career for several reasons. Although Pushkin disliked the *Messenger*'s Germanophilia, the journal did bring him up to date on the latest intellectual developments in Europe. He read a lot of Goethe, Jean-Paul Richter, E.T.A. Hoffmann, and other German authors with whom he was previously not very familiar.[42] Pushkin seems also to have read at least some German philosophy and criticism. This 'Germanophile' phase in Pushkin's acculturation deepened his understanding of the issue of national culture, with which he had been preoccupied since his return from exile. The stimulation Pushkin received from Pogodin and his collaborators also helped sustain Pushkin's interest in historiography. The historical studies by various Russian and German authors published in the *Moscow Messenger* provided models for Pushkin's own historical works, starting with the unfinished *History of Peter I* and going on to *The History of Pugachev's Rebellion*, composed in 1832. I also think that the *Moscow Messenger* and its editor did much to encourage Pushkin to turn his attention to provincial Russia and develop additional interests in ethnography and ethnology.[43] These new foci, already apparent in Pushkin's *Journey to Arzrum* (1828), played a major role in the composition of *The Captain's Daughter* – a novel set away from the metropolitan centres, on the north-eastern periphery of the empire.[44] Finally, Pushkin's short-lived collaboration with Pogodin helped prepare his own turn toward journalism and publishing, which

I see as a natural extension of his newly assumed role as a public educator and Karamzin's heir.

Pushkin's growing disappointment with the excessively theoretical direction of the *Moscow Messenger* was in fact directly related to his growing appreciation of Karamzin's idea of public enlightenment. For Karamzin, the spread of enlightenment meant first of all the cultivation of manners, and only secondly the development of philosophical or scientific (theoretical) knowledge. From this angle we can also take a fresh look at the long-standing issue of the relationship between *The Captain's Daughter* and *The History of Pugachev's Rebellion*, a historical work published in 1834. Critics have long debated which of these works was composed first and which one carries greater weight as a testament of Pushkin's historical and political beliefs. I agree with Svetlana Evdokimova, who argues that these works should be viewed separately, as two different examples of historical writing, belonging to two separate historiographic traditions. The novel is expressly designed to present us with an 'edifying fiction,' while the more dispassionate and 'scientific' *History of Pugachev's Rebellion* belongs to the post-Enlightenment tradition of 'objective' historiography.[45] While in the former the personality of the author or narrator comes to the fore and plays a didactic role, in the latter text the narrator hides behind the mask of complete disinterestedness and scientific objectivity.

In his own journal, Pushkin strove to emulate Karamzin as he understood him – as a man whose journals and almanacs pursued the task of contributing to knowledge within the more general project of shaping the public sensibility. Pushkin saw his journal as the means for shaping young Russians from the 'middling' gentry background, in whom Pushkin vested his hopes for Russia's future. Had he published the novel as a separate volume, as he did with *The History of Pugachev's Rebellion*, the price would have put it out of reach of the less affluent and provincial readers upon whom Pushkin counted.

We can assume that Pushkin wrote *The Captain's Daughter* with a particular audience in mind. Presented from the first-person perspective and framed as a family memoir, Grinev's biography is addressed to provincial nobles whose background is similar to Grinev's (and Pushkin's). The novel unfolds a fiction of self-formation centred on the character of the ideal Russian gentleman. Given the intimate, even confessional tone of this narrative (modelled on the didactic fiction of the age of sensibility and in particular on Karamzin), the readers of Pushkin's journal were expected to identify with the autobiographical hero/narrator.[46]

This presumed connection between the author and his audience is reaffirmed rhetorically through an apostrophe in chapter 6: 'When I reflect that this happened in my own lifetime and that since then I have lived to see Emperor Alexander's mild reign, I cannot help marvelling at the rapid progress of enlightenment and the spread of humane principles. Young man! If my notes fall into your hands, remember that the best and most permanent changes are those arising from a betterment of mores without violent shocks' (PSS 8:318–19; Debreczeny 305). The narrator's cast of mind, that of the gallant from the 'gentle reign' of Alexander I, is supposed to reinforce the moral and psychological ideals of the age of sensibility. Thus Grinev's persona brings to mind Karamzin, whose legacy was being actively appropriated and canonized in the 1830s. For Pushkin in the 1830s, casting himself as the educator of the Russian gentry, Karamzin's idea of 'sensibility' seems well adapted to the spread of enlightenment within the limits of Russia's organic institutions. In this way, Pushkin can champion aristocracy as the guarantor of cultural continuity and growth. Grinev's sensitivity and responsiveness, as well as his willingness to take chances and bravely confront destiny, make him an embodiment of the idea of aristocracy or *dvorianstvo*, which Pushkin conceptualized in his 'Memorandum On National Education' and dramatized in *Boris Godunov*. In taking this side, Pushkin demonstrates his loyalty to Karamzin.[47]

Narrated retrospectively from a standpoint of sixty years after the events in question occur, Grinev's memoir recollects the historical background against which the hero's personality takes shape, while simultaneously accounting for the hero's actions. In this connection, we are reminded of Bakhtin's distinction between 'author' and 'hero' in a literary work. The 'author,' by virtue of being located outside of the story, can order or 'finalize' the biography of the hero, which the latter experiences as a flux.[48] The hero's life gets carefully etched out against the landscape of history, his conscious actions as well as his accidental and instinctive reactions (such as the famous gift of the hare-skin coat to a 'muzhik' who turns out to be Pugachev incognito) being re-evaluated in light of his completed life story. Because Grinev does in the end fare well, his life story comes across as a moral exemplum through which the author projects his values and ideals on his implied readers, who are projected by the text as Grinev's grandchildren. This device is reminiscent of seventeenth- and eighteenth-century memoirs – a genre that was comparatively less developed in eighteenth-century Russia due to the small size of the reading public as compared to Europe. By stylizing his novel from the time of the Pugachev rebellion in this way, Pushkin contributed to the development of this literary form, whose popularity in early modern Europe was tied to the spread of the humanistic idea of self-cultivation.

If we compare *The Captain's Daughter* to Pushkin's earlier prose works, including *The Queen of Spades*, with its romantic and 'frenetic' elements, or even if we compare it to other historical novels written in the 1820s and 1830s, *The Captain's Daughter* does strike us as a bit quaint. I think that Pushkin stylized Grinev's persona very carefully to convey what could be taken for a 'grandfatherly' point of view, which marks him as a member of the generation of Karamzin and Dmitriev.[49]

Thinking of *The Captain's Daughter* as a stepping stone to the long-awaited phase of independent journalism, when Pushkin would be able to exercise some freedom as an arbiter of public taste, allows us to appreciate the unusual (for the 1830s) choice of genre and the novel's somewhat quaint rhetorical style, evidently calculated to strike the contemporary reader as a departure from the widespread Romantic-era prose.[50] At first taken by surprise, readers and critics eventually came to realize that *The Captain's Daughter* was a milestone in Pushkin's career. It was Apollon Grigor'ev who first recognized that this novel, along with *The Tales of the Late Ivan Petrovich Belkin*, which the critic saw as ideologically and stylistically similar to Grinev's 'memoirs,' were in fact a kind of literary manifesto in which Pushkin announced his mature credo, which consisted of the acceptance and even celebration of Russian everyday life.

My goal in the rest of this chapter will be to revisit and re-evaluate Grigor'ev's critique in order to achieve a better understanding of what the later Pushkin was doing. For Grigor'ev, Pushkin's unique breadth of vision and feeling symbolized Russia's burden of, as well as opportunity for, becoming the privileged site where the global 'semiosphere' or *Weltliteratur*, as Goethe has called it, could emerge.[51] As I said in the previous chapter, the reaction of Tolstoy and Dostoevsky (among others) to Grigor'ev's claim helped launch the Russian Bildungsroman and provoked a long debate over Russia's special cultural role as a missionary of transcultural dialogue and liberating 'polyphony.'

Pushkin as a Poet of Everyday Life: Apollon Grigor'ev on Pushkin's Prose

It was Apollon Grigor'ev who first saw in Pushkin's prose works, particularly *The Tales of the Late Ivan Petrovich Belkin* and *The Captain's Daughter*, a shift away from the intensely self-critical 'negative' tendency that had swept Russian literature in the wake of Romanticism.[52] Unlike Onegin, Aleko, and other characters inspired by Byron, the heroes projected by Pushkin's prose are neither misanthropic nor deracinated. Grigor'ev particularly stresses the significance of Belkin as Pushkin's new quasi amanuensis. While in his youth Pushkin was, according to Grigor'ev, an apprentice to European Romantic poets (particularly Byron), in his later work he was able to gain full independence from foreign ideals and artistic models: hence the emergence of the new 'Belkin' style. Anticipating the formalists, Grigor'ev realizes that Belkin, whose autobiography Pushkin began to write but never finished, is important mostly as a device or a certain stylistic and aesthetic principle:

> What is Pushkin's Belkin [...]? Pushkin's Belkin is simply common sense and a wholesome feeling, meek and gentle, – a kind of common sense that rebels against every brilliant lie, a feeling which rebels, quite reasonably, against our abuse of our natural ability to understand and feel broadly. Thus, in essence, Belkin is only a negative principle, and is true (justifiable) only as a negative principle. Give it independence, it is capable of turning into stagnation or dull inertia, into the crudeness of a Famusov or the merry corruption of a Iusov.[53]

Grigor'ev's view of Pushkin's Belkin can be understood if we take into account his idea of Russian 'breadth,' which I discussed in chapter 1. What the critic means by 'our ability to understand and feel broadly' is the Russian predilection for sympathy with different cultures, ideas, and currents, which Grigor'ev sees, *pace* Herder, as a direct consequence of Russia's geographical and socio-cultural breadth. The recognition of this authentically Russian charactesristic constituted a major advance in Pushkin's development. Grigor'ev goes on to argue that *The Tales of the Late Ivan Petrovich Belkin* and *The History of the Village of Goriukhino* constitute a new phase in Pushkin's art – one during which he attains complete self-consciousness as a *Russian* author. We should not, however, identify Belkin with the entire scope of Pushkin's vision. Rather, Grigor'ev says, Belkin should be seen as the 'critical aspect of Pushkin's soul':

> And such tales as *Dubrovsky* and the family chronicle of the Grinevs, this predecessor of all our family chronicles, which still has not lost its freshness, are all narrated to us in the skin of Belkin and with Belkin's tone. For

Pushkin, Belkin was not just a hero, but rather the critical side of his soul. We would have been not so well-endowed (by nature) as a nation if had we only had Belkins as our heroes, or even the honest captain in Tolstoy's 'The Wood-Felling.' These characters are important insofar as they provide a contrast to the glamorous and, so to speak, 'predatory' type, whose greatness and glamour turned out to be fake from the standpoint of our spirituality.[54]

The expression '"predatory" type,' which Grigor'ev introduced to Russian criticism, survived and found a rich resonance all the way to Dostoevsky. According to Grigor'ev, a 'predatory' type is a Romantic 'Byronic' hero endowed with ardent but selfish passions. Grigor'ev views the emergence of a new, Russian, and 'meek' voice in Pushkin as an overcoming of his Byronic phase dominated by the 'predatory' un-Russian images. Incidentally, the idea that the predatory type is not intrinsic but alien to Russian culture can be traced back to Hegel's *Philosophy of History*, where Hegel describes nations in terms of their hereditary character traits, linking them to geographical and climatic conditions.[55]

Extrapolating from Grigor'ev, Dostoevsky in the late 1860s and throughout the 1870s would also try to create literary plots centred on the 'predatory' type. The drafts to *The Idiot, The Devils,* and *The Adolescent* show that this character type occupied a prominent place in Dostoevsky's creative laboratory. Among all the characters created by Dostoevsky, it is Stavrogin who serves as the fullest embodiment of the 'predatory' type. Versilov from *The Adolescent* also represents a toned-down version of this type, which Dostoevsky linked to the spread of European ideas and in particular the Romantic cult of the Byronic hero. Following Grigor'ev, Dostoevsky spoke about the pernicious domination of the predatory hero image during what he calls the 'Petersburg' phase of Russian culture (i.e., the period of Westernized culture, stemming from the Petrine reforms). In order to tame this 'predatory' type and reduce his influence in society, so these early pochvenniki believed, Russian authors need to restore their contact with the Russian 'soil,' with its essentially 'meek' and 'gentle' spirit.

It was Pushkin, the pochvenniki agreed, who first freed himself from the spiritual dependence on foreign ideals and clichés. Pushkin's work, particularly of the last phase of his life, seemed to announce to the pochvenniki the coming of a new cultural age, when our broad and conflicting spiritual and psychological tendencies would come together and form a coherent (if not intrinsically homogeneous) culture. Of course, this would not happen without much agony and strife. While other Russian critics still saw Pushkin as a light-headed, effortlessly brilliant poet, Grigor'ev recognized Pushkin's inner struggles. He also believed that it was only in his last phase that the poet began expressing a completely new perspective, but died before he finished expressing it:

> There exist natures whose task is to indicate once and for all the outlines of historical processes, to outline, even if only schematically, robust ideals. This is the kind of nature that Pushkin possessed. Pushkin experienced all our feelings, from nostalgic love for the repressed, old Russian culture to sympathy for the [Petrine] reforms, from our fascination with passionate, poetically charming ideals to the humble service of Savel'ich, from our debauchery to our need for concentrated self-reflection and 'motherwilderness.' Only death kept him from realizing our high spiritual calling, [such as those embodied in] the meek, loving and spiritually edified image of Tazit. The same death that carries away most creators of multifaceted and hopeful ideals, which carried away Mozart and Raphael, has also carried away Pushkin. For there is some kind of mysterious law, according to which all broad phenomena do not last long, while one-sided profundity puts down roots like an oak tree.[56]

Grigor'ev's allusion to *The Captain's Daughter, Tazit,* and several other late works by Pushkin seems to presage Dostoevsky's novels, with their psychological oscillations between exalted passions and asceticism, the suffering of the 'petty' individuals trapped in their squalid everyday lives and the unearthly joy of mystical transport. As I will show in chapter 7, among Russian writers it was Dostoevsky who was most deeply taken by Grigor'ev's characterization of Pushkin's mature phase as one marked by broad sympathy – a trait Grigor'ev believed to be the hallmark of the Slavic or Russian culture in particular. Moreover, Dostoevsky's only completed novel of education, *The Adolescent,* is implicitly in dialogue with *The Captain's Daughter.* But before we can appreciate Dostoesky's response to this novel (mediated by Grigor'ev's criticism) – which will be the subject of my last chapter – we need to get a better idea of how Pushkin's himself understood Russian everyday life.

As Grigor'ev astutely pointed out, what distinguishes *The Captain's Daughter* from Pushkin's other stories is the protagonist. Gone are the Byronic features, the brooding over the past, the injured pride and a sense of thwarted life. While Byronic 'Romanticism' implied a certain solipsism and lack of common sense, Pushkin's new 'realistic' attitude implies a more grounded and balanced view of things. Pyotr Grinev is a perfect vehicle for Pushkin's new philosophy of life, because he combines a firm moral backbone and a secure sense of identity with the kind of openness and responsiveness to the world that characterizes especially the very young, the curious, and poets. Grinev is flexible, but he is not a chameleon. He makes room for chance, yet never stoops to sheer opportunism. Interestingly, in the first drafts of the novel Grinev and Shvabrin were one and the same character. One of the most respected Soviet Pushkin scholars, Yu.G. Oksman, believed that Pushkin rendered Grinev's character less ambivalent under pressure from censorship.[57] Thus, according to Oksman, Shvabrin is what is left over after the novel's protagonist was cleansed of his ideological and moral doubts and hesitations and turned into a fully loyal subject. Shvabrin is indeed a rather weak and unconvincing character, either a pale shadow of the Byronic anti-hero or a somewhat contrived receptacle of all the negative qualities originally possessed by Pushkin's psychologically and politically ambivalent hero, who was then split into two different characters. Nevertheless, it is difficult to agree with Oksman's hypothesis. Although the cases of noblemen who defected from the Empress Catherine's army to join the rebels did interest Pushkin greatly, the entire artistic and rhetorical architectonic of *The Captain's Daughter* is centred on a hero who does not swerve from the path of honour, where 'honour' is understood as the moral code of the gentry culture that this hero embodies. Pushkin virtuosically manages to twist his story without undermining its moral kernel, reminiscent of the *contes moraux* popular in the eighteenth century. For example, he endows his protagonist with a gentle soul that makes him capable of feeling sympathy for Pugachev. This motif of sympathy becomes more pronounced toward the end of the story, when Grinev is imprisoned for 'treason' and realizes that Pugachev will soon be or has already been captured by the imperial troops.

Yet, Grinev's humane feelings toward and even, occasionally, romantic fantasy about Pugachev as a powerful embodiment of freedom does not blur his rational vision or his memory of the murders committed by Pugachev's band. The narrator's image of Pugachev is softened and humanized to create the possibility of a humane relationship (or even 'sentimental traffic') between Grinev and Pugachev – while in another context, in the *History of Pugachev's Rebellion* for example, Pushkin has no compunction about presenting Pugachev as a quite horrifying figure.

His Romantic fantasies notwithstanding, Grinev remains at his core a loyal son, subject, and *honnête homme et gentilhomme Russe* (without the diminishing irony, with which Dostoevsky's Versilov in *The Adolescent* would use this expression to describe himself). The hero's sensitivity makes him capable of reconciling these feelings. In fact, upon a closer analysis, the very essence of this story is to convey Grinev's highly developed sensibility and make us privy to his experiences and his judgments, which represent a very careful balancing of his feelings and moral ideals, sensuality and rationality. Apollon Grigor'ev's intuition about the later Pushkin's tendency to experience and sympathetically convey different points of view, which, I think, was suggested to a large degree by *The Captain's Daughter*, ought to steer us toward a more aesthetically and psychologically cogent explanation of how Grinev manages to maintain and even strengthen his moral centre while respecting his father's precepts (even in the breach) and the internalized image of the law (even as he appears to be in the wrong). Indeed, I think that what Grigor'ev means when he talks about Pushkin's 'breadth' is not quite the schizophrenia to which Versilov eventually succumbs, but rather something more like Keatsian 'negative capability.'

Speaking of Pushkin's artistry, we would do well to follow up another of Grigor'ev's suggestions, which posits a relationship between Pushkin and Karamzin as two major Russian prose writers. The social conditions in which the Karamzinian tale of sensibility was produced were those of Russian salon society. Pushkin, however, wanted to transcend the salon-centred culture of Karamzin's age and (to use Grigor'ev's term) to 'broaden' both his own and his readers' cultural consciousness. Thus, while employing certain of the devices of the Karamzinian tale (and of the novel of sensibility in general), Pushkin subtly employs new means to express his desire to expand his hero's consciousness. Essentially, Pushkin is creating the type of hero who would eventually look a complete stranger in the rarefied atmosphere of the Petersburg salon – just as Tolstoy's Pierre Bezhukhov does later.

The passing from the elite culture with its refined sensibility toward mass readership was accompanied by many challenges. For Russian reality was indeed dramatically uneven, and in the decades following the inception of mass literature it would drive quite a few authors and critics (including Grigor'ev himself) to the verge of madness, if not further to sheer insanity.[58] Pushkin, however, managed to steer his way between the Scylla of cultivated aesthetics and the Charybdis of popular literature without losing his wits. Grigor'ev's insight was taken up over a hundred years later by Lotman, who stressed that Pushkin's remarkable sanity and unfailing sense of balance was to a large extent a product of his poetic consciousness.[59] While mastery in lyric poetry was the milestone of his youth, literary prose – the art that involved the translation of poetic thinking to the medium of the everyday language of common prose, rather than a withdrawal from poetry – was the achievement of Pushkin's maturity. Denigrated or misrecognized by many contemporaries, Pushkin's prose came to be valued in the next generation, thanks to Grigor'ev, as a new stage in Pushkin's creativity and, by extension, of Russian literary culture as a whole.[60]

This is not to deny the continuity between Pushkin's poetry and his prose. Indeed, as critics have shown apropos of *The Captain's Daughter*, an elegant symmetry reminiscent of poetic structures guides this narrative practically on every ideological and architectonic level. For instance, on the thematic level, Grinev's story unfolds in a series of gestures that consistently push the limits of the provincial gentry estate culture in which Grinev was born and raised. The novel employs, at its core, the familiar fairy tale plot of the weak son who goes out into the world in order to win his fortune, and whose 'weaknesses,' as they are viewed by the father or Savel'ich (for example, his generosity or his passion for Masha Mironova), end up as the key to his fortune. Thus, Grinev's gift of the coat (which his servant, using no doubt the words Grinev's father would apply, hates), ends up saving him from hanging and eventually allows him to save and marry Masha Mironova. Furthermore, as several critics have pointed out, Masha's accidental encounter with the Empress Catherine II incognito at the park in Tsarskoe Selo mirrors perfectly Grinev's encounter with Pugachev (also incognito) on his way to the remote fortress in the Orenburg steppes. We could find many other examples of symmetrical composition in this text. Nonetheless, while structured in a perfectly symmetrical way, the narrative does move forward ideologically and psychologically. Indeed, upon closer examination, the story, which begins in the idyllic setting of the patriarchal country estate, is really neither an idyll nor a parable, both of which would have a cyclic chronotope, but is rather a Bildungsroman, which implies historicity of consciousness. To capture this subtle transition from the closed and circular chronotope to a historicist one we need to carefully observe the way Pushkin handles the plot of maturation, which in his hands becomes at once a narrative of one generation replacing another (the trope of tradition), and a narrative of progress (a trope of 'enlightenment').

The Dialectic of Enlightenment in *The Captain's Daughter*

As Caryl Emerson has pointed out, in Pushkin's novel the quest for maturity is thematized as the hero's struggle to receive his father's blessing to marry the girl of his own choice.[61] He falls in love and chooses to marry Masha Mironova, a poor captain's daughter who is even more deeply rooted in Russian life than Tatiana Larina, the heroine of *Eugene Onegin*. Thus Masha's main dowry consists of her 'organic' Russian values. Grinev's father, standing for patriarchy built upon inherited wealth and status, absolutely opposes such a match. In the end, however, in a moment rich with symbolism, Pushkin will reconcile the contradictions between Grinev and his father, or between traditional common sense and sensibility, through the deus ex machina: the intervention of Catherine II, who gives Masha a dowry.

There is an instructive contrast here between Masha and Tatiana Larina, Pushkin's most celebrated heroine. The latter becomes a fashionable lady and a hostess of a salon, a transformation that William Mills Todd III has interpreted as a female version of a successful Bildungsroman.[62] The former comes to Petersburg at the end of the story with a single purpose in mind: to rescue her beloved. Masha deliberately avoids all distractions and fascinating sites of the capital, and after successfully pleading Grinev's case before the Empress, she immediately leaves the fashionable city to return to the countryside, where she and Grinev will spend the rest of their life together.

This gesture is extremely revealing. It shows that even though Pushkin has appropriated Karamzin's view of literature as the vehicle of moral and social amelioration, he rejects the polite society of the capital as the absolute arbiter of good taste. Pushkin wanted to create a broader cultural community beyond the narrow circle of the high-born and wealthy gentry who could afford to live in the capitals. His new target audience included middling provincial gentry as well as the low-ranking service gentry (those who benefited from Peter's table of ranks). Potentially it also included the rising bourgeoisie and the professional class. In this respect, the marriage of the scion of an old albeit obscure clan, Grinev, to Masha Mironova, obviously only a second-generation gentlewoman appears symbolic of the new social order Pushkin was trying to envision. It reflects, as well, one of the more salient aspects of the ideology of legitimacy in post-Napoleonic Europe, in which many of the gains of the bourgeoisie during the Revolutionary and Napoleonic periods were tacitly recognized by the new order. Hence, the title of the novel emphasizes directly the social standing of Grinev's bride.

Goethe, Walter Scott, Jane Austin, and other leading European novelists – contemporaries of the French Revolution and the Napoleonic Wars – also turned to the motif of a *mésalliance* as a way of codifying the changes that were taking place in the class structure of Europe and of expressing their hope that class warfare might dissolve in a nonviolent way.[63] Pushkin's theme in *The Captain's Daughter* can be viewed in this light; yet it is here that we can trace the sort of capillary fractures that separate Pushkin's work from the 'classical' Bildungsroman in Franco Moretti's sense of the term. While the realization of the proscribed love affair constitutes the hero's ostensible object, the real motor of Grinev's maturation is his relationship with Pugachev, whom he encounters in chapter 2. As Grigor'ev astutely saw, Grinev's relationship with Pugachev emblematizes the experience of the top strata of Russian society when they began to confront a completely different Russia – the Russia of the people, that is, the social stratum that had remained untouched by Peter's reforms. This Russia remained an intellectual terra incognita until it was, as it were, rediscovered in the late eighteenth and nineteenth centuries by such democratically minded thinkers as Radishchev, Karamzin (particularly as the author of 'Poor Liza'), the Decembrists, and some others.[64] From this angle, the 'strange friendship' between Grinev and Pugachev could even be seen (roughly) as a symbolic echo of the liberal demand for the democratization of Russia's political and social institutions, which pervaded Russian sentimentalism and the Decembrist-era political poetry.[65] As Grinev's horizon and psyche broaden, the reader, too, begins to experience sympathy with the side of national character, which had previously barely lent itself to high culture and literature, remaining in the domain of myth and oral memory. Thus the novelist's motive in sending his hero to complete his sentimental education in a provincial garrison, instead of in Petersburg, is to throw him into the wholly unfamiliar, politically volatile milieu of the Orenburg steppes.

Assuming that Grinev's core character is based on such inherited gentry virtues as honour, courage, sympathy, and respect for traditions, it would be interesting to trace the transformation of this ideological vertebrae as the hero's life story grows and acquires more flesh.[66] At this juncture, I shall reintroduce Lotman's approach to *Bildung*. As I showed in part 1, this approach can be traced back to Grigor'ev's view of Pushkin as a poet of 'universal responsiveness.' Using Lotman's semiotic terminology, we can call the whole complex of moral and cultural norms and ideals inculcated in Grinev's consciousness a certain 'code.' Indeed, what distinguishes Pushkin's hero from the more 'opportunistic' (*pace* Moretti) Western Bildungsroman heroes like Wilhelm Meister is his unswerving loyalty to his class and kin. But Pushkin's hero is not 'finalized' until the very end of the story. He continues to evolve: he learns how to respond to life's unpredictable challenges and expands his horizon, without, however, unlearning the language (or, as Lotman would say, 'code') of honour, which was his original mother tongue (or, perhaps, father tongue). This 'code' is constitutive of Grinev's identity, but this identity is flexible. Thus Pushkin's hero comes to embody the very essence of cultural evolution.

Given that the narrative of *The Captain's Daughter* is presented to us as Grinev's autobiography, or *zapiski*, we can approach Grinev's maturation as an example of autocommunication, which Lotman discusses in his essay 'On Two Models of Communication' (*'O dvukh modeliakh kommunkatsii'*).[67] In this essay Lotman distinguishes between ordinary information exchange, which he calls 'I-he' communication, and autocommunication, or 'I-I communication.' The first type of communication, from 'I' to 'he,' uses the same code to transmit a certain idea. Lotman's concept of auto-communication takes up messages transmitted by the subject back to himself. Lotman's examples of this type of communication include diary jottings, which help one revisit and mentally clarify a certain segment of experience, thereby changing the 'rank' of this information. Through this retransmission of information to oneself, the original 'code' – a broad and flexible term in Lotman's writings, which can mean anything from one's 'natural' language to the original point of view or even entire identity – undergoes a transformation. Lotman explicitly suggests that auto-communication allows the human intellect to step outside of the ready-made notions and begin to act improvisationally. Thus auto-communication leads to the 'restructuring of the subject of communication, the original "I".'[68] In other words, auto-communication is essentially a step toward self-creation (*obrazovanie, Bildung*).[69]

In part 1 I demonstrated the salience to my project of Lotman's vision of cultural dynamic as an open-ended, uncontrolled process necessarily concerned with contingency. Among other scholars it was Grigor'ev, I argue, who inspired Lotman to create a model of culture as a growing and perpetually evolving organism. Grigor'ev was the first major Russian thinker to understand that what distinguished Russian modernity from the middle-class cultural norm that was developing in contemporary Europe was that Russia, unlike Europe, was never and could never become a homogeneous monolith. In Russia both individual identity and culture as a whole were perpetually subject to redefinition or, to use Grigor'ev's favourite term, 'broadening.' Lotman's vernacular for understanding cultural evolution took its final shape in the 1970s, when he turned to semiotics. However, his earlier pre-semiotics essays, such as his article on *The Captain's Daughter*, already contain some of his crucial semiotic insights, such as the insight into the mechanism of code-switching and self-translation.

Writing in the wake of Lukács, Lotman presents the basic 'ideological structure' of his novel as a juxtaposition of the two mutually alienated social classes or worlds, each of which is endowed with its system of values and its own 'code.' On the one hand, there is the culture of the gentry, whose chief spokesmen in the novel are Grinev and his father. Opposed to it is the world of the peasant and Cossack rebels, represented firstly by their leader Pugachev. Thus, the accidental encounter between Grinev and Pugachev results in the intersection of these 'codes.' Grinev's consciousness becomes the site of this semiotic 'explosion,' which can be analysed in terms of 'I-I communication.'[70] In short, we could say that the novel demonstrates Lotman's idea of how genuine change can occur within the semiosphere. Even if we insist that 'Pugachevshchina' is not actually represented by a single man, Pugachev, and that Pushkin's representation of this event is a bit more nuanced and even chaotic than Lotman describes it, I think we can still adopt Lotman's idea of 'auto-communication' as a basic model for thinking about Grinev's *Bildung*.

Importantly, Lotman sees code-switching and 'auto-communication' not only as an ideological, but also as a psychological or even spiritual process. That is to say, the hero of Pushkin's tale emerges from the ordeal of Pugachevshchina not only with more knowledge of the world, but, presumably, also as a more mature person with a qualitatively different mind. Thus Lotman's approach illuminates the very essence of organic historicity, which consists of a qualitative change in the hero's consciousness. Without the subjective dimension in which such transformation can take place, history would be mechanistic, viewed only as a series of arbitrary changes. It is easy to agree with Lotman on this point, since, as Pushkin understood very well, the major flaw in the Petrine reforms was that they flowed from the very top level and imposed new customs and administrative principles on all levels of society without taking into account national customs and intellectual habits. The Russian subjects did not have a chance to develop the inner need for these changes, did not develop an identity around them, and so became uprooted without being enlightened. Therefore, for both Karamzin and Pushkin, who saw Peter as an ambiguous figure and his reforms as a mixed blessing, the task was to re-naturalize the uprooted educated Russians into a grounded community with which to identify.[71]

A great scholar of Karamzin, Lotman understood Pushkin's debate with his predecessor's spirit. In fact, we can argue that Lotman, like Karamzin or Pushkin, endorsed an organicist vision of history, which he recasts in his semiotic theory as the semiosphere. A more detailed discussion of theory, however, should be left for another occasion. Here it is important only to point out that the central point of Lotman's 'The Ideological Structure of *The Captain's Daughter'* is the reaffirmation of the idea of history as an organic change in world view, which is illustrated by Grinev's maturation and growth. Thus *The Captain's Daughter* not only gives history a concrete face but also shares this historical experience with those who are supposed to benefit from it – that is, Grinev's heirs, being by implication not only the hero's fictional heirs (the grandsons of Pyotr Grinev and Masha Mironova), but also the narratees in the broader sense, including the readers of Pushkin's *The Contemporary* and later readers. It is not surprising, then, that there evolved a whole critical tradition that stressed that *The Captain's Daughter* is firstly a Russian family chronicle, which presents readers with a lesson, before being a historical romance.[72]

Reading for the Plot

The story of Petrusha Grinev begins in the idyllic *locus amoenus* of the provincial country estate and then swiftly brings us out of it, in a journey that keys the entire narrative (as it is on a journey, in transit, that Grinev first meets Pugachev) through the culturally diverse region of the steppes surrounding the military fortress Orenburg. This area was populated by Cossacks as well as by semi-nomadic peoples like the Bashkirs, the Kalmyks and the Tartars, all of whom were colonized by the Russians in the course of the seventeenth and eighteenth centuries. In the eighteenth century the indigenous peoples struck back in several major uprisings, which provided the raison d'etre of the fortress to which Grinev is assigned. In choosing this frontier region rather than Petersburg as the setting for the real education of his hero, Pushkin demonstrates his desire to forego habitual paths (i.e., Petersburg and/or the grand tour) and chart out a new path for his hero's apprenticeship. Grinev, then, is destined to confront the real Russia in all its violent splendour.

It is here that Walter Scott, the poet of the borderland, serves as Pushkin's poetic guide. Like Scott, Pushkin has devised a plot that allows us to experience the pleasure of adventure and the sublime confrontation with real danger. Also like the author of *Waverley* and *Rob Roy*, Pushkin assures his reader from the beginning that the tale will end well by stylizing it as a chronicle of a man who is narrating the events lived in the past by a point in the future relative to these events. This is the position of the traditional storyteller. By resorting to this typical eighteenth-century (or Gothic) device, Pushkin offers his readers a 'narrative contract' that firmly locates them in the present while opening up the past's possibilities in an adventure that casts that present, in the course of its unfolding, into doubt. The only striking difference between Pushkin's narrative and a typical Scott novel is the fact that Pushkin's hero is not a typical 'middling hero' cast in the median between struggling political camps, whose function is merely to reflect on the historical events. Pushkin's Grinev is an active hero who shapes his own destiny and takes charge of his life, even as he is taken charge of. He leaves home a naïve child explicitly under the watchful eye of his servant, Savel'ich, and comes back not as a prodigal son anxious for his father's forgiveness, but as a man who has earned the right to his happiness and his father's blessing. It is significant that Grinev returns home after his father already receives a letter from the Empress urging the elder Grinev to pardon his son. This royal sanction forces the father, whom Grinev has disobeyed (wanting to marry Masha and enduring all kinds of ordeals that compromised his honour in the eyes of the state),[73] to accept his son as an equal and as his genuine heir. Thus, like so many eighteenth-century moral fictions, Pushkin's story ends with a homecoming. Yet this homecoming signals not only the completion of one life cycle and the beginning of another, but the replacement of one generation – that of Grinev's father – with its uncouth lack of cultivation, its insensibility to sentiment, with another – Grinev's – with its 'softened' manners, its sympathy, and its breadth. To use Grigor'ev's favourite metaphor, Grinev's consciousness has been 'broadened.'

As Grigor'ev implies, it is precisely Grinev's ability to broaden himself (i.e., to broaden both his mind and his soul) that makes him a more developed Russian literary hero than were his predecessors in Pushkin's works, the superfluous men like Onegin and Aleko, whose growth was stunted by their demonic and self-chosen isolation from Russian reality.

In *The Captain's Daughter* this reality is presented in all its touching and sometimes brutal honesty. The realism of the tale is not confined to the description of the dreary everyday life on a provincial estate, in a backward garrison, or in a still more remote fort. In Pushkin's novel we also see the obverse of the slothful Russian everyday: its immense propensity for violence, which is typically hidden beneath the surface of submission. Interestingly, Savel'ich, Grinev's servant, offers us a psychological glimpse into this level of society. Because Savel'ich belongs to this lower class and knows it better, he tries to oppose Grinev when the latter gives the 'Guide' (Pugachev) his cloak at the inn – an act of generosity that actually saves both Grinev and his servant in the end. Pushkin does not romanticize Pugachev's troops, but, on the contrary, emphasizes their roughness. They are a ragtag assortment of former Cossacks, serfs who have escaped from their masters, various semi-nomadic indigenous peoples resisting Russian imperialism, and other people who for one reason or another find themselves at odds with the authorities. They embody the contradictions of the Russian people, unleavened by the chivalric values and culture Grinev brings, and their brief sovereignty is entirely destructive.

The epigones of pochvennichestvo emphasized Pushkin's sympathy with Pugachev as the embodiment of nature's demonic power. Marina Tsvetaeva went so far as to compare it to the kind of irresistible charm that attracts children to the evil hero of the fairy tale.[74] In this connection, it is worth bearing in mind that Grigor'ev himself, while praising Pushkin's desire to get closer to Russian reality – to the 'soil' and its 'elemental powers' – was rather cautious about these powers, which he called *stikhiia* or *stikhiinye nachala*.[75] Seeing both the creative and the destructive potential of the demonic forces, or, as he calls them, 'peripheral' forces of the human soul, he praises Pushkin for being able to keep these powers in balance.[76]

Undoubtedly, this balance is a testimony to the poet's remarkable willpower. The amazing energetic potential that we sense behind Pushkin's prose suggests great internal pressure hidden just beneath the surface. Post-Freudian critics, including Caryl Emerson and David

Bethea, have surmised that this energy has to do with Pushkin's Oedipal battles. This insight can be brought to bear on Grigor'ev's vision of Pushkin as a poet who, constricted by the narrow tastes of the salon, engineered his escape by reaching out to the more popular audience. Pushkin's efforts to overcome literary inauthenticity and his pursuit of a more authentic *narodnost'* were clearly both personally and politically motivated, especially considering the circumstances of Pushkin's life during exile and afterwards. After all, it is during this time that Pushkin's own father complied with Alexander's order to spy on his son while the latter was under house arrest in Mikhailovskoe. We should also keep in mind Pushkin's personal ties and enmities with Nicholas I and his infinite frustration at his position as a court poet. Clearly, Pushkin's imagination was fed by his intense desire to move beyond the court culture in which he was kept perpetually in a position of dependence and inferiority, without, however, losing the benefit of firm identity that this hierarchical culture granted. In short, Pushkin's transcendence of the older poetic persona marked by the 'genre consciousness' of eighteenth-century poetics was not simply a contingent result of his discovery of the mass audience and popular prose literature. It was refined in the whole complex of ideological and psychological changes that occurred in this writer's life after he managed to survive the repressions of 1825–6.[77]

I do not want to exaggerate, in the manner of Marxist critics, Pushkin's sympathy with Pugachev. However, I do believe that this element of the plot cannot be read as a simple tribute to or mimicry of Scott. The dynamic of Grinev's strange relationship to Pugachev – one that oscillates between friendliness and antipathy or even horror – makes Pugachev more than a mere adventure in Grinev's life. Continuing to develop Grigor'ev's insight, we can say that it is thanks to his almost magical relationship with Pugachev that Grinev achieves a truly unique as well as robust identity. It is also with Pugachev's help that he wins Masha in a contest with his demonic double, Shvabrin. This point needs more explanation, and I will offer it by turning to Caryl Emerson's essay, which interprets Grinev's dream in chapter 2 of the novel.

As Emerson shows, Grinev's dream provides a key for understanding the psychological dynamic of the hero's confrontation with his own father on the one hand and, on the other hand, with the muzhik whom he encounters on the road to Belogorskaia fortress, who later turns out to be Pugachev.[78] In this dream he sees himself as arriving home and finding his father near death. His mother urges him to go ask for the father's last blessing:

> I was in that state of mind and feeling in which reality yields to reveries and merges with them in the nebulous vision of approaching sleep. The blizzard, I fancied, was still raging, and we were still floundering in the snow-covered wilderness, but I suddenly beheld a gate and was driven into the courtyard of our manor-house. My first thought was an apprehension that my father might be angry with me for this unintentional reentrance under the paternal roof, construing it as deliberate disobedience. I jumped out of the wagon with anxiety and saw my mother coming off the porch to meet me with an air of deep sorrow.
> 'Quiet,' she says to me, 'your father is on his deathbed and wants to bid farewell to you.'
> Struck by fear, I follow her into the bedroom. I see a dimly lit chamber and people standing around the bed with a sad expression on their faces. I tiptoe up to the bed, mother raises the bed curtain and says, 'Andrei Petrovich, Petrusha has arrived: he's heard of your illness and come back home; give him your blessing.'
> I go down on my knees and raise my eyes to the invalid. But what did I see? Instead of my father, I behold a muzhik with a black beard, looking at me gaily. I turn to mother in bewilderment, saying, 'What's the meaning of this? This is not father. And why should I ask a muzhik for his blessing?'
> 'It's all the same, Petrusha,' answers mother; 'this is your father by proxy: kiss his dear hand and let him bless you.'
> I could not agree to that. The muzhik jumps out off the bed, draws an axe from behind his back and starts flourishing it in all directions. I want to run, but I can't; the room is filling with dead bodies; I stumble over the corpses and slip in the pools of blood. The terrifying muzhik calls out to me kindly, 'Don't be afraid, come to receive my blessing.'
> Horror and bewilderment overwhelm me. (8:289; Debreczeny 276)

This dream exerts a symbolic power over every level on which the events of the next two chapters unfold. Emerson makes much of the Freudian implications of Grinev's dream, which, she says, manifests an extreme anxiety about authority both on the socio-political and the family levels. Indeed, one could interpret all the social upheavals of the story in terms of the portents in the dream. On the level of the state, it portends Pugachev's revolt, fanned not by any Republican ideology, but by his claim to the throne as a Tsar, the 'father' of the people; on the local level – the fall of Belogorskaia fortress and the murder of the Captain, a patriarchal figure who by the end of the book becomes Grinev's father-in-law; and finally, on the personal level, where Grinev's 'crime' (with which he is officially charged) consists in resorting to Pugachev's help in rescuing Masha and accepting his blessing, as though he were Grinev's own father. This is where the split between Grinev and Shvabrin becomes more than a fact of the text's compositional history. While Grinev contains a Shvabrin in his soul without giving him reign, Shvabrin cannot contain a Grinev. That is to say, Grinev is able to both feel Pugachev's seductive power and resist it. He does not desert to Pugachev's side, because this would permanently damage his gentleman's honour that provides him with an identity, which I earlier compared to a 'father tongue.' It is very significant for the story that Pushkin's *Bildungsheld* enters life equipped with a set of basic moral principles and rules of conduct. As we remember, when Grinev's father sends his son away to begin his military career in a remote garrison, he, as befits a nobleman, gives his son a set of instructions. Thus the 'Grinev code' gets imprinted in the memory of the reader as deeply and firmly as it is imprinted in Grinev's consciousness: 'Good-bye, Petr. Serve faithfully the Sovereign to whom you swear allegiance; obey your superiors; don't curry favor with them; don't volunteer for duty, but don't shirk it either; and remember the proverb: Take care of your clothes while they are still new; cherish your honor from a tender age' (8:282; Debreszeny 269).

If Grinev's legitimate father can be said to represent the 'code' of the enlightened nobility whose rational order is contiguous with the state and deep-rooted social institutions (such as hereditary nobility), then Petrusha's encounter with the Guide seems to answer his deep-seated desire to subvert this order.[79] Thus, when the Guide has safely brought Petrusha to the nearest tavern, he looks for the first time at his new friend, and Petrusha sees his piercing eyes and black beard. A Romantic at heart, Marina Tsvetaieva read this as one of the most powerful moments in the novel, conveying the magic of spontaneous 'elective affinity' that suddenly and powerfully takes a hold of one's psyche.[80] Grinev, who up to this point has lived an extremely sheltered life, experiencing only very simple and tame emotions, such as his mother's timid tenderness and his father's authority mitigated by love, suddenly feels the brunt of real passion, which has to do with violence and prohibition. Pugachev takes a liking to the young man and tries to win him by showing his power, magnificence, and generosity. Interestingly, this brings out the stubborn manly side of Grinev. Instead of yielding to Pugachev's power, he holds his line, acting like a born nobleman whose rank does not permit stooping down to the pretender. By so doing, he challenges Pugachev to act honourably too. He even dares seek Pugachev's help when he tries to rescue Masha from the clutches of the vicious Shvabrin, and Pugachev, miraculously, does help. At the end of chapter 11, which describes this third encounter between the heroes, Grinev takes the liberty to advise Pugachev to quit his band. He dares to lecture Pugachev, warning him about his future and comparing him to Grishka Otrep'ev. Here Grinev acts almost like a 'rigourist' out of an eighteenth-century moral tale, trying to reform his 'friend' Pugachev. Yet the latter also does not relent. He tells Grinev a 'Kalmyk tale' about the eagle and the raven, which explains the morality he lives by:

> Once the eagle asked the raven, 'Tell me, raven-bird, why is it that you live three hundred years in this bright world, and I am allotted only three and thirty?' 'It's for this reason, my friend,' answered the raven, 'that you drink live blood while I feed on carrion.' Thought the eagle, 'Let me try to feed on the same.' Very well. Off flew the eagle and the raven. Suddenly they saw a fallen horse; they descended and alighted on it. The raven started tearing at it, praising it. The eagle pecked at it once, pecked at it twice, then flapped its wings and said to the raven, 'No, friend raven: rather than live on carrion for three hundred years, I'll choose one good drink of blood, and then what'll come will come.' (8:353; Debreszeny 336–7)

In response to this tale, Grinev says curtly: 'In my opinion, to live by murder and plunder is the same as pecking carrion.'[81] Pugachev's surprised glance, which ends this scene, conveys the utter incomprehension between their two points of view, which ultimately leads the nobleman, whose life is driven by the idea of honour, to return to the side of the legitimate monarch, and the leader of the rebellious Cossacks to continue on his path until his death on the executioner's block. This scene ends on a harsh note of miscommunication and sadness: 'We both fell silent, each engrossed in his own thoughts. The Tatar struck up a melancholy tune' (8:353; Debreszeny 337.). To be empathetic or psychologically and intellectually 'broad' is not the same as accepting moral chaos.

All of these elements of the plot are foretold in the dream, which hinges on the (non)substitutability between Grinev's father and the terrifying muzhik – Pugachev. That Grinev can, even unconsciously, treat his father and the thief as equivalents shows that, at the beginning of the novel, Grinev is not yet what Bakhtin would call a 'finalized' (or 'completed') character in possession of a firm self-image. Thus the drama that is played out in the larger, historical sphere will be played out, too, in his own psyche. Eventually he will indeed choose the paternal order, codified as the culture of 'honour,' and refuse to kiss Pugachev's hand, that is, acknowledge him as a legitimate father-figure.

In this connection, I want to point out that although some critics have interpreted Pugachev's initial decision to spare Grinev as a testimony to his humanness – for he supposedly is acting out of gratitude to the young *barich* – I think that the scene in front of the gallows actually underscores the sheer arbitrariness of Pugachev's authority. The perfect way for the pretender to demonstrate his limitless power is by sparing one prisoner – just because he so desires. And this is exactly what neither Pushkin nor his novelistic alter ego Grinev can accept as the rule of civic life.

Surviving this auto-da-fé with power brings home to us and to the hero the difference between raw power, steeped in instincts and terrifying when left to its own devices, and power channelled through various rational and historically tested institutions, which is therefore 'civilized.' Guided by his belief in legitimate power, Grinev is determined to win his father's blessing for his marriage to Masha, the captain's daughter. For ultimately it is as unreasonable to suppress sensibility as it is to let sensation take over life. Grinev grasps the moral of this *conte* when he sees that the eagle's path of blood is no different than the vulture's path of carrion. In the end of the adventure at the heart of the novel, Pushkin's hero comes back home, having won the Empress's recognition and the right to marry whom he wants.

Conclusion

We do not know exactly when *The Captain's Daughter* was actually finished. The ending bears the date 'October 19th, 1836.' This date is highly symbolic: October 19 is the day of the Lyceum graduation, which Pushkin and his classmates celebrated every year. Pushkin typically wrote a poem to celebrate this occasion. In 1836 he addressed his friends scattered all over the Empire with a prose work. Thus Pushkin's novel can be linked to the body of lyric texts addressing the issues of memory, maturation, and self-recognition as agents in history. In this connection Masha's trip to Tsarskoe Selo, where she meets the

Empress and receives a pardon for Grinev – the magical conclusion to the novel – seems charged with more symbolism than the critics have so far granted it. A trip to Tsarskoe Selo being the crucial *lieu de mémoire* for Pushkin and his cohort, like a symbolic pilgrimage, sanctifies Masha's and Grinev's marriage. The fact that Masha does not care about seeing Petersburg and rushes home to the Grinevs' provincial estate separates the *locus amoeunus* that Tsarkoe Selo represents for Pushkin from the banal and cruel world of politics, court, and professional competition represented by Petersburg. By virtue of neglecting to visit the capital, Masha avoids being tainted by it, returning back to her fiancé with the same unspoiled wholesome character as she had from the beginning. They spend the rest of their lives together in on this estate, which gets symbolically framed as a genuine matrix of organic culture and purebred national values, shielded from the harsh and vulgar reality of historical existence. This conclusion seems to suggest that whatever historical experience Petrusha and Masha needed to make themselves whole was provided by the adventures leading up to their marriage. Now they must only protect their hard-won happiness and translate their success down the line by breeding numerous robust offspring.

The story about Masha's trip to see the empress, with its Walter Scottian echoes, is related not by the memoirist himself, but by the 'editor' who steps in to bring the story to its denouement and 'finalize' Grinev's tale. Thus the fictional world, in which Grinev experiences Pugachevshchina, with all its terror, lust, and wonder, is placed at a remove from the everyday reality where the Grinev homestead continues to exist (and which the 'editor' supposedly visits in search of materials related to the Pugachev uprising). The device of the 'editor' creates an aesthetic distance in order to emphasize a qualitative shift in the form and conditions of experience where there is no geographical gap.[82] For the Grinevs, the heirs of our hero, reside in the very same provincial Russia where some of Pushkin's nineteenth-century readers lived. Perhaps, by stressing the ubiquity or ordinariness of the Grinevs' country house Pushkin wants to bring home to every reader that his or her dwelling place may also harbour some untold tales, and there is a lot of wonderment concealed under every roof, at the heart of every Russian hearth and home. To bring out this secret spark is the task of literature, which helps ennoble and enrich life, no matter how quotidian and unenlightened it may seem to be outwardly.

This re-enchantment of daily life through literature and fiction is essential to the success of Pushkin's overall program for the humanistic education of his contemporaries, because the susceptibility to culture and morality requires a soul that is sensitive to its narrative possibilities – a soul that is self-reflective without being egotistical. Therefore, when Lotman says that in Pushkin's imagination the idea of historical progress was inseparable from the development of 'humanity,' what he means is first of all the development of sensibility. Like Pushkin, Lotman believes that sensibility is the only power capable of forestalling violence on both a local and a global scale. The idea that human beings share some basic propensity for understanding even if they do not share a language underlies the relentless quest for community and for more effective translation that energizes both Pushkin's artistic quest, particularly toward the end of his life, and Lotman's semiotics.

This point requires some emphasis. When speaking about Pushkin or Lotman, the majestic term 'Humanity,' which brings to mind the philosophy of the *Aufklaerung*, should never be mistaken for an empty accolade. As Lotman points out in his article 'Ideinaia struktura "Kapitanskoi Dochki,"' 'Back when he was creating the ode *Liberty*, Pushkin considered the rule of law a force that stands above the people and the government, [a force that] embodies justice. But now he discovered that people who live in a socially divided society inevitably find themselves under the power of one or the other of the two mutually exclusive concepts of lawfulness and justice, because what is legal from the perspective of one social force is considered unlawful from the perspective of the other.'[83]

We are reminded here of Pushkin's rejection of 'theory' (favoured by the generation of the Lovers of Wisdom) and his preference for concrete poetic action. Lotman goes on to conclude that Pushkin generalized from his inability to formulate uniform concepts of truth and justice that this was not a failure of culture but rather a symptom of its vitality. Abstraction actually distorts an emergent quality of human communities. Following that emergent quality, we come to understand that 'historical progress is inseparable from humanity' ('istoricheskii progress neotdelim ot chelovechnosti').[84] Lotman's analysis of *The Captain's Daughter* strives to illustrate this quest for humanity not only insofar as Grinev's older self incarnated in the perfectly self-controlled, well-measured voice of the narrator is obviously broader, wiser, and less prone to passions than the young hero of the tale, but also insofar as his tale succeeds in shedding some light on one of the darkest pages of Russian history. Transformed into a tale of personal maturation and quest, history becomes more amenable to personal experience in the sense of what Walter Benjamin called 'narratable experience' or *Erfahrung*.[85] In this sense, we can say that within Pushkin's work we find a countermeasure Benjamin pointed to in his dictum about the decline of experience in modern societies, where the speed of biological and informational reproduction exceeds the speed of cultural critique, self-comprehension, and what Lotman called 'auto-communication.'[86] If we agree with Benjamin's shocking diagnosis of modernity as a form of cultural inertia, where action becomes limited to the routine repetition of mechanical processes, then in Pushkin's novel we find both an awareness of these modern tendencies and an artistic attempt to counteract them.

In reawakening the movement of the past that led to the present, we counter the conformism – the lack of the capacity to imagine things being otherwise – that, according to some critics, determines the modern tendency toward spiritual apathy. And this is where the Russian cultural and literary traditions added their own unique twist to European ideas about culture and cultivation.

6 Educating Russia, Building Humanity: Tolstoy's *War and Peace*

Prologue: Tolstoy's *Lehrjahre*

When Lev Tolstoy entered the public sphere, Russian literature was undergoing a major change. The deaths of Gogol (in 1845) and Belinskii (in 1848), as well as Herzen's emigration in 1847, brought to a close a major chapter in Russian literary history. The memory of this epoch, which P.V. Annenkov famously dubbed 'the remarkable decade,' was still fresh.[1] The influential journal *The Contemporary* (*Sovremennik*), once led by V.G. Belinskii (1811–48), was now in the hands of N.A. Nekrasov, I.F. Panaev, V.P. Botkin, P.V. Annenkov, and I.S. Turgenev. The journal's political orientation in the early 1850s could be described as progressive/liberal. However, the appearance of N.G. Chernyshevskii (1828–89) as the journal's leading critic in 1854 and 1855 influenced its whole orientation, transforming it into the organ of the radical left. Seeing himself as the chief heir to Belinskii, Chernyshevskii proceeded to attack his liberal colleagues.[2] The ensuing civil war within the editorial board of *The Contemporary* was fought over different philosophical and aesthetic conceptions. While the generation of the 1840s was still largely wedded to Hegel's idealism, Chernyshevskii was influenced by left Hegelians (particularly Feuerbach) and British utilitarianism. Chernyshevskii first challenged the idealists of the 1840s in a review article published in *The Contemporary* in March 1855. He followed this with the publication of his master's dissertation, *The Aesthetic Relations of Art to Reality* (*Esteticheskie otnosheniia iskusstva k deistvitel'nosti*, May 1855). In this thesis Chernyshevskii questioned Hegel's aesthetics, with its emphasis on the transformative role of Spirit in human history, and offered his own materialist interpretation of art as part and parcel of objective material reality. Chernyshevskii's assault on the beliefs of the generation of the 1840s proved successful in the short term, for he practically displaced his liberal opponents on the editorial board of *The Contemporary*. He also found two strong followers in N.A. Dobroliubov (1836–61) and D.I. Pisarev (1840–68). The second half of the 1850s saw a bitter confrontation between these radical critics and those who remained faithful to the ideals of the 1840s.

It was in this highly charged atmosphere that the twenty-seven-year-old Tolstoy found himself upon his return, in November of 1855, to St Petersburg from Sevastopol. After an eleven-month siege this naval stronghold was surrendered to the allied forces of France, Britain, and the Ottoman Empire. As they were leaving, the Russians had to sink their entire fleet to prevent it from falling into the hands of the enemy. Thus the Crimean War – up to that point the most inglorious war in the history of the Russian Empire – came to a close. Tolstoy, who served as an artillery officer in Sevastopol from November 1854 to November 1855, described the defence of this Black Sea port in a series of sketches published in *The Contemporary*, the same journal where Tolstoy had made his literary debut in 1852 by publishing *Childhood*.[3]

Tolstoy's autobiographical trilogy, *Childhood, Adolescence* (1854), and *Youth* (1857), and the *Sevastopol Sketches* (1855) were very well received by Petersburg critics. When Tolstoy himself arrived in the capital, he was immediately embraced by the publisher of *The Contemporary*, N.A. Nekrasov, and his collaborators, including the writer I.S. Turgenev and critics A.V. Druzhinin, V.P. Botkin, and P.V. Annenkov. During the winter of 1855–6, which Tolstoy spent in Petersburg, he became an intimate in the literary circle led by Druzhinin. He also met with a number of other prominent writers and intellectuals, including the Slavophiles K.S. and S.T. Aksakov (who were visiting from Moscow), I.A. Goncharov, I.F. Panaev, and A.K. Tolstoy.[4]

Chernyshevskii, too, was well disposed toward the young Tolstoy. Thus, in December 1856, Chernyshevskii published a most flattering review of Tolstoy's *Sevastopol Sketches*, in which he coined the expression that was destined to survive the 1850s: he called Tolstoy's method of psychological analysis 'the dialectics of the soul' [*dialektika dushi*] (*The Contemporary*, December 1856).[5] As Donna Orwin has pointed out, Chernyshevskii recognized that there was some common ground between himself and Tolstoy insofar as both of them were wedded to 'analysis' and rationalism. The fact that Tolstoy attacked contemporary society with such passion and tenacity must have also appealed to

Chernyshevskii. Some evidence suggests that in 1857 Chernyshevskii was seeking to obtain influence over Tolstoy.[6] Tolstoy, however, kept his distance.

The three critics with whom Tolstoy formed a close association during this period of his life, A.V. Druzhinin, V.P. Botkin, and P.V. Annenkov, were all opposed to the radicals in general and to Chernyshevskii in particular. This group, whom Tolstoy called his 'priceless triumvirate' [*bestsennyi triumvirat*], claimed just like Chernyshevskii to be Belinskii's literary descendants. However, the Belinskii they continued to revere was the earlier, idealist Belinskii, rather than the later Belinskii, a Utopian socialist and admirer of George Sand.

Not all of Tolstoy's intellectual interests and alliances of 1856–7 proved lasting. For example, for a time Tolstoy considered himself a follower of the 'Art for Art's Sake' movement. This was the position he openly embraced in his acceptance speech to the Society of the Lovers of Russian Literature [*Obshchestvo Liubitelei Rossiiskoi Slovesnosti*].[7] Yet by the beginning of the 1860s, Tolstoy no longer saw himself as a 'pure artist.' Nonetheless, certain predilections developed during this period; for example, a distaste for the utilitarian ethic and aesthetics remained crucial to Tolstoy's outlook throughout his literary career. In this respect Druzhinin, one of the key defenders of idealist aesthetics and, throughout the 1850s and 1860s, an active propagandist of Shakespeare and contemporary English writers, must have played an important role in shaping Tolstoy's taste. As several critics have remarked, the English novel, particularly the subgenre of the 'family novel,' played a major role in Tolstoy's artistic development.[8] Druzhinin also succeeded in transferring his own misgivings about Chernyshevskii to Tolstoy. Tolstoy's correspondence with Druzhinin (who had left *The Contemporary* and joined *Library for Reading* [*Biblioteka dlia chteniia*] in 1852) contains a number of biting remarks directed against Chernyshevskii's 1856 *Sketches of the Gogolian Period of Russian Literature* (*Ocherki gogolevskgko perioda russkoi literatury*).[9]

In his own public response to Chernyshevskii, entitled *The Sketches of the Gogolian Period of Russian Literature and Our Attitudes to It* (*Ocherki gogolevskgko perioda russkoi literatury i nashi k nim otnosheniia*), Druzhinin attacked Chernyshevskii as well as the ostensible source of his inspiration, the later Belinskii.[10] Belinskii (in his phase as an advocate of George Sand) had accused Pushkin's Tat'iana of not following her heart and staying with an unloved old husband instead of abandoning him for Onegin, whom she loved.[11] Belinskii's criticism, according to

Druzhinin, betrayed a lack of taste as well as a misunderstanding of Pushkin's chaste poetic ideal. Druzhinin also caustically commented on what was perhaps the most scandalous aspect of Belinskii's legacy: his mistranslation of Hegel's terminology. As is well known, Belinskii translated Hegel's term *Wirklichkeit* (actuality), from the *Phenomenology of Spirit*, as *deistvitel'nost'*, giving rise to a long and vehement polemic about Belinskii's own arguable 'reconciliation with reality.'[12] Chernyshevskii's own thesis about the equality of the beautiful with the real rested on Belinskii's conception of reality, which Druzhinin and other nineteenth-century critics who read Hegel in the original (unlike Belinskii) believed to be deeply flawed. Consequently, Chernyshevskii's aesthetic views were utterly indefensible in the eyes of these scholars reared on German idealism.

Although the young Tolstoy was hardly sufficiently versed in criticism or aesthetics to be able to follow the Druzhinin-Chernyshevskii dispute over Belinskii, the atmosphere of vigorous intellectual debate that surrounded him in Petersburg challenged him to catch up with the current intellectual trends. Tolstoy spent the winter of 1858 studying Russian and European literature, aesthetics, and criticism. He was compensating for years of disorganized reading and unguided literary experimentation. 'Now the period of *Lehrjahre* has begun for him, and he is thirsty for wisdom and knowledge,' Botkin wrote to Turgenev about Tolstoy on 3 January 1857.[13]

Indeed, reading Tolstoy's diary for 1856 and 1857 we see a record of an extremely intense intellectual development undergone by a young writer as he moved from the periphery to the centre of Russia's intellectual life. This apprenticeship was perhaps too rapid and intense. Boris Eikhenbaum makes a valid point when he suggests that Tolstoy never felt completely at home in Petersburg and eventually got so thoroughly fed up with professional literature that he was eager to escape back to the countryside.[14]

To be fair to Tolstoy, although he spent the entire summer of 1856 in Iasnaia Poliana, his ancestral estate, he did not simply resume the life of a country squire, but continued to work assiduously on both new and unfinished literary projects. One of these projects was the third part of his four-part quasi-autobiography, *Four Epochs of Development: Youth*. The first part, *Childhood*, hailed by the critics, described the idyllic life of the hero (named Nikolen'ka Irten'ev) at his family's country estate up to the point when the idyll is suddenly disrupted by the death of Nikolen'ka's mother.[15] The orphaned children and their father relocate to Moscow, where the next part of Tolstoy's work, *Adolescence*, unfolds. Here Tolstoy shows how the young hero makes a difficult transition from the world of the patriarchal noble family to the world of Moscow high society, describing his first faux pas, his disappointments, and his small misdemeanours caused by excessive wilfulness and *amour de soi*. The next part, *Youth*, was supposed to describe Nikolen'ka's encounter with the world of Moscow University students, many of whom were not of noble origin. These democratic students were both alluring and enigmatic for the young aristocratic hero. In the last chapters of *Youth*, as in *The Cossacks* (1857–8) and the first few stories from peasant life (*narodnye rasskazy*), which Tolstoy also attempted to write in 1861–2 (i.e., 'Tikhon and Malan'ia,' 'Polikushka,' 'The Idyll,' and some others), the writer first posed the problem with which he continued to wrestle for the rest of his career: how to bridge, or at least reduce, the gap between people of vastly different cultural backgrounds, or, as the case was in Tolstoy's Russia, between 'society' [*obshchestvo*] and the 'people' [*narod*].

As judged by its title, *The Four Phases of Development* [*Chetyre Epokhi Razvitiia*], conceived as early as the 1840s, was a tribute to Tolstoy's early fascination with Jean-Jacques Rousseau (1712–78), Johann Heinrich Pestalozzi (1746–1827) and other mostly eighteenth-century authors who focused on the idea of human life as a continual inner development and self-perfection.[16] The age of Sensibility and German *Aufklaerung* were among the first and most lasting intellectual impressions of Tolstoy's life. We must also note the lasting influence of Laurence Sterne (1713–68), as well as Tolstoy's interest in the work of a lesser-known Swiss author and follower of Rousseau and Sterne, Rudolf Toepffer (dates unknown), whose work *My Uncle's Library* (1832) apparently influenced Tolstoy's *Childhood, Adolescence*, and *Youth*.[17] These were Tolstoy's earliest exercises in the form of the Bildungsroman.

Youth was eventually completed and published in *The Contemporary*, but the critical reaction to this work was mixed, and Tolstoy himself was not entirely satisfied by this work. When, almost fifty years later, in 1903, he reread *Youth*, Tolstoy accused himself of lack of sincerity. As he wrote in his *Recollections*, there was something contrived about the autobiographical hero's demonstration of his democratic sympathies.[18] The fourth part of the projected four-part book on the development of the self was never written. It is plausible to suggest that Tolstoy could not bring this project to completion, because his own Weltanschauung was not yet fully formed. Tolstoy also suffered from the narrowness of his education and upbringing and was beginning to feel constrained by the aesthetic ideology of the 'art for art's sake' movement, which his friends Fet and Druzhinin pushed him to join. To complete his own apprenticeship Tolstoy needed to go abroad. On 29 January 1857 he set off for Europe.

The main destination of Tolstoy's first European trip was Paris. Once in France, Tolstoy immersed himself in the reading of French literature, frequently attended the theatre (especially opera, which he loved), and enjoyed his first encounter with 'that social freedom' about which, as he wrote to Botkin, he had 'no idea in Russia.'[19] Soon, however, Tolstoy's mood changed. The event that precipitated Tolstoy's rejection of France and modern Europe as a whole was the strong impression made upon him by witnessing a public execution by guillotine in Paris on 6 April 1857.[20] This incident, to which Tolstoy reacted with disgust and indignation, lodged itself so firmly in Tolstoy's mind that decades later he would again comment on it in his *Confession*.[21] How could the French, arguably the most enlightened people in the world, condemn a human being to execution by guillotine and transform murder into a spectacle? This shocking experience prompted a series of works, including 'Luzerne' and *Family Happiness*, in which the young Tolstoy rages against the modern European nation states dominated by the spirit of usury and selfishness.

Undoubtedly, Tolstoy's anti-French animus was also fuelled by his recent experience as an officer in the besieged Sevastopol. Furthermore, as Kathryn Feuer has shown, during his European trip and afterwards Tolstoy was appalled by the cult of Napoleon I in the new Empire of Napoleon III.[22] Whether or not the young Tolstoy was politically savvy enough to understand that the successful reconstruction of the European economy in the wake of the Napoleonic Wars, supported by autocratic Russia (this 'policeman of Europe,' to use Herzen's phrase), had actually paved the way for the flourishing and political strength of Napoleon III's empire, his disillusionment with French society and France's political system seem to run much deeper than wounded national pride. Tolstoy saw the economic and socio-political system that had emerged in Europe since the French Revolution as deeply flawed, because it reduced a human being to a self-interested agent, a prisoner of the social contract, disregarding his emotions and higher spiritual aspirations. As a result, human beings had become spiritually impoverished and therefore inept in situations that called for humane feelings. This is, in a nutshell, the main idea behind the story 'Luzerne,' where

Tolstoy indicts wealthy British tourists at a fashionable Swiss resort because they seem unable to show charity toward a poor Tyrolese singer who entertains them with his singing.[23]

Tolstoy spent the remainder of his first European trip in Switzerland, where his cousin, the lady-in-waiting Countess A.A. Tolstaya, was living at the time. He first went to stay with her in Geneva, but soon he abandoned this city, which was full of aristocratic Russians, and went to Clarens, the town described by his beloved Rousseau in *Julie, or the New Heloïse*, then to Bern, and finally to the depths of rural Switzerland, where he rejoiced in observing nature and the lives of peasants.[24] He returned to Russia by way of Baden-Baden, where he saw Turgenev, who at the time was still one of Tolstoy's major literary allies.

Tolstoy's first trip to Europe broadened his horizon and increased his literary ambitions. Having studied *The Iliad*, *The Odyssey*, and Goethe's *Hermann und Dorothea*, Tolstoy developed a desire to write an epic based on Russian material.[25] In the meantime, he kept reworking his novel about an aristocrat, Olenin, who escapes from Petersburg in order to seek happiness among the Cossacks. Tolstoy's unfinished novel *The Cossacks* was finally published in Mikhail Katkov's journal *Russian Messenger* (*Russkii Vestnik*) in 1863. However, it took a few more years and a good deal more experience and work before Tolstoy's rather vague idea about a Russian epic began to take shape, leading eventually to *War and Peace*.

In the meantime, Russia was on the threshold of a major economic and social transformation. In March 1856, in an address to the Moscow gentry, Alexander II had called upon landowners to cooperate in the emancipation of the serf population 'from above,' lest the serfs try to emancipate themselves 'from below.'[26] Indeed, at the time there were widespread fears of a new Pugachevschina. Tolstoy welcomed this opportunity to participate in the reforms. In June 1856 he proposed to his peasants a plan whereby he would give them their freedom and also a portion of land, for which they would reimburse him. The peasants, thinking that the emperor's announcement meant that they would soon receive from the government both freedom and land without any further obligations toward their master, rejected Tolstoy's offer. The young count was dismayed.[27]

Alexander II's speech to the Moscow gentry also called upon the gentry to assist the government in the difficult task of educating the peasants. In fact, in all levels of society education emerged as a crucial problem confronting post-Reform Russia. Tolstoy was by no means the only intellectual who made this issue his central concern for a number of years. Thanks to the efforts of N.I. Pirogov, K.D. Ushinskii, and others, pedagogy emerged as a separate field during this era and began to attract more and more bright minds.[28] Borrowing the title from N.I. Pirogov's famous article, we can say that education became the 'vital question' of post-Reform Russia. In this connection, I wish to contest Boris Eikhenbaum's claim that teaching peasant children at Iasnaia Poliana was for Tolstoy only a temporary diversion from literature, in which he became involved when his works 'Luzerne,' 'Al'bert,' and *Family Happiness* failed to attract much critical attention.[29] While it is true that in the late 1850s Tolstoy felt dissatisfied with his literary productions, particularly with *Family Happiness,* his passion for pedagogy was quite genuine and ran deeper than Eikhenbaum presents it. Tolstoy believed that without understanding the minds and souls of the peasants it was impossible to reform Russia. Ambitious though he was, he realized that Russia could not be reformed overnight, but that a gradual social transformation would have to accompany economic and political reforms.

Obrazovanie (Bildung) According to Tolstoy

Since the late 1840s, Tolstoy had been teaching the children of his peasants during his stays in Iasnaia Poliana. In the fall of 1859 he opened an official school on his estate and hired several students to serve along with him as teachers. He dedicated much of his spare time to studying European education theories. Tolstoy recorded his thoughts and impressions as a teacher and eventually composed a series of pedagogical tracts, which he published in the journal he edited, *Iasnaia Poliana*. Tolstoy's journal received mixed reviews in the press. Notably, the most glowing reviews of Tolstoy's pedagogical activities were published in M.M. and F.M. Dostoevskys' journal *Time*. The unnamed author of these reviews was Nikolai Strakhov, a person who was responsible for introducing Apollon Grigor'ev to the brothers Dostoevsky and who later, in the 1870s, became Tolstoy's intimate friend and main correspondent.[30]

In 1860–1 Tolstoy made a second trip to Europe. One of the main goals of this trip was to study European educational establishments. In France and England Tolstoy visited numerous schools and met with leading pedagogues. Another important stop in Tolstoy's itinerary was Weimar, the intellectual capital of eighteenth-century Germany, which Karamzin had visited seventy years earlier. In his *Letters of a Russian*

Traveller Karamzin described his visit to Weimar, including his conversations with Herder and Wieland, in great detail.³¹ Following in the footsteps of the famous eighteenth-century pilgrim, Tolstoy also spent several days in Weimar. However, his diary suggests that this trip had more sentimental significance than practical usefulness. While in Weimar, Tolstoy visited Goethe's house, which was already open to visitors and functioned as a museum, the Duke's palace, and the local gymnasium. However, he disliked what he saw at the court and in the gymnasium, finding the local pedagogues dogmatic and narrow-minded.³²

Reading Tolstoy's pedagogical essays written shortly after his return from Europe, we sense that he came away with the impression that the spirit of genuine Enlightenment had been nearly extinguished in contemporary Germany. His impressions of the city schools of London and Marseille were no better. Tolstoy rejected all forms of external coercion or guidance in education, and tried to put this theory into practice in his own school for peasant children. Anticipating J.S. Mill's theory of originality, Tolstoy's essays argue against the parochial notion of *Erziehung* (upbringing, education) (translated by Tolstoy as *vospitanie*), which still dominated contemporary German schools.³³ Tolstoy maintains that every individual, including every peasant child, has his own path to follow and personal ideal to fulfil. In short, he maintains that since there are no universal norms or criteria to guide human intellectual development, each and every individual must blaze his own trail to maturity. In contrast, the schools in contemporary Germany, he claims in his 1862 essay 'On Popular Education' ['*O narodnom obrazovanii*'], were viewed by average peasants as 'institutions for torturing children.'³⁴ Tolstoy goes on to suggest that 'in Germany, nine tenths of the school population take away from school a mechanical knowledge of reading and writing, and such a strong loathing for the paths of science traversed by them that they never again take a book into their hands.' But, even more importantly, 'in these six years [of schooling] these pupils are inculcated with the hypocrisy and deceit that arises from the unnatural position in which the pupils are placed, and that condition of incoherence and confusion of ideas, which is called the rudiments of education.'³⁵ And finally, at the heart of the essay, there is this: 'Every instruction ought to be only an answer to the question put by life, whereas school not only does not call forth questions, but does not even answer those that are called forth by life. It eternally answers the same question which had been put by humanity several centuries back, and not by the intellect of the child, and which he is not interested in.'³⁶

Looking carefully at Tolstoy's pedagogical writings from 1860 to 1863, the period immediately preceding *War and Peace*, we can see that the topic of personal formation or obrazovanie gradually becomes the nexus of several major intellectual issues, including personal and national identity, the meaning of life, freedom, and religious faith.[37]

When his brother Nikolai died from tuberculosis in September 1860, Tolstoy was plunged into the first of his deep spiritual crises in which his own faith was truly put into question. Two deaths he witnessed, that of Nikolai and the criminal he saw guillotined in Paris, became touchstones for Tolstoy's vision of *obrazovanie*. He thought that everyone's life should be aimed at full self-realization and enjoyment of one's individuality, taking the latter not in its mundane sense (i.e., welfare), but in the spiritual sense, as serenity and even blessedness. Tolstoy's understanding of obrazovanie was in fact close to the original meaning of Bildung as it was understood by many eighteenth-century German enlighteners, and before it became an instrument, in the age of constitutional liberalism, for shaping loyal subjects of the Prussian state. Importantly, Tolstoy's understanding of *Bildung* was disconnected from the ideology of 'official nationality,' which was once again on the rise in the post-Reform Russia. This explains his negative reaction to contemporary British educational establishments, many of which were aimed at shaping citizen-subjects.[38] In Britain, the German theory of cultivation, mediated through Coleridge, Carlyle, Arnold, and Ruskin, was combined with a powerful native utilitarian tradition, a combination Tolstoy totally rejected. It is thus not surprising that Tolstoy would claim that in the 1860s genuine *obrazovanie* or *Bildung* could be found only in Russia and, to a very limited extent, in Germany. For instance, in his essay entitled *'Vospitanie i obrazovanie'* (typically translated 'Education and Culture'), Tolstoy writes:

> Education, French *éducation*, German *Erziehung*, are conceptions which are current in Europe; but *obrazovanie* [culture] is a concept which exists only in Russia and partly in Germany, where there is an almost exact correspondence in the word *Bildung*. But in France an in England this idea and the word do not exist at all. *Civilization* is enlightenment, and *instruction* is a European idea that cannot be translated into Russian, but which means the wealth of scholarly scientific knowledge and the transmission of this knowledge. But instruction should not be confused with true formation, for the latter includes the arts and physical development as well as scientific knowledge.[39]

Throughout his essay Tolstoy draws a line between genuine *obrazovanie* on the one hand, and such terms as *vospitanie* (*Erziehung*, *education*) and *obuchenie* (technical education or instruction) on the other, because only genuine formation, or obrazovanie, promotes freedom, whereas both education and instruction keep a human being under the yoke of dogma. This type of formation rejects all forms of cultural authority and tutelage, relying entirely on a free dialogue between a teacher and his students.

The Organic Concept of *Bildung* and the Genesis of *War and Peace*

The fact that Tolstoy considered unfettered self-development the true end of human life reveals his affinity with an intellectual movement that crystallized in Germany in the late 1780s and whose lasting import consisted in promoting an organic view of life. As Fredric Beiser explains, the organic conception of life combined Kant's notion, expressed in the *Critique of Judgment*, of natural purpose or *Naturzweck* with a pantheistic vitalism derived from late eighteenth-century interpretations of Spinoza.[40] The champions of organicism understood in this sense included Herder, Jacobi, Novalis, Friedrich Schlegel, Schelling, and a number of other influential thinkers who were well known in Russia. Schelling was especially influential at the time when the young Tolstoy began to attend university. Thus some scholars have suggested that Tolstoy had studied both Schelling and Herder as a student in Kazan'.[41] This suggestion appears plausible if we look at some of Tolstoy's diary entries from 1847.[42]

From the standpoint of intellectual history, Tolstoy's familiarity with the German philosophical tradition in general and with the organicist paradigm in particular is hardly surprising. The majority of Russian thinkers of Tolstoy's generation, including Grigor'ev and Strakhov, were attracted to this school of thought. As for Herzen, even after his break with Hegelianism, he remained committed to the organic conception of nature and to the idea of *Bildung* as the proper vocation of a human being.[43] Another propagandist of German philosophy and especially *Naturphilosophie* in Russia was Mikhail Pogodin. In this connection, I should say that Eikhenbaum's hypothesis about Pogodin's possible influence on *War and Peace* is quite astute.[44] Tolstoy's relationship with Pogodin at the time when he began to compose *War and Peace* deserves further investigation. Evidently, after Tolstoy left Petersburg and cut his ties with his liberal friends there, he needed a new intellectual circle.

A well-established historian like Pogodin would make an excellent ally and a stepping stone to influential Moscow intellectuals and publishers like Katkov. It is likely that Tolstoy also found Pogodin's personality intellectually stimulating. A self-chosen heir to Karamzin, Pogodin was a living link between the epoch of Karamzin and Pushkin and Tolstoy's own age.

Pogodin shared Tolstoy's enthusiasm for organicism and his dislike of mechanistic explanations of history.[45] Thus Eikhenbaum cites Pogodin's 1836 book *Historical Aphorisms* as a possible influence on Tolstoy's philosophy of history. According to Eikhenbaum, Prince Urusov, who was trying to work out a mathematical theory that would explain the pattern of history, might have brought Pogodin's book to Tolstoy's attention.[46] This book, intentionally composed as a collection of aphorisms unconnected by any kind of unified argument, does indeed contain some statements that sound like quotations from various works by Herder or his followers, such as, for example, Wilhelm and Alexander von Humboldt.[47] Evidently, Pogodin was taken by the ideas of these German thinkers, but was either too cautious or intellectually unable to produce his own theory. It was one of Pogodin's students and protégés, Apollon Grigor'ev, who was bold enough to develop his own theory of 'organic criticism,' which in some sense represents a systematization of Pogodin's prolific but ultimately failed attempts to devise a cultural paradigm specific to Russia.[48]

We should probably trust Eikhenbaum's suggestion that Pogodin was one of the main instigators of Tolstoy's semi-fictional, semi-historiographic project, which eventually grew into *War and Peace*. Of course, the idea of writing a large-scale prose work about the history of Russia's fight against Napoleon came to Tolstoy not only as a result of befriending Pogodin and Urusov. In fact, many scholars believe that it was Tolstoy's meeting with Herzen in London in 1861 that led to his decision to write an *epopeia* about Russia's 'awakening' and maturation during the struggle against Napoleon. The conversations between Tolstoy and Herzen ranged over a broad array of topics, including the collapse of the Hegelian philosophical school, Herzen's own painful disappointment in Hegelianism and in the revolution of 1848, and the fate of post-Reform Russia.[49] These conversations were continued in correspondence, only part of which (Tolstoy's letters to Herzen) has survived. One of these letters is especially important for understanding Tolstoy's state of mind at the time when he was beginning to conceive the future *War and Peace*. Responding to Herzen's essay 'Robert

Owen' (which was later incorporated into *My Past and Thoughts*), Tolstoy wrote:

> Your article about Owen is, alas! too close to my heart. Although in our time this [becoming like Owen?] is possible only for a denizen of Saturn who came down to Earth or for a Russian. There are many people, and 99/100 Russians too, whom fear will keep from believing your idea (and, in parenthesis, it is easy to disbelieve you because of the light tone of your article. You seem to address yourself only to intelligent and brave people). Those who are not intelligent and brave will tell you that it is better to keep silent when you came to such results, that is, came to the conclusion that the entire path was wrong. And you a little bit encourage them to say this by placing life itself, the pattern of life as you call it, in place of the old idols. In lieu of the great hopes of immortality, eternal perfectibility, historical laws etc. – this pattern is nothing, a little button in place of a colossus.[50]

First of all, we should note Tolstoy fascination with Herzen's description of Robert Owen's personality. Herzen portrays Owen as a fully mature individual who has reached 'rational consciousness' (*razumnoe soznanie*) and is therefore no longer in need of social approval. The notion of 'rational consciousness' will reappear in Tolstoy's treatise *On Life* (1887), where it pertains to the final stage of human development, which Tolstoy seems to understand somewhat differently from Herzen. In Tolstoy, the attainment of 'rational consciousness' puts man's soul at peace by overcoming the yoke of 'general will' as well as the fear of death.

A similar schema of maturation is offered in Tolstoy's major theological treatise, *The Kingdom of God Is Within You* (1893), where human ontogenetic development is grafted onto a philogenesis of humanity as a whole. Thus all life is divided into three stages. The first state is called personal [*lichnoe*] because the main motivation for action at this time is the 'satisfaction of personality' [*volia lichnosti*]. This stage revolves around the satisfaction of desires of the individual as an 'animal self.' The second stage is called 'social' [*sotsial'noe*]. If in the 'personal' stage man recognized life only in himself, now he recognizes it in the 'aggregate of personalities.' In short, he comes to understand society and power. According to Tolstoy, both youth and part of middle age are spent in the service of society. Only the third stage of life, at which a human being can arrive after he transcends social constraints and becomes fully mature (here we can think back to Herzen's portrayal of Robert Owen) does one achieve what Tolstoy calls the 'universal' or 'divine' (*vsemirnoe* or *bozheskoe*) stage.[51] Richard Gustafson, who thinks that this vision of life as a development from an animal to a 'divine'-like being can be detected already in *War and Peace*, has a good point.[52] Indeed, we can assume that Tolstoy did not simply abandon his 'Four Epochs of Development,' but transferred this project onto a new, much broader scale, combining individual life stories with a vast panorama of Russian society and history in the epoch of the Napoleonic Wars.

Throughout his pedagogical treatises Tolstoy continually insists on the idea that life should be understood not in mechanistic but in organic terms, as a growth toward a better self. The best education is the one that allows the mind to simply grow in the school of life, which will naturally lead it toward gradual self-perfection, hopefully culminating in the attainment of complete spiritual freedom. The Utopian colouring of this theory is fully understandable, taking into account Tolstoy's long-lasting attachment to eighteenth-century humanism, with its optimistic belief in self-perfection. It is likely that Tolstoy's predilection for this rather outmoded school of thought served as a shield (and perhaps also as a weapon) in his ideological duel with Herzen, whose despair of finding a rational order in history shocked Tolstoy. In the above-quoted letter to Herzen, Tolstoy goes on to argue against Herzen's historical scepticism, suggesting that as a practical man he cannot live without some kind of regulative ideal. For Tolstoy himself this ideal is what he calls 'his Russia' – a vision of history he himself has built and which he regards as a true and real piece of knowledge: 'You are saying that I do not know Russia. Not true. I know my Russia subjectively, the way I see it through my little prism. Since for both you and me the soap bubble of "history" has been burst, this only proves that we are already beginning to blow a new bubble, one we cannot yet discern. For me, this new bubble represents a firm and precise knowledge of my Russia.'[53] Tolstoy concludes this letter by telling Herzen about his new literary project: a novel about a Decembrist who is coming back to Russia from Siberia after thirty years of exile. 'My Decembrist,' says Tolstoy, 'must be an enthusiast, a mystic, a Christian, returning to Russia in '56 with his wife, son and daughter and testing his own stern and somewhat idealistic point of view against the new Russia.'[54] This is one of the first references to the future *War and Peace* in Tolstoy's correspondence.

An enthusiast and mystic of the older generation is chosen to serve as what Henry James would call a 'vehicle of consciousness' or a 'window in the house of fiction.' It is through him – a future Pierre Bezukhov – that we, Tolstoy's readers, are supposed to envision Russia. Even in the published version of the novel (which, as we know, went through many redactions and revisions before it became *War and Peace*) Pierre is an enthusiast and an idealist, whose ultimate deed is the creation of the Russian Tugendbund, a prototype of the pre-Decembrist 'Union of Welfare.' Pierre's life is a striving toward virtue, very much in the manner of an eighteenth-century German Bildungsroman like Wieland's *Geschichte des Agathons*. There is a metaphysical dimension to Pierre's life, revealed to the hero only through dreams. These dreams, however, are not to be dismissed as mere phantasms. Rather, they represent those things that do not lend themselves to cold scientific reason but, as Henry James put it, 'can reach us only through the beautiful circuit and subterfuge of our thought and our desire.'[55]

As Donna Orwin has pointed out, the Tolstoyan fictional universe has a metaphysical anchor. The entire fictional edifice of *War and Peace* rests on a belief that there is an inextricable tie between history and nature: 'Properly interpreted, political history becomes a part of God's will which affects every individual (and which every individual affects) but which remains ultimately mysterious. Its meaning lies hidden in that part of metaphysics – by far the greater part – that the student of the Savoyard Vicar regarded as inaccessible to human reason. It was when Tolstoy reached this outer limit of the conceivably natural and discovered the natural equivalent of what historians call history that his novel took off.'[56]

Tolstoy's fascination with Rousseau was surely of great help to the writer as he set out to wrestle with Herzen's profound historical scepticism. I think that Herder, whom Tolstoy may have known already as a student in Kazan' and whom he would most likely re-encounter in Pogodin's circle, was another important source for Tolstoy when, faced with the pessimism and atheism of many of his contemporaries, he was trying to conjure the image of the youthful Russia that emerged victorious from the war of 1812. This suggestion in no way undermines the continual significance of Rousseau for Tolstoy, since Herder himself was a follower of Rousseau.

Patricia Carden has already argued for the importance of Herder's idea of human life as gradual 'self-expression' of our rational and linguistic faculties for the ideological shape of *War and Peace*.[57] As Carden notes, the entire world according to Herder constitutes a single 'chain of *Bildung*,' where humans occupy an intermediary position between inanimate nature and Spirit. A key to this interpretation can be found in several drafts to the novel (when it was still *1805*), where the officers on the eve of the battle discuss the idea of immortality. These conversations revolve around Herder's work, *Ideas for the Philosophy of History of Humanity* (1784–1804). A segment of this work was translated by Karamzin and published in his journal *Messenger of Europe* in July of 1804, only a few months after Herder's death. In one draft, officers Belkin and Tushin discuss these ideas with a group of other officers on the eve of the battle of Schoengraben.[58] In another draft, the issue of death and immortality are discussed by Belkin, Anan'ev, and Tushin.[59] In all these drafts Belkin is a significant figure. Later on he disappears from the novel or becomes merged with another character (probably Tushin or Timokhin).

In the published version of the novel the argument over Herder's piece becomes one of the key scenes of the entire work. In the final text of the novel, the conversation between Pierre and Prince Andrei occurs in the course of a visit made by Pierre to the Prince's estate, Bogucharovo, shortly after Prince Andrei's return from French captivity, and in the first spring of Pierre's enthusiasm for the Masonic brotherhood, which he has recently joined. Pierre is now travelling all around Russia, visiting his estates and engaging in what he believes to be socially beneficial activity. Prince Andrei, on the other hand, has become bitterly disenchanted with his former idol, Napoleon, and has lost his former ambition. Moreover, he has also recently lost his wife, who died in childbirth. In contrast to Pierre's cheerfulness, Prince Andrei has succumbed to bitter pessimism. Trying to dispel the spirit of alienation and cold irony that has emerged between the two friends, Pierre says to Prince Andrei:

> 'You say that you cannot see a reign of truth and goodness on earth. Nor could I, and it cannot be seen if we regard our life here as the end of everything. On earth, here on this earth' (Pierre pointed to the fields), 'there is no truth – all is evil and deception. But in the universe, in the whole universe, there is a kingdom of truth, and we who are now the children of the earth are, in the eternal sense, children of the universe. Do I not feel in my soul that I am part of that vast, harmonious whole? Do I not feel that I constitute one link, one step from the lower to the higher beings in this infinite multitude of beings in which the Godhead – the Supreme Power, if you prefer – is manifest? If I see, clearly see, the ladder leading from plant to man, then why should I suppose that this ladder, the beginning of which I cannot discern below me – why should I suppose that it breaks off

with me and does not go farther up to higher beings? I feel not only that I cannot vanish, since nothing in the world vanishes, but that I shall always exist, always have existed. I feel that besides myself, above me, there are spirits, and in the world there is truth.'

'Yes, that is Herder's theory,' says Prince Andrei in response.

'But it is not that, my dear fellow, which will convince me;' Prince Andrei goes on to say. 'Life and death – that is what convinces. What convinces is when you see a being dear to you, whose life is bound up with yours, to whom you have done a wrong and had hoped to expiate ... and all at once this being is suffering, is in agony, and ceases to exist ... Why? There must be an answer!'[60]

In both voices in this dialogue we can recognize two different Tolstoyan alter egos. Prince Andrei represents Tolstoy's more sceptical side. Like this character, Tolstoy was deeply shaken by the Crimean War and by the loss of his brother Nikolai, and for a time he also retreated from public life to the refuge of a landowner's round of duties. Pierre, on the other hand, represents Tolstoy's more enthusiastic self, the popular educator and mediator between the gentry and the peasants.

Significantly, this encounter between Andrei and Pierre has a beneficial effect on Prince Andrei, reviving his soul and relieving his *accedia*, which gives a practical form to Pierre's optimistic statement, 'in the world there is truth.' During this encounter the roles between the friends are reversed for the first time, and we see Pierre, who was once the Prince's admiring student, assuming the leading role. Infected by Pierre's optimism, Andrei eventually decides to go on the trip during which he meets Natasha on old Count Rostov's estate and, moved by her singing, experiences a return to life, a complete revival of his spiritual forces. Although Prince Andrei does not immediately give up his materialistic views or the sceptical disposition he inherited from his father, the encounter at Bogucharovo is still a significant benchmark in Prince Andrei's spiritual life. As a result of his conversation with Pierre, Prince Andrei will finally open his heart to authentic emotion and fall in love with Natasha. This love will cause him still more suffering (after Natasha breaks her faith), but it will also propel him further on the path of his spiritual *Bildung*.

In the published version of Tolstoy's novel both Pierre and Prince Andrei emerge as intellectually and spiritually striving heroes, whose life is propelled by a quest for truth, love, and God. The dialogue between these two plot lines is arguably one of the strongest motors of novelistic action, which is not an uncommon novelistic device. For example, in Balzac's novels we frequently find two life stories narrated side by side, where the reader's interest in the narrative is perpetually stirred by the constant juxtaposition of the two lines (Goriot and Rastignac, Lucien and David Sechard). But while Balzac's heroes seek success or simply worldly happiness, Tolstoy's heroes have loftier ambitions. Tolstoy's heroes are metaphysical seekers, whose *Bildungsromane* (deliberately placed by Tolstoy in an earlier historical era and thus protected from the charge of being anachronistic) defy the fashionable Balzacian novel, with its preoccupation with wealth and glory within the narrow (by Tolstoy's standards) confines of Parisian society. Tolstoy's world is both broader and airier than the world of the French novel and less socially conservative and rigid than the world of the British novel, another important generic antecedent to *War and Peace*. These, I think, are the main distinctions Tolstoy had in mind when he insisted, in 'Several Words Apropos of the Book *War and Peace*,' that his work is not to be confused with a conventional European 'novel,' 'chronicle,' 'epic poem,' or any other established genre (16:7–16).[61] In his search for an authentic Russian story, Tolstoy absorbed the lessons of nineteenth-century European authors, but ultimately looked back to the eighteenth century, finding illumination and a source of spiritual sustenance in the works of Rousseau, Herder, Wieland, Goethe, and other humanists concerned with the spiritual well-being, and not merely with the material welfare of their heroes.

Pierre as Tolstoy's 'Little Prism'

In the earliest drafts of the opening scene of Tolstoy's novel, which takes place in the salon of Anna Pavlovna Scherer, there appears a young man named Léon, who is said to be an illegitimate son of the immensely rich Count Bezukhov. Pierre's original name – Léon – may be an allusion to Karamzin's unfinished Bildungsroman, *The Knight of Our Time* (*Rytsar' nashego vremeni*).[62] The first example of the Bildungsroman genre in Russian literary history, Karamzin's semi-autobiographical work describes the early youth of a provincial nobleman, whose refined sensibility reminds us of another quasi-autobiographical character created by Karamzin: the narrator of his *Letters of a Russian Traveller*. The presence of Karamzin in the drafts to *War and Peace* is hardly surprising. Karamzin's name was in vogue in the 1850s thanks to the recent biography by Mikhail Pogodin, who made the case for canonizing

Karamzin as Russia's first real man of letters who could compete with European contemporaries.⁶³ Karamzin's journal *Messenger of Europe* was one of the sources that Tolstoy consulted to evoke the Napoleonic era while he was working on the novel.⁶⁴ In the final redaction, few traces of Karamzin remain. There is, of course, the allusion to a text by Herder translated by Karamzin, which I discussed earlier. There is also the connection between these authors on the level of character construction and the generic form. Thus, Pierre, as Tolstoy's most clearly delineated emerging hero, bears a vague resemblance both to the hero of Karamzin's *Knight of Our Time* and to his European traveller. It is not merely coincidental that on his first appearance in the first scene of the novel Pierre is described as a young man who has just returned from Switzerland, since this would make him one of the rare Russians of the era to have, like Karamzin's traveller, experienced Europe. At the outset of the novel he is on his way to experience Russia. This transition is precisely the pattern that unfolds for us within the plot, which from the earliest versions had been focused on Pierre's *obrazovanie*.

There are other links between the image of Pierre Bezukhov and eighteenth-century literature, particularly the classical Bildungsroman. We can detect in Pierre's life story many overlaps with the plot of Christoph Martin Wieland's *Agathon*, a story about a young Scythian educated in Greece. Like Agathon, Pierre begins his novelistic career by making missteps and undergoing ordeals. Mistaking lust for love, he marries Hélène Kuragina, who turns out to be utterly superficial and amoral or even immoral. However, after multiple trials and tribulations, Pierre, like Wieland's Bildungsroman hero, finds a woman whom he truly loves and who deserves that love, his Psyche, so to speak.⁶⁵ Her name, Natasha or Natalia (which, incidentally, coincides with the name of Wilhelm Meister's bride in Goethe's *Wilhelm Meisters Lehrjahre*), apparently symbolizes the hero's moral rebirth after their marriage.

One of Tolstoy's original inspirations for a national narrative was Goethe's *Hermann und Dorothea*. As his project took off, however, Tolstoy became more and more interested in describing a developing hero, someone more akin to Wilhelm Meister than to Hermann, who is more of an allegorical figure – a symbol of the young German nation, rather than a modern novelistic character. Wilhelm Meister, on the other hand, represents a somewhat idealized, yet fully plausible from the psychological point of view, type of modern German bourgeois citizen undergoing socialization. Tolstoy would eventually reject Goethe's idea of socialization and ultimately transformed his work into a riposte to the

Bildungsroman aimed at socialization. Nonetheless, the parallel between Pierre as a model modern Russian hero and Wilhelm Meister as a quintessential German Bildungsroman hero is instructive insofar as we are tracing the ideological dialectic of Tolstoy's project as it passed through various generic stages. Let us outline this transformation step by step.

Tolstoy's portrayal of a Petersburg salon as a mechanism that strips whoever enters it of all naturalness and spontaneity reveals his animus against the French novel of worldliness, including its modern heir, Balzac, whose tendency to equate the fictional world with Parisian society was one of the novelistic conventions that Tolstoy was eager to undo. It is not surprising that Pierre is completely out of place in Anna Scherer's salon, looking and acting like a 'bear.' He rudely intervenes in a conversation about Napoleon Bonaparte and dares to argue against the royalist French viscount Mortemart, defending Napoleon and calling him a 'great man.' A few scenes later the metaphor of the bear will be actualized, as we hear about Pierre's carousing among the 'golden youth' of Petersburg, including Hélène's brother Anatole Kuragin, his friend Dolokhov, and several other men famous for debauchery. One of their 'pranks' is to tie a policeman to the back of an actual bear and release the bear to swim in the Neva. From the outset Tolstoy thus underscores the wild side of Pierre's character. We soon come to understand, however, that Pierre is rather introverted, shy, and extremely kind-hearted. We also see that he is prone to attacks of self-assertion and rage, which mark him as a true son of his natural father, the once all-powerful Count Bezukhov. Pierre's naïveté, his weakness of will, his lack of self-control and occasional outbursts of temper all make him an ideal subject for a pedagogical novel, and this is indeed how Tolstoy envisioned Pierre's story. Since the unfinished project 'Four Epochs of Development,' *Family Happiness* (1859), and *The Cossacks* (1862), Tolstoy had experimented with the novel of apprenticeship, but these earlier exercises did not fully satisfy him. *Youth* remained unfinished, as did *The Cossacks*. These works were coolly received or ignored by the critics,[66] with one important exception: *Family Happiness* was complimented by Apollon Grigor'ev.[67] Tolstoy's goal in all of these works was to show the progressive liberation of the human soul from the moral servitude of societal conventions to the point when one can attain genuine *eudaimonia*. Thus, for example, in *Family Happiness* Tolstoy wanted to counterpoise the organic life of the family to the life in society, oriented toward outward success, as typically depicted by Western novelists. Only Grigor'ev recognized Tolstoy's true goal and hailed his work as a perfectly 'organic' work of art – an adjective that qualified Tolstoy's work as a genuine expression of the Russian cultural spirit.[68]

In the two articles devoted to Tolstoy's work, which appeared in *Time* in 1862, Grigor'ev discussed the *Sevastopol Sketches*, the trilogy *Childhood, Adolescence*, and *Youth*, 'The Three Deaths,' 'Albert,' 'Luzerne,' and *Family Happiness*. The critic complimented the young writer on his desire to break free from the narrow-minded aristocratic milieu. He discerned in the young Tolstoy's attacks on the mores of high society a thirst for a broader audience and a more authentic cultural ideal. Grigor'ev welcomed Tolstoy as an artist who could potentially overcome the so-called negative tendency [*otritsatel'noe napravlenie*] in Russian literature – a tendency that the critic associated with the Byronic Romanticism widespread in the Russian literature of the 1830s and 1840s. Lermontov, Herzen, and others, according to Grigor'ev, were still beholden to the essentially foreign aesthetic ideal, even as they struggled with this ideal's demonic charisma. Characterizing this generation of writers, Grigor'ev says:

> All our attempts to ridicule our intellectual 'fermentation,' including both the healthy and the unhealthy attempts, all these attempts to defeat the charming type that was emerging in front of our eyes and which, when embodied in Pechorin, recognizes that it possesses 'limitless' powers and wastes them on trifles – in short all our attempts to defeat the type of the powerful and passionate man proved useless. Our comical literature destroyed only the false and conditional aspects of this type. Our attempts to substitute this type with another one – with the type of a positive and active personality – also proved futile. Alas! We still have not gone beyond the protagonists who quite their service as soon as they barely started to serve.[69]

Tolstoy appealed to Grigor'ev as a genuinely post-Romantic author (in the sense of being interested in moving beyond the 'superfluous man' predicament). The critics especially lauded Tolstoy's interest in humble characters, such as the common soldiers in the *Sevastopol Sketches* or the nurse from *Childhood*, and remarked that Tolstoy's early work showed a desire to seek inspiration from the native soil. At the same time, Grigor'ev was alarmed by Tolstoy's psychological analysis, which, he thought, bordered on 'nihilism':

> This analysis, which, not leaning on the soil, culminates in the love of the meek type, chiefly out of distrust for the dazzling predator type, ultimately leads to some kind of pantheistic despair, which is quite obvious

in 'Luzerne,' 'Albert' and even in the earlier work 'The Notes of a Billiard-Marker.' Thirdly, at last, this analysis turns into some kind of pointless analysis of analysis. Because it is so pointless, it leads to scepticism and undermines all spiritual feelings. The key episode showing where this analysis leads is the death of the oak in 'The Three Deaths,' a death which the narrator's consciousness puts higher than the death of a simple man. From here there is one step to nihilism.[70]

Concluding his reviews of Tolstoy's works, Grigor'ev charged the young author with the task of continuing in the spirit of the work left unfinished by Pushkin's early death, that is, to take Russian literature beyond the narrow sphere of the genteel reader's social niche and transform it into a vehicle of a truly national self-consciousness. Following in the footsteps of the later Pushkin, whose pseudo-autobiographical fictional Belkin, the 'editor' of *The Tales of the Late Ivan Petrovich Belkin* and the historiographer of Goriukhino, was, according to Grigor'ev, capable of encompassing in his heart and mind a broad spectrum of Russian 'types' and ideologies. Grigor'ev begged Tolstoy to create characters with genuinely Russian souls – that is to say, characters who would no longer reproduce foreign cultural clichés in Russian form, but would instead be possessed of an inwardness reflective of their true historical origins. This did not mean that Tolstoy had to exclude from his purview the aristocratic types. Rather, what Grigor'ev wanted was a more thoroughgoing analysis of the collective psychological process that began to occur during the Napoleonic Wars – the fermentation of a new national self-consciousness.

That Tolstoy did not remain unresponsive to Grigor'ev's ideas, which began to gain broader audience after the publication of his most famous essay, '*Ob organicheskoi kritike*,' in 1858, is attested by the fact that Tolstoy names at least two of his characters 'Belkin' – a name that Grigor'ev saw as symbolic of the organic Russian character. Thus, in addition to the 'Belkin' who appears in the drafts of *War and Peace*, in the earlier version of *Family Happiness* the heroine is named Liza Belkina (eventually she is called Masha and her last name is dropped). The whole thrust of this story, where the heroine, after becoming disillusioned with the life of high society, returns to the country in order to start a new life there with her husband and sons, suggests a movement in the direction of the 'native soil.'

Whether Tolstoy kept in mind Grigor'ev's suggestions when he was creating the image of Pierre Bezukhov, this character's life story is consonant with Grigor'ev's desire to see some kind of rapprochement between the simple Russian people, the *narod*, and the gentry. It is significant, for example, that Pierre is a bastard, a son of Count Bezukhov and a mother who is probably a serf (her identity is never disclosed). At the same time, by his kind heart and noble soul Pierre reminds us of Petrusha Grinev, Pushkin's hero whom Grigor'ev saw as one of the beacons of a new organic Russian culture. Even though Pierre does not have a strict and conscientious father to guide him – indeed, his birth and breeding result from the vices of his natural father, who seems to care little for his son's feelings and who sends him away as a child, to be raised by tutors in Switzerland – Tolstoy's hero does have one secure guide in life: his conscience. We can understand why the representation of Pierre's entrance into the 'world' of Petersburgian society is accompanied by a scene of drunken raillery (culminating in a trip to the gypsies). While he yields to desire, Pierre's conscience awakens.[71] His temptations only increase once he inherits the fortune and the name of Count Bezukhov, but Pierre never gets inured to his situation, or comfortable in his vices – even if they are the approved vices of society. The voice of conscience becomes more and more audible in Pierre's soul even as his potential for vice increases. Imperfection – the openness to the visceral pleasures of the animal life – is a necessary adjunct of the ideal – spiritual development. The sense of shame grows within Pierre until he is moved to shake off his moral inertia. The catalyst for change comes about due to one of Hélène's routine infidelities, which precipitates a duel between Pierre and one of his wife's lovers, Dolokhov. The inexperienced Pierre, to his own astonishment, wounds Dolokhov, an expert duellist, and comes away unharmed. The fact that he has nearly killed a human being (which Tolstoy subtly underlines by suddenly upending the reader's expectations about Dolokhov, who ultimately turns out to be a loving son who supports his mother, who he fears will be broken by his death) triggers Pierre's first profound moral crisis. It is at this point in his life that Pierre encounters a person whom he will later call his 'Benefactor' – Osip Alexeyevich Bazdeev.

Bazdeev is a fictional representative of that small circle of people who formed the kernel of the Enlightenment in early nineteenth-century Russia. By joining the Masonic brotherhood, Pierre enters into this small circle. Of course, the Lodge as an institution will turn out to be deeply disappointing to him. Corruption and hypocrisy reign there as much as they do in society. Yet these facts don't besmirch the figure of Bazdeev, who stands above this milieu and symbolizes the best and most culturally and morally useful aspect of Masonry.[72] In this connection, it would be appropriate to cite A.N. Pypin's characterization of the Muscovite freemasonry of the last two decades of the eighteenth century as the first phase of the Russian Enlightenment:

> Culture [obrazovannost'] was still too weak in Russia: the only university, which was founded as late as 1755, was hardly larger than a secondary school; literary culture was limited to a small group of readers. And while at this level of culture there was already a desire to ponder difficult questions about humanity and nature and the first steps in the direction of moral self-awareness were being made, it is quite natural that mysticism appeared as an appealing form in which all of these strivings could be expressed. Our culture was all borrowed in a variety of forms and movements that came to us from European sources. Russians digested what they could, what corresponded to its current cultural level and appealed to the taste.[73]

In this stage of his life, Pierre Bezukhov becomes a classic example of this early nineteenth-century Russian man of culture, subject to long bouts of inertia but at the same time keen on improving his education and expanding his horizon. The meeting with Bazdeev revives Pierre's soul and gives his life a new direction. As a result of this transformation, Pierre leaves Hélène and his Moscow circle and begins to travel all over Russia. It is in this mood of guilt and renewal that he comes to visit Prince Andrei in Bogucharovo, where they have their memorable conversation on the raft, which, in turn, revives Andrei's soul.

At this point in the story Pierre is no longer the classic novelistic naïf. His experience with his wife's circle, and then his dealings with the Petersburg Masons, have opened his eyes to the inauthenticity bordering on sheer evil that dominates high society. But despite having gained in experience and worldly wisdom, Pierre has not entirely lost his Rousseauesque genuineness and spontaneity. It should be pointed out that he lacks the kind of personal vanity or *amour propre* that constantly torments Prince Andrei. A simple heart, Pierre is not prone to theatricality and therefore his actions and words convey an immediacy that gives him a natural charisma. This power is so great that he manages to bring out the innocent, childlike side of Prince Andrei. Thus, in response to Pierre's profession of faith, Prince Andrei looks at Pierre with radiant eyes, which throughout the novel serve as a special characteristic of Prince Andrei's spiritually inclined sister Marya: 'Prince

Andrei sighed, and with a tender, radiant, child-like glow in his eyes he glanced at Pierre, whose face was flushed with triumph, though he still was diffident, conscious of his friend's superiority' (420).

What threatens to destroy Pierre's simplicity is the Masonic habit of self-accounting.[74] Keeping a journal is supposed to discipline Pierre, help his reason keep a reign on his passions. However, it also becomes a trap, for Pierre's newly developed habit of self-analysis transforms him into a 'sentimental' hero (in Schiller's sense of the term), thus distancing him from nature and happiness.[75] Indeed, as several critics have shown, the ideal of the 'beautiful soul' espoused by the Pietists and their disciples from among the Russian Masons easily veers into dangerous self-delusion and inner inauthenticity (i.e., theatricality), threatening to turn a subject of Bildung into an aesthete or even into an outright hypocrite.[76]

That Pierre's incessant self-accounting leads to a state of dangerous self-delusion bordering on madness becomes obvious when war breaks out again in 1812 and Pierre starts dreaming about the great role he is destined to play in this world-historical confrontation between Russia and the West. While most denizens of Moscow flee from the city that is about to be occupied by the French, Pierre decides to stay behind. Steeped in the esoteric science he derives from the Masonic books he has found in the library of Bazdeev (who has recently died of cancer), Pierre tries to decode his destiny and finally, by manipulating letters of his name, comes up with what he takes to be a heaven-sent omen: he, *le russe Bezuhoff*, ought to become the slayer of the Antichrist – Napoleon. Living in the same house with the late Bazdeev's insane brother intensifies the atmosphere of madness that threatens to engulf Pierre completely. Indeed, throughout the scenes in occupied Moscow Pierre behaves like a lunatic or an intoxicated person.[77] It is in a paroxysm of passion that he rushes to save a little girl from fire. Enthused by his own heroism, Pierre blithely lies to the French officer, who suspects him of being an incendiary, in saying that the girl whom he has saved from the burning fire is his own daughter.[78] Only a profound shock can interrupt a stream of Pierre's delusional thoughts and reckless actions, forcing him to drop his heroic pretensions and confront reality. This new shock occurs when the French arrest him along with other Russians suspected of being incendiaries and Pierre finds himself face to face with imminent execution.

By a miracle, Pierre escapes death. He is saved by a sudden, almost whimsical outburst of sympathy on the part of Marshal Davout, otherwise notorious for his cold-blooded cruelty. When Davout's eyes meet

Pierre's, Davout's soul, all but extinguished through many years of unchecked power over people's lives and deaths, suddenly stirs:

> Davout looked up again and stared closely at Pierre. For several seconds they looked at one another, and it was this look that saved Pierre. The business of staring at each other took them beyond the realm of warfare and courtrooms; they were two human beings and there was a bond between them. There was a single instant that involved an infinite sharing of experience in which they knew they were both children of humanity, and they were brothers. (1069)

It is likely that Davout spent more than a second staring at Pierre – long enough for a humane feeling to awaken in his soul – because he recognized in Pierre a disguised aristocrat, a man of quality, so to speak, rather than one of the 'rabble.' While the shadow of class definitely falls over this miracle, at the same time, this amazing scene anticipates the later Tolstoy's idea of human brotherhood attained spontaneously, through love and mutual kindness, rather than through social contract. On this reading, Davout's momentary and unexplainable kindness toward Pierre resembles that moment in the story *Master and Man* in which the usually self-serving master suddenly feels impelled to go back to a place where he had abandoned his servant in the middle of the snowstorm and try to bring the poor half-frozen man back to life by warming him with his own body.[79] These are moments of metanoia that can befall anyone, but which have no permanence unless they are followed by a change in one's way of life. The irony in *Master and Man* is that the poor man is indeed rescued, whereas the master, who had spent his entire life as a greedy and self-serving man, dies. However, Tolstoy would have us believe that the greater reward went to the man who experienced a genuine conversion and recovered his humane soul on the threshold of his death.

Returning to Pierre and Davout, there is no indication in the novel that Davout's outburst of humane feeling would indeed be followed by a change of character. However, within the architectonic of Tolstoy's novel, this miraculous outburst of humanity in Davout is not an inconsequential episode. It foreshadows other spontaneous expressions of goodness, some of which will indeed lead to metanoia – a conversion or a leap of faith that would bring the spiritual dialectic of Tolstoy's heroes to a certain closure. For, as I have made clear earlier, in Tolstoy's world peace and justice rely on goodwill or the recognition of individuals that they are 'brothers' (and sisters) rather than simply participants in a 'social contract.' This faith in human goodness jibes with Tolstoy's view that the liberal construal of human beings as rational self-interested subjects is wrong both as ideal and reality; actually, they are much more complex and confused beings, subject to the twofold pull of reason and emotions, or the animal vitality of the self. The task of *obrazovanie*, as Tolstoy describes it in his pedagogical tracts of the 1860s, is first of all to awaken the individual's soul and bring about the self-realization that one is a complex and contradictory being, which should impel the properly educated person to seek spiritual harmony and happiness.[80]

While in his pedagogical tracts of the 1860s Tolstoy, still beholden to the idea of gradual 'perfectibility,' never presses the point, in his fiction there is increasingly an orientation toward the experience of a moment of sudden spiritual awakening, which can result in a conversion, purging the soul of all negative feelings of jealousy, enmity, and rancour toward others, and their replacement by an all-encompassing feeling of love. In *War and Peace* he demonstrates that this is precisely how an individual can bring his spiritual quest to completion. It turns out, in other words, that a glimpse of the divine grace, manifested through an unexpected and inexplicable act of kindness performed by someone whose heart has long been hardened, is the pivotal 'spring' that supports the entire architectonic of human life. Dostoevsky's conviction that in seeing a repenting sinner God smiles (one of the parables that Grushen'ka tells Alyosha Karamazov) refers to a similar or essentially the same idea – that is, the hope that divine forgiveness and grace are open to anyone at any time. This hope is indispensable for an organic community bound together by love, but structurally open to the power of evil.

Indeed, looking ahead to the next chapter, I want to suggest that in writing the drafts of *War and Peace* Tolstoy came to realize that he had more and more in common with his contemporary and literary rival, Dostoevsky. Consequently, the character of Pierre Bezukhov, originally conceived along the lines of a typical Germanic Bildungsroman hero, changes through the drafts until, like Dostoevsky's Gorianchikov from *The Notes from the House of the Dead*, he becomes capable of undergoing a *metanoia*. As is well known, Tolstoy was deeply impressed by Dostoevsky's fictionalized memoir, in which Dostoevsky's own experiences were transposed to the nobleman convict Alexander Petrovich Gorianchikov, under guard in a Siberian labour camp where he is forced to live shoulder to shoulder with low-class criminals.[81] What impressed

Tolstoy was the way Dostoevsky shows that his Siberian experiences did not undermine, but on the contrary strengthened, Dostoevsky's belief in humanity. Gorianchikov's experience in *The House of the Dead* can be seen as a possible precursor to Pierre Bezukhov's wartime experiences, the end result of which is to bring him closer to the simple soldiers – the Russian people – and reveal to him their humanity.[82]

Pierre and Platon

Pierre's encounter with Platon Karataev is pivotal not only to Pierre's life story, but to Tolstoy's goal of showing that the duality between the Russia of the educated nobles and the organic Russia of peasants, soldiers, and other 'simple' people, untouched by the upper-class cultivation, can be bridged through empathy. A simple soldier, Platon Karataev becomes one of Pierre's most important teachers. There are two texts that seem to be echoed here, one being Herzen's 'Robert Owen,' where the rich and aristocratic Herzen feels humbled and at the same time edified in the presence of that eponymous self-made man, and the other being *Notes from the House of the Dead*, in which Gorianchikov resurrects his humanity by revering the memory of the peasant who once showed him kindness. The motif of a plebian teaching a disillusioned aristocrat the true meaning of freedom and love of life is recapitulated in Pierre's prison experience, when Pierre comes to see (and love) life in a completely new way thanks to Platon. Indeed, Tolstoy and Dostoevsky's artistic and spiritual views overlapped when it came to representing a figure from the *narod* as an agent of divine grace. Thus, for example, in her analysis of Dostoevsky's 'Peasant Marei,' a chapter from Dostoevsky's *Diary of the Writer* (written much later than *War and Peace*, in 1876), Harriet Murav draws attention to Marei's feminine and maternal features – the characteristics that Tolstoy also attributes to his Platon Karataev.[83] Another piece of evidence to this effect is the character of Makar Dolgorukii from *The Adolescent*, who is often (and justly) seen as an emulation of Platon Karataev.

Pierre's experience in the prisoner of war camp teaches him to see the world in a new light, one stripped of the kind of artifice that pervades court and aristocratic society. And yet, at the same time, Pierre never fully understands Platon or the other soldiers, nor do they fully understand him. A certain degree of difference and even alienation prevails in Pierre's communicative relationship with the Russian people even while he is in the camp. For the other prisoners, he remains a *barin*, that is, a member of the serf-owning class, but one who is deserving of and happily receives their compassion.

In terms of the formal development of the plot, Tolstoy has already prepared us for Pierre's prison experience by showing him, in the previous chapters set in Moscow and then in the field of Borodino, acting like a 'middling hero' or a go-between for the upper echelons of society and the folk. The fact that Pierre is a very rich civilian during the war facilitates his movement among different groups of people. Since Pierre (like one of his real-life prototypes, Count Matvei Dmitriev-Mamonov) equips a whole military unit at his own expense, he is allowed to be present at the battlefield and observe the war from whatever location he chooses. This lets Tolstoy show us, through a civilian's gaze, how military action is experienced from below, from the point of view of grunts and low-ranking officers directly engaged in action.

Somewhat earlier, in Mozhaysk, a town outside of Moscow where Pierre falls asleep at an inn on the eve of the battle, his dream imagery persistently revolves round the image of a simple soldier. Pierre unconsciously wishes to trade places with a simple soldier – a man who does not waste his time thinking but simply acts:

> 'Thank God it's all over!' thought Pierre, burrowing down again. 'Fear – what a terrible thing it is. It got to me straightaway. I feel so ashamed! But they ... they were rock solid and perfectly calm all the way through,' he thought. *They*, in Pierre's mind, were the soldiers, soldiers on the battery, soldiers who had fed him, soldiers who had prayed to the icon. *They* – those strange people, completely unknown to him before – *they* stood out from everybody else, etched clearly and sharply in his mind.
>
> 'Oh, to be a soldier, just an ordinary soldier!' thought Pierre as he nodded off. 'To enter into the communal life with your whole being, to be absorbed into whatever it is that makes them what they are. But how can you cast off everything that doesn't matter, everything sent by the devil, the whole burden of the outer man? There was a time when I could have been one of them. I could have run away from my father. God knows I wanted to. And after that duel with Dolokhov I could have signed on as a soldier.' (935)

Pierre dreams of uniting himself with these soldiers who come from a social stratum 'completely unknown to him before.' He desires to cast off the trappings of his upper-class culture, to get closer to these simple men, to become one of them. This reminds us of the way Olenin, in

The Cossacks, strives to regain his personal integrity by going outside of 'civilized' society, where the subtle power dynamic is based on inequalities and artificial distances between human beings. In Tolstoy's earlier story, Olenin fails to become accepted by the Cossacks. Pierre, too, frets that he will never be able to separate himself from the group of people he associates with in the Masonic Lodge and the English club – the inauthentic, pompous people – and will never find his way to the other side, that of the simple people. The following sequence of dream images is quite revealing of Pierre's anxiety about 'going over to the people':

> And in his imagination Pierre pictured that dinner at the club when he had challenged Dolokhov, and then his benefactor at Torzhok. And in his mind he saw another picture: a grand dinner of the lodge members at the English Club. And someone he knew, someone close to him, some dear friend was sitting at the end of the table. Yes, him! My benefactor. 'But isn't he dead?' thought Pierre. 'Yes, he did die, and I did not know he was still alive. I'm so sorry he died, and I'm so glad he is alive again!' Down at one side of the table sat Anatole, Dolokhov, Nesvitsky, Denisov and others of that ilk (this category of people was as sharply delineated in Pierre's dream as the other category of men that he referred to as 'them'), and that lot, Anatole and Dolokhov, were shouting and singing at the tops of their voices, but through all their racket he could just hear the voice of his benefactor that refused to be drowned out, and the sound of his voice was as insistent and meaningful as the roar of the battlefield, though also sweet and soothing. Pierre couldn't make out what his benefactor was saying, but he knew that he was talking about virtue and the possibility of being like *them*. And *they* with their simple, good, stolid faces stood all round the benefactor. They meant well, but they took no notice of Pierre; they didn't know him. Pierre wanted them to notice him, and he wanted to speak, he tried to get up, but instantly his legs felt cold and all exposed.
>
> 'It's getting light,' thought Pierre. 'But that's not it. I've got to listen to the benefactor and understand what he is saying.'
>
> When he remembered these thoughts afterwards, although they had been stimulated by the impressions of that particular day, Pierre was certain that they had come to him from outside. He really believed that in his waking moment he could never have thought those thoughts or expressed them in that form. 'War is the subjection of man's will to the law of God at its most agonizing extreme,' said the voice. 'Simplicity is submitting to God's will. You cannot escape Him. And they are simple. They don't talk,

they do things. Spoken words are silver, unspoken words are gold. A man can be master of nothing while ever he fears death. And the man that fears not death possesses everything. Without suffering the man would know not his limits, would know not himself.' (935–6)

The 'they' of Pierre's dream are the soldiers, who are naïve in the Schillerian sense of the term, which is to say that they are free from the burden of excessive self-consciousness. This allows them to engage in action and enjoy what Rousseau called the 'sentiment de l'existence.'[84] It is this sentiment that Pierre craves, but cannot achieve sheer naturalness due to his habit of perpetual self-analysis. Carried away by his patriotic élan, he later decides to save Russia by assassinating Napoleon, even if it means sacrificing his life. Subsequently, his being taken prisoner, and his exchange of glances with Davout, shocks Pierre out of his solipsism. The train of events that follows, his imprisonment, sickness, and recuperation under Platon's kindly gaze, will enable Pierre's transformation from a self-absorbed person sealed in his narcissism into a more simple, humane being capable of receiving as well as giving love.

Pierre's experience in the French POW camp bears similarity in its psychological development to Gorianchikov's experience in Dostoevsky's 'House of the Dead' (1862). Both characters begin as high-minded idealists. Both plunge, at the beginning of their careers, into scepticism bordering on despair. And both eventually regain faith and achieve a deeper appreciation of humanity. In both cases, in order for their psychological transformation to take place, the characters must be first reduced to what a contemporary philosopher calls 'bare life.'[85] Importantly, however, it is not the fact of being stripped of his noble privileges and civil rights and deprived of the habitual comforts of life that wounds Pierre's soul. What prompts a real crisis in him is the execution of the innocent Russians suspected of arson by the French. This is how Tolstoy describes the pivotal moment in Pierre's Bildungsroman (recalling Tolstoy's own impressions after witnessing the execution in Paris):

From the moment Pierre had witnessed the grisly murder carried out by men who had not wanted to do it he had felt as if the mainspring of his soul that kept everything in him balanced and working and gave him a semblance of life had been torn out, and it all seemed to have collapsed into a pile of meaningless rubbish. Without Pierre fully realizing it, all his faith had been undermined, faith in the good order of the universe, in the souls of men, in his own soul, even in God. This was something Pierre had experienced before, but never with this kind of intensity. Whenever he had been assailed by doubts like these in the past they had arisen from a sense of his own guilt, and at the bottom of his heart Pierre had always known that salvation from this kind of despair and doubt lay in his own hands. But now he felt that he wasn't to blame for the world collapsing before his eyes and leaving nothing but meaningless ruins behind. He felt powerless; there was no way back to his old faith in life. (1074)

The fact that the French soldiers, despite their natural sympathy for their victims, are nonetheless still able to murder them forces Pierre to recognize the error of his earlier (Masonic) assumption of a necessary correlation between human feelings and actions. This scene is Tolstoy's most powerful indictment of Napoleon I and his war machine. But does Pierre's crisis mean that all faith has vanished from his soul? It is at this crucial juncture in Pierre's life that his dark reflections are suddenly interrupted by the stooping little man who makes his presence felt by the stench of sweat wafting from him every time he moves. Because of the darkness in the barrack, Pierre at first cannot see this man, but he somehow involuntarily feels attracted to this stranger – Platon Karataev. 'Pierre was aware of something rather pleasant, something rounded and reassuring, in those neat, circular movements, the man's nicely tidied corner, even the very smell of him. He couldn't take his eyes off him,' says the narrator (1075). When Platon talks to Pierre, he sounds almost like a cooing Russian peasant woman trying to console a baby:

> 'Seen a lot o' trouble in your time, sir, have you?' said the little man suddenly. And there was so much concern and such simplicity in the sing-song voice that Pierre couldn't get an answer out through the trembling of his jaw and his rising tears. Barely a second later, leaving no time for Pierre to start looking embarrassed, the little man went on in the same pleasant tones: 'There you are, sweetie, don't you worry.' He said, in the gently soothing sing-song voice of an old Russian peasant woman. 'Don't you worry, old pal. Trouble's short, life is long!' (1075)

Platon and Pierre engage in a conversation that, despite the cultural gap separating them, is very comforting to Pierre. As the narrator points out, up until this point Pierre found it difficult to talk to other Russian prisoners, because for him the most natural way to express himself was in French and he did not want to use French with his fellow Russians. Pierre's anxiety about language is, of course, a symptom of his identity crisis. Platon's speech, by contrast, flows naturally as if he does not need to think about how to formulate his thoughts, as if there were no gap between concept and expression. His Russian is, in Herder's sense, his natural mother tongue: the medium through which the human being grows organically from infancy toward maturity and which he continues to use for self-expression throughout his life. Under Platon's kindly gaze Pierre gradually loses his self-consciousness and begins to talk, answering Karataev's simple questions about his life and family. Platon's kindness, a miracle in this dark world full of enmity and suffering, gradually revives Pierre's soul.

The fact that Pierre has never known his mother – which, we may notice in parenthesis, up until this moment in the story has never been discussed at any length – now acquires a great significance. Platon, with his feminine roundness and motherly kindness, is distressed to hear that Pierre is an orphan who never had any close relationship with his father and never knew his mother. Platon himself has survived spiritually by always thinking of his own family and rejoicing in their happiness, even as it was bought at the price of his self-sacrifice: he willingly allowed himself to be drafted instead of his older brother, because the latter had a big family. Such is the sad background of the simple soldier's life that Pierre had cosily dreamt about in the past. But Platon has not been barbarized by his experience and there is no rancour in his soul. He offers Pierre a simple familial or even maternal affection – the simple gift that at this point in Pierre's life proves more necessary than any lofty idea or theory. Pierre happily accepts Platon's love, and, for the first time in his life, he experiences genuine happiness.

In the meantime, the narrator makes it clear that ideologically and intellectually Pierre and Platon remain worlds apart, as Platon cannot understand Pierre's life and Pierre listens with wonderment to Platon's stories and his nonsensical prayers: 'Lord Jesus Christ, holy Saint Nikola, Frola and Lavra, Lord Jesus Christ, holy Saint Nikola, Frola and Lavra, Lord Jesus, have mercy and save us!', he concluded, bowed down to earth, got up, sighed and sat down on his heap of hay' (1078). When Pierre enquires about the meaning of this strange prayer, Platon is already asleep.

When Platon is shot by the French, Pierre deliberately tries not to pay any attention to this incident. Pierre's strange inattention to Platon's death has shocked many readers of *War and Peace*. Tolstoy calls

Pierre's strange lapse of attention a 'safety-valve' of consciousness and describes it as a natural ability of our psyche to displace traumatic impressions with pleasant memories and dream imagery (1179). So, suddenly, instead of thinking about his friend's disappearance, 'a memory emerged in Pierre's soul, coming from God knows where, of an evening he had spent with a beautiful Polish woman on the balcony of his house in Kiev. And still not connecting the memories of that day and not drawing any conclusions about them, Pierre closed his eyes, and the picture of summer nature mixed with the memory of bathing, of the liquid, wavering ball, and he sank somewhere into water, so that the water closed over his head' (1185).

Pierre's soul attempts to find refuge from further trauma in the watery imagery. This is again quite natural, considering that water and bathing are usually among our earliest pleasant childhood memories. In fact, as Lydia Ginzburg reminds us, Tolstoy's own earliest memories were associated with being bathed in a tub at the age of about one and half.[86] To interpret Pierre's psychology at this crucial phase in his Bildungsroman we may also want to recall the Romantic notion of life as an ocean or Freud's assertion that the religious sentiment is connected to an 'oceanic' feeling. Examples of this kind of imagery pervade Romantic poetry, particularly the metaphysical poetry of Tolstoy's friend Fyodor Tiutchev.

Pierre's epiphanic dream, the last of his important dreams in the novel, presents us with an image of life as a great liquid globe, composed of many bubbles that constantly emerge and then burst, to be replaced by ever new bubbles. It is in this dream, rather than in waking life, that Pierre realizes that Platon has died:

> Once again real events mingled with his dreams; once again a voice either his own or someone else's was murmuring thoughts in his ear, some of the same thoughts he had heard in his dream at Mozhaysk. Life is everything. Life is God. Everything is in flux and movement, and this movement is God. And while there is life there is pleasure in being conscious of the Godhead. To love life is to love God. The hardest and the most blessed thing is to love this life even in suffering, innocent suffering.
>
> 'Karataev!' The memory flashed into Pierre's mind. And suddenly Pierre had a vision, like reality itself, of someone long forgotten, a gentle old teacher who had taught him geography in Switzerland. 'Wait a minute,' said the little old man. And he showed Pierre a globe. This globe was a living thing, a shimmering ball with no fixed dimensions. The entire surface

of the ball consisted of drops closely compressed. And the drops were in constant movement and flux, sometimes dissolving from many into one, sometimes breaking down from one into many. Each drop was trying to spread out and take up as much space as possible, but all the others, wanting to do the same, squeezed it back, absorbing it or merging into it.

'This is life,' said the little old teacher.

'It's so simple and clear,' thought Pierre. 'How could I have not known that before? God is in the middle, and each drop tries to expand and reflect Him at the largest possible scale. And it grows, gets absorbed and compressed, disappears from the surface, sinks down into the depths and bubbles up again. That's what has happened to him, Karataev: he has been absorbed and he's disappeared.' (1184–5)

This pivotal scene in *War and Peace* is rife with literary and philosophical allusions. As Inessa Medzhibovskaya points out, Pierre's visionary dream actualizes the metaphor of 'engulfing the divine' ['*zakhvatyvan'e bozhestva*'], which, as we learn from Tolstoy's diary, appeared in one of his own dreams. In this dream it was the German poet Schiller who told him that happiness consists in the 'engulfing of the divine.'[87] Interpreting Pierre's dreams alongside Tolstoy's, we could say that the little drops – individual selves – struggle to engulf as much divinity as 'deeply' and 'broadly' as they can. Once they have attained happiness, they burst and other drops come to the fore, and the same game begins again.

Tolstoy's description of Pierre's response to Platon's death – or, rather, Pierre's self-protective avoidance of Platon once he subconsciously realizes that Platon is going to get shot, followed by his subconsciously deliberate inattention to the fact of Platon's disappearance – raises important ethical issues. While in the camp, Pierre seems to acquire a kind of amoral or pantheistic attitude to life and death, which, no doubt, shields his psyche from excessive trauma, but which also verges on nihilism. The fact that Pierre is able to let Platon go without remorse or guilt vividly illustrates what one of Tolstoy's pedagogical articles calls a 'natural law,' according to which a child (a pupil) needs her parents (teachers) only as long as she is still dependent on them and is learning from them.[88] Once the individual reaches self-sufficiency, she no longer needs those who nurtured her and can allow the bond of pedagogical eros to dissolve. Thus, when Pierre, earlier in the story, needed Platon to show him by personal example that even the simplest life full of deprivations and hardships can be full of dignity, he established a close emotional bond with the peasant sage. However, as soon as Pierre has learnt everything that Platon can teach him – namely, how to rejoice in mere existence without enquiring into its causes or consequences, free from anxiety, curiosity, or desire – he can do without Platon and turns away from him precisely at the moment when Platon lets go of his quietism and starts clinging to life. Withholding his compassion, Pierre manifests the kind of selfishness that, according to Tolstoy, characterizes every happy and healthy being who enjoys his or her own existence too much to take notice of death or the sufferings of others. The narrator of *War and Peace* does not condemn Pierre's callousness, but tries to explain it, naturalistically, as the normal reaction of a healthy organism, which shrinks away from suffering and death. As Tolstoy would some years later tell Strakhov, 'I define life as the separation of a part that loves itself from the whole [...] A human being knows only that which is alive. That is what a living being can comprehend only that which is likewise living, that which is like himself.'[89]

Pierre's Bildungsroman comes to a happy ending. However, at the end of the story Pierre does not become 'one of the people.' Pierre's post-war career, which we can glimpse in the epilogue, suggests that he has transformed from a dreamer into a man capable of action, a founder of a secret political society modelled on the German secret societies (like the *Turmgesellschaft* described in Goethe's *Wilhelm Meister's Apprenticeship*), and, implicitly, a future Decembrist. Most importantly, Pierre has succeeded in the task that Tolstoy regarded as the hardest and most important task in life: he has built a happy family. Having won Natasha's love, he marries her and together they build a large family nest where they breed a robust clan of young Bezukhovs.

Pierre's story is presented as only one strand within Tolstoy's complex and multilayered narrative about Russia's awakening and maturation during the Napoleonic Wars. At this juncture, a methodological disclaimer is in order. An analysis focused on individual characters and the narrative spaces that emerge around them – that which has been my analytical strategy thus far – inevitably runs the risk of destroying the organic unity of the text.[90] Indeed, contrary to what many critics have said about this novel, Tolstoy intends *War and Peace* to be an organic unity that mirrors life itself, which Tolstoy saw as a great self-renewing organism, or a liquid globe consisting of an infinite number of little bubbles that appear, grow, burst, and then reappear as new bubbles. In Tolstoy's text different narrative strands or layers enrich, clarify, and amplify one another, contributing to our understanding of the whole without converging on the single representative individual or family, as is often the case in Western, particularly British, novels.[91] However, to discuss a work of such immense scope some kind of methodological reduction is inevitable. Therefore I chose to focus this chapter on the analysis of only two heroes, who seem to me to be the most dynamic 'vehicles' of the artist's consciousness, and therefore, the broadest windows in the house of fiction constructed by Tolstoy.

As Tolstoy admitted in the above-quoted letter to Herzen, he could only imagine his Russia through his own 'little prism.' He knew that he could not immediately understand or speak on behalf of the Russian nation as a whole. Therefore he chose to focus on the inner *Bildung* or *obrazovanie* of those characters who were culturally, socially, and psychologically closest to himself.[92] However, rather than presenting us with a single model of a Russian apprenticeship (of the sort that he had attempted earlier in works like *The Cossacks*, 'The Gentleman's Morning,' and *Family Happiness*), in *War and Peace* Tolstoy has created a multifocal prism through which he looks at 'his Russia.' Andrei, Pierre, Nikolai Rostov, Natasha, and Princess Marya all represent different angles of vision or *prizmochki*. The novel's female heroines, such as Natasha and Princess Marya, also develop, but in a different direction from their male counterparts. Like Psyche in *Agathon*, Dorothea in *Hermann und Dorothea*, or the numerous heroines of *Wilhelm Meister's Apprenticeship*, these female figures help the male heroes to attain their purposes and in doing so become psychologically indispensable to them. As mothers, sisters, muses, and the like, these heroines are indeed crucial to the life of the world envisioned as an organism. However, the women themselves are hardly independent historical agents. The author of *War and Peace* was no feminist.

Among the central male figures Nikolai Rostov appears to me to be the least dynamic character. It is true that Nikolai most accurately represents the type of the Russian landowner of Tolstoy's father's generation. He embodies a cultural mentality that Tolstoy knew well and regarded as typically Russian. In this sense Nikolai, as Gary Saul Morson has argued, could be seen as the novel's main character.[93] However, I think that, notwithstanding Tolstoy's widely trumpeted sympathy for the 'old landowner' type, in analysing *War and Peace* we should not lose sight of Tolstoy's democratic sentiments and his fascination with Russia's first revolutionaries, the Decembrists. In this regard, I fully agree with Victor Shklovskii, who says that 'his entire life Tolstoy thought about how to connect the Decembrists, who were so far from the people, with the people (the folk); he kept creating literary plots that show how a gentry revolutionary, or simply a kind gentleman, finds himself in the peasant milieu, how he and the peasants live together and gradually find a common language.'[94]

It is clear from the epilogue that Nikolai Rostov would be in opposition to the Decembrists. As a spokesman for the status quo, rather than an expression of the 'spirit of the age,' Nikolai, too, is part of the work's organic whole. However, it is not his story that makes *War and Peace* resemble a Bildungsroman. Through his marriage to Princess Marya, Nikolai restores his family's fortune and recreates the kind of organic cell that is properly described by the idyllic chronotope, rather than by the chronotope of the Bildugsroman.[95]

In my discussion of *War and Peace* as a Bildungsroman, however, I have so far focused on Pierre, the hero around whose development into a Decembrist Tolstoy originally intended to weave his entire story. In describing Pierre's path to happiness, which takes him first through multiple falls and mistakes to the spiritually liberating and edifying experience of imprisonment, Tolstoy has implicitly answered the demand posed by organic criticism: he has shown that the social and moral malaise these critics dubbed 'superfluity' was not incurable and that a Russian hero was capable of a non-'predatory' personal happiness. However, if we take seriously the idea, first expressed by Carden, that Tolstoy took much of his philosophical inspiration from Herder, a thinker who believed that earthly and spiritual forces are intertwined and mutually influence each other, then Pierre's story, which ends in the attainment of happiness on this earth, must be balanced out by another story, one that takes a more sceptical view of this life and strives toward a less earthly and human-centred conception of happiness. In the philosophical dialogue between himself and Prince Andrei it is Pierre who points beyond this world, invoking the idea that a human soul need not be imprisoned in a body and social life and can aspire to a higher, more spiritual form of being. In the end, however, it is Prince Andrei who oversteps the boundary of this life and touches the realm of immortality. Thus, ultimately, it is through the narrative arc of Andrei's career that Tolstoy irrevocably parts company with the type of Bildungsroman in which youthful experiment – the sentimental education – ends in the attainment of earthly happiness. Andrei's heroic confrontation with death helps us understand that for Tolstoy the ultimate end of personal development is not happiness, but freedom. Later in his career Tolstoy would define this stage of development as 'rational consciousness.' Having borrowed Herzen's term, Tolstoy injects it with his own meaning. For a Tolstoyan 'rational consciousness' means both a freedom from the yoke of social convention and freedom from the fear of death.

Andrei's Path to Immortality

'For the scene at Austerlitz I needed a brilliant young man,' wrote Tolstoy in a private letter, explaining the genesis of the character of Prince Andrei.[96] Andrei's heroic behaviour at the battle of Austerlitz was modelled on that of Ferdinand Tizenhausen, Kutuzov's son-in-law, who died in this battle. Unlike his real-life prototype, Prince Andrei does not die but experiences an epiphany: the first of Tolstoy's attempts in this novel at representing the soul's transport beyond the realm of worldliness and toward the eternal realm (whose existence, we might add, the sceptically inclined Tolstoy for a long time doubted). Andrei, too, is a sceptic. Tolstoy allows Andrei's characteristic scepticism to play itself out by having him face the boundary separating this world from the world beyond death not once, but three times: first on the field of the battle at Austerlitz, then at the time of his wife's death, and finally after he receives a mortal wound at Borodino.

Thus, Prince Andrei's first 'epiphany,' which occurs when he realizes the futility of earthly glory and the pettiness of Napoleon in the face of the 'infinite, lofty sky' he is gazing at, lying on the battlefield of Austerlitz, does not translate into a leap of faith. Andrei does, however, understand the insignificance of his earlier desire for 'glory' and becomes disenchanted in his former idol, Napoleon, who embodies this glory. Prince Andrei's next brush with death, experienced vicariously through his wife Liza who dies in childbirth, plunges Prince Andrei into utter despair about the freedom of the individual to control his fate. A series of fortuitous events rescues Andrei from spiritual death (or utter nihilism): first, his conversation with Pierre on the raft – a conversation that inspires him and gives him a certain hope despite his intellectual resistance to love and life; and then in his meeting Natasha, with whom he falls in love even against his own rational will, and certainly against his father's wishes.

What stands in the way of Andrei's happiness is pride or excessive *amour propre*, his own and his father's, for, as Tolstoy demonstrates, pride is the main characteristic that distinguishes the old and the young Princes Bolkonsky. Thus, it is wounded pride that forces the old prince – nicknamed *le roi de Prusse*, presumably for his love of order and his predilection for Voltaire's philosophy – into a self-imposed exile on his estate. Likewise, pride is the main motivation behind Prince Andrei's quest for military glory. In Anna Scherer's salon, where most other characters act like automata, the self-assured Prince Andrei Bolkonsky cuts a noble figure, especially against the background of courtiers and sycophants (such as, for example, the Kuragins). From the beginning of the novel, Prince Andrei and his father seem to stand – *faute de mieux* – for the flower of the Russian nation: a sense of aristocratic honour, personal courage, and military prowess. And yet, already in the early chapters of the novel Prince Andrei looks too blasé to be genuinely sympathetic.

In portraying Prince Andrei (who possesses certain Lermontovian or Romantic features), Tolstoy is deepening and broadening the familiar 'dazzling' or 'Byronic' literary type, as Apollon Grigor'ev dubbed it. But instead of following Grigor'ev in categorizing this type of hero as alien to the Russian soil and casting him down, Tolstoy, who, we might add, was infinitely better acquainted with Russian aristocratic society, its history, and traditions than Grigor'ev, shows that Prince Andrei, too, can and will be transformed through suffering and participating in the great war. Indeed, it is not simply his love for Natasha that helps Prince Andrei achieve blessedness or redemption. He must also undergo a complete moral transformation, which coincides with and is caused by the 'people's war.'

But before Prince Andrei can earn his moral rebirth, he has to fully live out the destiny allotted to his prideful 'dazzling' type, and only then, through extreme suffering and on the brink of death, become liberated from the shackles of his inauthentic 'outer man' and embrace real love. Tolstoy stages Andrei's conversion as a multiple-act drama. The first act comes to a head on the field of Austerlitz, when Prince Andrei sees Napoleon standing over his body and saying to his aide-de-camp, 'A fine death this one!' (310). In Prince Andrei's consciousness, however, the voice of his former idol sounds like the buzzing of a fly, whereas his thoughts are fixated on the high and eternal sky.

The second act begins when Prince Andrei, now disappointed in worldly glory and full of remorse about the cold way in which he had treated his late wife, tries to reinvent himself and his life by marrying Natasha. However, the old Prince deems the Countess Rostova, whose family is nearly ruined, a poor match for his son, and refuses to bless the union. The father's obstinacy in this case reminds us of the elder Grinev's withholding of his paternal blessing, which propels the entire plot of Pushkin's *The Captain's Daughter*. In *War and Peace*, however, the son does not dare seek help from 'chance' (which in *The Captain's Daughter* is embodied in Pugachev's volatile figure). Instead, the two men reach a compromise – to postpone the wedding for a year, which Prince Andrei will spend travelling in Europe – a delay that proves fatal to Natasha's and Prince Andrei's love. The episode of Natasha's elopement with Anatole, which Tolstoy plotted very carefully and considered the pinnacle of the entire novelistic plot, becomes the next crucial test not only for Natasha, but also for Pierre as well as for Prince Andrei himself. This is a crucial juncture in the text, which should be examined more closely before we can go any further.[97]

When Pierre, having heard of the scandalous rupture between his friend and Natasha, comes to see Prince Andrei, he is shocked by his coldness and composure. The author emphasizes Andrei's reserve and Pierre's amazement at the fact that his magnanimous friend could not find it in his heart to forgive the inexperienced young woman who made an unfortunate misstep. Pierre reminds Prince Andrei of their conversation from a while ago, probably alluding to Rousseau's *Julie, ou la Nouvelle Héloïse* (one of the most popular books at the time): ' "Listen. Do you remember that difference of opinion we had in Petersburg?" said Pierre. "Remember what we . . . ?" "Yes, I do," Prince Andrei answered hastily. "I said that a fallen woman should be forgiven, but I did not say I could forgive her, and I can't" ' (660).

In Rousseau's novel, the more open-minded M. de Wolmar, as a true follower of the Enlightenment, forgives his wife Julie when he finds out that she has had an affair with Saint-Preux. Prince Andrei, however, shows himself unable to act in conformity with the rationalists' ethical principles and forgive Natasha out of utilitarian necessity. Nor can he forgive her simply out of compassion. The Bolkonsky family trait, excessive *amour propre*, undermines Prince Andrei's fragile return to life, and once again plunges him into the cold condition of seeking a socially acceptable death by returning to the army and seeking out danger (prefiguring Vronsky in the epilogue to *Anna Karenina*). Pierre, in the meantime, becomes Natasha's true friend, winning her heart by his genuine spiritual generosity and kindness.

Prince Andrei goes out to the theatre of war with the intention of finding Kuragin and challenging him to a duel. He enlists in the army once again and apparently is seeking his own death. Ironically, death will catch him unawares. Thus he gets mortally wounded while waiting with his regiment in the reserves on the outskirts of Borodino.

132   Nineteenth-Century Russian Novels of Emergence

The climax of Prince Andrei's moral drama begins in the medical station near Borodino, where Prince Andrei suddenly sees his enemy, Anatole Kuragin, and watches the doctors amputate Anatole's leg. After finishing with Anatole, they operate on Prince Andrei, causing him to lose consciousness. Upon regaining consciousness, Prince Andrei awakens to a new life, which will last only a fortnight:

> After all the pain he had endured Prince Andrei now felt blissfully at peace; he had not felt like this for a very long time. The nicest and happiest moments of his life, especially his earliest childhood, when he had been undressed and put to bed, and his nurse had sung lullabies over him, and he had burrowed down under pillows feeling happy just to be alive, floated through his imagination, and instead of seeming like past events they seemed like the here and now.
> [...] it was all too much for Prince Andrei; he broke down in tears of love and tenderness for his fellow men, himself, his own silly misdoings and everybody else's. Sympathy and love, for our brothers, those who love us and those who hate us, for our enemies. Yes, the kind of love that God preached on earth, that Marie told me about and I could not understand – that's why I was so sorry to let go of this life, that's what would have been left for me if I had lived. (904)

Prince Andrei's newly awakened feeling of brotherly love continues to grow within his soul as he is carried away from the camp and is taken, along with other wounded officers, to Moscow and then to Mytishchi, where he is accidently placed at the peasant hut next to the one occupied by the Rostov family. Prince Andrei's spiritual transformation prepares him for his final encounter with Natasha, who has also grown spiritually since the day she wrote the fateful letter breaking her engagement with him. Only now, when both of them are humbled by suffering and the sense of their mutual moral failure, can Prince Andrei and Natasha truly come together as human beings. Lying awake in a peasant hut in the village of Mytishchi, while Moscow burns and the refugees can see the dome of smoke rising above the horizon, Prince Andrei experiences a genuine conversion. The new feeling of love in his soul brings him genuine joy and peace:

> 'Yes, it's love ...' (his thoughts were lucidity itself), 'but not the kind of love that loves for a reason, a purpose, a cause, but the kind of love I felt for the first time when I was on my death-bed and I saw my enemy and loved

him. I experienced the feeling of love that is the essence of the soul, love that seeks no object. [...] How many people I have hated in my life! And there is nobody I loved more and hated more than her.' And he formed a clear mental image of Natasha, though not as he had seen her in the past, with all the charm that had given him such joy. For the first time he caught an image of her soul. And he could understand all her feelings, suffering, shame and remorse. For the first time he could sense the full cruelty of his rejection of her, the break between them. 'If I could only see her one last time ... just once, to look into her eyes and say ...' (1021)

It is at this point that Natasha visits the peasant hut in which she knows Prince Andrei is lying. In response to Natasha's plea to forgive her, Prince Andrei says: 'I love you more than I did, better than before' (1022). We accept the miraculous encounter between the hero and the heroine because we know that the two have come together due to the historical circumstance of the retreat of the Russian army and the abandonment of Moscow by its denizens, which has made all chance encounters possible. Tolstoy thus creates an intersection between the two dramatic stories he is telling, one of which unfolds in the sphere of private life while the other takes place in the public, epic sphere of world history. The reconciliation between Prince Andrei and Natasha symbolizes the dissolving of differences between people in the war. Humbled by their suffering, they give up their *amour propre* and experience *agape*.

At this point Prince Andrei has completely cast off the garb of a socialized being and risen above the limitations imposed by his bodily self (his 'mortal coil,' so to speak), finally being able to embrace his metaphysical essence. In other words, he has come to realize what Tolstoy would describe as the feeling of identity combined with the feeling of unity with the rest of being. Tolstoy puts this idea in one of his diary entries from the time when he just completed *War and Peace*: 'All philosophical theories (modern ones, since Descartes) include an error. The error of these philosophers is that they admit only the consciousness of oneself as an individual (the so-called subject), whereas in fact the consciousness of the entire world, of the so-called object, is as undoubtedly true as individual self-consciousness.'[98]

True self-consciousness and the path of life that leads to its attainment became the subject of Tolstoy's philosophical treatise *On Life* (1887), where he summarized many decades worth of reflection on a proper way to lead one's life. To my mind, this treatise, and subsequent theological and moral treatises by Tolstoy, including *The Kingdom of God*

Is Within You (1893), grow out of the author's earlier thinking about self-perfection and *obrazovanie*. For the mature Tolstoy, the ultimate goal of self-perfection is to redeem one's immortal self or soul – a feat that only a few Tolstoyan heroes accomplish. In this regard, the death of Prince Andrei deserves special attention as one of Tolstoy's most elaborate analyses of death from within the dying man's consciousness. Tolstoy will repeat this tour de force in the story *The Death of Ivan Il'ich* (1884), which was written only a few years before *On Life*. In all three analyses of the process of dying, Tolstoy is most interested in how the spirit or soul, accustomed to being housed in the particular body into which it was born, exits this 'animal' body and leaves the physical world behind. As he gradually removes himself from life and distances himself from his loved ones, Prince Andrei can no longer see the world the way they see it, nor can he sympathize with them. The fact that he is already half-dead, that his soul has already half-abandoned his body, is brought home painfully to Princess Marya, when she comes to see her dying brother and brings along Prince Andrei's son Nikolushka: '"Andrei, would you ..." Princess Marya began with a catch in her voice, "would you like to see Nikolai? He never stops talking about you." For the first time Prince Andrei smiled the ghost of a smile, but Princess Marya, who knew his face so well, was horrified to realize it was not a smile of joy, not of tender affection for his son, it was a smile of quiet, gentle mockery as his sister made one last, desperate attempt to bring him back to sensitivity' (1088).

Princess Marya is shocked by her brother's lack of emotional reaction to this meeting with his son – their last meeting. Death is a radical alienation of the spiritual being from the three-dimensional world of embodied objects. In this passage Prince Andrei has already become alienated from his flesh and from everyone who was connected to him by ties of flesh and blood, including his son. However, Tolstoy does not follow Andrei's thoughts any further. Like Herder, who believed in the supersensible but eschewed mysticism, Tolstoy carefully draws a wedge between the consciousness of the man who is about to depart this earth and those who stay behind.[99]

7 Dostoevsky on Individual Reform and National Reconciliation: *The Adolescent*

> Из Христа выходит та мысль, что главное приобретение и цель человечества есть результат добытой нравственности. Вообразите, что все Христы, – ну возможны ли были бы теперешние шатания, недоумения, пауперизм? [. . .] Если бы люди не имели ни малейшего понятия о государстве о ни о каких науках, но были бы все как Христы, возможно ли, чтоб не было рая на Земле тотчас же?
>
> Ф.М. Достоевский, из *Записных книжек* к *Бесам*, 11:192–3

> Christ suggests that mankind's main acquisition and its goal stem from its morals. Imagine that all men are Christs – would there be room for contemporary wavering, perplexity, pauperism? [. . .] If people had no idea about the state or about any sciences, but were all Christ-like, could the paradise on earth fail to come right away?
>
> F.M. Dostoevsky, from the notebooks to *The Possessed*

When Fyodor Dostoevsky returned to Russia in 1859 after the amnesty announced by the new emperor on the eve of the Great Reforms, he found himself in a rather different ideological climate from the one he had left a decade earlier. The critic to whom the young Dostoevsky owed his fame, Vissarion Belinskii, was gone. The dispute over his legacy and over the future of the journal *The Contemporary* polarized the St Petersburg literati. Entering this debate would mean siding with one of the camps. Dostoevsky, however, dreamed of a certain degree of independence in this turbulent public sphere that could only be obtained if he had his own journal. With the help of his brother Mikhail, Dostoevsky was able to realize this long-term desire and in 1861 opened the journal called *Time* (*Vremia*).[1] This journal became the organ of the new 'native soil' or *pochvennichestvo* movement. The *pochvenniki* – a relatively small group whose core included, in addition to the Dostoevsky brothers, Apollon Grigor'ev and Nikolai Strakhov – believed that Russia's acute social issues could be resolved primarily by encouraging the educated classes to take the leading role in encouraging and designing cultural and educational reforms. Eager to contribute to nation building at this crucial historical juncture, the *pochvenniki* offered a new vision of national culture that took only the most fruitful elements of the Westernizing and Slavophile positions and rejected their drawbacks. In the manifesto for the new journal Dostoevsky wrote:

> We are not talking about the Slavophiles or Westernizers. Our era is completely indifferent to their domestic quarrels. We are talking about the reconciliation of civilization with the national principle. We believe that both sides must finally come to an understanding of one another, must clear up all the misunderstandings that had amassed in such incredible numbers between them and then advance in concord, with uncompromisingly combined forces, along a new, broad, and glorious path. Union at all costs, in spite of all sacrifices and as quickly as possible – that is our motivating idea, that is our motto.[2]

In this piece Dostoevsky argues that the most urgent task facing the intelligentsia at this momentous time is to find a common language with the mass of people, who, newly emancipated from serfdom, are still poorly prepared for independence and citizenship. The intellectual elite should return to the 'native soil' not simply in order to share their skills and knowledge with the people, but also to learn from them, to establish a genuine two-way dialogue. Borrowing one of Grigor'ev's cherished ideas, Dostoevsky argues that this movement back to the soil would solve the predicament of the so-called 'superfluous man' (an educated and liberal-minded aristocrat alienated from his own country).[3] Now was the time for all those who felt homeless and useless in their native, Russia like Pushkin's Aleko or Lermontov's Pechorin, to apply themselves to the practical task of educating peasants and their children – just as Count Lev Tolstoy did in his country house, Iasnaia Poliana. Not surprisingly, Tolstoy was highly regarded by the *pochvenniki* and his pedagogical activities and writings were very favourably reviewed in *Time*.[4] In the writings of Apollon Grigor'ev, we frequently come across a still more ambitious idea. He suggests that a new phase in world history would emerge once the representatives of the 'Petersburg stage' in Russian history (i.e., hyper-self-conscious men whose theories found no application in reality) experience a genuine homecoming and forge a true union with their fellow-Russians who may still be illiterate and lacking self-awareness, but who nonetheless possess great spiritual resources.[5] This dialogue, according to Grigor'ev, would give rise to a completely new culture. There is, of course, a good deal of romantic dreaminess in Grigor'ev's vision of Russia's future. The very term *pochva* or 'native soil' was borrowed from the vocabulary of German Romanticism.[6]

One of the commonest tropes used by the Russian *pochvenniki* of the 1860s was 'reconciliation.'[7] This idea must have come to Russia by way of Germany and Britain, where it was actively used by cultural figures like Matthew Arnold, who was also concerned with the problem of internal distrust and lack of dialogue between different social strata of his country.[8] 'Reconciliation' implied a non-militant, open-minded approach to various ideological and class conflicts that were tearing the social fabric. According to this (admittedly rosy-coloured) view, through sympathy and mutual forgiveness different groups of society would be able to build a modern form of organic national community.

It is not surprising, then, that pochvennichestvo immediately invited acute critical attacks from the radicals who clustered around N.G. Chernyshevskii's *Contemporary* (and later around N.A. Nekrasov's *Notes for the Fatherland*). Dostoevsky's article 'Two theoretical camps' (*'Dva lageria teoretikov'*) was written as a rebuttal of M.A. Antonovich's attack on pochvennichestvo in the December 1861 issue of *The Contemporary* (5:27). In this piece Dostoevsky responds to his radical critics, arguing that the complex issues facing Russia during the age of the Great Reforms will be resolved if, instead of battling with each other on the pages of periodicals, the Russian intellectuals join their efforts and fuse their energies in the difficult task of bringing literacy and enlightenment to the peasants. He accuses Antonovich and other radical intellectuals of elitism for arguing that the people had to be brought up-to-date through the imposition of European standards of reason and science, as though they had nothing to offer themselves.[9] Echoing Tolstoy's pedagogical essays, Dostoevsky writes in 'Two theoretical camps':

> We think that it is physically impossible to make the people disavow everything they have accumulated and developed in the course of their history and make them embrace, say, the pan-human ideal, which was developed in other countries. Consequently, if we want our people to

become more enlightened and developed, it is inevitable that we pay attention to *narodnost'*, because the people's instincts [*narodnye instinkty*] are extremely sound. The people are sensitive to all external influences. Sometimes what is considered 'panhuman' turns out to be completely useless in a given country and can only stunt the development of the people.[10]

Without doubting the peasants' ability and eagerness to learn, the author of *The House of the Dead* does not think that the peasants should simply passively accept European culture and science, thereby forfeiting their organic national customs. He believes that the peasants should be taught only the most basic things like grammar and arithmetic, but that in every other respect they should be allowed to rely on their innate common sense, which will steer them toward the knowledge of what is truly useful and applicable to their native soil. Essentially the same idea is expressed in the two articles Dostoevsky published in *Time* under the title 'Pedantry and Literacy' ('*Knizhnost' i gramotnost'*'). Here too he argues that the main task of the educated class is to spread literacy.[11] The peasants themselves will figure out how to apply this knowledge to their lives. For the pochvenniki, just as for L.N. Tolstoy, there is nothing more pernicious than forcing European cultural standards and norms on the Russian peasant.[12] The utilitarian approach did not require a student to develop his personality, but made him into a useful unit in the social whole, a practical person able to rationally perform a set task. From the *pochvennik*'s point of view, however, this excessively pragmatic approach impeded the natural growth of the human personality and threatened to undermine the spiritual potential of the Russian people.[13]

Dostoevsky and his colleagues in *Time* were justified in their fears that without the intelligentsia acting as a unified front, the successful implementation of reforms was in question, for both the younger generation and the former serfs were in need of moral and intellectual guidance. Student insurrections were a common occurrence in the early 1860s. One of the most colourful episodes from this period of Russian history is known to historians as the 'epoch of proclamations,' which culminated with the printing and distributing of a proclamation on behalf of the organization that called itself 'Young Russia.' As police later discovered, this proclamation was authored by a student named Zaychnevskii who did not represent a powerful political movement.[14] Yet his proclamation, full of terrorist threats, along with the unexplained fires that raged in St Petersburg in the summer of 1862 and that some believed to be connected to 'Young Russia's' activities, helped to spread panic among the population.

Joseph Frank masterfully describes Dostoevsky's courageous behaviour under these extraordinary circumstances. As a former convict, the writer knew that he was surely watched by the secret police. And yet he paid a visit to the house of N.G. Chernyshevskii, whom he and many others believed to be the most authoritative figure among the young radicals. Dostoevsky apparently pleaded with Chernyshevskii to address those who stood behind 'Young Russia' in order to pre-empt a real civil war. Luckily, this time Dostoevsky himself was untouched by the police, whereas Chernyshevskii was soon arrested and the publication of *The Contemporary* suspended.

In the meantime, *Time* was on its way to becoming a very successful journal. Undoubtedly, Dostoevsky's own contributions – *The Humiliated and the Wronged, Notes from the House of the Dead, Winter Notes on Summer Impressions* – contributed to the journal's success. Just as the Dostoevsky brothers were beginning to feel that they were in good shape both professionally and financially, the censorship vetoed N.N. Strakhov's article that could be described as a comparative anthropological study of Russian and Polish cultures as two separate branches of the Slavic tribe. Although Strakhov's piece, written in the cold voice of a scientist, was completely free from any political commentary, the journal was closed down. This sudden blow was all the more devastating considering the personal circumstances in the lives of Mikhail and Fyodor Dostoevsky. M.M. Dostoevsky was already ailing and would die of liver failure in July of 1864, just months after the brothers started a new journal, *Epoch*. F.M. Dostoevsky's first wife, Marya Dmitrievna, whom he had married in Siberia, died of tuberculosis after a protracted agony in March of 1864 – just as her husband was hard at work on *Notes from the Underground*. Another death that goes unmentioned in Frank's otherwise full account of Dostoevsky's life and work is that of Apollon Grigor'ev, who died suddenly of a stroke on 25 September 1864. Before he died, the critic had passed on the text of his memoirs, *My Literary and Moral Wanderings*, which were printed in *Epoch*. After the deaths of his brother, wife, and his chief critic, Grigor'ev, Dostoevsky did not manage to keep his journal afloat for long. The last issue came out in March 1865.

Dostoevsky and the Bildungsroman

Seeking at least a temporary respite from the gloom of his St Petersburg life, Dostoevsky went to Europe in the summer of 1865. Returning to Petersburg in mid-October, Dostoevsky plunged back into the depressing atmosphere of financial difficulties and family squabbles. Mikhail's widow, whose family Dostoevsky was now obligated to support, and his own stepson Pasha Isaev, who continued to be Dostoevsky's dependent, placed constant demands on the writer, who was thus forced to work on several projects simultaneously. The love affair with Apollinaria Suslova must have provided some emotional relief from this otherwise gloomy existence. However, this affair, which inspired *The Gambler*, was bittersweet at its best, and ended up becoming emotionally draining. And yet despite all these obstacles, or perhaps out of the necessity to constantly battle them, Dostoevsky's talent and productivity were continually on the rise. *Crime and Punishment*, serialized in Katkov's *Notes for the Fatherland*, became the literary sensation of 1866. The writer had fully regained his popularity and was beginning to rebuild his life when a shattering event occurred that wreaked havoc in Russian politics. On 4 April 1866 a student named Dmitrii Karakozov fired a shot at Alexander II, the 'Tsar-liberator.'

Whether the student was a poor marksman or whether someone else had jostled his arm – a tradesman named Osip Komissarov has been mentioned in this regard – Karakozov missed his target. There followed series of police investigations. The most apparent suspects were the Poles, yet Karakozov asserted repeatedly that he was a pure Russian. Although Alexander II remained convinced that the attempt on his life must have originated in a Polish plot, he dismissed a relatively liberal minister of education, A.V. Golovnin, and replaced him with Count D.I. Tolstoy, a conservative bureaucrat who immediately curtailed the students' and gymnasium pupils' civic freedoms. On 26 May 1867 the new minister issued a decree demanding closer cooperation between police and school authorities and greater limitation on student extracurricular activities. Dismayed by the fact that Karakozov, despite his role in the 1861 disorders, could re-enter the University of Kazan' two years later and then transfer to Moscow, the government required education officials to provide the police with detailed information about all students and put an end to all concerts, spectacles, readings, and other public assemblies.[15]

This background is essential for understanding why Dostoevsky's art in the next decade and a half of his life will almost obsessively return to the questions of Russian boyhood, youth, and adolescence. Of course, these were the problems that Dostoevsky had also encountered in the works of his beloved Western authors, from Rousseau to Dickens, as well as in those of his Russian rivals, pre-eminently Tolstoy and

Turgenev. As Donna Orwin pointed out, 'Dostoevsky first noticed Tolstoy as a pseudonymous author of *Adolescence* while in exile in Siberia, which he read in *The Contemporary* in 1855. Starting with his novel *The Humiliated and the Wronged*, Dostoevsky referred in print a number of times, directly or indirectly, to passages from Tolstoy's trilogy.'[16] I suspect that it was both a sense of rivalry as well as a sense of shared responsibility for the future of their country that perpetually drew Tolstoy and Dostoevsky to similar topics, thereby also inciting them to enter into an intertextual dialogue. Not surprisingly, they were both drawn to the genre of the Bildungsroman as Franco Moretti describes it, that is, a story that captures the period of youthful experimentation in search of happiness and a steady vocation.

In fact, as attested by Konstantin Mochul'skii as early as 1863–4, Dostoevsky was already at work on a Russian Bildungsroman resembling Goethe's *Wilhelm Meister's Apprenticeship*, but focused on the personality of a quintessentially Russian hero. The biography of this hero would be symbolic of Russia's historical advance in the nineteenth century.[17] As we know, during his European sojourn Dostoevsky developed plans for two different large-scale epic works or even cycles of works. The first project, entitled *Atheism*, was supposed to tell a story of an upper-class Russian man who suddenly, in the middle of his life, loses religious faith and then spends years trying to rediscover his faith. As A.L. Bem has pointed out, although *Atheism* was never written, the image of its central hero resurfaced in several other novels, including, for example, *The Idiot*, where the figure of Prince Myshkin's benefactor Pavlischev resembles the image of the atheist.[18] The second project, entitled *The Life of a Great Sinner*, also remained unrealized. However, critics concur that the last four major works by Dostoevsky – *The Idiot*, *The Devils*, *The Adolescent*, and *The Brothers Karamazov* – all bear the impress of this project, which was to have described the life of a quintessential Russian sinner who ultimately reforms himself.[19]

Both works were conceived as large-scale epics on a par with Tolstoy's *War and Peace*, exceeding the scale of any of Dostoevsky's works so far. This ambition forced the writer to rethink his aesthetic and compositional approach to the novel. Dostoevsky's penchant was to concentrate the entire action of his novels in several highly dramatic scenes. Yet, on the epic scale, Dostoevsky foresaw problems with this method and was eager to overcome the limits it placed upon him, in order to find the kind of pacing necessary for the epic genre. From this vantage point, Mikhail Bakhtin's influential view of Dostoevsky as a novelist who does not portray his characters' diachronic *Bildung*, but rather focuses on the synchronic analyses of their consciousness, appears to be inadequate. Debating against B.M. Engel'gardt,[20] whose study of Dostoevsky's ideological novel served Bakhtin as a point of departure for formulating his view of Dostoevsky as a polyphonic author, Bakhtin writes:

> The fundamental category in Dostoevsky's mode of artistic visualizing was not evolution, but *coexistence* and *interaction*. He saw and conceived his world primarily in terms of space, not time. Hence his deep affinity for the dramatic form [. . .] The possibility of simultaneous coexistence, the possibility of being side by side or one against the other, is for Dostoevsky almost a criterion for distinguishing the essential from the nonessential. Only such things as can conceivably be linked together at a single point in time are essential and are incorporated into Dostoevsky's world; such things can be carried over into eternity, for in eternity, according to Dostoevsky, all is simultaneous, everything coexists. That, which has meaning only 'earlier' or 'later,' which is sufficient only unto its own moment, which is valid only as past, or as future, or as present in relation to past and future, is for him nonessential and is not incorporated into his world. That is why his characters remember nothing, they have no biography in the sense of something past and fully experienced. They remember from their own past only that which has not ceased to be present for them, that which is still experienced by them as the present: an unexpiated sin, a crime, an unforgiven insult [. . .] Thus there is no causality in Dostoevsky's novels, no genesis, no explanations based on the past, on the influences of the environment or of upbringing, and so forth. Every act a character commits is in the present, and in this sense is not predetermined; it is conceived of and represented by the author as free.[21]

In juxtaposing the 'unconsummated' Dostoevskian hero who implicitly never develops a stable identity and the typical novelistic or Bildungsroman hero who acquires such an identity by accumulating experience and self-consciousness,[22] Bakhtin wants to draw our attention to Dostoevsky's preoccupation with freedom from all forms of determinism. Bakhtin actually follows his predecessor Engel'gardt in arguing that Dostoevsky's characters embody particular ideological positions ('ideas' or 'idea-feelings'), yet he disagrees with Engel'gardt's attempt to detect a Hegelian dialectic in Dostoevsky's poetics.[23] Bakhtin insists on looking at Dostoevsky's architectonic only in spatial terms, denying the existence of a temporal and evolutionary dimension in Dostoevsky's plots.[24] This, I think, is a misapprehension that can be easily corrected if one looks at the notebooks to *The Idiot*, *The Devils*, *The Adolescent*, and *The Brothers Karamazov*. All of them contain, in various stages of development, sketches for a novelistic plot centred on a sinful hero who undergoes moral suffering and in the end regains faith. A born dramatist whose best plots so far always centred on dramatic collisions, Dostoevsky recognized that this new task would be a challenge.[25] Nonetheless, he was determined to master the epic genre. In the spring of 1870, he confessed to Strakhov: 'I have made this idea [the idea of a large-scale narrative of apprenticeship] the goal of my whole future literary career' ('Po krainei mere, iz etoi idei ia sdelal tsel' vsei moei budushchei literaturnoi kar'ery').[26]

In a certain way, the figure of Raskol'nikov, which according to Joseph Frank was conceived as a response to Turgenev's Bazarov, is a precursor to the figure of the sinner that became Dostoevsky's obsession in the 1870s. However, Raskol'nikov's conversion in Siberia occurs too suddenly. It lacks the kind of narrative motivation that Dostoevsky was trying to work out in his subsequent plots. Raskol'nikov is indeed a caricature of a nihilist hero, and Frank is completely right to foreground Turgenev's *Fathers and Sons* as a key intellectual source of *Crime and Punishment*.[27] There is, however, another important influence that we have to take into account when analysing Dostoevsky's intellectual and artistic development in the 1860s and 1870s: Apollon Grigor'ev. Different scenarios involving what Grigor'ev called a Byronic or a 'predatory' type pervade Dostoevsky's notebooks to *The Idiot*, *The Devils*, and *The Adolescent*. In most of these sketches Dostoevsky tries to work out a plan in which this 'predatory' type undergoes a moral reform. I suggest that what allows this negative type to undergo such a radical transformation and become a real Russian hero is his psychological 'breadth' – a complex (and at first sight, even ambiguous) notion with which every reader of Dostoevsky's novels is familiar from the text of *The Brothers Karamazov*.[28] Grigor'ev ascribed the breadth of the Russian soul to Russia's peculiar historical and geopolitical conditions. According to him, Russia's troubled history (including a major rupture caused by the reforms of Peter the Great) as well as this country's geographical and cultural extensiveness shaped a unique ethos.

For Dostoevsky, the Russians' ability to endure extreme suffering and even succumb to sin and moral corruption while still holding on to the high spiritual ideals of Christianity (or, as Dmitrii Karamazov puts it, to combine the ideal of Sodom with that of Madonna) is a highly auspicious and integral part of this unique national character. Although, especially in the case of reflective personalities, excessive 'breadth' could paralyze the will and lead to self-hatred and inertia (as it does in the case of the Underground Man), under the right conditions it could become a source of incredible strength and power, building truly remarkable characters. In his most ambitious statements Dostoevsky suggests that 'breadth' would eventually lead to a total regeneration of the Russian nation, making it a messianic nation that will help regenerate humanity as a whole. Incidentally, 'breadth' is precisely the term that Dostoevsky's first biographer Nikolai Strakhov uses to describe the writer's own personality. Strakhov uses this word to point out the writer's remarkable intellectual openness and ability to think from different points of view as well as his unusual emotional and spiritual tenacity. What Strakhov finds most noteworthy about Dostoevsky's personality is his ability to dwell on the most problematic and contradictory aspects of human nature without losing faith in humanity.[29]

At this point in their lives, Dostoevsky was particularly close to Strakhov, who after Grigor'ev's death in 1864 became Grigor'ev's self-appointed legatee and keeper of the flame. As A.S. Dolinin suggested, Dostoevsky's collaboration with Strakhov had played a crucial role in Dostoevsky's intellectual life.[30] Strakhov not only kept Dostoevsky interested in Grigor'ev's ideas, but interested Dostoevsky in many ideas of his own. What were, then, the most crucial points of intersection among these three thinkers?

Trained as a natural scientist, Strakhov came to literary criticism and philosophy with a strong background in natural history and evolutionary theory.[31] A sworn enemy of positivism, Strakhov developed his own theory of the organic evolution of the earth, in which he drew on the romantic writers on science: Goethe, Wilhelm v. Humboldt, and other German thinkers who subscribed to the idea of life as a unified organism. Strakhov argues that life on earth is the effect of a constant activity of spirit, which gradually ascends up the ladder of creation, giving rise to ever more sophisticated organisms. Sophistication is measured by the degree of interpenetration of matter and spirit, of the 'ideal' and the 'real.' In higher organisms, matter is suffused with spiritual energy, enlivened by spirit's activity, while the lower organisms are less spiritualized and therefore more inert. History (or culture), according to Strakhov, displays a gradual ascent of humanity toward a more spiritualized state.[32]

Conceived as a narrative of reformation or *perevospitanie*, *The Life of a Great Sinner* was supposed to transpose into narrative form an idealist vision of personal *Bildung* and spiritual ascent.³³ This vision bears a close resemblance to Strakhov's conception of culture as a development from mere nature toward spiritualized humanity. This vision lacks the moment of ascetic denial of the flesh, which is indispensable for spiritual progress in the more traditional Orthodox approach to spiritual salvation. At the time of the writing of *Crime and Punishment* (1863), Dostoevsky was clearly leaning toward the Orthodox vision of moral regeneration, hence Raskol'nikov's purely spiritual romance with Son'ia Marmeladova. However, as I will show in the second half of this chapter, the history of Arkadii Dolgorukii's self-formation in *The Adolescent* is markedly different insofar as the adolescent's path to a purer, better self does not obliterate passions and erotic stirrings, but rather purifies and raises them to a higher level. Likewise, in The *Brothers Karamazov*, Dostoevsky's final attempt to compose a Bildungsroman, Zosima's stinking corpse does not undermine the sublimity of Zosima's spirit, just as Alyosha's erotic stirrings in the presence of Grushen'ka are not a sign of impending corruption and fall, but rather a sign of his humanity.³⁴ The task of *Bildung* is to suffuse our organic nature with spirit, not to exorcize it. At the end of his Bildungsroman, Alyosha will presumably attain a higher form of Eros, which will mean the reconciliation of the material and spiritual drives.³⁵

By boldly merging Christian eschatology with the Herderian or romantic idea of self-accruing 'Humanity,' Dostoevsky goes further than Strakhov, who carefully abstained from speculation about the end of human evolution. Nevertheless, Dostoevsky's humanistic Utopianism unavoidably brings up the issue of Dostoevsky's familiarity with Strakhov, who remained one of the chief followers of romantic *Naturphilosophie* in Russia in the 1860s and 1870s.³⁶

In various notebooks dating from 1867 to 1870, Dostoevsky envisions human life as a chain of *Bildung*, where new and more spiritualized forms are constantly being created; however, this is not an evolutionary struggle for existence in which the older forms are annihilated, but rather one in which they are absorbed and redeemed through the process of higher synthesis. Perhaps originally the approach to the sinner's *Life* was entirely Orthodox and presupposed a traditional Christian conversion. However, this idea metamorphosed into a narrative of gradual spiritual self-formation or *Bildung* along the lines of romantic *Naturphilosophie*. It is telling that the characters in the drafts to the *Life* so often debate the idea of *Bildung* as a gradual perfection and divinization of nature. I will cite only one especially striking dialogue between the figure of the sinner, who in these drafts is called 'the Prince' (he will eventually metamorphose into Stavrogin in *The Devils*), and the character named Shatov. Both the Prince and Shatov are obsessed with the question of life beyond material existence. The Prince defends the view that a human being is at the centre of creation, at the point where physical or material nature begins to convert into spirit. Human history is thus both a continuation of organic natural evolution and a stepping stone to a new, supersensual nature. Shatov, however, is a sceptic who wants to believe in the possibility of immortal spiritual life but lacks faith. This dialogue drives home the idea that reason is insufficient for the progress of our 'Humanity.' One can grow beyond the material self and transform into a spiritual being only if one has faith in oneself as well as in the ultimate meaningfulness of creation:[37]

> Shatov: If human beings transform – how will they use their minds? The kind of intelligence we have corresponds only our current state as organisms.
> The Prince: How do we know whether or not one will need our current intelligence?
> Shatov: What then? Something higher, of course?
> The Prince: Without doubt, something much higher!
> Shatov: Can there be any thing higher than intelligence?
> The Prince: This is how science has it. For example, a bedbug is crawling on your body. Science knows that the bedbug is an organism, that it is living some kind of life and has impressions, and even has its understanding and God knows what else. But can science discover and tell me what constitutes the essence of the bedbug's life, consciousness and sensations? It never will! To discover this, one must become a bedbug for at least a minute. But if science cannot tell what it is like to be a bedbug, then it also cannot inform us of the essence of another, higher organism or being. Consequently, it cannot tell us what state humanity will reach as it transfigures in the millennium, whether or not there will be intelligence by that point.
> Shatov: – My mind is a whirlwind! But I won't leave you alone.
> The Prince: I don't understand why you consider having an intelligence, i.e., consciousness, the highest of all forms of beings? In my opinion, this is no longer science but faith. There is a natural focus here, which consists in that valuing of oneself (as a whole, i.e., every

man must value humanity as a whole) that is necessary for self-preservation. Every being must consider itself the highest form of being; a bedbug probably considers itself higher than you, and even if he could have become a human being, he probably would not want to, but would rather remain a bedbug. A bedbug is a mystery, and there are mysteries everywhere. Why do you deny mysteries? Note also that, perhaps, human beings are inclined toward faithlessness because they value intelligence above all, and since intelligence is only a quality of the human organism, human beings do not understand and do not want another form of life, i.e., life after death, they do not believe that that other form of life is higher. On the other hand, a human being has by nature a proclivity for despair and [self?] condemnation, since the human mind is made in such a way that every minute it loses faith in itself, it becomes dissatisfied with itself, and therefore a human being considers its existence insufficient. Hence the desire to believe in life after death. Evidently, we are transitional beings, and our life on earth is evidently the existence of a caterpillar transforming into a butterfly.[38]

Because *The Life of a Great Sinner* was never written, we can only speculate whether the character Shatov in this book would escape the confines of his materialism. His namesake in *The Devils* is an idealistic *intelligent* who becomes a hapless victim of the conspirators, and not a hero aspiring to 'Mangodhood.' However, another character from this book, Kirillov, is so anxious to test his manly will that he commits suicide – a sublime act that momentarily releases him from his metaphysical angst. But is suicide the only way to escape from the nihilistic lack of certainty in the meaningfulness of existence? In my opinion, *The Adolescent* and *The Brothers Karamazov* answer this difficult question negatively. In these works, Dostoevsky tries to shows that a person can reconcile the material and spiritual drives of his human nature. By undergoing this reform, one can discover a true path toward God.

A Reading of *The Adolescent*

In the remainder of this chapter I will argue that *The Adolescent* represents Dostoevsky's sole completed Bildungsroman. At the same time, *The Adolescent* represents a very condensed version of the Bildungsroman trilogy centred on the figure of Alyosha Karamazov. In other words, I will read Dostoevsky's penultimate novel as a sketch for the magnum opus that he never completed.

In *The Adolescent* Dostoevsky the artist and Dostoevsky the member of the *pochvennichestvo* movement come together in order to shape a plot of Russia's reformation (*perevospitanie*) during the post-reform period, which involves a twofold dialectic: first, the reconciliation between the Russian intellectuals of the so-called Petersburg period and their sons, the populists of the 1860s; and second, the reconciliation between the educated classes and the *narod*. Arkadii Dolgorukii's illegitimacy and his mixed origins (his father is a noble while his mother is a former serf) make him an heir of Russia's past contradictions and a genuine representative of the coming community. In this regard, Arkadii represents a Dostoevskian riposte to Tolstoy's Pierre Bezukhov – also an illegitimate offspring of a count and an unnamed (and probably peasant) mother, destined to become a leader of the Decembrists.[39]

We can distinguish several subordinate plot lines within the main plot of *The Adolescent*. One of these stories is focused on the *agon* between the young *raznochinets* Arkadii and his natural father, the nobleman Versilov. The story begins with their alienation one from each other, but as it proceeds, the father and son gradually come together and attain a genuine spiritual closeness, in contrast to the other father/son couple who represent different generational and intellectual directions, Stepan Trofimovich and Pyotr Verkhovenskii in *The Devils*. Although this closeness does not last, it is enough to allow Arkadii to get to know and forgive his sinful father. Another crucial idea underlying *The Adolescent* is that the maturation of the new generation of Russians, the generation of the *raznochintsy*, differs in some crucial ways from the maturation narratives composed by the authors who belong to the nobility like Pushkin and Tolstoy (who, according to Dostoevsky, were themselves products of the 'Petersburg' period). In contrast, Arkadii's maturation unfolds as he confronts the multifarious, chaotic world into which he is thrust by dint of his illegitimacy. Arkadii's 'accidental' upbringing, a consequence of his illegitimacy, also accounts for the unusually complex and even somewhat chaotic structure of the *Bildungsroman* of which he is the protagonist. As I will argue, this narrative structure with its multiple intertwined subplots was deliberately devised by Dostoevsky to emphasize the point about Arkadii's background and his complex identity. Arkadii is not a hero by virtue of his social position, but is, on the contrary, a hero because his mixed origin and his hectic upbringing partakes of all social strata and absorbs all ideological currents (*veiianiia*) of contemporary Russian life. In the course of his *Bildung*, Arkadii confronts various strata of the Russian society and gets fully involved in the contemporary social-historical process of disintegration (*razlozhenie*).[40] And if, at the end of his apprenticeship, Dostoevsky's hero does finally emerge as an integral personality with a robust sense of identity, it suggests that Russian society as a whole is capable of emerging from crisis and rebuilding itself as a unified nation.

Before we look more closely at the plot of Dostoevsky's penultimate novel it is helpful to survey, at least briefly, the literary and historical context surrounding its composition. In writing *The Adolescent*, Dostoevsky saw himself to a large degree as a legatee of the novelistic tradition created by Pushkin and carried forward by Dostoevsky's contemporaries, Turgenev and Tolstoy. However, he also intended to critique his predecessors. The history of *The Adolescent*'s creation takes us back to 1868, which saw the writing of Strakhov's celebrated essays on Tolstoy's *War and Peace*, in which he tried to establish Tolstoy's reputation as a leading national storyteller and consequently Pushkin's most faithful heir among contemporary authors.[41] Taking a cue from Apollon Grigor'ev, Strakhov suggested that *War and Peace* represents an authentically Russian epic tradition, embodied in an earlier generation by Pushkin's *Tales of Ivan Petrovich Belkin* and, especially, *The Captain's Daughter*. According to Strakhov, they were all essentially Russian family chronicles (*predan'ia russkogo semeistva*), which captured the true spirit of the Russian national character. The fact that Strakhov stresses the 'family' side of these epics and says almost nothing about their public or political dimension reveals his intellectual dependence on Grigor'ev's idea about the intrinsic 'meekness' of the Russian national character. It should be clear from my own analyses of *The Captain's Daughter* and *War and Peace* that these works were not only family chronicles, but genuine epics where everyday life is embedded in a larger historical framework. And yet, Strakhov is right to draw our attention to the fact that in these Russian epics, familial values prove indestructible even when subjected to the harshest historical trials. Rather than being overwhelmed and defined by history, the Russian family triumphs over history. In this sense, it is telling that even such strongly individualized heroes as Pierre Bezukhov are in the end nearly subsumed by the family ethos represented by the Rostov clan.

It was not until the spring of 1871 that Dostoevsky, travelling in Europe with his second wife, Anna Grigor'evna, in order to escape his creditors, read and responded to Strakhov's essays, which were published in 1870 in a newly established journal *Zaria* (*Dawn*).[42] Apparently, it was Dostoevsky's critical view of Tolstoy's *War and Peace* and his disagreement with the laudatory tone of Strakhov's essays that stirred a conflict between the two *pochvenniki*. Dostoevsky, who had already published *The Idiot* and was at work on *The Devils*, disagreed with Strakhov's enthusiasm for Tolstoy's national *epopeia*, calling it an example of 'landowner's literature' (*pomeschich'ia literatura*), an epithet that obviously offended Strakhov.[43]

Obviously the controversy over *War and Peace* was more than an expression of Dostoevsky's involuntary resentment against Tolstoy, his chief literary rival, with whom he had been fiercely competing since the late 1860s. By calling Tolstoy's work a piece of 'landowner's prose,' Dostoevsky draws attention to Tolstoy's underdeveloped social and class consciousness. In Dostoevsky's eyes, even Tolstoy's masterful portrayal of the Russian peasants in *War and Peace* cannot make him a genuinely national or *narodnyi* author. Arguing against Strakhov, Dostoevsky suggests that as a result of Tolstoy's 'lordliness,' that is, his sheltered position in life, he possesses a narrowed sense of reality. We can surmise from Dostoevsky's criticism of Tolstoy that Dostoevsky found Tolstoy's work lacking in a realistic vision of the Russian social structure. By situating his epic in the past, Tolstoy escaped from confronting the most difficult contemporary issues. Thus he avoided bringing on stage and scrutinizing the type of hero of whom he knew little and toward whom he felt an unconscious repugnance: the *intelligent-raznochinets*. Another aristocratic-born contemporary author, Turgenev, was audacious enough to focus his attention on this type of hero in his epochal work, *Fathers and Sons* (1862). Dostoevsky's novel focusing on the hero-*raznochinets* – an attempt to create an alternative to the Pushkinian and Tolstoyan 'family chronicles' set in noble clans – was possibly inspired by Turgenev. Even the first name of Dostoevsky's protagonist, Arkadii, reminds us of Turgenev's *Fathers and Sons*, although, of course, Dostoevsky's hero is socially and psychologically closer to Bazarov than to the weak and comparatively bland Arkadii Kirsanov.[44]

Prompted in part by his disagreement with Strakhov, Dostoevsky started recasting his plan for writing the life of the Russian everyman, the *Great Sinner*, as an epic based on the theme of 'fathers and sons.'[45] The first finished product that reflects this reorientation is the novel-pamphlet *The Devils*, in which Dostoevsky offers for the first time a historical explanation for nihilism, Russia's contemporary moral predicament. Through the use of an archetypal father-son pair, Stepan Trofimovich and Pyotr Verkhovenskii, Doestoevsky dramatizes his idea that the foundations for contemporary nihilism were laid by the liberal intelligentsia of the 1840s generation, that is to say, by those who, like himself, sought the truth in the works of Charles Fourier and Ludwig Feuerbach, instead of turning their attention to their native culture. As Joseph Frank has shown, *The Devils*, whose story centres on a well-known political conspiracy that received broad coverage in the Russian newspapers, is certainly more than a lampoon of the revolutionary Sergei Nechaev and the circle known as *nechayevtsy*.[46] In this novel Dostoevsky puts on trial both the younger generation of the Russian intellectuals and the generation of their fathers, who stand indicted for their inability to provide a genuine lesson and good guidance to their sons. The destiny of 'young Russia' – not the failed political organization mentioned earlier, but the whole young generation of Russians – is what is ultimately at stake in Dostoevsky's novel.

The Devils, Dostoevsky's darkest work, does not represent Dostoevsky's last word on the subject of 'father and sons,' nor does it offer a wholly pessimistic diagnosis of Russian modernity. As can be gleaned from the epigraph to this novel, whose symbolic significance is revealed in the deathbed scene of Stepan Trofimovich Verkhovenskii, the multiple deaths at the end of this novel symbolize the purgation of Russia's demonic spirit. This spirit of the age – represented through the figure of the father Verkhovenskii, a prototypical westernizer modelled on T.N. Granovskii – emerged in Russia as a result of Peter the Great's reforms and spread with renewed intensity after the War of 1812. This 'Petersburg period' (to use Grigor'ev's term) was the period of negation. However, following the dialectical law of spirit's evolution, this epoch of negativity would eventually have to be subjected to negation, yielding some positive results.[47] Thus a hopeful spirit can be discerned in some of the entries in the notebooks to *The Devils*.[48]

Dostoevsky's drafts and notebooks from his sojourn in Europe (1869–74) show that he was in fact constantly at work on a macroscopic novelistic plot in which he would be able to express his hopeful vision of Russia's future within the dramatization of its troublesome present. Thus, one of the recurrent motifs in Dostoevsky's notebooks from this period is the motif of childhood, for children organically embody the human future.[49] Yet children are, of course, under the rule of the adult world, and are organized in families and school according to the principles laid down by adults. Dostoevsky played with the paradox of the theme of the 'children's club' in which a children's 'conspiracy' would actually effect adult society. This was originally meant to be one of the leading themes in *The Idiot*, the novel that greatly pleased Strakhov. However, in its final version, the role of the children is relatively limited as compared to the original plan. The protagonist of *The Idiot*, who is raised away from society in a Swiss mental asylum and thus remains a kind of an overgrown child, is also transformed in the course of the writing from a sublime into a tragicomic figure. These changes suggest that Dostoevsky met with significant difficulties when he tried to reconcile his optimistic vision of Russia's future, which he connected with the idea of the 'children's club,' and the image of Prince Myshkin, with his sober awareness of the actual socio-political and cultural environment. Prince Lev Nikolaevich Myshkin, who in the drafts of *The Idiot* is presented as the head of this club and in the final version ends up becoming a leader of the children in a Swiss village, organizing them on a crusade against the philistinism of the adults, recalls the Lev Tolstoy whose work as the educator of peasant children and publisher of *Iasnaia Poliana* was supported by *pochvenniki*.[50] This echo of Tolstoy's pedagogic activities suggests the respect Dostoevsky felt for Tolstoy as a pioneer of popular education. Dostoevsky was impressed by Tolstoy's repeated attempts to go to the 'people,' genuinely trying to immerse himself in the world of peasant life and thus forge a link between European culture and the *narod*.

As I showed in my analysis of *War and Peace* in the previous chapter, Tolstoy and Dostoevsky were both confronted with the same aesthetic question, namely, how to represent the budding 'young Russia,' in whose existence they both believed. But if Tolstoy chose to look back to 1812, by all accounts the most glorious and hopeful year of Russia's modern history, Dostoevsky focused on the contemporary life and on the future, often centring his narratives on themes that concern childhood and adolescence either directly or indirectly. Dostoevsky's national narratives are future-oriented and possess an eschatological dimension. His fascination with the theme of the 'children's club' bespeak his desire to use the child as a symbol of the world's openness to redemption, a correlate to the biblical injunction that 'a child would lead them.'[51] In this sense, the child is the most concrete manifestation of what Hannah Arendt calls 'natality,' the potential for a new beginning, which is always present in our world before the end of time.[52]

The notebooks to *The Life of a Great Sinner*, which provided material for *The Idiot*, *The Devils*, and *The Adolescent*, show Dostoevsky's eagerness to infuse the images of adult heroes with childishness, to merge the adult and the child in one character, or to create a truly childlike hero. Such a hero is at once father and son, a figure both of wisdom and of innocence. In creating such a hero, Dostoevsky sought to stage the development of a character who would represent the polarities of Russian history, the painful divides between the elite and the peasants, enlightenment and faith, the generation of the 1840s and the generation of the 1860s, but also be capable of transcending them and making a genuinely new beginning. And although Dostoevsky (by contrast with Tolstoy, who portrays childhood in idyllic terms) typically focuses on the more troubled and dark aspects of Russian childhood, one can always sense in Dostoevsky's fiction a desire to negate the negative and arrive at happiness and maturity.

Bakhtin has tried to sever Dostoevsky from the Bildungsroman tradition. However, if we are attentive to the temporal regime crystallized in Dostoevsky's use of children and adolescents, who represent human potentiality for growth, it appears that Bakhtin's elevation of the hero of *Notes from the Underground* as a quintessential Dostoevskian hero is rather biased. For Bakhtin, the Underground Man, with his acute self-consciousness, is a kind of gloss on all future Dostoevskian heroes, a key as to how to read them. Undoubtedly *Notes from the Underground*, written while Dostoevsky was keeping vigil at the deathbed of his first wife, struck its author as an important stage in his maturation, and has struck his readers since as representing the pinnacle of his critical self-consciousness. Dostoevsky's famous diary entry, in which he identifies spiritual damnation or sin with the inability to genuinely love another soul, sheds light on this painful moment in the writer's life.[53] However, in Dostoevsky, the deeper the consciousness of one's sinfulness, the stronger one's desire to achieve redemption. As the narrator of *The House of the Dead* makes clear, the hope of spiritual regeneration survives even in the souls of the cruellest of criminals. The Underground Man, too, secretly seeks redemption, although his sadomasochistic attachment to pain prevents him from trying to reform himself. In the last decade of his life, however, Dostoevsky tried as it were to rewrite *Notes from the Underground* as a Bildungsroman, where the underground consciousness undergoes reform and re-education. While Dostoevsky's heroes are stubbornly protective of negation in the face of various kinds of false enlightenments, from political radicalism to the liberal contempt for the people, the negation is ultimately instrumental: the heroic quest is for redemption and reconciliation.

The Adolescent can be read as a revision of *Notes from the Underground*. Both works are structured as first-person autobiographical narratives that portray heroes suffering from alienation. In this regard both works bear a resemblance to Rousseau's *Confessions*. However, as evidenced by the drafts of *The Adolescent*, there are some new motifs in this work that were absent from *Notes from the Underground*. One of these new motifs is the motif of childhood, which was originally supposed to become one of the leitmotifs of the novel. In drafting his Bildungsroman, Dostoevsky tries to imagine the world free from underground anxiety and *ressentiment*, a world populated by children or childlike persons; this is how I would interpret the jottings that refer to the 'children's republic' or 'children's monarchy.'[54] This dream of a childlike state will ultimately culminate in the famous 'Dream of a Ridiculous Man.'

In *The Adolescent* Dostoevsky not only puts the underground mentality on trial, but finally – toward the very end of the novel – transcends it. Unlike the hero of *Notes from the Underground*, who exemplifies alienated self-consciousness, Arkadii Dolgorukii is a *growing* youth[55] who actively works through his painful memories, overcoming his hatred for his father and liberating himself from the 'underground' in both the social and a moral-philosophical senses of the term.[56] In the afterword to *The Adolescent*, Nikolai Semyonovich, Arkadii's 'mentor' (whom we never meet in the novel itself), compares Arkadii's autobiography with similar autobiographies written by the representatives of 'landowner's literature' (*pomeschich'ia literatura*) and argues that the story written by Arkadii, a typical representative of the *raznochintsy*, is a genuinely new step in the history of Russia's self-consciousness.[57] The author of *The Adolescent* sets out to transcend the negative 'Petersburg period' in the history of Russian literature and culture, the stage that produced such authors as Pushkin, Lermontov, Turgenev, and Tolstoy (as the author of *War and Peace*). While these aristocratic authors approached their literary characters with very specific, classical biographical norms in mind – the forms that corresponded to the aristocratic conventions of honour and duty – Dostoevsky brings onstage a protagonist who is thrown into the world without any such moral or aesthetic compass. A representative of what Dostoevsky calls an 'accidental family,' Arkadii Dolgorukii represents a qualitatively new type of personality, one that has emerged in post-reform Russia. Arkadii overtly expresses his desire for a new literary form – one that is not conventionally 'literary' – in order to give a candid account of his experience. Arkadii's desire is for a form that necessarily differs both from Dostoevsky's earlier works and from the 'family chronicles' and narratives of apprenticeship by other Russian authors.

The connection between *The Adolescent* and Tolstoy's *War and Peace* has been thoroughly analysed by the critics.[58] However, upon a more careful examination of the sources, it appears that the target of Dostoevsky's polemic in *The Adolescent* is not only or perhaps not even so much Tolstoy himself, but rather his former fellow *pochvennik* Strakhov. Thus when Dostoevsky's Nikolai Semyonovich attacks the 'landowner's' literary tradition confined by the aristocratic 'forms of honour and duty' (*formy chesti i dolga*), he clearly alludes to Strakhov's essays on Tolstoy, where Strakhov compares *War and Peace* to *The Captain's Daughter* as genuine Russian family chronicles.[59] These works, says Strakhov, depict the formation of Russian national identity as one based on the hereditary norms of honour and duty. Stressing the liberal-conservative side of Pushkin's ideology, which underlay Pushkin's presentation of the Grinev family as an idealized noble family and a core of the Russian nation in *The Captain's Daughter*, Strakhov argues that this aristocratic tradition represents the most vital contemporary tendency.[60] Dostoevsky, for all his respect for Strakhov's unfailing commitment to the conciliatory ideology of *pochvennichestvo*, could not agree with this particular claim, because it went against his own firm conviction that the future of the Russian nation depended on the cultural synthesis of the 'Petersburg period' and the traditional Russia. This synthesis would produce a major qualitative change in the Russian mentality, erasing deeply ingrained feelings of social difference and inequality.

Ultimately, the clash between Dostoevsky and Strakhov, which becomes evident in the afterword to *The Adolescent*, has to do with the different positions that these two former *pochvenniki* occupied in the debate on national education, which broke out with new vigour and intensity in 1873–4. In this new debate, Strakhov remained in the camp of aristocratic conservative liberals, whereas Dostoevsky sought to realize his dream of the pan-national synthesis by acting as a conciliator between the liberals and the radicals, who by this time had transformed themselves into populists. As A.S. Dolinin has argued, although Dostoevsky may not have originally intended to publish *The Adolescent* in the progressive journal *Sovremennik*, his willingness to do so bespeaks his readiness to engage in a conversation with the audience of *Sovre-*

mennik, an audience sharply opposed to that of the arch-conservative *Grazhdanin* (*The Citizen*), on whose editorial board Dostoevsky had served just months before the publication of *The Adolescent*.[61]

But how can we explain Dostoevsky's sudden attempt to fling himself into the left-wing debates at the risk of losing a number of his old friends and loyal readers?

Again, I believe the answer to this thorny problem can be found by examining Dostoevsky's penultimate novel in the context of the national debate surrounding the issue of national education (*narodnoe obrazovanie*). In 1873 Alexander II published an imperial manifesto to the nobility in which he solicited their help in the most urgent task of educating the masses. This was a delicate manoeuvre on the part of the Tsar, who was aware of the disgruntled mood among an aristocracy that had seen many of its privileges curtailed or lost as a result of the Great Reforms.[62] (Alexander II's 1856 appeal to the Moscow gentry, cited in the previous chapter, included a similar point about the crucial role of the nobles in educating the serfs and preparing them for freedom.) This new appeal certainly did not amount to the restoration of the traditional estate privileges, but was intended as a way of assuaging the nobility by restoring their magnanimous aristocratic self-image.

The spokesmen for the more conservative nobles, General Rostislav Fadeev, responded to the imperial manifesto by publishing an article that celebrated the role of the nobility in the history of Russia's enlightenment and attacked the democratic intelligentsia as usurpers trying to hijack the educational system in order to lead the country away from its authentic cultural roots. Outraged by Fadeev's attack on the intelligentsia, the populist Nikolai Konstantinovich Mikhailovskii mounted a counter-attack on the conservatives on the pages of *The Contemporary*. He argued that, Fadeev and *Vestnik Evropy* to the contrary, the Russian culture (*obrazovannost'*) and the Russian intelligentsia were not two separate movements led by different groups of people, but in fact mutually interpenetrated one another. The intelligentsia that had emerged over the course of the struggle to create a Russian culture included both the best representatives of the hereditary nobility, those who came from the middle ranks, and even those who came from the peasantry. These people were united in their sense of a shared responsibility for Russia's fate and a will to serve the Russian people. True nobility, according to Mikhailovskii, consisted in generosity of spirit and a readiness to sacrifice one's privileges for the sake of the entire nation. Therefore, instead of trying to assert their privileges, the hereditary nobles would do better to join those democratic intellectuals like himself and his colleagues from *Sovremennik* who were engaged in the task of improving the people's lot.

The Adolescent allows us to surmise that Dostoevsky largely agreed with Mikahilovskii's point and thus found himself in opposition to Strakhov, a conservative and anti-populist. Dostoevsky, unlike Strakhov and Fadeev, became convinced that in Russia the 'aristocracy' should not be seen as a social status based on hereditary privileges, but was, rather, a special noble disposition of the mind acquired either through family traditions or through self-cultivation, or both. This is the message that Prince Myshkin, an impoverished bearer of one of Russia's most ancient names, tries to convey to a group of aristocratic guests gathered at the Epanchins' party.[63] The fact that *Sovremennik* took a firm stand in the debate on education, calling on the hereditary nobility and the intelligentsia to join their efforts in the task of educating the people, must have produced a very positive impression on Dostoevsky, who had expressed very similar views in the essays he published in *Time* in 1861–2.[64]

Like Pushkin's *The Captain's Daughter*, *The Adolescent* is stylized as the memoirs written from the superior vantage point of age and maturity and describing the youth of their author, Arkadii Dolgorukii. But unlike Pushkin's Grinev, who is proud to be the son of his dignified father, and also unlike Turgenev's Arkadii Kirsanov, who, underneath his veneer of intellectual superiority and condescension, still loves and respects his father, Dostoevsky's Arkadii suffers from an acute identity crisis stemming from the fact that he is the illegitimate son of a landowner named Versilov and his former serf, Sophia, although Sophia is legally married to a much older serf named Makar Dolgorukii.[65] Versilov's and Sophia's son bears Makar's last name, which also happens to be the name of one of Russia's princely families – a detail that plays an important role in the development of Arkadii's self-consciousness, for in society Arkadii is constantly made to feel ashamed of being a Dolgorukii without being a prince.

However, as Arkadii's first name suggests, the hero of *The Adolescent* is destined for happiness. The term that Dostoevsky uses to define the goal of Arkadii's quest is *blagoobrazie*.[66] A semantic fusion of *blago* (the good) and *obraz* (the image or, in German, *Bild*), the term *blagoobrazie* implies both ethical and aesthetic perfection. Its antonym is *bezobrazie*, another keyword that we frequently encounter on the pages of Dostoevsky's notebooks to *The Life of a Great Sinner* and *The Adolescent*, where it functions as a synonym of *besporiadok* or 'chaos,' which was supposed to be the novel's original title.[67] 'Society is undergoing a chemical dissolution' (*obschestvo khimicheski razlagaet'sia*), claims Dostoevsky in the notebooks to *The Adolescent*,[68] echoing a theme in Grigor'ev and Strakhov, who also frequently claimed that contemporary Russian society was caught up in a process of dissolution, which continually brings to the surface situations that appear both chaotic and aesthetically formless or ugly (*bezobrazno*).[69]

The task of the novelist under these conditions is to discern within this chaos the image of a new order that will emerge once the old forms of life completely disappear from view. In *The Adolescent* the apocalyptic imagination is intertwined with the pedagogical dream, allowing Dostoevsky to pursue a new artistic and intellectual goal: to show a hero whose soul has been malformed as a result of an 'accidental' upbringing re-educating himself. Thus the hero who will emerge as a result of the moral and aesthetic re-education will also represent a qualitatively new personality, one possessed of *blagoobrazie*. In this connection, it is important to bear in mind that the root of *blagoobrazie* and *bezobrazie*, the Russian word *obraz* (which means both 'image' and 'icon'), also constitutes the root of *obrazovanie*, education. In *The Adolescent*, Dostoevsky masterfully plays on the semantic breadth of the word *obraz* and its various cognates, demonstrating how they simultaneously have theological, aesthetic, pedagogic, and socio-historical implications. Through the prism of Arkadii Dolgorukii's identity crisis and its resolution, Dostoevsky wants to provide us with a blueprint for the re-education as well as the spiritual resurrection of the entire Russian society as it undergoes the transition of the Reform era.

Given Dostoevsky's image of the Russian community divided between an elite and a peasantry who are both fragments of one whole, Dostoevsky's choice of a hero like Arkadii Dolgorukii, an illegitimate son of a nobleman and a peasant, obviously satisfies his criteria for finding a symbol of young Russia to serve as a testing ground for the formation of a new personality. Arkadii's self-possessed maturity – the starting point for his memoirs – is the result of his coming to terms with his dual identity as half-peasant and half-noble. In writing his memoirs, Dostoevsky's hero transforms his social marginality into a viable new identity. Of course, Dostoevsky was not the first Russian author to concern himself with the plight of those who found themselves outside of traditional estate identities and, having acquired self-consciousness and some education, struggled to shape a new identity, one that came to be associated with the idea of the intelligentsia. Indeed, as I have suggested earlier, Arkadii Dolgorukii represents Dostoevsky's attempt to address the issue of *raznochintsy*, which had already been tackled by Turgenev, Chernyshevskii, and other authors. In this connection, A.S. Dolinin's suggestion that the editor of *Sovremennik*, the poet Nikolai Nekrasov, might have served as the prototype for the character of Arkadii Dolgorukii seems historically appropriate.[70]

However, there is another important connection that so far has not been mentioned by the critics, that is, the connection between Dostoevsky's representation of the accidental upbringing of Arkadii Dolgorukii in *The Adolescent* and Apollon Grigor'ev's autobiography, *My Literary and Moral Wanderings*.[71] Like Arkadii Dolgorukii, Grigor'ev was born as an illegitimate son of a noble father and a peasant mother. Although he was educated at home, rather than at a French boarding school, his unhappy childhood has much in common with the 'accidental' education of Dostoevsky's hero. One of Grigor'ev's ideas that Dostoevsky absorbed and used not only in *The Adolescent* but also in *The Brothers Karamazov* is that an 'accidental' upbringing and a life full of diverse experiences and adventures can create a truly 'broad' personality. Under certain conditions, this kind of experiential and spiritual breadth can result in greatness:

> According to Sand's deep observation, there exist *des hommes forts* – strong people, and *des hommes grands* – great people. According to a deep observation of Ernst Renan, one of the most original and independent contemporary thinkers, there are *des pensées étroites* – narrow thoughts, and *des pensées larges* – broad thoughts. 'Only narrow thoughts rule the world,' adds Renan, and he is quite justified. And if we cannot conclude Sand's idea in the same way, we can find an affinity between his idea and Renan's. There are broad people: they become either great people or the Oblomovs; and there are strong people, who can sometimes and even oftentimes become great people, but can never become the Oblomovs.[72]

In portraying his own maturation, which occurred in the 1840s, as a series of 'wanderings,' Grigor'ev suggests that he is a 'broad' personality. As a student of Hegel, Grigor'ev views his own autobiography as a single example of a larger historical process. Thus Grigor'ev comes to view his 'wanderings' as a symptom of Russia's social, ideological, and spiritual crisis. Whether or not Grigor'ev's personality and, by implication, his entire generation attain genuine 'greatness' is the question that the author leaves open, inviting the reader to reflect on the legacy of the 1840s and on the destiny of the generation of *raznochintsy* who came of age during this time. Echoing Grigor'ev, Dostoevsky comes to see the psychological and spiritual 'breadth' acquired through a troubled, non-traditional upbringing as a sign of an unusually talented and even messianic personality. 'Breadth' in Dostoevsky means the ability to sympathize with a wide range of emotions and moral sentiments. In a much-cited passage from *The Brothers Karamazov* Dmitrii will argue that a human being is too broad and has too many contradictory sides to her character. Thus, foreshadowing Dmitrii Karamazov, Arkadii Dolgorukii wonders whether human 'breadth' is an advantage or a curse, whether it can serve as a stepping stone to greatness or just keeps one from making a moral choice: 'I've marveled a thousand times at this ability of man (and it seems of the Russian man above all) to cherish the highest ideal in his soul alongside the greatest baseness, and all that in perfect sincerity. Whether it's a special breadth in the Russian man, which will take him far, or simply baseness – that's the question!'[73]

Assuming that Grigor'ev's autobiography served as one of the inspirations for *The Adolescent,* we can make a hypothesis that Dostoevsky's intention was to portray a personality who, in the course of his apprenticeship, scales the depths of human nature and acquires a broad vision of human experience in order then to convert this 'breadth' into a positive spiritual force. This assumption would explain the structure of the narrative, which many critics consider rather unpolished and chaotic.[74] I would argue, however, that the narrative shape of *The Adolescent* accords with Dostoevsky's idea of *Bildung*. Arkadii's emergence as a Russian 'new man' (*novyi chelovek*, in the sense this term was used by the 1860s authors, but given a slightly new sense) constitutes the main narrative axis. However, this story consists of a number of separate subplots, all of which contribute to the ultimate goal of Arkadii's emergence from the negativity, or contradiction, of his hybrid upbringing. The most well developed among these subplots centres on Arkadii's relationship with his newly rediscovered father, Versilov. The other stories develop in parallel to this central story and sometimes intersect with it. Thus Arkadii falls romantically in love with the same woman whom Versilov has been following across Europe, Mme Akhmakova. Without knowing it, he becomes entangled in the blackmailing of Akhmakova organized by his school friend Lambert. He gets to know Akhmakova's father, the old Prince Sokol'skii, who instructs the youth in atheism. He also encounters and befriends the young Prince Sokol'skii, a penniless adventurer who seduces Arkadii's sister Liza.

By chance, he is entangled by his half-sister Anna Andreevna Versilova in the intrigues surrounding the old Prince Solkol'skii's will. Finally, he gets involved with a group of revolutionaries and becomes privy to their ideological waverings (*shatan'ia*).

By entering into such a number of frays, Dostoevsky's 'accidental' youth exposes himself to various instructive, helpful, confusing, and harmful influences that help him acquire the kind of depth that Dostoevsky requires of the new Russian hero. In being so marginal, he also, paradoxically, becomes representative of the Russian youth of the 1870s. Compared to the heroes of Pushkin, Tolstoy, and Turgenev, he emerges from the pages of his account as a qualitatively new person in Russian literature.

The main challenge facing Dostoevsky's hero is to acquire this wisdom without losing his sense of direction or telos. As Strakhov points out in *The World as Whole* (published as a monograph in 1872, at the time when Dostoevsky was working on *The Adolescent*), the strength of an organism is measured by its capacity for assimilating the various environmental influences it becomes exposed to. A weak organism or a weak person may not survive such exposure, which inevitably involves structural changes within its own core. Strakhov's book is now nearly forgotten, but in it he articulates a metaphysics of organisms (including both natural organisms and humanity, which for Strakhov constitutes the intermediary stage between nature and spirit) that is certainly congenial to Dostoevsky's vision of humanity as an organism evolving toward the Christian moral ideal:

> The more elements influence a stone and the longer they influence it, the more they destroy the stone. It is rather the contrary with human beings: different influences not only fail to destroy a person, but rather fortify his individual personality. Indeed, they assist his development. We can express this idea simply and correctly by saying that a human being adopts something when someone influences him. To adopt means to appropriate, to add to one's own nature and to one's own essence. So the essence of a human person grows as this person experiences various influences. This is not a mechanical accumulation that heaps everything into a single pile, but rather a self-propelled, internal growth.[75]

Arkadii and Versilov

Inspired by the figures of the intellectuals of the 'Petersburg period,' in particular A.I. Herzen and P.Ia. Chaadaev, Versilov is a complex and intriguing character. The figure of Versilov is also genealogically linked to Stavrogin and the putative protagonist of *The Life of a Great Sinner*.[76] At the outset of the narrative, Arkadii, who saw his natural father only once as a child, is painfully curious about Versilov, but tries to hide his curiosity by assuming an air of independence and even superiority. Nonetheless, deep down Arkadii is pained and ashamed by various rumours that have reached him, such as the one that Versilov had once dishonourably refused to fight a duel. Arkadii believes that his own illegitimacy is proof of his father's dishonourable behaviour toward his mother (Versilov enjoyed her youth and beauty, but never married her and tried to marry other women in the meantime). Therefore, when father and son meet in Petersburg in part 1 of the novel, Arkadii assumes that Versilov is a scoundrel whom he must despise. However, it turns out that Versilov is not so easily understood and assigned a precise identity, for he, too, is a 'broad' personality, swayed by emotions and driven toward contradictory ends. As soon as he enters the stage, Versilov – to use Mikhail Bakhtin's terms – begins to resist his adolescent son's attempt to 'finalize' ('consummate') his character.[77] In fact, Versilov's powerful ego threatens to hijack the position of narrative centrality and relegate Arkadii to the status of a mere witness of Versilov's egotistical adventures. Their relationship turns into a duel of consciousnesses and wills.[78]

The confrontation between Arkadii and Versilov, a typical Grigor'evan Russian 'Byronic' hero, plays out as a competition for the role of the protagonist, which, as Alex Woloch convincingly argues, undermines the narrator's claims to omniscience and creates narrative asymmetry.[79] Woloch considers this type of narrative structure to be one of the commonest in the modern European novel, serving to frame, on the level of representation, the emergence of psychologically and intellectually distinct characters endowed with unique inwardness and personal identity, which unfolds on the level of content. As Woloch shows, in many nineteenth-century novels it is usually the character with a stronger, more compelling inwardness or 'ego' who ends up becoming the centre of the narrative's attention, relegating others to the status of secondary characters.[80] Indeed, in Dostoevsky's novel, Versilov's enigmatic and charming ego powerfully claims our attention, threatening to marginalize Arkadii (who is so preoccupied with Versilov's mysterious personality that this enigma becomes constitutive of Arkadii's own inwardness). As we learn from the story, Versilov is indeed accustomed to playing leading roles. It is a telling detail that the adolescent's only recollection of his father – one that is practically etched into his memory – is that of Versilov playing the role of the brilliant yet tragic (or tragicomic) Chatskii from Alexander Griboiedov's *Woe from Wit* at the home theatre.

How, then, does Arkadii manage to share 'his' narrative space with Versilov, and assert himself as the protagonist in his own story? At first he tries to assert his own identity – to set his own tune, so to speak – by dreaming about becoming rich like a Rothschild. The idea of wealth is Arkadii's own theme, one that distinguishes him and his generation from the generation represented by the reckless landowner Versilov. However, this 'idea' does not carry him very far. Even Arkadii's immature attempts to assert his own individuality by adopting a 'monomaniac' idea to become 'as rich as a Rothschild' is subverted by the appearance of Versilov, which powerfully takes a hold of Arkadii's psyche. The competition for narrative centrality between Arkadii and Versilov drives home the idea that in a psychological novel a character is destined to be marginalized if not completely misrepresented unless he himself somehow seizes control over representation and, rather than acquiescing to a story that someone else is telling, begins to author his own narrative. If we look into Dostoevsky's creative laboratory – the notebooks to *The Adolescent* – we discover that Dostoevsky hesitated before deciding which of these two heroes was to become 'the narrative centre' of the novel. Ultimately he decided to make Arkadii the main narrator. In this way, Arkadii's very position as the teller of the story allows him, as the son, to 'consummate' his father's narrative and thus finally ascend to the position of the protagonist. Only after a painstaking artistic search and experimentation did Dostoevsky decide to transform the novel, originally entitled *Disorder* (*Besporiadok*) and intended as a drama depicting the dissociation of a Russian family and, by extension, society, into a more optimistic Bildungsroman that portrays the transformation of an unhappy, alienated adolescent into a self-possessed personality.[81] Throughout the novel, the emergence of Versilov in, as it were, Arkadii's consciousness is one of the great events of Arkadii's inner as well as exterior life, thus helping Arkadii himself to emerge from his mental 'underground' and acquire self-respect. Indeed, if at the outset of the novel Arkadii, much like the Underground Man, feels resentful against his father and the entire world, in which his father cuts a notable figure while he, the illegitimate son, is condemned to marginality and perpetual minority, in the course of the narrative Arkadii comes to shake off his minority, becoming a hero on par with Versilov; to use Bakhtin's terms, he attains complete polyphonic equality with Versilov. In the end, Arkadii completely liberates himself from Versilov's influence, winning the struggle for the role of the protagonist. However, the image of Versilov that emerges in the course of the narrative is much more favourable and nuanced than the one with which we are presented at its outset. As the son 'consummates' his father and leaves him behind, he also forgives him.

Michael Holquist's observation that in order to reach maturity novelistic sons must become fathers, made in connection with *The Brothers Karamazov*, seems apropos in the case of *The Adolescent* as well.[82] As Arkadii Dolgorukii's story makes clear, becoming a father means not so much literally fathering a child (for this evidently does not in itself promote self-consciousness and responsibility) as it does overcoming one's insecurity and learning to stand upright on one's two feet, like a true hero.[83] In Dostoevsky, maturation also means learning how to respect and care for others. As Arkadii outgrows his adolescence, he comes to recognize Versilov's point of view as valid and also to forgive Versilov on an emotional level.[84] The intellectual and emotional dialectics unfold hand in hand throughout the novel. The first one aims at polyphony, whereas the second one aims at love or *agape*.

At this juncture, both Bakhtin and Engel'gardt contribute useful points to our discussion. I have already used Bakhtin's notion that a character can be 'finalized' or 'consummated' by another. Similarly, I have shown that Dostoevsky, far from rejecting Hegel's philosophy, engaged with it, as did Grigor'ev and Shakhov. Thus, I can see that there is an angle from which Engel'gardt is right to interpret the dynamic in *The Adolescent* as an instance of the Hegelian dialectic of consciousness. However, neither of them is fully accurate. As I have mentioned earlier, Bakhtin's theory shows its limitations insofar as it fails to take into account the historiosophical dimension of Dostoevsky's later novels, which were intended as allegories of Russia's coming of age as a nation. Engel'gardt's interpretation of *The Adolescent* as an instance of the Hegelian dialectic of consciousness is limited, because it does not recognize the presence of polyphony in this novel.[85] Thus, while it is the adolescent's goal to come to understand Versilov and accept his legacy, father and son retain distinct identities. Versilov's narrative retains its unique signifying potential, one that Arkadii can 'consummate' only in his capacity as a narrator, but never as a hero within the story.

Dostoevsky never completely erases alterity from his *Bildungsgeschichte*. As soon as Arkadii attains his full independence from Versilov, who eventually falls apart as a personality, turning prematurely senile like the older Prince Sokol'skii, a new strong father figure – Makar Dolgorukii – emerges on the horizon. At the end of the story, Arkadii is only just venturing into his new life. Presumably, mature self-consciousness is not the end point of Arkadii's Bildung. The ultimate end of Bildung, according to Dostoevsky, is a transformation into a higher, more spiritual being. Leaving behind his 'underground' self, Arkadii completes the preliminary stage of Bildung as outlined in Dostoevsky's drafts to this novel and to his projected *The Life of a Great Sinner*. To attain the next stage, he must strive toward a loftier, transcendent ideal.[86]

To get a better sense of Arkadii's unfinished *Bildungsgeschichte*, let us trace the development of the Arkadii-Versilov subplot through the rest of the novel. To show the gradual narrowing of distance between father and son, Dostoevsky infuses Arkadii with a feeling of intense curiosity about everything that concerns Versilov. Arkadii is especially anxious to grasp the essence of Versilov's relationship with Arkadii's mother because understanding and forgiving his father's relationship with the former serf Sophia is the key to resolving his own identity crisis and conquering his own 'underground' instincts. Is he a child of love or rather a progeny of sin, exploitation, and perhaps even violence? This crucial question is raised in the first part of the novel, when Versilov and the seventeen-year-old Arkadii meet in Petersburg for the first time in many years. Arkadii has just finished his studies at Touchard's boarding school in Moscow and has moved to Petersburg in order to realize his monomaniac dream to become as rich as a Rothschild. Versilov tries to persuade the adolescent that his relationship with Sophia was completely natural and spontaneous – not a passing fancy, or an exercise of the ancient droit de seigneur. But despite his lifelong closeness to Sophia, Versilov is still perplexed by her. He tells Arkadii that throughout their twenty-year long-liaison, he and Arkadii's mother never developed any intellectual connection, never even discussed anything or quarrelled; and yet there was a deep and unaccountable intimacy that kept them together despite their unbridgeable culture gap:

> 'All these twenty years, your mother and I have lived in complete silence,' he began his palaver (affected and unnatural in the highest degree), 'and all that has been between us has taken place in silence. The main quality of our twenty-year-long liaison has been – speechlessness. I don't think we even quarreled once. True, I often went away and left her alone, but in the end I always came back. *Nous revenons toujours*, that's a fundamental

quality of men; it's owing to their magnanimity. If the matter of marriage depended on women alone, no marriage would stay together. Humility, meekness, lowliness, and at the same time firmness, strength, real strength – that is your mother's character. Note that she is the best of all the women I've met in the world. And that there is strength in her – that I can testify to; I've seen how that strength nourishes her. Whether it's a matter, I wouldn't say of convictions, there can be no proper convictions here, but of what they consider convictions, which, to their minds, also means sacred, there even torture would be to no avail. [. . .] I'll say, by the way, in parenthesis, that for some reason I suspect she never believed in my humanness, and therefore always trembled; but while trembling, at the same time she never yielded to any culture. They somehow know how to do it, and there's something here we don't understand, and generally they know better than we how to manage their own affairs. They can go on living in their own way in situations that are most unnatural for them, and remain completely themselves in situations that are most not their own. We can't do that.' (125)

By 'they' Versilov means the Russian peasants or *narod*, of which Sophia is a typical representative. Despite her 'sin' (she abandons her lawful husband Makar Dolgorukii and becomes Versilov's common-law wife), Sophia possesses dignity and commands respect from everyone, including Versilov himself. Sophia remains largely silent in the novel and is represented only through the points of view of others – Versilov, Arkadii, and Makar – so that her willingness to give herself to Versilov is never quite explained. Sophia's quiet devotion, which bespeaks her typically Russian selflessness and kenotic self-abnegation, can hardly be accounted for in rational terms. Therefore her and Versilov's mysterious bond can never be reduced to the terms of a marriage contract, which, in any case, is absent. As Versilov points out, Sophia and he never culturally approach each other, each retaining his or her own separate worlds and values. And yet their liaison, devoid of any kind of intellectual or legal foundation, can never dissolve because it rests on a deep organic foundation. No matter how many other women tempt Versilov and stir his vivid imagination, the uprooted nobleman cannot help but return to his peasant lover, his single anchor in the world.

This organic marriage is presented in terms that are recognizably borrowed from the *pochvenniki* thesis of the divide between, on the one hand, Russia's uprooted cultural elite, who display features of what Grigor'ev called the 'predator' type, and, on the other, their native soil, which produces typically 'meek' persons. The task of accounting for this mysterious, albeit fully natural union falls to Versilov's and Sophia's son, Arkadii, who needs to justify or at least come to terms with his parents' 'sin' in order to attain a more wholesome identity.[87] Thus Arkadii keeps thinking about Versilov and his mother throughout the novel, as he witnesses a number of other affairs that unfold in front of him, such as his sister Liza's affair with the young Prince Sokol'skii, which seems to repeat motifs in their mother's affair with Versilov. Moreover, even the young Prince has the air of being a bad copy of Versilov, a double with much less brilliance and magnanimity than the original; as it turns out, Liza, unlike her mother Sophia, does have some degree of self-consciousness and pride, for she suffers intensely when the Prince turns out to be a scoundrel involved in illegal financial machinations. The subplot involving Liza and the young Prince offsets Versilov's twenty-year-long liaison with Sophia, making it look more dignified by comparison. This subplot also forces Arkadii to confront his chief enemy, his father, as the youth associates his sister's dishonour and acute moral suffering with his own experience of his 'underground feelings,' that is, his shame, self-hatred, and anger against his oppressors.

Inwardly, Versilov secretly longs to be redeemed, but outwardly, he acts with aplomb and boldness, treating his son with condescension and at first even cruelly mocking him. Under this guise, he lets the insecure adolescent know that he, Versilov, can see through him and guesses his grand 'idea' – to become rich, independent, and aloof from others. Versilov's insight troubles Arkadii. He does not realize that it is in fact Versilov who is acting out of insecurity – he does not dare seek his son's forgiveness. Dismayed and undermined by Versilov, the adolescent begins to falter and finally loses his resolve to live for the sake of his 'idea.' In part 2 of the novel he seems to have abandoned his plan altogether. Instead of saving money in order to become rich and aloof, Arkadii is now living carelessly and foppishly. Taking advantage of the adolescent's naïveté and his disturbed, vulnerable state of mind, the young Prince Sokol'skii generously starts lending him money, without informing him that his sister Liza has been the Prince's mistress for several months and is now pregnant. The adolescent remains ignorant about the motivations behind the Prince's spurious generosity until the Prince's treachery becomes revealed through a public scandal.

The incident, which the narrator calls a 'catastrophe,' occurs in the casino, where Arkadii is taken by the young Prince Sokol'skii. Chapters

5 through 8 of part 2 is reminiscent of *The Gambler* both thematically and in terms of how they portray the feverish state of the 'underground' hero's mind, as he struggles to surmount his perpetual inferiority complex by playing roulette. The theme of roulette throws into higher relief the adolescent's moral and psychological instability, his 'breadth,' as he tries to come to terms with his difficult identity. Like the hero of *The Gambler*, Arkadii does get unbelievably lucky, winning large sums of money several times in a row and attracting attention to himself. Emboldened by his success, Arkadii feels that he has finally overcome his inferiority complex. But he suffers a cruel blow when the young Prince, out of spite for the winner, throws in his face the truth about his sister Liza. Indignant, Arkadii rushes back to the casino in order to win more money and pay off the debt he owes the Prince. This time around he notices that his luck has only won him the hatred of other players, who start assaulting him from all sides. Finally, he ends up being thrown out of the casino. Exhausted and spiritually destroyed, he spends the night on the street, falling asleep in the snow and almost freezing to death.

In the course of these adventures, Dostoevsky's hero is all the while experiencing a profound moral ordeal that tests his character by bringing him face to face with various forms of human evil and misery, including his own. It is here that the notion of breadth gains its moral salience, for it is due to this putatively quintessentially Russian characteristic that the ordeal does not shatter Arkadii. Instead, the new, more mature Arkadii of part 3 is no longer haunted by adolescent shame, the inferiority complex of a bastard, or the slavish instincts he acquired at Touchard's boarding school. Of course, Arkadii's emotional and psychological maturation in part 3 must be seen as only a stepping stone to his ultimate resurrection and entrance into the realm of higher spiritual being. The ultimate *blagoobrazie* represented by Christ's divinely human personality (*bogochelovecheskaia lichnost'*) still lies ahead. Nonetheless, when Arkadii, after spending a night on the snow, falls dangerously ill and the recovers from his illness, his nearly miraculous recovery brings along a fundamental regeneration of his moral being.

Who and what are responsible for Arkadii's miraculous transformation? While he, like a heroine in Nikolai Nekrasov's *Frost-the Red Nose*,[88] is sleeping in the snow on the threshold between life and death, a dream descends on him that brings back a long-forgotten memory from his childhood. In this dream, Arkadii remembers how one Easter week his mother came to visit him at Touchard's. Humbly and lovingly she offered him some gifts and treats, which he, out of false pride, rejected. Bathed in the warm evening sunlight, the image of the mother with her quiet, unassuming beauty provides a striking contrast to the action-packed, melodramatic, and thrilling narrative of the preceding chapters.[89] While on the thematic level this dream introduces a new theme – that of selfless and unconditional love – it also introduces an entirely new stylistic register, one characterized by the blend of Orthodox and folkloric elements. This stylistic shift is meant to suggest not only Arkadii's regeneration on the abstract intellectual level, but also to represent this regeneration through a radical change of mood as it changes the totality of his existence.[90] Thus the image of the dignified yet humble peasant mother is reminiscent of the image of Christ's mother in Russian popular lore. As a woman who has sinned much and loved much, Arkadii's mother is also reminiscent of Sonya Marmeladova, one of the first characters in Dostoevsky writings whose language and imagery are deeply rooted in biblical text. Both Sonya and Arkadii's mother (also a Sophia) are saints-martyrs whose life stories lend themselves to allegoric interpretation as stories of Christ-like passion. It is all the more appropriate then that in Arkadii's dream his mother's image is connected to the Easter holidays.

Instead of a crude transition from the dream to the reality principle, Dostoevsky's hero awakens to find himself in a dreamlike atmosphere. How does the author manage to infuse waking reality with the aura of the quasi-prophetic or redemptive dream? To answer this question, we ought to take a closer look at the figure of Makar Dolgorukii, Sophia's husband and Arkadii's legal father. After many years of wandering (*strannichestvo*) throughout Russia, Makar returns to Sophia's house in order to die there in peace. His return coincides with Arkadii's recovery after his illness and contributes to his regeneration.

Makar (whose first name is etymologically related to the Greek *makarios*, meaning 'blessed') is an emblematic figure reminiscent of Tolstoy's Platon Karataev. He also foreshadows the Elder Zosima in *The Brothers Karamazov*. Like Tolstoy's Platon, Makar represents a perfected, almost self-sufficient human being whose spiritual essence is fully at peace with his nature and the world. This noble peasant has travelled far and wide, has presumably witnessed all forms of human joy as well as suffering, and has emerged from his experiences not only a broader but also a more integral, stronger person. Makar's joyful acceptance of life, with all its trials and sorrows, stems not only from the Orthodox glorification of kenotic saints and wise elders, but also from

Romantic pantheism. Indeed, the passages that Dostoevsky devotes to Makar bring to mind the *Naturphilosophical* visions of early Romantics and Schelling, as well as Schiller's ideal of an improved, harmonized humanity.[91] Makar's luminous presence and his tales, grounded in the collective wisdom of the people, have a soothing effect on Arkadii's troubled soul. They help ease the pain of the adolescent's painful memories and orient his entire being toward the future. As scholars have pointed out, the image of Makar is associated with sunlight, the force that makes the natural world flourish and grow.[92]

If Makar's most memorable trait is a spontaneous and unswerving love of life, Versilov is a character with a strong tragic or pessimistic streak. His tendency toward inertia is conveyed through the recurrent image of the dying sun.[93] However, the aura of love and reconciliation emanating from Makar has a miraculous effect on Versilov as well. It moves Versilov to seek reconciliation with his illegitimate family.[94] Trying to win his son's confidence and forgiveness, Versilov opens his heart to Arkadii in a famous confession that represents a summary of his spiritual and intellectual wanderings. Through this confession (whose socio-political significance has been linked to the ideas of Russian liberals of the 1840s and specifically to Herzen's political philosophy), Versilov finally realizes his dialogic potential, emerging as a complex and interesting personality and not merely a petty demon like his antecedents, Stavrogin and Stepan Verkhovenskii.[95] Together with Arkadii, we come to realize that Versilov's wanderings were indeed a quest prompted by genuine spiritual longing.[96] Although Versilov never found his ideal, we discover that his love for Sophia had a lot to do with his intense quest for the truth and goodness. Deeply moved by Sophia's quiet devotion and her constant self-abnegation, Versilov developed a deep love-pity, which would have led to his marrying her, had he not encountered Akhmakova, who provoked his uncontrollable passion. By opening his heart to Arkadii in his daring confession, Versilov shows his need and desire to be redeemed in his son's eyes. He actually wins our sympathy and convinces us – at least momentarily – that he was neither wicked nor shallow (the traits that would make him most despicable in Dostoevsky's eyes), but rather a man of strong and genuine feelings. These feelings pulled him in several directions at once and in the end destroyed him. Versilov's multifaceted character, which lacks inner integrity, comes to serve as a caution for his adolescent son, who is seeking to resolve his own identity crisis. And yet, we have to concede that Versilov, too, was endowed with certain 'breadth,' which he failed to transform into 'greatness' (to use Grigor'ev's terms).

The feat of transforming 'breadth' into a genuinely strong identity is reserved for Arkadii. Versilov, on the other hand, does not manage to sustain his newly established closeness with his son. In an act of self-laceration that recalls Nastas'ia Filippovna's madness in *The Idiot*, Versilov cuts short his budding redemption narrative by snatching an icon (*obraz*) bequeathed to him by the dying Makar and violently breaking it into two pieces. The symbolic significance of this act is obvious: the divine and the demonic sides of Versilov's personality will not be reconciled in this life. Like Nastas'ia Filippovna, Versilov finally gives in to his demonic drive, which precipitates his complete self-destruction. However, in Versilov's case it is not masochism, but erotic temptation (by Akhmakova) that functions as the catalyst for the hero's final downfall.

In the denouement, Arkadii acts as a witness of his father's ultimate destruction. This experience, which evinces his deepest sympathy, provides him with an especially deep insight into the human soul, maximally expanding his psychic and spiritual 'breadth.' When Vesilov, having smashed the icon, madly runs off to a secret rendezvous with Akhmakova, in order then to blackmail her into loving him, Arkadii follows along as though he can read his father's mind. The swiftly unfolding action emphasizes the danger implicit in the extreme psychological closeness that has developed between father and son. Thus, while throughout the novel Arkadii has struggled to dissociate himself from his father and gain recognition as an independent self, at this juncture he cannot resist Versilov's charm and acts unconsciously as his double.[97] Given that he, too, is madly in love with Akhmakova, it is natural to expect that his ideas and gestures would mimic Versilov's and that he would end up fighting with him. And yet, unlike *The Brothers Karamazov*, where the erotic rivalry between Fyodor Pavlovich and Dmitrii produces a merciless Oedipal clash, *The Adolescent* stays short of parricide or even parricidal fantasies. Instead, Arkadii ends up rescuing Versilov from the crime of murder (he was about to shoot Akhmakova) and then carries him back home to the all-suffering and forgiving Sophia. The father collapses and turns into a child, whereas the son transforms into a caring, loving father figure.

These chapters of *The Adolescent* affirm that Arkadii is finally a stronger and more viable psychological type than Versilov. He does become the hero of his story – a type who can truly make use of his 'breadth.' After Versilov's confession he begins both to respect Versilov and genuinely care for him. Are Arkadii's last attempts to 'save' Versilov from his own passion for Akhmakova motivated by charity or by jealousy?

These emotions seem to struggle in his soul as he observes and sympathetically co-experiences Versilov's violent outbursts; yet in the end, Arkadii avoids such complete identification with Versilov as to be absorbed by his father's demon, which would mean self-destruction.

In the course of his Bildungsroman, Arkadii has grown spiritually. He has completely abandoned his 'underground' self-hatred as well as hatred of others and has emerged as a person with his own identity and a powerful personality capable of sympathizing with every side of human nature without losing a sense of inner balance and integrity. The epilogue describes Arkadii as the caretaker and protector of his family, including Versilov, his mother, his sister Liza, and Liza's soon-to-be-born child. Just when Versilov's story comes to a crushing end, Arkadii's new life is about to begin. He has undergone a transformation from a budding Underground Man into a responsive and responsible personality. He can now become a true man of action.

According to Dostoevsky's initial design, Arkadii represents a genuinely new type of character that has emerged among Russia's post-Reforms generation. Arkadii's life story does not reach its completion by the end of *The Adolescent*. The plot of this novel covers mainly Arkadii's *agon* with himself, that is, with his own demonic side that threatens to transform the adolescent into an 'underground man.' Because there are sociological reasons for Arkadii's inner split (his illegitimacy), for a long time the *agon* between the Christian and the demonic factions within the hero's soul is projected outside, transforming into an agonistic struggle between Arkadii and his natural father Versilov. But as Arkadii conquers the demonic drive present within his hyper-self-consciousness he also discovers the real Versilov – a 'Byronic' type full of lofty dreams, also burdened by self-consciousness and recognizing his uncertain, almost marginal place in the world, but above all, a father tormented by guilt and desiring forgiveness.

The story also contains a phantasmagoria of other demonic doubles and faulty role models, like Vasin, Dergachev, Lambert, and the younger Prince Sokol'skii, all of whom seem to have been conjured up by Russia's social disintegration. None of these secondary models have as much influence as Versilov, although they do contribute to the 'broadening' of Arkadii's horizons and his soul, helping him to overcome his monomaniac tendencies (e.g., the idée fixe to become another 'Rothschild') and acquire a more polyphonic consciousness.

Makar, too, emerges as a powerful spiritual influence and father figure. He is the projection of Arkadii's most idealistic vision of humanity.

Like the Elder Zosima in *The Brothers Karamazov*, Makar represents the ideal Teacher providing his son-in-spirit with an ideal toward which he can strive his entire life.[98] This ideal, however, remains beyond our reach at the end of the novel. Consequently, Arkadii Dolgorukii's *Bildungsgeschichte*, and by implication the Russian national Bildungsroman, remain still in progress. Indeed, as the narrator of his own story of apprenticeship, Arkadii 'consummates' (in Bakhtin's sense of the term) his portrait as a young man, but he also lets us know that his *Bildung* is still under way. At the end of the novel we begin to hope that Arkadii, like Alyosha at the end of *The Brothers Karamazov*, might some day become a Teacher, a spiritual model for somebody else.[99]

Assuming that *The Adolescent* was indeed a sketch for the projected tripartite Bildungsroman centred on the figure of Alyosha Karamazov, we can venture a guess why Alyosha's emergence is punctuated with the parricide, in which he personally takes no part, but in which one of his brothers is accused and the other brother is psychologically and intellectually implicated. Indeed, why should the innocent youngest son witness and partake of his brothers' spiritual torments? If we assume that Arkadii Dolgorukii – a character who does not kill his father but nonetheless is guilty of hating him, and who does actually watch his father's terrible collapse – represents in seminal form all four sons of Fyodor Pavlovich Karamazov (including the illegitimate son Smerdiakov), we can surmise where the trilogy about Alyosha Karamazov is headed. In the course of his apprenticeship, Alyosha, like Arkadii, must acquire a consciousness of sin and an almost unbearable guilt. Although he does not kill his father, he is fully implicated in a terrible family and identity crises, which in Dostoevsky's mind were synonymous with the crisis of the Russian historical consciousness. As a Russian 'Everyman' or 'universal man' (*vsechelovek*), the Dostoevskian hero must partake of every kind of misery and come to sympathize with many kinds of human behaviour. His tenacious soul will be able to endure these trials and ordeals. In the end he will grow stronger and will become what Zosima had been for him: a true Teacher.

Conclusion

In *Dostoevsky's Unfinished Journey* Robin Feuer Miller suggests that Dostoevsky hesitated in his fiction to say his last word or to state, directly, any final conviction.[1] Miller is thinking of the contrast with Dostoevsky's journalistic prose, where he never hesitated to speak *in propria persona*. As Miller points out, the only novel where Dostoevsky tries to create similar closure is *The Brothers Karamazov*. Dostoevsky's last novel concludes with a moving and memorable speech given by Alyosha Karamazov to the group of schoolboys for whom he has served as teacher throughout most of the novel.[2] Gathered together at the funeral of their classmate Iliushechka, the boys listen to Alyosha's passionate speech, in which he explains to them the significance of this day: they will always remember it as the single moment in their lives when they all felt united by their shared feelings of grief and brotherly love. At this point, Alyosha Karamazov seems to lose any distance from his creator, Dostoevsky, as he shares with his readers his conviction that the most effective way to raise good people is by imprinting children's souls with bright and happy memories.[3]

When I first sketched out this project, I intended to conclude my study of the Russian Bildungsroman by focusing on the final chapter of Dostoevsky's last novel, which replays many of the themes that I have discussed throughout my study. After all, there is a genetic connection between *The Adolescent* and *The Brothers Karamazov*, which both arose from the same materials and sketches. However, upon reflection I decided that Alyosha's speech about education would not provide a fitting conclusion to my study of the Russian Bildungsroman. For Alyosha's sermon, no matter how touching it is, serves as a kind of 'coda' that, in musical terms, finalizes all thematic developments and ends the polyphony.

At this juncture I can explain why I removed Dostoevsky's final novel from my discussion. It is true that from an artistic standpoint *The Adolescent* has multiple imperfections, whereas *The Brothers Karamazov* stands out as one of Dostoevsky's masterworks – perhaps indeed *the* masterwork. However, I feel that *The Adolescent*, with all its flaws, offers a more straightforward insight into what I would call Dostoevsky's artistic laboratory, where he carried out his fearless investigation of social, cultural, and psychological crises of modern society. Igor' Volgin and others have suggested that the finished text of *The Brothers Karamazov* represents only the first part of a projected trilogy, in which the hero, Alyosha, would eventually commit some kind of horrible crime (possibly a regicide), repent for it, and ultimately find forgiveness.[4] Indeed, the current scholarly consensus seems to be that *The Brothers Karamazov* is likely just the beginning of Dostoevsky's great *epos* centred on the Russian hero who touches the extremes of 'Sodom' and 'Madonna' and is finally reborn to a new life. If this is indeed the case, then the young hero whom we find preaching to a group of schoolboys at the end of the first novel is indeed the Messiah, whom Dostoevsky tried but ultimately failed to represent in the figure of Prince Myshkin in *The Idiot*. The dialectical moment that Pushkin, Grigor'ev, and Tolstoy had all resisted, in which Russian difference is construed in redemptive and eschatological terms, would overwhelm Dostoevsky's scruples.

Had Dostoevsky indeed succeeded in transforming Alyosha into the Russian Messiah, destined to hasten the regeneration of the world, what would have happened to his famous 'polyphonic' method, which rests precisely on the relative equality of different voices within the narrative? Alyosha's speech at the grey stone projects so much authority that it makes one wonder whether, at the end of the day, Dostoevsky was in fact fully committed to 'dialogism.' Indeed, both Alyosha's eloquence in the final scene and his silent kiss given to Ivan in imitation of Christ's kissing the Great Inquisitor disarm, overwhelm, and silence the audience. Or, to put it in Bakhtinian terms, they fill in the reader's response.

The monologic voice also prevails in Dostoevsky's famous 'Pushkin speech,' despite the fact that most of its crucial ideas are borrowed from Grigor'ev. It is important for us to recognize that in presenting the image of Pushkin not only as the protean genius capable of 'universal responsiveness' (*vsemirnaia otzyvchivost'*), but also as a 'prophetic event' in Russia's history, foretelling Russia's messianic role in world history, Dostoevsky actually misrepresents one of Grigor'ev's crucial ideas.[5]

As I explained in part 1, Grigor'ev, like his German predecessors Herder and Goethe, was not interested in a synthesis of all cultures and languages in a single global culture or a single universal tongue. On the contrary, he believed that Russia, given its geographical expanse and ethnographic variegation, could give birth to a new cultural consciousness capable of encompassing different values and ideals precisely because its diversity could not be reduced without destroying it.

Dostoevsky's speech allows us to surmise that in his final creative phase (which was interrupted by his sudden death in 1881), he was moving away from Grigor'ev's vision of global humanistic dialogue and was ready to embrace the dangerous idea of Russia's 'messianic' role in the world. Looking at Dostoevsky's drafts to his Pushkin speech, we can see that he is still operating with Grigor'ev's words and texts, but gives them his own interpretation, which diverges from Grigor'ev's humanism. Here is a particularly telling extract from one of the drafts of the Pushkin speech:

> The great road presupposes involvement with the great humanistic ideals, which is precisely the Russian calling. Slavophilism – and Westernism. There are no strict divisions, it's an organism. [. . .]
>
> The spirit of the people is to appropriate everything universal (all-human). One is allowed to think that nature or mysterious destiny, which has arranged for such a spirit for the Russian nation, did so with a purpose. What is this purpose? It consists precisely in the fraternal unification and the apotheosis of the last word of love, brotherhood, equality and the highest spiritual freedom kissing each with fraternal tenderness. And this is the beggarly Russia! The Lord of Heaven dressed as a slave. And Christ too was born in the manger.[6]

This draft allows us to see how Dostoevsky forms in his mind the association between the prospect of reconciliation among various mutually antagonistic parts of Russian society (which he describes in *The Adolescent*) and universal reconciliation among nations. Then Dostoevsky makes a conjectural leap from reconciliation within a single nation, where the uprooted sons have found their way back home and have been reconciled with their roots and the 'soil,' to the world as a whole, where, he hopes, all ethnic, religious, and economic rivalries and enmities can be resolved through brotherly love. This emotional élan will sweep away all barriers that keep people from embracing one another in a brotherly way, enacting the epoch of 'eternal peace.'

In the terrorism-prone atmosphere of 1880, Dostoevsky's passionate plea for reconciliation can be very well understood, and may even seem admirable. However, looking from the standpoint of what Bakhtin called 'great time,' Tolstoy's decision to abstain from speaking at the opening of the Pushkin memorial seems to me wiser.

Although *War and Peace* was motivated by the desire to produce a national epic along the lines of Goethe's *Hermann und Dorothea* or even *The Iliad*, as he grew older Tolstoy became more and more wary of the potential danger implicit in all nationalistic ideologies.

As I showed in chapter 6 of part 2, already in the epilogue of *War and Peace* Tolstoy shows his ambivalence with regard to the liberal ideals motivating his hero Pierre Bezukhov. At the same time, it is not without a dash of irony that Tolstoy describes the family happiness enjoyed by Marya and Nikolai Rostov, whom a successful marriage has transformed into an old-style landowner. Only Platon Karataev – a saintly muzhik – stands out as a possible model of the good life, pointing toward Tolstoy's later, post-conversion oeuvre. A more careful discussion of Tolstoy's intellectual trajectory after the completion of *War and Peace* transcends the scope of my present study. However, I should point out that among all nineteenth-century Russian thinkers, it was Tolstoy who saw most clearly that a country as vast and diverse as Russia could not be transformed into a modern nation state on par with the leading European nation states. In Tolstoy's view, if Russia were to grow and change, it had to blaze its own trail to modernity. Given that the 'Pushkin celebration' in Moscow in 1880 was intended as a reaffirmation of the nationalistic cultural policy of the Romanov Empire, we can easily understand Tolstoy's decision not to attend this event. And thus, unlike Goethe and Schiller (to whom Thomas Mann compares them), Tolstoy and Dostoevsky never met in real life.[7]

Nonetheless, in the minds of readers and critics of subsequent generations, Tolstoy and Dostoevsky remain juxtaposed, or even coupled together, as indicated by Vladimir Nabokov's famous rhetorical coinage: 'Tolstoyevsky.' My book revisits this celebrated topos in order to contribute more intellectual and cultural historical data that, I hope, will shed new light on the texts by Tolstoy, Dostoevsky, and their common predecessor, Pushkin. The need for such a reassessment of the familiar texts stems from the current ideological and economic climate, where artistic achievements are increasingly subject to re-evaluation in terms of their global intellectual 'worth.' In the United States and in Europe (and, very slowly, in Russia too), national canons are being subjected to critiques aimed at depoliticizing them. I dare say, however, that even if we approach Russian literature without any preconceived idea of a canon, the works that I analysed in the preceding chapters would still appeal to our imagination. Indeed, 'the intellectual capital' earned by Pushkin, Tolstoy, and Dostoevsky was hardly due to the political strength of the Russian Empire, toward which all three authors bore feelings that we may best describe as 'ambivalent.' It is true, however, that on occasion all three of them entertained a Romantic desire to see Russia transform into the realm of brotherly love and humanness. This Utopian wish was one of the vestiges of the Enlightenment that found such a hospitable reception in Russia.

However, it is not only the Utopian side of the Enlightenment that the Russians found congenial. As Melchior de Vogüé has noted apropos of the realistic method employed by the Russian novelists, 'it [their realism] is ennobled by moral emotion, by anxiety about the divine, and by sympathy for human beings. None of these novelists sets himself a purely literary goal. All their work is governed by a double concern: for truth and for justice.'[8] Even as these authors adopted the genre of the *Bildungsroman*, a form famously ridiculed by Hegel for its bourgeois narrow-mindedness,[9] they managed to broaden it in such a way that it came to reflect the breadth of their own concerns and awareness.

Thus, while for Hegel the European novel signalled the decline of the chivalrous ethos that underlay Romantic art, for Russian novelists concerns for truth, justice, and authentic love remained vital. Hegel saw in modern European novels an expression of the new spirit of bourgeois liberalism, with its twin faces of individualism and conformism, where the hero's quest was placed in a context from which sacrifice and revelation had been excluded, and he was oriented, instead, to the internal totality of his ego. This kind of ego-centredness, cut off from the adventures of chivalry, had to take social success as its goal, leading to the disappointing conclusion that the novelistic hero, 'however much he may have quarreled with the world, or been pushed about in it, in most cases at last he gets his girl and some sort of position, marries her, and becomes as good a Philistine as others.'[10]

Yet, once transposed to the Russian soil, where social ills and inequities were more dramatic than in Europe, while traditional forms and institutions of society were rapidly turning obsolete, the prose novel, including the genre of the Bildungsroman, received a new bout of inspiration. Feeling on their shoulders the weight of Russia's unsolved problems spurred writers on toward brave artistic experimentation.

At this point I would allow myself to disagree with de Vogüé's pronouncement, repeated by many subsequent critics, that the writings of the Russian authors were 'devoid of taste and method.'[11] Both taste (as *sensus communis*) and method, which emerge as a result of an uninterrupted cultural or scholarly tradition, were already available to Pushkin, Tolstoy, Dostoevsky and other authors who were the beneficiaries of the so-called Petersburg period in Russian culture. The later Pushkin, Tolstoy, and Dostoevsky all chose to transcend the cultural horizon and aesthetic sensibility of polite society, because they felt compelled to broaden their cultural community, including in it other kinds of people with their own viewpoints, beliefs, and anxieties.

It is with Yurii Lotman's conviction that reading should be not merely a pastime or an exercise aimed at inculcating a certain taste, but must first and foremost broaden one's sympathy and improve one's ability to understand other human beings, that I want to conclude this book. Lotman's hope that the coming world culture would resemble the 'semiosphere,' where constant encounter with new images and ideas would provoke everyone to become 'unfinalized,' brings to mind the world of the nineteenth-century Russian novel. It is there that any attempt to build a sense of identity involved a radical estrangement from the expectations imposed by one's social class (or estate) and an exercise in empathy and interpretation. In his books, essays, and interviews Lotman constantly drives home to us the fact that genuine *gumannost'* (*humanity*) is not an instinct, but a result of enculturation that requires intense and constant intellectual effort; it is an ongoing heroic adventure that requires more energy than mastering a single art or foreign language. Lotman thinks that human beings are capable of this heroism. He leaves us with a stubbornly optimistic view of the human intellect, psyche, and cross-cultural communication.

Appendix

The Russian Texts

Listed below are the original texts of the quotations from Russian given in translations. All quotations from Apollon Grigor'ev, Nikolai Strakhov, Alexander Pypin, and Yurii Lotman are included, as well as several key quotations from non-fictional works by Tolstoy and Dostoevsky.

Chapter 2

Grigor'ev (from a letter to Mikhail Pogodin):

Приехал Тургенев и мы с ним сидим ночи и говорим, говорим. Я читал ему написанное мною за границей. Он, вложивши перст в самое больное место моей личности, в разбросанность мысли, в ее неудержимость розлива, тем не менее сказал, что 1) только у меня, в настоящую минуту, есть сила, что только во мне есть полнота какого-то особенного учения, которое вовсе неисключительно, как Славянофильство (. . .); 2) что, для успеха, я должен *долбить*, как покойник Виссарион, ограничить себя, повторять без малейшего зазрения совести: одним словом, долбить, долбить, долбить, 3) что долбить мне, в настоящую минуту негде, ибо ни к одному из существующих направлениий я пристать не могу, т. е. что ни одно меня не примет и ни одному я не могу по чести и совести делать уступок, ибо у меня выработано свое крепкое и цельное.[1]

Grigor'ev:

Пока эта природа с ее богатыми стихийными началами и с беспощадным здравым смыслом живет еще сама по себе, то есть живет бессознательно, без столкновения с другими живыми организмами, как то было до петровской реформы, – она еще спокойно верит в свою стихийную жизнь, еще не разлагает своих стихийных начал (...). И вдруг этот веками сложенный тип, эта богатая, но еще нетронутая стихийная природа поставлена – и поставлена уже не случайно, не на время, а навсегда – в столкновение с иною, дотоле чуждою ей жизнью, с иными, столь же крепко, но роскошно и полно сложившимися идеалами (...). Тронутые с места стихийные начала встают как морские волны, поднятые бурею; начинается страшная ломка, выворачивается вся внутренняя бездонная пропасть. Оказывается, – как только разложился старый, исключительный тип, – что у нас есть сочувствие ко всем идеалам, то есть существуют стихии для создания многообразных идеалов (...).[2]

Chapter 3

Lotman:

Искусство является средством познания и, в первую очередь, познания человека. Это положение так часто повторяется, что превратилось в тривиальность. Однако что следует разуметь под выражением 'познание человека'? Сюжеты, которые мы определяем этим выражением, имеют одну общую черту: они переносят человека в ситуацию свободы и исследуют избираемое им при этом поведение. Ни одна реальная ситуация – от самой бытовой до самой неожиданной – не может исчерпать всей суммы возможностей и, следовательно, всех действий, обнаруживающих потенциально заложенное в человеке. Подлинная сущность человека не может раскрыться в реальности. Искусство переносит человека в мир свободы и этим самым раскрывает возможности его поступков. Таким образом, любое произведение искусства задает некоторую норму, ее нарушение и установление – хотя бы в области свободы фантазии – некоторой другой нормы. Циклический мир Платона, уничтожая неожиданность в поведении человека и вводя непререкаемые правила, тем самым уничтожает искусство.[3]

Если коммуникативная система 'Я-Он' обеспечивает лишь передачу некоторого константного объема информации, то в канале 'Я-Я' происходит ее качественная трансформация, которая приводит к перестройке самого этого 'Я.'[4]

Механизм передачи информации в канале 'Я-Я' можно описать следующим образом: вводится некоторое сообщение на естественном языке, затем вводится некоторый добавочный код, представляющий собой чисто формальную организацию, определенным образом построенную в синтагматическом отношении и одновременно или полностью освобожденную от семантических значениий, или стремящуюся к такому освобождению. Между первоначальным сообщением и вторичным кодом возникает напряжение, под влиянием которого появляется тенденция истолковывать семантические элементы текста как включенные в дополнительную синтагматическую конструкцию и получающие от взаимной соотнесенности новые – релятивные – значениия.[5]

Chapter 4

Lotman:

(. . .) последовательность семантико-стилистических сломов создает не фокусированную, а рассеянную, множественную точку зрения, которая и становится центром надсистемы, воспринимаемой как иллюзия самой действительности. При этом существенным именно для реалистического стиля, стремящегося выйти за пределы субъективности семантико-стилистических 'точек зрения' и воссоздать объективную реальность, является специфическое соотношение этих множественных центров, разнообразных (соседствующих или взаимонаслаивающихся) структур: каждая из них не отменяет другие, а соотносится с ними.[6]

Lotman:

(. . .) роман создает пространство 'третьего лица.' По лингвистической структуре оно задается как объективное, расположенное вне мира читателя и автора. Но одновременно оно переживается автором как нечто им создаваемое, т. е. окрашенное всей интимностью родственных цветов, а читателем как лично переживаемое. Третье лицо обогащается эмоциональным ореолом первого лица.[7]

Chapter 5

Grigor'ev:

Что же такое этот пушкинский Белкин (. . .)? Белкин пушкинский есть простой здравый толк и здравое чувство, кроткое и смиренное, – вопиющий законно против злоупотребления нами нашей широкой способности понимать и чувствовать: стало быть, начало только отрицательное – правое только как отрицательное, ибо представьте его самому себе – оно перейдет в застой, мертвящую лень, хамство Фамусова и добродушное взяточничество Юсова.⁸

Но ведь в коже Белкина, в духе Белкина, в тоне Белкина рассказаны еще нам поэтом такие рассказы, как 'Дубровский,' как семейная хроника Гриневых, эта нимало не потерявшая своей свежести родоначальница всех наших 'семейных хроник' (. . .). Белкин для Пушкина вовсе не герой его, а больше ничего как критическая сторона души. Мы были бы народ весьма нещедро наделенный природой, если героями нашими были пушкинский Белкин, и даже честный кавказский капитан в ' В рубке леса' Толстого. Значение всех этих лиц в том, что они – критические контрасты блестящего и, так сказать, хищного типа, которого величие оказалось на нашу душевную мерку несостоятельным, а блеск фальшивым.⁹

Есть натуры, предназначенные на то, чтобы наметить зараз грани процессов, набросать полные и цельные, хотя только очерками обозначенные идеалы, и такая-то именно натура была у Пушкина. Пушкин все наше перечувствовал (. . .), от любви к загнанной старине ('Рословная моего героя') до сочувствий реформе ('Медный всадник'), от наших страстных увлечений блестящими, эгоистически-обаятельными идеалами до смиренного служения Савелья ('Капитанская дочка'),* от нашего разгула до нашей жажды самоуглубления, жажды 'матери-пустыни,' и только смерть помешала ему воплотить наши высшие стремления, весь дух кротости и любви в просветленном образе Тазита, смерть, которая почти всегда уносит преждевременно набрасывателей многообъемлющего и многосодержащего идеала, Рафаэля Санцио и Моцарта. Ибо есть какой-то тайный закон, по которому недолговечно все разметывающееся в ширину, и коренится как дуб односторонняя глубина . . . (. . .)¹⁰

Lotman:

Когда-то, создавая оду 'Вольность,' Пушкин считал закон силой, стоящей над народом и правительством, воплощением справедливости. Сейчас перед ним раскрылось, что люди живущие в социально разорванном обществе, неизбежно находятся во власти одной из двух

---

* Grigor'ev misnames 'Savel'ich,' a character from Pushkin's *The Captain's Daughter*, calling him 'Savelii.'

взаимоисключающих концепций законности и справедливости, причем законное с точки зрения одной социальной силы оказывается беззаконным с точки зрения другой.[11]

Chapter 6

Tolstoy:

Воспитание – французское *éducation*, английское *education*, немецкое *Erziehung* – понятия существующие в Европе, образование же есть понятие, существующее только в России и отчасти в Германии, где имеется почти соответствующее слово – *Bildung*. Во Франции же и Англии это понятие и это слово вовсе не существует. *Civilisation* – есть просвещение, *instruction* есть понятие европейское, непереводимое по-русски, означающее богатство школьных научных сведений или передачу их, но не есть образование, включающее в себя и научные знания, и искусства, и физическое развитие.[12]

Tolstoy (from a letter to Herzen):

Ваша статья об Овене, увы! слишком близка моему сердцу. Правда – quand même, что в наше время возможно только для жителя Сатурна, слетевшего на землю, или Русского человека. Много есть людей, и русских 99/100, [которые] от страху не поверят вашей мысли (и в скобках буде сказано, что им весьма удобно, благодаря слишком легкому тону вашей статьи. Вы как будто обращаетесь только к умным и смелым людям). Эти люди, т.е. не умные и не смелые, скажут, что лучше молчать, когда пришел к таким результатам, т.е. к тому, что такой результат показывает, что путь был неверен. И вы немного даете право им сказать это – тем, что на место разбитых кумиров ставите самую жизнь, произвол, узор жизни, как вы говорите. На место огромных надежд бессмертия, вечного совершенствования, исторических законов и т.п., этот узор ничто – пуговка на месте колосса.[13]

Вы говорите, что я не знаю России. Нет, я знаю свою субъективную Россию, глядя на нее с своей призмочки. Ежели мыльный пузырь истории лопнул для Вас и для меня, то это тоже доказательство, что мы уже надуваем новый пузырь, который еще сами не видим. И этот пузырь есть для меня твердое и ясное знание моей России, такое же ясное как знание России Рылеева может быть в 25 году. Нам, людям практическим, нельзя жить без этого.(. . .)[14]

186 Appendix

Pypin:

Образованность была еще слишком слаба; единственный университет, основанный только в 1755 году, едва выходил из размеров средней школы; литературное влияние, в смысле просвещения, ограничивалось небольшим кружком читающей публики, – и если при этом уровне образования в обществе являлась уже некоторая потребность вдумываться в трудные вопросы о человеке и природе и зарождалась первая попытка нравственного самосознания, то мистицизм довольно естественно представлялся той формой, в которую могли уложиться эти стремления. Образование наше было вообще заимствованное, и из тех различных форм и направлений, которые к нам приходили из европейского источника, оно усваивало более или менее то, что соответствовало существующему уровню умственной зрелости, что было по вкусу и по силам.[15]

Tolstoy:

Все теории философии (новой от Картезиуса) носят ошибку, состоящую в том, что признают одно сознание себя индивидуума ([так] [называемого] субъекта), тогда как сознание – именно сознание всего мира, [так] [называемого] объекта, так же несомненно .[16]

Chapter 7

Dostoevsky:

Мы говорим здесь не о славянофилах и не о западниках. К их домашним раздорам наше время совершенно равнодушно. Мы говорим о примирении цивилизации с народным началом. Мы чувствуем, что обе стороны должны, наконец, понять друг друга, должны разъяснить все недоумения, которых накопилось между ними такое невероятное множество, и потом *согласно и стройно общими силами двинуться в новый широкий и славный путь. Соединение во что бы то ни стало, несмотря ни на какие пожертвования, и возможно скорейшее – вот наша передовая мысль, вот девиз наш.*[17]

    (. . .) И думается, что если физически невозможно заставить народ отрешиться ои всего им нажитого и выработанного в пользу, положим, и общечеловеческого идеала, только добытого в других странах, то неизбежно надобно обращать внимание на народность, если мы хотим какого-нибудь развития народу (. . .) Народные инстинкты слишком чутки ко всякому посягательству со стороны, потому что иногда рекомендуемое общечеловечным как-то выходит никуда негодным в известной стране и только можнт замедлять развитие народа, к которому прилагается . . .[18]

Шатов: 'Если изменится человек – как же он будет жить умом? Имение ума соответствует только теперешнему организму.'

Князь: 'Почем Вы знаете, нужен ли будет теперешний ум?'

Шатов: 'Что же будет? Конечно, высшее ума?'

Князь: 'Без сомнения, гораздо высшее!'

Шатов: 'Да разве может быть что-нибудь высшее ума?'

Князь: 'Так по науке, но вот у вас ползет клоп. Наука знает, что это организм, что он живет какою-то жизнию и имеет впечатление, даже свое соображение и бог знает что еще. Но может ли наука узнать и передать мне сущность жизни, соображений и ощущений клопа? Никогда не может. Чтоб это узнать, надо самому стать на минуту клопом. Если она еще этого не может, то я могу заключить, что не может передать и сущности другого, высшего организма или бытия. А стало быть, и состояние человека при вырождении в milennium'е, хотя бы там и не было ума.'

– Закружили вы меня! – говорит Шатов, но я от вас не отстану.

Князь: 'Не понимаю, для чего Вы имение ума, т.е. сознания, считаете высшим бытием из всех, какие возможны? По-моему, это уже не наука, а вера, и если хотите тут фокус-покус природы, а именно: ценить себя (в целом, т.е. человеку в человечестве) необходимо для сохранения его. Всякое существо должно считать себя выше всего, клоп, наверно, считает себя выше вас, если не может, то наверно, не захотел бы быть человеком, а остался клопом. Клоп есть тайна и тайны везде. Почему же вы отрицаете другие тайны? Заметьте еще, что может быть, неверие сродно человеку именно потому, что он ум ставит выше всего, а так как ум свойствен только человеческому организму, то и не понимает и не хочет жизни в другом виде, т.е. загробной, не верит, что она выше. С другой стороны – человеку свойственно по натуре чувство отчаяния и проклятия, ибо ум человека так устроен, что поминутно не верит в себя, не удовлетворяется сам собою, и существование свое человек потому склонен считать недостаточным. От этого влечение к вере в загробную жизнь. Мы, очевидно, существа переходные, и существование наше на земле есть, очевидно, беспрерывное существование куколки, переходящей в бабочку. (. . .)[19]

Grigor'ev:

Есть, по глубокому слову, кажется Занда, *des hommes forts* – люди сильные и *des hommes grands* – люди великие; есть по глубокому же замечанию одного из оригинальнейших и самостоятельнейших мыслителей нашей эпохи, Эрнеста Ренана, *des pensées étroites* – мысли узкие и *des pensées larges* – мысли широкие. 'Только узкие мысли управляют миром,' добавляет Ренан, и это совершенно справедливо. . .Если так же нельзя закончить мысль Занда, то можно все-таки найти в ней сродство с мыслью Ренана. Есть люди широкие; из них делаются или великие люди, или Обломовы, и есть люди сильные, крепкие, кряжевые, из которых великие люди бывают, и даже часто, но Обломовы никогда.[20]

Strakhov:

Чем больше влияний действует на камень, чем дольше они на него действуют, тем значительнее разрушение камня, тем ближе он к своему уничтожению. У человека наоборот: различные влияния не только не уничтожают его, но еще более усиливают его самостоятельность. В самом деле, они его *развивают*. Мы выражаем это чрезвычайно просто и верно, говоря, что человек нечто *усвоивает* себе, когда что-нибудь на него действует. Усвоивать значит делать своим, вносить в собственную природу, прибавлять к своей сущности. Так-что сущность человека растет по мере того, как претерпевает различные влияния. Притом это нарастание не механическое, не складывание в одну кучу, но самодеятельное, внутреннее.[21]

Conclusion

Великая дорога – это соприкосновение в великими идеалами человечества, это и есть назначение русское. Славянофильство и – западничество. Нет строгих разделений, организм. (. . .)

Дух народа – усвоение всего общечеловеческого. Позволительно думать, что природа или таинственная судьба, устроив так дух русский, устроила его с целью. С какой же? А вот именно братского единения в апофеозе последнего слова любви, братства, равенства и высшей духовной свободы – лобызания друг друга в братском умилении. И это – нищяя-то Россия. Царь небесный в рабском виде. И Христос родился в яслях.[22]

Notes

Introduction

1 Astolphe de Custine, *La Russie en 1839* (Paris: Librairie d'Amyot, 1843), 240. Earlier travellers to Russia, like Mme de Staël, noted the beauty of the Russian language and Russian peasants' songs and expressed hope that Russia would one day develop a literary culture and society on a par with Europe. See Germaine de Staël, *Ten Years of Exile*, trans. Avriel H. Goldberger (De Kalb: Northern Illinois University Press, 2000), 174.
2 See Prosper Mérimée, *Stat'i o russkoi literature* (Moscow: IMLI RAN, 2003). See also David Baguley, 'Pushkin and Mérimée, the French Connection: On Hoaxes and Impostors,' in *Two Hundred Years of Pushkin*, vol. 3. *Pushkin's Legacy*, ed. Joe Andrew and Robert Reid (Amsterdam: Rodopi, 2004), 177–91.
3 Virigia Woolf, 'The Russian Point of View,' in *The Essays of Virginia Woolf*, ed. Andrew McNeillie (London: Harcourt Brace 1987), 2:240–343, 341.
4 See Peter Holquist, *Making War and Forging Revolution: Russia's Continuum of Crisis, 1914–1921* (Cambridge, MA: Harvard University Press, 2002); David L. Hoffmann and Yanni Kotsonis, eds., *Russian Modernity: Politics, Knowledge, Practices* (New York: St Martin's Press, 2000).
5 E. Melchior de Vogüé, *Le roman russe* (Paris: Plon, 1892), see Avant-propos, XIV–XVII. For a recent discussion of this topic, see William Mills Todd III, 'The Ruse of the Russian Novel,' in *The Novel*, Volume 2: *Forms and Themes*, ed. Franco Moretti (Princeton, NJ: Princeton University Press, 2006), 401–23.
6 Much work has been done by historians analysing the influence of Voltaire's project of 'civilization' on Catherine II's enlightened absolutism. See, for example, Carolyn H. Wilberger, *Voltaire's Russia; Widow on the East*,

Studies in Voltaire and the Eighteenth Century 164, ed. Theodore Besterman (Oxford: Voltaire Foundation at the Taylor Institution, 1976). See also Isabel de Madariaga, *Russia in the Age of Catherine the Great* (New Haven, CT: Yale University Press, 1981); and Dmitri von Mohrenshildt, *Russia in the Intellectual Life of Eighteenth-Century France* (New York: Columbia University Press, 1936). There is also a rich and still growing body of work analysing the influence of Rousseau on Russian culture and literature. See, for example, Thomas Barran, *Russia Reads Rousseau, 1762–1825* (Evanston, IL: Northwestern University Press, 2002); and Priscilla Meyer, *How Russians Read the French: Lermontov, Dostoevsky, Tolstoy* (Madison: University of Wisconsin Press, 2008).

7 V.V. Vinogradov, *Istoriia slov* (Moscow: Akademiia Nauk Rossiiskoi Federatsii, 1999), 792. There was another Russian term that up until the 1850s was frequently used in the contexts where we would now use *obrazovanie: obrazovannost'*.

8 On the history of English debates about the term 'culture,' see also David Lloyd and Paul Thomas, *Culture and the State* (New York: Routledge, 1998).

9 J.G. Herder, *Journal meiner Reise im Jahr 1769*, in *Werke in zehn Bunden* (Frankfurt am Mein: Deutcher Klassiker Verlag, 1997), v. 9/2:9–126.

10 Ibid.

11 Jean-Jacques Rousseau, *On the Social Contract with Geneva Manuscript and Political Economy*, ed. Roger D. Masters, trans. Judith R. Masters (New York, Boston: St Martin's Press, 1978), 71.

12 Ibid.

13 For a detailed discussion of this polemic, see Larry Wolff, *Inventing Eastern Europe: The Map of Civilization on the Mind of the Enlightenment* (Stanford, CA: Stanford University Press, 1994), 195–283.

14 Herder, *Journal meiner Reise im Jahr 1769*, 21.

15 See works by Arsenii Gulyga and E.P. Zhukova.

16 N.M. Karamzin, *Pis'ma russkogo puteshestvennika. Sochineniia Karamzina*. 3 vols. Izd. A. Smirdina (St Petersburg: Karl Krai, 1848). 2: 138–54.

17 See especially Karamzin's essays 'O novom obrazovanii narodnogo prosveshcheniia v Rossii' and ' Nechto o naukakhm iskusstvakh i prosveshchenii,' in *Sochineniia Karamzina* 3: 348–57; 373–403.

18 For an eloquent discussion of Herder's pluralism see Isaiah Berlin, 'Herder and the Enlightenment,' in *Three Critics of The Enlightenment: Vico, Hamann, Herder*, ed. Henry Hardy (Princeton, N.J.: Princeton University Press, 2000), 168–242.

19 F.M. Dostoevsky, 'Pushkin' (Ocherk), in *Polnoe sobranie sochinenii v tridsati tomakh* (Leningrad: Nauka: Leningradskoe otdelenie, 1972–1990), 26:136–48.

20 Franco Moretti, *The Way of the World: The Bildungsroman in European Culture*, trans. Albert Sbragia (London: Verso, 1987), 3–13. The term *Bildungsroman* was put in broad circulation by Wilhelm Dilthey, who discussed *Bildung*, a notoriously untranslatable word that denotes image and image-making, culture and cultivation, and the German novelistic tradition that unfolded simultaneously with the tradition of *Bildung* in his *Poetry and Experience*. In Wilhelm Dilthey, *Selected Works* ed. Rudolf Makkreel and Frithjof Rodi (Princeton, NJ: Princeton University Press, 1985) 5. It has been established, however, that the term Bildungsroman was coined by Karl Morgenstern, a German scholar who was a professor at the Russian University of Dorpat (now Tartu). See Karl Morgenstern, 'On the Nature of the *Bildungsroman*,' trans. and intro. Tobias Boes, *PMLA* 124, no. 2 (March 2009): 647–59.

21 Yu.M. Lotman, *Struktura khudozhestvennogo teksta* (Providence, RI: Brown University Press, 1971), 333. In his short biography of Pushkin, Lotman even states that this vacillation between viewpoints constitutes the 'formula of the Russian novel.' See Yu.M. Lotman, *Pushkin: ocherk tvorchestva* (St Petersburg: Iskusstvo-SPb, 1995), 196.

22 For a different vision of enculturation, which he sees as simultaneous with socialization, see Moretti, *The Way of the World* 96–9. Here Moretti claims that Lotman's vision totally ignores the reality principle for in reality most readers seek pleasure and relaxation, not constant work. Lotman's theory, says Moretti, is 'founded on a dream' (99).

23 Herder's title alludes polemically to Voltaire's *La philosophie de l'histoire* (1765).

24 See especially Yu.M. Lotman, 'Besedy o russkoi kul'ture (televizionnye lektsii),' in *Vopsitanie dushi* (St Petersburg: Iskusstvo SPB, 2003), 348–597.

25 I completely agree with B.F. Egorov that Lotman's essay on *The Captain's Daughter* (written in 1962) was a milestone in Lotman's career, leading from a purely philological approach to a semiotic one. See B.F. Egorov, Zhizn' i tvorchestvo Lotmana (Moscow: Novoe literaturnoe obozrenie, 1999), 88–92.

26 See, for example, Elena Krasnoschekova's recent monograph *Roman vospitaniia-Bildungsroman na russkoi pochve: Karamzin Pushkin, Goncharov, Tolstoy and Dostoevsky* (St Petersburg: Izdatel'stvo Pushkinskogo fonda, 2008), 20–47.

27 See Franco Moretti, *Atlas of the European Novel, 1800–1900* (London, New York: Verso, 1998), 35–7.

1. Russian Literature from the National Awakening of the 1800s to the Rise of *Pochvennichestvo* in the 1850s

1 N.D. Kochetkova, *Nikolay Karamzin* (New York: Twain, 1975), 95–118.
2 William Mills Todd III, *Fiction and Society in the Age of Pushkin: Ideology, Institutions, and Narrative* (Cambridge, MA: Harvard University Press, 1986). Among recent Russian studies on this subject, see N.L. Brodskii, ed., *Literaturnye salony i kruzhki: pervaia polovina XIX veka* (Moscow: Agraf, 2001). Russia's first political society in this era was 'The Order of the Russian Knights,' founded by the young General Count Mikhail Orlov, hero of the anti-Napoleonic campaign and signatory of the capitulation of Paris, and Count Matvei Dmitriev-Mamonov, one of the prototypes for Pierre Bezukhov.
3 Nicholas Riasanovsky offers a good overview of this period in the history of Russian education in *Russian Identities: A Historical Survey* (Oxford: Oxford University Press, 2005), 111–29.
4 A.N. Pypin, *Masonstvo v Rossii: XVIII v. i pervaia chetvert' XIX v.* (Petrograd: OGNI, 1916), 190–9.
5 Germaine de Staël, *Ten Years of Exile*, trans. Avriel H. Goldberger (De Kalb, IL: Northern Illinois University Press, 2000), 138–80. The relationship between Mme de Staël and Russia has been detailed by S. Durylin in 'Gospozha de Stal' i ee russkie otnosheniia,' *Literaturnoe nasledstvo* 33–4 (1939): 215–330.
6 Alexander Martin, *Romantics, Reformers, Reactionaries: Russian Conservative Thought and Politics in the Reign of Alexander I* (DeKalb: Northern Illinois University Press, 1997), 57–142. See also Boris Gasparov, *Poeticheskii iazyk Pushkina kak fakt istorii russkogo literaturnogo iazyka*, part 1, 'Apokalipticheskaia bitva (Messianisticheskaia ritorika 1810-kh gg. kak pitatel'naia sreda poeticheskogo iazyka Pushkina)' (Vienna: Wiener Slawistischer Almanach, 1992), 83–117.
7 Martin, *Romantics, Reformers, Reactionaries*, 122–42.
8 See an extremely valuable study of the *Beseda* in M.G. Al'tshuller, *Beseda liubitelei russkogo slova: u istokov slavianofil'stva* (Moscow: Novoe literaturnoe obozrenie, 2007), 10–89.
9 See Andreas Schoenle, 'Modernity as a "Destroyed Anthill": Tolstoi on History and the Aesthetics of Ruins,' in *Ruins of Modernity*, ed. J. Hell and A. Schoenle (Durham, NC: Duke University Press, 2010), 89–103.
10 Martin, *Romantics, Reformers, Reactionaries*, 16, 21. The question of Herder's influence on Shishkov is analysed in Al'tshuller, *Beseda liubitelei russkogo slova: u istokov slavianofil'stva* (Moscow: Novoe literaturnoe obozrenie,

2007), 268–89. A recent bibliographical summary of the translations from Herder and critical studies on Herder is E.P. Zhukova, *Gerder v Rossii: Bibliograficheskii ukazatel'* (Moscow: Universitetskaia kniga, 2007). See also E.P. Zhukova, *Gerder i filosofsko-kul'turologicheskaia mysl' v Rossii* (Moscow: Universitetskaia kniga, 2007), 75.

11 Zhukova argues quite convincingly that Karamzin's support for Russia's cultural independence from Western Europe (which he states as the main reason for protecting Russia's national sovereignty during the Napoleonic Wars) in his *Memoir on Ancient and New Russia* (*Zapiska o Staroi i Novoi Rossii*) is inspired by Herder. Zhukova, *Gerder i filosofsko-kul'turologicheskaia mysl' v Rossii*, 78–142.

12 For a more detailed discussion of Shishkov's and Karamzin's projected linguistic reforms, see Boris Gasparov.

13 Nicholas V. Riasanovsky, *Nicholas I and Official Nationality in Russia, 1825–1855* (Berkeley: University of California Press, 1959), 10–50.

14 An interesting discussion of this issue can be found in Andrei Zorin, *Kormia dvuglavogo orla: literatura i gosudarstvennaia ideologia v Rossii v poslednei treti XVIII-pervoi treti XIX veka, veka* (Moscow: Novoe literaturnoe obozrenie, 2001), 350–66.

15 F.M. Dostoevsky, *Polnoe sobranie sochinenii v tridsati tomakh* (Leningrad: Nauka, 1972–90), 5:46–98.

16 Uvarov was a graduate of the Göttingen University, educated in the classical and modern traditions. Although he preferred Racine to Shakespeare, he was well read in contemporary literature and philosophy. During diplomatic service in Vienna he became acquainted with a number of European luminaries, including Mme de Staël.

17 Andrei Zorin, *Kormia dvuglavogo orla: literatura i gosudarstvennaia ideologia v Rossii v poslednei treti XVIII-pervoi treti XIX veka*, 364.

18 Ibid., 364.

19 The term *narodnost'* is notoriously difficult to translate given that Russian also has the term *natsional'nost'*. A recent article that discusses the historical semantics of both terms is by Alexei Miller, 'Natsiia, Narod, Narodnost' in Russia in the 19th Century: Some Introductory Remarks to the History of Concepts,' *Jahrbuecher fuer Geschichte Osteuropas* 56, no. 3 (2008): 1–12.

20 According to Lotman, the first Russian poet to introduce the idea of '*narodnost''* into the literary-critical polemics was Andrei Turgenev (who was educated in Germany). He accused contemporary poets of lacking *narodnost'* at the meeting of the *Druzheskoe literaturnoe obschestvo* (Literary Society of Friends) in 1801. See Lotman's foreword (*Predislovie*) to *Poety*

1790–1810hs godov, ed. Mark Alt'shuller (Leningrad: 1991), 9. Turgenev's early death prevented him from elaborating on his views of *narodnost'*.

21 L.Ia. Ginzburg, 'O probleme narodnosti i lichnosti v poezii dekabristov,' in *O russkom realizme XIX veka i voprosakh narodnosti literatury*, ed. Pavel Gromov et al. (Moscow-Leningrad: Khudozhestvennaia literatura, 1960), 52–93.

22 This acerbic title was invented by Herzen, who used it in *My Past and Thoughts*. However, some European thinkers who were interested in Russia, e.g., Stendhal, shared Herzen's sentiment. See Tatiana Kochetkova, 'Stendhal, Viazemski et les décembristes,' *Stendhal Club* 8 (1960): 311–19.

23 Astolphe de Custine, *La Russie en 1839* (Paris: Librairie d'Amyot, 1843).

24 See L.N. Kiseleva, 'Pushkin i Zhukovskii v 1830-e gody (tochki ideologicheskogo sopriazheniia),' in *Pushkinskaia konferentsia v Stenforde*, ed. L. Fleishman et al. (Moscow: OGI, 2001), 171–85.

25 A.S. Pushkin, *Polnoe sobranie sochinenii* (Moscow and Leningrad: Nauka, 1937–59), 11:43–4.

26 *The Lovers of Wisdom* gathered in the home of writer and musicologist Prince V.F. Odoevskii. The main figure cultivated by this circle was Schelling. However, the group was also familiar with Fichte, Friedrich Schlegel, Novalis, and other Romantic authors.

27 I make this conclusion on the basis of historical analyses of the 'Moscow Romanticism' found in two recent works by K. Iu. Rogov: 'Iz istorii uchrezhdeniia *Moskovskogo Vestnika*,' in *Pushkinskaia konferenistia v Stanforde*, ed. L. Fleishman et al., (Moscow: OGI, 2001), 106–32; and 'K istorii moskovskogo romantizma: kruzhok i obschestvo S. Ie. Raicha,' in *Lotmanovskii sbornik*, ed. E. Permiakov (Moscow: Garant, 1995), 523–676.

28 For example, the first issue of Pogodin's journal opens with a scene from *Boris Godunov*. *Moskovskii Vestnik* also published the seventh chapter of *Engene Onegin* and many shorter poems by Pushkin. However, his contributions became less frequent after 1828, due not only to Pushkin's marriage and resettlement in Petersburg in 1831, but also to his growing intellectual disagreements with the theoretically inclined Moscow thinkers. In the 1830s, Pushkin also became interested in publishing his own journal, and I suspect this was the key reason behind his gradual withdrawal from Pogodin's venture.

29 P. Ia. Chaadaev, *Polnoe sobranie sochinenii i izbrannye pis'ma*,. ed. and intro. Z.A. Kamenskii, 2 vols. (Moscow: Nauka, 1991), 1: 320–38.

30 Pushkin became familiar with this text as early as 1831 and, allegedly, even wanted to publish it in his journal, *The Contemporary*. See Chaadaev's letter to him in A.S. Pushkin, *Polnoe sobranie sochinenii*, 14: 225–8.

31 P.Ia. Chaadaev, *Lettres philosophiques adressèes à une dame. Lettre Première*. In *Polnoe sobranie sochinenii i izbrannye pis'ma*, ed. and intro. Z.A. Kamenskii (Moscow: Nauka, 1991) 2 vols., 1:90–1.
32 M.O. Gershenzon, 'P. Ia. *Chaadaev: Zhizn' i myshlenie*,' in *Izbrannoe*, 4 vols. (Moscow and Jerusalem: Universitetskaia kniga, Gershsarim, 2000), 381–562.
33 Chaadaev, *Polnoe sobranie sochinenii i izbrannye pis'ma*, 1:331.
34 See Gershenzon, 'P. Ia. *Chaadaev: Zhizn' i myshlenie*,' 562. See also Andrzej Walicki, 'Petr Chaadaev,' in *A History of Russian Thought from the Enlightenment to Marxism*, trans. Hilda Andrews-Rusiecka (Stanford, CA: Stanford University Press, 1979), 81–91. This study contains a good bibliography of Western and Russian works on Chaadaev. See also Chaadaev's letter to Pushkin in Pushkin, *Polnoe sobranie sochinenii*, 14:225–8.
35 Chaadaev, *Polnoe sobranie sochinenii i izbrannye pis'ma*, 523–38. According to Raymond McNally, the change of Chaadaev's attitude in the 1830s is partly related to his disillusionment with contemporary Western society and the rise of Russophobia in France. See Raymond T. McNally, 'Chaadaev's Evaluation of Peter the Great,' *Slavic Review* 23, no. 1 (March 1964): 31–44, 36.
36 Chaadaev, *Polnoe sobranie sochinenii i izbrannye pis'ma*, 400–1. For a nuanced discussion of what he calls 'The Paradox of Chaadaev,' see Walicki, *History of Russian Thought*, chap. 5, 'Petr Chaadaev,' 81–91.
37 Walicki, *History of Russian Thought*, 83–90.
38 Walicki, *The Slavophile Controversy: History of a Conservative Utopia in Ninteenth-Century Russian Thought*, trans. Hilda Andrews-Rusiecka (Notre Dame, IN: University of Notre Dame Press, 1989), 333.
39 Ferdinand Toennies, *Community and Society*, trans. Charles P. Loomis (East Lansing: Michigan State University Press, 1957).
40 A.S. Khomiakov, *Izbrannye sochineniia* (New York: Izdatel'stvo imeni Chekhova, 1955), 119.
41 For an excellent intellectual biography of Belinskii, see Victor Terras, *Belinskii and Russian Literary Criticism* (Madison: University of Wisconsin Press, 1974).
42 Nikolai Barsukov, *Zhizn' i trudy M.P. Pogodina* (St Petersburg: tip. Stasiulevicha, 1888–1907), 21 vols.
43 This hypothesis was first expressed by Boris Eikhenbaum. See B. Eikhenbaum, *Lev Tolstoy*, Her. D. Tschizewskij, 2 vols. (Muenchen: Wilhem Fink Verlag, 1968), 2:326–49. In chapter 6 I return to this issue.
44 Karamzin's biography could be considered Pogodin's life's work. He published a sketch entitled '*Detstvo, vospitanie i pervye literaturnye opyty Karamzina*' ('Childhood, Education and the First Literary Attempts of Karamzin') in the almanac he edited, *Utro* (Moscow: tip. Stepanovoi, 1866),

1–58. That year he also published *Nikolai Mikhailovich Karamzin po ego sochineniiam, pis'mam i otzyvam sovremennikov* (Moscow: tip. Mamontova, 1866), 2 vols. See N.P. Barsukov, *Zhizn' i trudy M.P. Pogodina* (St Petersburg: tip. Stasiulevicha, 1888–1907).
45 Barsukov, *Zhizn' i trudy M.P. Pogodina*, 7:52–5.
46 Ibid., 2:369.
47 On the concept of *Weltliteratur* as a key intellectual motto of the day, see V.A. Avetisian, *Poslednie sobesedniki Pushkina: eshche raz o probleme Pushkin-Goethe* (Moscow and Izhevsk: R and C Dynamics, 2009). On Goethe's personal connections with the Princess Volkonskaia and several of the Lovers of Wisdom, see S.V. Durylin in his seminal work 'Russkie pisateli u Gëte v Veimare,' in *Literaturnoe nasledstvo* 4/6 (1932): 83–504.

2. Apollon Grigor'ev's Theory of Russian Culture

1 See B.F. Egorov, 'Khudozhestvennaia proza Ap. Grigor'eva,' in *Apollon Grigor'ev, Vospominaniia*, ed. B.F. Egorov (Leningrad: Nauka, 1980), 355–7.
2 Whittaker, *Russia's Last Romantic: Apollon Grigor'ev, 1822–1864* (Lewiston, NY: Edwin Mellen Press, 1999). 58.
3 Egorov, 'Khudozhestvennaia proza Ap. Grigor'eva,' 345. See also Whittaker, *Russia's Last Romantic*, 58–9.
4 Whittaker, *Russia's Last Romantic*, 37–41.
5 Egorov, 'Khudozhestvennaia proza Ap. Grigor'eva,' 342.
6 Whittaker, *Russia's Last Romantic*, 65
7 *Apollon Grigor'ev: Materialy dlia biografii*, ed. V. Kniazhnin (Petrograd: Tipografiia Ministerstva Zemledeliia, 1917), 227–8. My translation; italics are in the original.
8 Whittaker, *Russia's Last Romantic*, 279–80.
9 For an in-depth historical analysis of Grigor'ev's career as a critic, see Wayne Dowler, *An Unnecessary Man: The Life of Apollon Grigor'ev* (Toronto: University of Toronto Press, 1995); and Robert Whittaker, *Russia's Last Romantic*. See also B.F. Egorov, *Apollon Grigor'ev* (Zhizn' zamechatel'nykh liudei) (Moscow: Molodaia gvardiia, 2000).
10 Apollon Grigor'ev, 'Narodnost' i literatura,' *Estetika i kritika*, intro. and notes A.I. Zhuravleva (Moscow: Iskusstvo, 1980), 169–99.
11 Apollon Grigor'ev, *Sochineniia v dvukh tomakh*, ed. B.F. Egorov (Moscow: Khudozhestvennaia literatura, 1990), 2:364–5.
12 In an interesting essay, Whittaker discusses Grigor'ev's disagreement with the rural fixation of the Slavophiles. See Robert Whittaker, '"My Literary and Moral Wanderings": Apollon Grigor'ev and the Changing Cultural

Topography of Moscow,' *Slavic Review* 42, no. 3 (Autumn 1983): 390–407. Grigor'ev's autobiography was clearly modelled on Goethe's *Wilhelm Meisters Wanderjahre*, a work that he evaluates highly in his 1854 essay 'Stat'ia Lorda Jeffrey o *Vilgelme Meistere*' ('Lord Jeffrey's Article on *Wilhelm Meister*'). This essay, where Grigor'ev defends Goethe's work against the biting criticism of the prominent English critic, was published in *Moskvitianin* 2, no. 8 (April 1854). For a detailed discussion of Grigor'ev's attitude toward Goethe, see V.M. Zhirmunskii, *Gëte v russkoi literature* (Leningrad: Nauka, 1981), 304–21.

13 V.G. Belinskii, *Sochineniia Aleksandra Pushkina*. In *Polnoe sobranie sochinenii V.G. Belinskogo*, ed. S.A. Vengerov, 12 vols. (St Petersburg: tipografiia Stasiulevicha, 1900–17) 11:187–410.

14 See A.V. Druzhinin, *Sobranie sochinenii* (St Petersburg: Imperatorskaia akademiia nauk, 1865–67), 8 vols., 7:232.

15 See Lotman's articles 'Blok i narodnaia kul'tura goroda' and 'Chelovek prirody' v russkoi literature XIX veka 'tsyganskaia tema' u Bloka' (the latter is co-authored with Z.G. Mints). Both articles appear in Yu.M. Lotman, *Izbrannye stat'i*, 3:185–200 and 246–93, respectively.

16 D.I. Blagoi, 'Blok i Apollon Grigor'ev,' in *Tri veka: iz istorii russkoi poezii XVIII, XIX i XX vv.* (Moscow: Sovetskaia literatura, 1933), 269–300; Z.G. Mints, *Lirika Aleksandra Bloka*, repr. in *Poetika Aleksandra Bloka* (St Petersburg: Iskusstvo SPb, 1999), 12–232, 241.

17 B.F. Egorov's most significant works on Grigor'ev were published in *Uchenye Zapiski Tartusskogo Gosudarstvennogo Universiteta*, the periodical where Lotman also published regularly. Their essays often appeared side by side. Z.G. Mints's articles also appeared frequently in *Uchenye Zapiski*. Thus, even a quick perusal of Tartu University publications helps us see how the dialogue between nineteenth-century organic criticism of Grigor'ev and modern semiotics and cultural theory has emerged. Egorov's publications in *Uchenye Zapiski Tartusskogo Gosudarstvennogo Universiteta* include 'Apollon Grigor'ev – kritik. Stat'ia 1' 3 (1960): 194–246; 'Apollon Grigor'ev – kritik. Stat'ia 2' 4 (1961): 58–83; 'Materialy ob Apollone Grigor'eve iz arkhiva N.N. Strakhova' 6 (1963): 339–50; and 'Pis'ma A. Grigor'eva M. P. Pogodinu (1855–8)' 21 (1973): 353–88.

18 See B.F. Egorov, *Zhizn' i tvorchestvo Iu.M. Lotmana* (Moscow: Novoe literaturnoe obozrenie, 1999), 49–76. See also Egorov, 'Lotman kak chelovek i iavlenie'; V.G. Shchukin, 'Dukh karnavala i dukh prosveshcheniia'; L.N. Kiseleva, 'Iu.M. Lotman: ot istorii literatury k semiotike kul'tury,' in *Yurii Mikhailovich Lotman*, ed. V.K Kantor (Moscow: Rasspen, 2009), 13–81; 132–90; 282–93, respectively.

19 Interestingly, E.P. Zhukova omits Grigor'ev from her otherwise extremely rich account of Herder's presence in Russian philosophy and literature. In his book on Goethe in Russia, Viktor Zhirmunskii mentions Herder as a pivotal influence on the young Goethe and devotes a special chapter to Goethe's influence on Grigor'ev. However, neither here nor in his introductory essay to Herder's collection of poetry and essays translated into Russian does Zhirmunskii mention Herder's possible influence on Grigor'ev as a poet and critic. This topic, however, lies beyond the scholar's scope in each of these works. Moreover, given Zhirmunskii's interpretation of Grigor'ev as a right-wing nationalist and adept of official nationality, it would be illogical for him to draw any direct connections between the founder of *pochvennichestvo* and Herder, who was considered an 'internationalist' and paid lip service throughout the Soviet period. See V.M. Zhirmunskii, *Gëte v russkoi literature* (Leningrad: Nauka, 1981), 304–21. See also Zhirmunskii's introductory essay to I.G. Gerder, *Izbrannye prozivedeniia* (Moscow and Leningrad: Akademiia Nauk SSR, 1959), vii–lix.
20 See Apollon Grigor'ev, *Moi literaturnye i nravstvennye skital'chestva* in *Apollon Grigor'ev: materially dlia biografii*, 1–97.
21 See J.G. Herder, 'Critical Forests,' in *Selected Writings on Aesthetics*, trans. and ed. Gregory Moore (Princeton, NJ: Princeton University Press, 2006), 100–1.
22 *Estetika i kritika*, 117–33. 119.
23 *Literaturnaia kritika*, 527–40.
24 'Vzgliad na ruskuiu literaturu so smerti Pushkina,' *Sochineniia*, 2:47–124.
25 'Pushkin (Ocherk),' *Dnevnik pisatelia na 1880 god. Polnoe sobranie sochinenii v tridsati tomakh*, 26:136–48.
26 *Letters for the Advancement of Humanity* (1793–7) (excerpts), in *Philosophical Writings*, trans. and ed. Michael N. Forster (Cambridge: Cambridge University Press, 2003), 370–3.
27 On the connection between the rhetoric of Enlightenment humanism and the notion of the human right, see Joseph R. Slaughter, 'Enabling Fictions and Novel Subjects: The *Bildungsroman* and International Human Rights Law,' *PMLA* 121, no. 5 (May 2006): 1405–23.
28 Nikolai Strakhov, *Bor'ba s Zapadom v nashei literature* (Kiev: tipografiia Chokolova, 1897), 3 vols.

3. Yurii Lotman's Idea of the 'Semiosphere'

1 Karl Morgenstern, 'On the Nature of the *Bildungsroman*,' trans. and intro. Tobias Boes, *PMLA* 124, no. 1 (March 2009): 647–59.
2 See Tobias Boes, introduction to Morgenstern, 'On the Nature of the *Bildungsroman*,' 647–59.

Notes to pages 38–40   199

3   See B.F. Egorov, *Zhizn' i tvorchestvo Iu.M. Lotmana* (Moscow: Novoe literaturnoe obozrenie, 1999), 90–1.
4   One's of Lotman's key ideas, which I see as the starting point for his entire semiotic theory, is his interpretation of Russian realism as a philosophical breakthrough that makes literature a medium of a pluralistic world view. As I will show in the next chapter, Lotman first formulates this idea in 'Ideinaiia struktura *Kapitanskoi Dochki*.' He continues to refine this idea throughout his life, providing new examples and formulations in *Roman v stikakh A.S. Pushkina 'Evgenii Onegin.' Kommentarii* (see especially the chapter entitled 'Problema tochki zreniia v romane'), in *Struktura khudozhestvennogo teksta* (the chapter 'Tochka zreniia teksta'), and finally in his biography of Pushkin, where he credits Pushkin with creating not only the first truly multiperspectival novel, *Eugene Onegin*, but also the 'formula of the Russian novel': 'Pushkin oborval roman, ne "dogovoriv" siujeta. On ne khotel neischerpaiemost' zhizni svodit' k zavershennosti literaturnogo teksta. Vynosit' prigovor protivorechilo ego poetike. No v "Evgenii Onegine" on sozdal ne tol'ko roman no i formulu russkogo romana. Eta formula legla v osnovu vsei poseduiuschei traditsii russkogo realizma. Skrytyie v nei vozmozhnosti izuchali i razvivali i Turgenev, i Goncharov, i Tolstoy, i Dostoevskii.' ['Pushkin interrupted his novel before he finished telling us its story. He did not want to reduce life's inexhaustible possibilities to a finalized structure of a literary text. Passing verdicts was against his poetic principles. In "Eugene Onegin" he gave us not just a novel, but the formula of the Russian novel. The subsequent tradition of Russian realism, including Turgenev, Gonacharov, Tolstoy, and Dostoevsii, utilized this formula.'] [My translation.] Yu.M. Lotman, *Pushkin: ocherk tvorchestva*. In *Pushkin*, intro. B.F. Egorov (St Petersburg: Iskusstvo-SPb, 1995), 185–211; 196.
5   See Norbert Wiener, *The Human Use of Human Beings: Cybernetics and Society* (Boston: Houghton Mifflin, 1950), 92.
6   Yu..M. Lotman, *Pushkin*, 212–27.
7   Yu.M. Lotman, *Roman v stikhakh Pushkina 'Evgenii Onegin'* (Tartu, Estonia: Tartusskii Gosudarstvennyi Universitet, 1975). This work was later expanded. The new work was entitled *Roman A.S. Pushkina 'Evgenii Onegin.' Kommentarii*. In Yu.M. Lotman, *Pushkin*, 472–762.
    Among Lotman's most interesting narratological works are 'Proiskhozhdenie siujeta v tipologicheskom osveschenii,' 'Problema khudozhestvennogo prostranstva v proze Gogolia,' and 'Zametki o khudozhestvennom prostranstve,' all published in *Izbrannye stat'i v trekh tomakh* (Tallinn, Estonia: Alexandra, 1992), 1:224–42; 413–47; 448–63.
8   See David M. Bethea, 'Bakhtinian Prosaics versus Lotmanian "Poetic Thinking": The Code and Its Relation to Literary Biography,' *Slavic and*

Eastern European Journal 41, no. 1 (Spring 1997): 1–15; Amy Mandelker, 'Semiotizing the Sphere: Organicist Theory in Lotman, Bakhtin and Vernadsky,' *PMLA* 109, no. 3 (May 1994): 385–96. See also Caryl Emerson, 'Jurii Lotman's Last Book and Filiations with Bakhtin,' *Die Welt der Slaven* 48 (2003): 201–16.

9 This idea is expressed for the first time in Lotman's short book on *Eugene Onegin*. Here, Lotman acknowledges his colleague B.A. Uspenskii's work, *Poetika kompozitsii: Struktura khudozhestvennogo teksta i tipologiia kompozitsionnoi formy* (Moscow: Iskusstvo, 1970), whose interconnections with Lotman's *Struktura khudozhestvennogo teksta* are quite obvious to anyone familiar with these works.

10 The distinction between Schlegel's Romantic irony, which stems from scepticism, and what Lotman calls 'realistic irony' (*realisticheskaia ironiia*), which he traces back to Pushkin's 'mutiperspectival' perception of reality, comes across most clearly in *Roman v stikhakh Pushkina 'Evgenii Onegin'*, 425. As I argue, this idea is indebted to Grigor'ev, who stressed Pushkin's 'Protean' sympathy with various natural forces, human souls, and entire cultures.

11 See David Bethea, 'Bakhtinian Prosaics versus Lotmanian "Poetic Thinking,"' 5.

12 A good example of Lotman's influence on his friend is B.F. Egorov's 1973 article 'Slavianofil'stvo, zapadnichestvo i kul'turologiia.' I am deeply grateful to Galin Tihanov for bringing this work to my attention.

13 Yu.M. Lotman, 'O semiosfere,' in *Izbrannye stat'i*, 1:11–24.

14 V.I. Vernadskii, *Biosfera: izbrannye trudy po biogeokhimii*, ed. V.V. Dobrovol'skii (Moscow: Nauka, 1967). There are several English translations of this work. The most fluent of them is V.I. Vernadskii, *The Biosphere*, trans. Mark A.S. McMenamin (New York: Copernicus, 1998).

15 See Amy Mandelker, 'Semiotizing the Sphere: Organicist Theory in Lotman, Bakhtin and Vernadsky.'

16 Boas, of course, taught Margaret Mead and was a great influence in creating the liberal cultural relativism embraced by Rorty. See Bruce Knauft, *Genealogies of the Present in Cultural Anthropology* (New York: Routledge, 1996), 21.

17 Niklas Luhmann, *Social Systems*, trans. John Bednarz Jr, with Dirk Baecker (Stanford, CA: Stanford University Press, 1995).

18 Here I fully agree with Caryl Emerson, who places Lotman, along with Bakhtin, Vygotskii, and Lidiia Ginzburg, among staunch defenders of the human as a special category and value in the age of the post-totalitarian crisis of humanism. Caryl Emerson, 'Bakhtin, Lotman, Vygotskii, and

Lydia Ginzburg on Types of Selves: A Tribute,' in *Self and Story in Russian History*, ed. Laura Engelstein and Stephanie Sandler (Ithaca, NY: Cornell University Press, 2000), 20–45.
19 Translation is quoted from Juri Lotman, *Culture and Explosion*, ed. Marina Grishakova and trans. Wilma Clark (New York and Berlin: Mouton de Gruyter, 2009), 152.
20 For a particularly illuminating account of art as the modelling system that allows human beings to come to know themselves as free and capable of spontaneity, see Lotman, 'Chto daet semioticheskii podkhod,' in *Vospitanie dushi: vospominaniia, interviu, besedy; v mire pushkinskoi poezii; besedy o russkoi kul'ture (televizionnye lektsii)* (St Petersburg: Iskusstvo SPb, 2003), 113–15.
21 See Luhmann, *Social Systems*, 146, 218–21, 262–7.
22 Lotman, *Izbrannye stat'ii*, 1:76–89.
23 Human desire for creativity, which presents the stumbling block for structuralism, is the problem that preoccupied Lotman throughout his life and especially throughout his 'semiotic' stage. He usually explains creativity as a result of incomplete or imperfect translation between two different 'codes'; here the term 'code' stands not just for natural human languages but implies a whole world view or ideological system. One of the sources from which Lotman might have borrowed the term 'code' is Jakobson. The other is probably Roland Barthes, whose *Mythologies* was popular in the Moscow-Tartu semiotic circle. However, Lotman's task is to explain how 'codes' evolve from inherited 'mythologies' to more individualized and 'deautomatized' ideological positions. David Bethea has provided an illuminating account of the flexible relationship between the biographical self and multiple 'codes' in Lotman's biographies of Pushkin and Karamzin. See David M. Bethea, 'Iurii Lotman in the 1980s: the Code and Its Relation to Literary Biography,' in *Reconstructing the Canon: Russian Writing in the 1980s*, ed. Arnold McMillin (London: Harwood Academic Publishers, 2000), 9–32.
24 For Luhmann's analysis of 'double contingency,' see Luhmann, *Social Systems*, 103–36.
25 As David Bethea has shown in 'Bakhtinian Prosaics Versus Lotmanian "Poetic Thinking,"' over the course of the 1980s, Lotman gradually gave up the term 'code,' which implies a mechanistic view of language and communication. Following Bethea, a number of critics have argued that Lotman's move away from mechanical-structural semiotic 'modelling systems,' made famous in the works of the Moscow-Tartu school of the 1960s and 1970s, toward an organicist view of the semiosphere was largely due to his dialogue with Bakhtin. My intention is not to argue against this

assumption but to add one more context for understanding Lotman's organicist phase – his interest in Grigor'ev's organic criticism.
26 The first type of communication, from 'I' to 'he,' simply transmits a certain idea or information from one subject to another using the same code (a model completely rejected by Luhmann, always vigilant to crush all attempts to 'reify' consciousness).
27 Lotman, 'O dvukh modeliakh kommunikatsii v sisteme kul'tury,' in *Izbrannye stat'i*, 1: 76–89.
28 Ibid., 83.
29 Lotman, *Culture and Explosion*, 22–4.
30 The famous line of Tiutchev, 'A thought when uttered is a lie,' offers a correlate to Lotman's point. That suspension, in the moment before the thought is uttered, is romantically valued as the moment of authenticity.
31 For a more detailed analysis of Lotman's *Culture and Explosion*, containing a complete quotation of Blok's poem, see Lina Steiner, 'Toward Ideal Universal Community: Iurii Lotman's Revisiting of the Enlightenment and Romanticism,' *Comparative Literature Studies* 40, no. 1 (2003): 37–53,
32 See Luhmann, *Social Systems*, xxxxvi–liii.
33 Lotman, *Pushkin*, 375–90.
34 Raymond Williams, *The Long Revolution* (New York: Broadview Press, 2001), 12–99.
35 Williams's concept of culture can also be traced back to Herder's vision of *Bildung*. See Paul Jones, *Raymond Williams's Sociology of Culture: A Critical Reconstruction* (New York: Palgrave Macmillan, 2004), 97.
36 Raymond Williams, *Culture and Society: 1780–1950* (New York: Columbia University Press, 1958).

4. The Semiospheric Novel and the Broadening of Cultural Self-Consciousness

1 Yu.M. Lotman, *Aleksandr Sergeevich Pushkin: Biografiia pisatelia*, in *Pushkin* (St Petersburg: Iskusstvo-SPB, 1995), 196.
2 F.M. Dostoevsky, 'Pushkin (Ocherk),' in *Polnoe sobranie sochinenii v tridsati tomakh*, ed. G.M. Fridlender et al. (Leningrad: Nauka, 1972–90), 26:129–297.
3 See Lotman, *A.S. Pushkin: Biografiia pisatelia*, 196. Lotman first advanced this view of Pushkin's contribution to the novel (without calling Pushkin's innovation a 'formula') in the chapter 'Tochka zreniia teksta' in *Struktura khudozhestvennogo teksta* (Providence, RI: Brown University Press, 1971), 320–35.
4 See Lotman, 'Problema narodnosti i puti razvitiia literatury preddekabristskogo perioda,' *O russkom realizme XIX veka i voprosakh narodnosti literatury*,

ed. Pavel Gromov (Moscow-Leningrad: Khudozhestvennaia literatura, 1960), 3–49.
5 See Tobias Boes, 'Commentary' to Karl Morgenstern, 'On the Nature of the *Bildungsroman*,' *PMLA* 124, no. 2 (March 2009): 647–59, 647. In recent decades the aestheticist underpinnings of the traditional Bildungsroman came under severe critique especially from the scholars influenced by Paul de Man. Among these works, the most characteristic one is by Marc Redfield, *Phantom Formations: Aesthetic Ideology and the Bildungsroman* (Ithaca: Cornell University Press, 1996).
6 The English translation is quoted from Jurij Lotman, *The Structure of the Artistic Text*, trans. Ronald Vroon (Ann Arbor: Michigan Slavic Contributions, 1977), 277.
7 Jean-François Lyotard, *Le Différend* (Paris: Editions de Minuit, 1983), 128.
8 Yu.M. Lotman, 'Ideinaia struktura "Kapitanskoi Dochki,"' in *Izbrannye stat'i*, 416–29.
9 Lotman, *Izbrannye stat'i*, 1:11–24.
10 Lotman, *Culture and Explosion*, ed. Marina Grishakova and trans. Wilma Clark (New York and Berlin: Mouton de Gruyter, 2009), 117.
11 Caryl Emerson, 'Jurii Lotman's Last Book and Filiations with Bakhtin,' *Die Welt der Slaven* 48 (2003): 201–16.

5. Pushkin's Quest for National Culture: *The Captain's Daughter* as a Russian Bildungsroman

1 A.S. Pushkin, Polnoe sobranie sochinenii, 16 vols. (Moscow, Leningrad: Akademiia Nauk SSSR, 1937–49), 3/1:464. All further citations are from this edition. *Polnoe sobranie sochinenii* will be abbreviated as *PSS*. Trans. Ivan Eubanks.
2 Pushkin's ambivalence is registered in some of his lyric poetry (e.g., poems 'K Moriu,' 'Svobody seiatel' pustynnyi,' 'Andrei Schen'e), narrative fiction (*Bronze Horseman, Poltava, The History of the Village of Goriukhino*) and non-fiction prose, such as the materials toward the unfinished *History of Peter the Great* in vol. 9 of A.S. Pushkin, *PSS*.
3 The English translation is quoted from Alexander Pushkin, *Complete Prose Fiction*, trans. and intro. Paul Debreczeny (Stanford, CA: Stanford University Press, 1983), 361–440. All quotations from *The Captains' Daughter* in this chapter are from this edition and will be cited in the text, following the volume/page nos. from Pushkin, *PSS*.
4 For more detailed historical analyses of the Pugachev uprising in connection with Russia's imperialism – i.e., the 'civilizing' measures implemented

by the government since Peter the Great upon the Cossack population of the Russian north-east frontier – see, for example, Paul Avrich, *Russian Rebels, 1600–1800* (New York: Schoken Books, 1976); Geoffrey Hosking, *Russia: People and Empire, 1552–1917* (Cambridge, MA: Harvard University Press, 1997); Dietrich Geyer, *Russian Imperialism: the interaction of domestic and foreign policy, 1860–1914*, trans. Bruce Little (New Haven, CT: Yale University Press, 1987).

5 Throughout the 1830s, the period when he tried to become an independent journalist, Pushkin's energies were dedicated to the issue of national *prosveshchenie* (which I render in English, depending on the context and the established tradition of translating Pushkin's works, as 'culture,' 'enlightenment,' or 'education'). In addition to the above-mentioned works by Pushkin pertaining to the issue of public education, see his essay 'Mnenie M.Ie. Lobanova o dukhe slovesnosti, kak inostrannoi tak i otechestvennoi.' *PPS*, 12:67–74.

6 Anne Lounsbery, *Thin Culture, High Art: Gogol, Hawthorne, and Authorship in Nineteenth-Century Russia and America* (Cambridge, MA: Harvard University Press, 2007) shows how Gogol's quest for his artistic voice as a Russian national author was tied up with his quest for a broader readership, i.e., a genuinely national readership that would transcend the bounds of polite society as envisioned by Karamzin and the Karamzinists.

7 See V.G. Berezina, 'Iz Istorii "Sovremennika" Pushkina,' in *Pushkin: issledovaniia i materialy*, ed. M.P. Alekseev (Moscow: Izdatelstvo akademii nauk SSSR, 1956), 1:278–312. See also A.I. Reitblat, *Kak Pushkin vyshel v genii: istoriko-sotsiologicheskie ocherki o knizhnoi kul'ture Pushkinskoi epokhi* (Moscow: Novoe literaturnoe obozrenie, 2001). This study sheds additional light on the development of Russian journalism in the 1820s and 1830s and Pushkin's role in it.

8 The work by Todd that proved particularly influential on my entire study is *Fiction and Society in the Age of Pushkin: Ideology, Institutions, and Narrative* (Cambridge, MA: Harvard University Press, 1986). See also William Mills Todd III, ed., *Literature and Society in Imperial Russia, 1800–1914* (Stanford, CA: Stanford University Press, 1978).

9 Pushkin's growing social anxiety, reflected in poems like 'My Genealogy,' caused by the realization of the increasingly marginal status and constant impoverishment of the old boyar families (like the Pushkins) in the bureaucracy-run Petrine state, contributed to his ambivalence regarding Peter the Great as Russia's modernizer. It also contributed to Pushkin's growing interest in shaping a new cultural force out of these old but no longer politically powerful boyars. Pushkin was envisioning a new class of 'national

cultivators' along the lines of Coleridge's clerisy. See 'Zametki po russkoi istorii,' *PSS*, 12:202–4 and 'O dvorianstve,' *PSS*, 12:205–6. On Pushkin as a 'frondeur,' see M.G. Al'tshuller, 'Mistifikatsiia semeinogo predaniia ('A ded moi v krepost', v karantin . . .') in *Mezdu dvykh tsarei: Pushkin 1824–1836* (St Petersburg: Akademicheskii proekt, 2003), 186–200; and A.L. Ospovat, 'Imenovanie geroia *Kapitanski dochki*, in *Lotmanovskii sbornik*, ed. E. Permiakov (Moscow: ITS Garant, 2004), 261–7. Raeff discusses the traditions of aristocratic 'Fronde' in Russia in *Origins of the Russian Intelligentsia: the Eighteenth-Century Nobility* (New York: Harcourt and Brace, 1966).

10 In *The Fateful Question of Culture* (New York: Columbia University Press, 1997), Geoffrey Hartman addresses the legacy of the eighteenth- and nineteenth-century philosophical debates on 'culture' and *Bildung* in modern Anglo-American and European contexts.

11 Pushkin's critique of Peter the Great can be found in the drafts for his unfinished *History of Peter the Great*. See also A.S. Pushkin, 'Zametki po russkoi istorii XVIII veka,' in *PSS*, 11:14–17.

12 The Lyceum was opened on 19 October 1811. The Grand Dukes did not in the end enrol in the Lyceum. There is substantial literature devoted to the history of this school. One of the most valuable accounts of the history of this school in Pushkin's time is provided by B.I. Tomashevskii in *Pushkin* (Moscow: Khudozhestvennaia literatura, 1990), 1:113; 328–65.

13 For Pushkin's own account of this event and its influence on his subsequent life see A.S. Pushkin, *Avtobiografiia, vospominaniia, dnevniki*, in *PSS*, 12:304–336. See also Tomashevskii, *Pushkin*, 1:18–117.

14 Monika Greenleaf presents a strong case for interpreting Pushkin's poetry along the lines of the German Romantic conception of *Romantische Poesie* (with its stress on irony and fragmentariness) as well as for seeing Pushkin's literary self-image as that of a Romantic poet genius in *Pushkin and Romantic Fashion: Fragment, Elegy, Orient, Irony* (Stanford, CA: Stanford University Press, 1994).

15 For more nuanced discussion of these phases in Pushkin's life, see P.V. Annenkov, *Literaturnye vospominaniia* (Moscow: Pravda, 1989); Tomashevskii, *Pushkin*; and Lotman, *A.S. Pushkin: Biografiia pisatelia*.

16 Lotman, among other scholars, offers an extremely well informed synoptic account of this period in the poet's life. For a nuanced discussion of this issue see Yu.M. Lotman, *A.S. Pushkin: Biografiia pisatelia*, 56–112.

The issue of Pushkin's relationship with the Decembrists is an extremely tangled one. It has been discussed by most Soviet-era Pushkinists, as well as by some more recent ones. I discuss this issue at length in my essay

'"My most mature poèma": Pushkin's *Poltava* and the Irony of Russian National Culture,' *Comparative Literature* 61, no. 2 (Spring 1999): 1–45.
17 See Oleg Proskurin, 'Pushkin and Politics,' in *The Cambridge Companion to Pushkin*, ed. Andrew Kahn (Cambidge, UK: Cambridge University Press, 2006), 105–17. For a nuanced recent discussion of Pushkin's post-Decembrist conservative turn, see Sergei Davydov, 'The Evolution of Pushkin's Conservative Thought,' in *The Pushkin Handbook*, ed. David M. Bethea (Madison: University of Wisconsin Press, 2005), 193–208.
18 See P.V. Annenkov, *Materialy dlia biografii A.S. Pushkina*, ed. and intro. G.M. Fridlender, 2 vols. (Moscow: 'Sovremennik,' 1984), 1:115.
19 *PSS*, 11:44–7. L.N. Kiseleva provides substantial evidence for viewing Nicholas's decision to release Pushkin from exile as part of his plan to make him one of the leading intellectuals of the new reign in her essay 'Pushkin i Zhukovskii v 1830-e gody (tochki ideologicheskogo sopriazheniia),' in *Pushkinskaia konferentsia v Stenforde*, ed. L. Fleishman et al. (Moscow: OGI, 2001), 171–85.
20 The transformation of Pushkin's political and philosophical outlook during his two exiles has concerned many Pushkin scholars, and the literature on this issue is vast. In addition to the works by Tomashevskii, Blagoi, Vatsuro, Oksman, Eikhenbaum, Lotman, and Proskurin – to name only a few scholars who influenced my view of Pushkin's personal and intellectual Bildung – I also want to acknowledge several more recent studies on this topic: K. Iu. Rogov, 'Iz istorii uchrezhdeniia moskovskogo romantizma: kruzhok i obschestvo S.E. Raicha,' in *Lotmanovskii sbornik*, ed. E. Permiakov (Moscow: Garant, 1995), 523–676; Sergei Davydov, 'The Evolution of Pushkin's Political Thought'; and Natalia Mazur, 'Pushkin i "Moskovskie iunoshi" vokrug problemy geniia,' in *Pushkinskaia konferentsia v Stenforde*, ed. L. Fleishman et al. (Moscow: OGI, 2001), 54–105.
21 *PSS*, 11:44.
22 Along with many future Decembrists, Pushkin was a member of a conspiratorial literary and political society The Green Lamp (Zelenaia Lampa). However, he never formally joined any of the conspiratorial political societies. Yu.G. Oksman, however, insisted that Pushkin's formal non-participation was merely a historical accident. See Yu.G. Oksman, 'Pushkin i dekabristy,' *Osvoboditel'noe dvizhenie v Rossii* 1 (1971): 70–88.
23 Boris Tomashevskii discusses Pushkin's critical response to the July Revolution in 'Pushkin i Iul'skaia revoliutsia 1830–1831 gg,' in *Pushkin* (Moscow: Akademiia Nauk SSSR, 1956–61), 2:291–344. As Tomahsveskii makes clear, in order to understand Pushkin's sympathy for the French legitimists

one must bear in mind his earlier fascination with the works of European liberal theorists like Benjamin Constant. Pushkin owned the complete political works of Constant (*Collection complète des ouvrages publiés sur le gouvernement représentative et la constitution actuelle de la France*), as well as *Commentaire sur l'ouvrage de Filangieri* and *Du polythéisme romain*. See B.L. Modzalevskii, *Biblioteka A.S. Pushkina: bibliograficheskoe opisanie* (St Petersburg: Tipografiia Imperatorskoi Akademii nauk, 1910), 210–11.

24 Oleg Proskurin connects the composition of this tragedy and the conservative change in Pushkin's political orientation in 'Pushkin and Politics.' Pushkin's interest in conservative liberalism was probably influenced, among others, by Burke. See M.P. Alekseev, 'Epigraph iz E. Burka v *Evgenii Onegine*' and 'K stat'e Pushkina *Dzhon Tenner*,' in *Pushkin i mirovaia literatura*, ed. G.P. Makogonenko (Leningrad: Nauka, 1987), 560–71; 542–9.

25 Pushkin's argument against all disruptions of existing political systems can be traced back not only to Karamzin's *History*, but also to Burke and Scottish Enlightenment historiography. For a good discussion of this issue, see Alexander Dolinin, *Pushkin i Angliia* (Moscow: Novoe literaturnoe obozrenie, 2007), 15–53.

26 *PSS*, 7:3–98, 40–1. Pushkin discusses why he was interested in drawing a portrait of his ancestor, the boyar Gavrila Pushkin, in his draft to the projected preface to *Boris Godunov* ('Nabroski predisloviia k Borisu Godunovu') in *PSS*, 11:140–2.

27 In my essay 'My most mature poèma' I argue that the lessons of Montesquieu's political philosophy were never far from Pushkin's mind, even as he grew older and expanded his intellectual horizon beyond French philosophy. Montesquieu had argued that the moral foundations of a monarchical state are honour and glory. Pushkin tried to attribute these same qualities to Peter the Great in *Poltava* by stressing Peter's magnanimity toward the vanquished Swedes. See Montesquieu, *The Spirit of the Laws*, ed. Anne M. Cohler, Basia C. Miller, and Harold S. Stone (Cambridge: Cambridge University Press, 1989), 33.

28 *PSS*, 14:198.

29 See Yurii Druzhnikov, *Prisoner of Russia: Alexander Pushkin and the Political Uses of Nationalism*, trans. Thomas Moore and Iulia Druzhnikov (New Brunswick, NJ: Transaction Publishers, 1999), 62.

30 Puhkin writes: 'Poiavlenie *Istorii Gosudarstva Rossiiskogo* . . . nadelalo mnogo shumu i proizvelo sil'noe vpechatlenie. [. . .] Svetskie liudi brosilis' chitat' istoriiu svoiego otechestva. Ona byla dlia nikh novym otkrytiem. Drevniiaa Rossiia, kazalos', naidena Karamzynym, kak Amerika Kolumbom.' *PSS*, 11:57. ['The appearance of *The History of the Russian State* . . .

produced a real éclat and made a strong impression [on the public]. [. . .] People of the world rushed to read the history of their fatherland. It became for them a new discovery. Old Russia seemed to be discovered by Karamzin the way America was discovered by Columbus.'] My translation.

31 Pushkin's *Boris Godunov* is traditionally seen as a 'Shakespearean' Romantic drama. Pushkin's 'Shakespearean strides' during his imprisonment in his father's estate Mikhailovskoe may also have to do with his critical reassessment of Karamzin's legacy. Karamzin was the crucial Russian representative of 'Sensibility' (sometimes called 'pre-Romanticism') and, like all pre-Romantics, was deeply impressed by Shakespeare. See Rudolf Neuhauser, *Toward the Romantic Age* (The Hague: Martinus Nijhoff, 1974), 174–92. It is also worth mentioning that Herder was the author of one of the most influential studies of Shakespeare in pre-Romantic Germany. See J.G. Herder, 'Shakespeare,' in *Selected Writings on Aesthetics*, trans. and ed. Gregory Moore (Princeton, NJ: Princeton University Press, 2006), 291–307.

32 See Richard Pipes, 'Karamzin's Conception of Monarchy,' *Harvard Slavic Studies* 4 (1957): 35–58.

33 Karamzin's aesthetics and politics continue to attract scholarly attention. This issue seems to have become particularly vital since the collapse of the Soviet Union. Of special interest in this regard are several recent works, including Victor Zhivov, 'Chuvstvitel'nyi natsionalizm: Karamzin, Rastopchin, natsional'nyi suverenitet i poiski natsional'noi identichnosti,' *Novoe literaturnoe obozrenie* 91 (2008): 114–40; and Richard Pipes, *Russian Conservatism and Its Critics: A Study in Political Culture* (New Haven, CT: Yale University Press, 2005). See also N.M. Karamzin, *Karamzin: Pro et contra: lichnost' i tvorchestvo Karamzina v otsenke russkikh pisatelei, kritikov, issledovatelei* (St Petersburg: Iz-vo Russkoi Khistianskoi gumanitarnoi akademii, 2006).

34 N.M. Karamzin, *Istoriia Gosudarstva Rossiskogo* (St Petersburg: Zolotoi Vek, 1997), 11, chap. 3, vol. 3, 469–534.

35 Vadim Vatsuro, 'Povesti pokoinogo Ivana Petrovicha Belkina,' in his *Zapiki kommentatora* (St Petersburg: Akademicheskii proekt, 1994), 29–47. Alexander Dolinin, 'Historicism or Providentialism? Pushkin's *History of Pugachev* in the Context of French Romantic Historiography,' *Slavic Review* 58, no. 2. (Summer 1999): 291–309.

36 See Nikolai Barsukov, *Zhizn' i trudy M.P. Pogodina*, 21 vols. (St Petersburg: Tipografiia Stasiulevicha, 1888–1907), 2: 42. For a very interesting recent work on Pogodin, see Nicholas Riasanovsky, 'Pogodin and Shevyrëv in Russian Intellectual History,' in his *Collected Writings, 1947–1994* (Los

Angeles: Charles Schlacks, 1993), 72–85. Other essays from this collection that are pertinent to my discussion are 'Some Comments on the Role of the Intelligentsia in the Reign of Nicholas I of Russia, 1812–1855' and *'Nationality* in the State Ideology During the Reign of Nicholas I,' 86–95, 96–101 (respectively).

37 This circle, which emerged in 1823, included Prince Vladimir Odoevskii, Venevitinov, Ivan Kireevskii, Nikolai Rozhalin (the first Russian translator of Goethe's *Werther*), and some other 'archiaval youths.' Mikhail Pogodin and Stepan Shevyrev were not formally members of this circle, but were close to it. Some, scholars, for example, Zhirmunskii, have regarded Pogodin's *Moscow Messenger* as the journal of the Lovers of Wisdom. See V.M. Zhirmunskii, *Gëte v russkoi literature* (Leningrad: Nauka, 1981), 127.

38 Ibid., 43–4.

39 The intellectual climate that led up to the emergence of *Moskovskii Vestnik* is well covered in Kirill Rogov's article. A substantial amount of information concerning the Muscovites' (including Pogodin, Shevyrev, Rozhalin, and some others) connections to Goethe, Herder, Schelling, and the Romantic authors is provided by S.V. Durylin in 'Russkie pisateli u Gëte v Veimare,' *Literaturnoe nasledstvo* 4/6 (1932): 83–504. In regard to this connection, I should mention that in an essay L.N. Kiseleva suggests that Pushkin's decision to accept the role of Russia's 'national genius,' which determined his career in the late 1820s and the 1830s, was in fact prompted by the poet's ongoing correspondence with V.A. Zhukovskii during his second exile. Thus, throughout 1825 Zhukovskii time and again reminds Pushkin of his 'genius' and tells him that he ought to preserve his talent and dedicate it to Russia. After Nicholas I's ascension, Zhukovskii, who was at the time very close to Nicholas I as the tutor of Nicholas's son and a personal friend of the Tsarina, successfully petitioned the new Tsar to recall Pushkin. See also L.N. Kiseleva, 'Pushkin i Zhukovskii,' 171–85.

40 In this respect, one of Pushkin's letters to his lifelong friend Anton Del'vig, one of the so-called literary aristocrats (who were not thrilled with Pushkin's association with Pogodin), is quite telling. Pushkin writes: 'Ty peniaesh' mne za *Moskovskii Vestnik* – i za nemetskuiu metafiziku. Bog vidit kak ia nenavizhu i preziraiu eë; da chto delat'? sobralis' rebiata teplye, upriamye; pop svoie, a chort svoie. Ia govoriu: Gospoda, okhota Vam iz pustogo v porozhnee perelivat' – vse eto khorosho dlia nemtsev, presyschennykh uzhe polozhitel'nymi poznaniiami, no my ... *Moskovskii Vestnik* sidit v iame i sprashivaiet: verevka vesch' kakaia? (Vprochem na etot metafizicheskii vopros mozhno by i otvechat' da NB). A vremia vesch' takaia, kotoruiu ni s kakim *Vestnikom* ne stanu teriat'. Im khuzhe, esli oni

menia ne slushaiut.' *PSS* 13:320. ['You reprimand me for the *Moscow Messenger* and for German metaphysics. God can see how I hate and scorn it [metaphysics], but what can one do? A few warm, stubborn guys have gathered; the priest has his own truth, and so does the devil. I say to them: gentlemen, what's the use of beating the air? – all this is good for the Germans, who are already satiated with knowledge, but we ... *The Moscow Messenger* sits in a pit and asks: what kind of thing is a rope? (In fact, one could answer this metaphysical question, but [illegible]. As for time, it is the kind of thing which I am not prepared to waste on any *Messenger*. It's their problem if they are not listening to me']. My translation.

41 Pushkin's correspondence with Benkendorf (Head of the Third Section) regarding his petition to open his own journal is published under the rubric 'delovyie bumagi' ('business papers') in *PSS*, 14:278–83. In the same volume we can find a curious 'plan' for Pushkin's projected journal. This plan shows both Pushkin's willingness to make his journal an organ through which the state could address and thereby control the reading public. For example, he mentions that the journal might include 'Preliminary Expression of the Government's Opinion' (*'predvaritel'noe iz'avlenie mneniia pravitel'stva'*). The rest of the journal would be dedicated to literature. Pushkin concludes his 'plan' with these words 'Zhurnal moi predlagaiu pravitel'stvu kak orudie ego deistviia na obschee mnenie' ('I am offering my journal to the government as the means of its influence over public opinion'). 'Nabrosok plana' is dated, probably by Boris Tomashevskii, the end of March/early May 1831. *PSS*, 12: 284–5.

42 There is a recent study documenting Pushkin's interest in Goethe and Germany during this period by V.A. Avetisian: *Poslednie literaturnye sobesedniki Pushkina: eshche raz o probleme 'Pushkin-Gëte'* (Moscow and Izhevsk: R and C Dynamics, 2009).

43 Upon defending his thesis 'On the Origins of Rus',' which he sent, via I.I. Dmitriev, to Karamzin, Pogodin was personally introduced to Karamzin. He described this event in 'Moe predstavlenie istoriografu,' in *Russkii arkhiv* (1866) 3: lines 1766–70. In 1828 *Moskovskii Vestnik* published N.S. Artsybashev's critical commentary on the first volume of Karamzin's *History*. As a follower of Kachenovskii's 'sceptical' school in historiography, Artsybashev attacked some of the factual infelicities in Karamzin's account. This critique produced a scandal in the public sphere. The old Karamzinists, including Pushkin's friend P.A. Viazemskii, O.M. Somov, and M.A. Dmitriev, attacked Artsybashev for offending the memory of the venerable historiographer. As the editor of *Moskovskii Vestnik*, Pogodin defended Artsybashev. This scandal and Pogodin's defence of Artsybashev may have

contributed to the cooling of his relationship with Pushkin, which occurred around the same time. Pogodin reasserted his allegiance to Karamzin in 'Istoricheskoe pokhval'noe slovo Karamzinu, proiznesennoe pri otkrytii pamiatnika Karamzinu v Simbirske avgusta 23, 1845 goda akademikom Pogodinym.' See Karamzin, *N.M. Karamzin: Pro et contra*, 591–604.

44 For an insightful reading of the *Journey to Arzrum* that highlights these themes, see Monica Greenleaf, 'Pushkin's "Journey to Arzrum": The Poet at the Border,' *Slavic Review* 50, no. 4 (Winter 1991): 940–53.

45 Analysing Pushkin's poem 'Geroi' ('The Hero'), Svetlana Evdokimova suggests that in discussing Napoleon Pushkin insists on moving away from the strict distinction between 'poetry' and 'history' established by Aristotle and respected by neoclassical poets. Evdokimova argues that Pushkin's historical imagination is characterized by what she calls 'the principle of complementarity,' where different genres and forms of emplotments mutually enrich one another. See Evdokimova, *Pushkin's Historical Imagination* (New Haven, CT: Yale University Press, 1999), 128–35.

Evdokimova demonstrates how this principle works when applied to the analysis of *The Captain's Daughter* and *The History of Pugachev's Rebellion*. She corrects Andrew Wachtel's thesis, in *An Obsession with History: Russian Writers Confront the Past* (Stanford, CA: Stanford University Press, 1994), according to which these works ought to be viewed as two mutually dependent parts within the same 'intergeneric dialogue.' According to Evdokimova, Pushkin's perception of Russian culture and society is intrinsically polyvocal and therefore can lend itself to many genres or 'codes' (to use Lotman's term) at once. This reading agrees with Lotman's view of nineteenth-century Russian culture as an entity that gradually becomes more and more open and akin to what he calls the 'semiosphere,' as well as to his vision of Pushkin as the spokesman for this nascent pluralism.

46 Gita Hammarberg, in *From the Idyll to the Novel: Karamzin's Sentimental Prose* (Cambridge, UK: Cambridge University Press, 1991), interprets Karamzin's 'intimate style' as a symptom of the author's 'solipsism.' I would like to dispute the escapist implications of this reading. The creation of an intimate community between the narrator and his audience is a well-established rhetorical device practised by most authors of 'Sensibility' (including Karamzin) and their nineteenth-century pupils (including Pushkin).

47 In this respect an especially important text by Karamzin is his unfinished novel *The Knight of Our Time* (1803), where Karamzin describes the 'fraternity' organized by provincial noblemen. The protagonist's father is one of the co-founders of this *Tugendbund*. Karamzin cites '*Dogovor bratskogo*

obschestva' ('The agreement of the fraternal society'), which resembles the text of Herder's *Ueber eine ungesichstbar-gesichtsbare Gesellschaft*, Zwei Gespraeche,' which Karamzin translated for his *Messenger of Europe*. J.G. Herder, *Briefe zur Befoerderung der Humanitaet* Brief 26; translated in *Vestnik Evropy* 22, no. 6 (1802): 116–29.

48 M.M. Bakhtin, 'Author and Hero in Aesthetic Activity.' In *Art and Answerability: Early Philosophical Works by M.M. Bakhtin*, ed. Michael Holquist and Vadim Liapunov, trans. Vadim Liapunov (Austin: University of Texas Press, 1990), 4–256.

49 Pushkin and Pogodin were not the only intellectuals engaged in the project of Karamzin's canonization; other historians and publicists contributed to it as well. For example, in 1827 Nikolai Ivanchin-Pisarev published a collection of Karamzin's works and aphorisms entitled *Dukh Karamzina (The Spirit of Karamzin)* with a dedication to I.I. Dmitriev.

50 Indeed, as compared to other works by Pushkin, such as *The Queen of Spades*, which obviously bears traces of the 'frenetic' literature of the 1820s (under the influence of Balzac, Hofmann, Charles Maturin and others), *The Captain's Daughter* strikes a quaint note. This style has long puzzled critics. It signals a move away from sensationalism and fiction written for entertainment and in the direction of didacticism.

51 In the mid-1820s Goethe's idea of world literature or *Weltliteratur* was frequently discussed by the critics of the French journal *Le Globe*, which Pushkin, Pogodin, and their circle read regularly.

52 A.A. Grigor'ev, *'Vzgliad na russkuiu literaturu so smerti Pushkina,'* in *Sochineniia v dvukh tomakh*, ed. B.F. Egorov (Moscow: Khudozhestvennaia literatura, 1990), 2:48–91.

53 Ibid., 71.

54 Grigor'ev, *'Graf L. Tolstoy i iego sochineniia. Stat'ia vtoraia,'* in *Sochineniia*, 2: 344–74, 355.

55 G.W.F. Hegel, *The Philosophy of History*, trans. J. Sibree (Mineola, NY: Dover Philosophical Classics, 2004), 420.

56 Grigor'ev, *Sochineniia*, 2:342.

57 For the detailed analysis of the historical sources and evolution of the plot, see Yu.G. Oksman, 'Pushkin v rabote nad romanom "Kapitanskaia Dochka,"' in A.S. Pushkin, *Kapitanskaia Dochka. Literaturnyie Pamiatniki* (Moscow: Nauka, 1964), 149–208. The evolution of the text of *The Captain's Daughter* and the metamorphosis of the figure of Shvanvich into Basharin, and finally into two characters, a fully noble Grinev and the ignoble Shvabrin, is analysed in great detail by N. Petrunina in *Proza Pushkina: puti evoliutsii* (Leningrad: Nauka, 1987), 241–87.

58 One thinks here, first of all, of Gogol. Anne Lounsbery demonstrates how Gogol's struggles to create/envision a broader national reading public contributed to his mental demise. See part 2 of her study *Thin Culture, High Art: Gogol, Hawthorne, and Authorship in Nineteenth-Century Russia and America* (Cambridge, MA: Harvard University Press, 2007), 125–92.
59 See Lotman, *Struktura khudozhestvennogo teksta*, 75–242.
60 This view is expressed most cogently by Iu. N. Tynianov in 'Pushkin,' in *Istoriia literatury. Kritika* (St Petersburg: Akademicheskii proekt, 2001), 133–87.
61 See Caryl Emerson, 'Grinev's Dream: *The Captain's Daughter* and a Father's Blessing,' *Slavic Review* 40, no. 1 (Spring 1981): 60–76.
62 Todd, *Fiction and Society in the Age of Pushkin*, 132–3.
63 Franco Moretti, *The Way of the World: The Bildungsroman in European Culture*, trans. Albert Sbragia (London and New York: Verso, 2000), esp. chapter 1, 'The Comfort of Civilization,' 15–73.
64 Karamzin's democratic sympathy is summed up in the famous dictum, 'I krest'ianki liubit' umeiut' ('Peasant girls also know how to love'), from 'Poor Liza.' For an excellent recent discussion of Karamzin's sentimentalism and the question of the *narod*, see Viktor Zhivov, 'Chuvstvitel'nyi natsionalizm.'
65 See Lotman, 'Poeziia 1790–1810kh godov' (predislovie),' in *Poety 1790–1810kh godov*, ed. Mark Alt'shuller (Leningrad: Sovetskii pisatel', 1971), 5–62.
66 David Bethea in particular has argued that Grinev's life bears resemblance to Derzhavin's and that his character represents an improved and 'ennobled' version of Derzhavin's character. David M. Bethea, *Realizing Metaphors: Alexander Pushkin and the Life of the Poet* (Madison: University of Wisconsin Press, 1998), see esp. 212–13. The biographical connection between Derzhavin and Grinev (or, rather, his earlier version, Basharin) has been uncovered by Irina Reyfman in 'Poetic Justice and Injustice: Autobiographical Echoes in Pushkin's *The Captain's Daughter*,' *Slavic and East European Journal* 38, no. 3 (1994): 463–78.
67 Lotman, *Izbrannye stat'i*, 1:76–89.
68 Lotman, 'O dvukh modeliakh communikatsii v sisteme kul'tury,' in *Izbrannye stat'i*, 1:76–89, 77.
69 I have previously compared Lotman's understanding of creativity with the idea of auto-poeisis (*Bildung*) as understood by early German Romantic thinkers. See Lina Steiner, 'Toward an Ideal Universal Community: Yurii Lotman Revisiting the Enlightenment and Romanticism,' *Comparative Literature Studies* 40, no. 1 (2003): 37–53.

70 See also my analysis of Lotman's concept of 'explosion' (developed later, in *Kul'tura i Vzyrv/ Culture and Explosion*) in the introduction and chapter 1 of the present volume.
71 Karamzin's critical attitude towards Peter comes across most clearly in *Zapiska o staroi i novoi Rossii/ Memoir on the Old and the Modern Russia*. See Richard Pipes, *Karamzin's Memoir on Ancient and Modern Russia: A Translation and Analysis* (Cambridge, MA: Harvard University Press, 1959).
72 See N.N. Strakhov, *Kriticheskie stat'ii ob I.S. Turgeneve i L.N. Tolstom* (Kiev: tipografiia Chokolova, 1908), 1:179–310. Strakhov wrote his essay in aftermath of the emancipation of the serfs, when the role of the nobility in post-Reform society had become a hotly debated topic. See Nicholas Riasanovsky, *Russian Identities: A Historical Survey* (Oxford: Oxford University Press, 2005), 116–17.
73 Boris Tomashevskii has tried to prove this in the original (uncensored) version of the novel. According to him, Grinev's visit to Pugachev's headquarters in chapter 11 was voluntary, rather than accidental. In support of this claim, Tomashevskii draws our attention to the final sentence of chapter 10, which concludes with Grinev's conversation with the commander of the Orenburg fortress. Despite Grinev's desperate pleas to help mount a rescue operation, the prudent German general refuses to support such a risky affair. Grinev then addresses the reader, saying: 'I looked down; I was in despair. Suddenly a *strange idea* crossed my mind: what this thought was the readers will find out in the next chapter, as the old-fashioned novelists used to say.' *PSS*, 8:343. See B. Tomashevskii, 'Pervonachal'naia redaktsia XI glavy *Kapitanskoi dochki*,' in *Pushkin*, 2:281–90.
74 Marina Tsvetaeva, 'Pushkin i Pugachev,' in *Izbrannaia proza v dvukh tomakh: 1917–1937*, foreword Joseph Brodsky (New York: Russica Publishers, 1979), 2:280–301.
75 *Sochineniia*, 2:348–50.
76 *Sochineniia*, 2:365.
77 It is worth noting that while Pushkin's influence with Nicholas I waned, that of Uvarov increased. He became Minister of the Enlightenment in 1833, whereas Pushkin was forced to look for new allies and supporters in the fiercely competitive and volatile professional literary world of the 1830s.
78 Emerson, 'Grinev's Dream.'
79 I think it is plausible that Grinev's first name, Peter or Petrusha, is meant to emphasize his connection to Peter's state, which he, as a born nobleman, is supposed to serve and ameliorate. A.L. Ospovat discusses the significance of his last name, Grinev, as an old gentry name. Ospovat, 'Imenovanie geroiia.'

80 Marina Tsvetaeva 'Pushkin i Pugachev,' 283.
81 Ibid., 353.
82 Here, we are reminded of Lotman's prediction that the elimination of geographical barriers from our life (which is now occurring through the rapid development of information technology) will force us to seek and create new boundaries to cross in our minds, for without such boundary-crossing the creative aspect of human intelligence wanes. See the epigraph to chapter 1.
83 Lotman, 'Ideinaia struktura "Kapitanskoi dochki,"' in *Izbrannye stat'i*, 2:416–29; 422.
84 Ibid., 423.
85 Benjamin employs the concept of *Erfahrung* or 'narratable experience' in 'The Storyteller,' which (I think not accidentally) takes as its focus Nikolai Leskov. See 'The Storyteller,' in *Illuminations*, ed. and intro. Hannah Arendt (New York: Schoken Books, 1968), 83–110. For a broader intellectual historical discussion of the concept of 'Erfahrung,' see Martin Jay, *Songs of Experience: Modern American and European Variations on a Universal Theme* (Los Angeles: University of California Press, 2005), 312–60.
86 The importance of the Lotmanian 'auto-communication' for the development of 'open' liberal society has been recently discussed by several scholars of political science. See, in particular, Michael Urban, 'Post-Soviet Political Discourse and the Creation of Political Communities'; and Marek Steedman, 'State Power, Hegemony, and Memory: Lotman and Gramsci'; both are published in *Lotman and Cultural Studies: Encounters and Extensions*, ed. Andreas Schoenle (Madison: University of Wisconsin Press, 2006), 115–35, 136–58.

6. Educating Russia, Building Humanity: Tolstoy's *War and Peace*

1 See P.V. Annenkov, 'Zamechatel'noe desiatiletie, 1838–1848,' in *Literaturnye vospominaniia* (Moscow: Pravda, 1989), 111–352.
2 See Donna Orwin, *Tolstoy's Art and Thought, 1847–1880* (Princeton, NJ: Princeton University Press, 1993), 16–19.
3 *Sovremennik* no. 9 (1852).
4 See N.N. Gusev, *Letopis' zhizni i tvorchestva L.N. Tolstogo* (Moscow: Academia, 1936), 104–6.
5 See N.G. Chernyshevskii, 'L.N. Tolstoy's *Childhood* and *Boyhood* and *Military Tales*,' in *Belinsky, Chernyshevsky and Dobrolyubov: Selected Criticism*, ed. and intro. Ralph E. Matlow (Bloomington: Indiana University Press, 1962), 95–107.

6 Chernyshevskii wrote to Nekrasov on 5 November 1856: 'Na dniakh priedet Tolstoi i privezet "Iunost'" dlia pervogo nomera *Sovremennika*. Ia pobyvaiu u nego – ne znaiu, uspeiu li poluchit' nad nim nekotoruiu vlast'") [Tolstoy will stop by shortly and will bring his *Youth* for the first number of *The Contemporary*. I will visit with him – I don't know if I will have enough time to obtain some power over him']. My translation. See Gusev, *Letopis'*, 127. Tolstoy and Chernyshevskii met at Panaev's house on 18 December 1856. See Gusev, *Letopis'*, 134.
7 See *Polnoe sobranie sochinenii* [*PSS*] (Jubilee Ediition), 90 vols. (Moscow: Khudozhestvennaia literatura, 1928–58), 5:271–3. Henceforth I will refer to this edition as *PSS*.
8 Scholars since Eikhenbaum have stressed the influence of the British novel on Tolstoy. For example, Tom Cain draws a very convincing analogy between several key scenes and motifs from *War and Peace* and those in Charles Dickens's *David Copperfield*. See his 'Tolstoy's Use of David Copperfield,' in *Tolstoi and Britain*, ed. W. Gareth Jones (Oxford: Berg, 1995), 67–78.
9 See Tolstoy, *PSS*, 60:74–5.
10 See *Sobranie sochinenii A.V. Druzhinina*, ed. A.V. Gerbel', 8 vols. (St Petersburg: tip. Imperatorskoi Akademiii Nauk, 1865–7), 7:189–241. For a discussion of this work, see Boris Eikhenbaum, *Lev Tolstoj*, 2 vols. (Munich: Wilhelm Fink Verlag, 1968), 1:225.
11 Eikhenbaum, 1:213.
12 For a very interesting discussion of this famous incident see Ilya Kliger, 'Genre and Actuality in Belinsky, Herzen and Goncharov: Toward a Genealogy of the Tragic Pattern in Russian Realism,' *Slavic Review* 66, no. 1 (Spring 2011): 45–66.
13 N.N. Gusev, *L.N. Tolstoy: Materialy k biografii s 1855 po 1869 god* (Moscow: Izdatel'stvo Akademii Nauk SSSR, 1957), 157.
14 Eikhenbaum, *Lev Tolstoj*, 1:217–18, 278–80.
15 *PSS*, 1:84.
16 On Tolstoy's interest in the pedagogical writings of eighteenth-century authors, see Ie.N. Kupreianova, *Estetika L.N. Tolstogo* (Moscow, Leningrad: Nauka, 1966), 82.
17 The influence of Rousseau on Tolstoy has been discussed by several critics, most notably by Donna Orwin in *Tolstoy's Art and Thought*. The influence of Sterne has been analysed by, among others, Viktor Shklovskii. Eikhenbaum also stresses the influence of Toepffer on Tolstoy. See Eikhenbaum, *Lev Tolstoj*, 1:84. Elena Krasnoshchekova develops Eikenbaum's idea and makes a convincing case for regarding Toepffer as one of the key influences on

Tolstoy. See Krasnoshchekova, *Roman vospitaniia: Bildungsroman na russkoi pochve: Karamzin, Pushkin, Tolstoi, Dostoevskii*, 303–28.
18 Gusev, *L.N. Tolstoy: materialy k biografii*, 148–9.
19 Gusev, *L.N. Tolstoy: materialy k biografii*, 186.
20 See Gusev, *Letopis'*, 151.
21 Tolstoy, *Ispoved'*, in *PSS*, 23: 488–511.
22 Kathryn B. Feuer, *Tolstoy and the Genesis of* War and Peace, ed. Robin Feuer Miller and Donna Tussing Orwin (Ithaca, NY: Cornell University Press, 1996), esp. 168–206.
23 *PSS*, 5:3–36.
24 See Gusev, *L.N. Tolstoy: Materialy k biografii*, 222–6.
25 Gusev, *L.N. Tolstoy: Materialy k biografii*, 234–28.
26 See Gusev, *Letopis'*, 111.
27 See Feuer, *Tolstoy and the Genesis of* War and Peace, 26.
28 N.I. Pirogov was a military surgeon in Sevastopol, whose article 'Vital Questions,' published in *Morskoi sbornik* in 1856, removed pedagogy from the special preserve of the experts and made it a pressing concern for the general public. See Allen Sinel, *The Classroom and the Chancellery: State Educational Reforms in Russia under Count Dmitrii Tolstoy* (Cambridge, MA: Harvard University Press, 1973), 25. Ushinskii was Pirogov's follower as a pedagogue and administrator.
29 See Eikhenbaum, *Lev Tolstoj*, vol. 2, part 1, 'Tolstoy vne literatury,' 5–109.
30 See *Time* no. 3 (1862): 66, 71, 77.
31 See *Pis'ma russkogo puteshestvennika*, in *Sochineniia Karamzina*, 3 vols. (St Petersburg: Karl Krai, 1848), 2:139–52.
32 For a detailed description of this trip, see N.N. Gusev, *L.N. Tolstoy: Materialy k biografii*, 363–72.
33 J.S. Mill, 'On Genius' and 'Civilization,' in *Essays on Literature and Society*, ed. and intro. B. Schneewind (NY: Collier, 1965), 87–101, 148–82.
34 *PSS*, 8:11.
35 The English translation is quoted from Leo Tolstoy, *On Education*, trans. Leo Wiener and intro. Reginald D. Archambault (Chicago: University of Chicago Press, 1967), 14. The essay 'O narodnom obrazovanii' appears in the original Russian in *PSS*, 8:4–25.
36 Ibid., 15.
37 The essays in question are *'O publike,' 'O narodnom obrazovanii,' 'O znachenii opisaniia shkol i narodnykh knig,' 'Iasnopolianskaia shkola za noiabr' i dekabr' mesiatsy,' 'O metodakh obucheniia gramote,' 'O svobodnom vozniknovenii i razvitii shkol v narode,' 'Proekt obschego ustroistva plana narodnykh uchilisch,' 'Vospitanie i obrazovanie,'* and several others. Tolstoy's pedagogical works from this phase of his career are collected in *PSS*, vol. 8.

38 See Raymond Williams, *Culture and Society* (New York: Columbia University Press, 1958), 11–99. David Lloyd and Paul Thomas, *Culture and the State*, 3–20.
39 Tolstoy, *PSS*, 8:211–46. 212. The English translation is quoted from Leo Tolstoy, *On Education*, 110.
40 See Frederick Beiser, *The Romantic Imperative: The Concept of Early German Romanticism* (Cambridge, MA: Harvard University Press, 2003), 137–40. See also Beiser's *The Fate of Reason* (Cambridge, MA: Harvard University Press, 1986) and *German Idealism: The Struggle Against Subjectivism, 1781–1801* (Cambridge, MA: Harvard University Press, 2002), 81–180.
41 See G. Krasnov, 'Herder und Lev Tolstoj,' *Zeitschrift fuer Slawistik* 6, no. 3 (1961): 415–33. 416. One of Tolstoy's acquaintances from the University of Kazan', N.N. Bulich, wrote in 1886 that as a student Tolstoy was interested in Spinoza. See B. Eikhenbaum, 'Iz studencheskikh let Tolstogo,' in *O proze* (Leningrad: Khudozhestvennaia literatura, 1969), 91–116. 106.
42 See, for example, a diary entry dated 17 April 1847. Tolstoy, *PSS*, 46:30–1.
43 On this issue see Ul'rich Schmid, 'The Family Drama as an Interpretive Pattern in Aleksandr Gerzen's *Byloe i dumy*,' and Lina Steiner, 'Gertsen's Tragic *Bildungsroman*: Love, Autonomy and Maturity in Aleksandr Gertsen's *Byloe i dumy*,' both in *Russian Literature* 61 (2007): 67–102; 139–74 (respectively).
44 Eikhenbaum, *Lev Tolstoj*, 2:330–3.
45 This can be gleaned from a perusal of *Moskovskii Vetsnik*. See also Pogodin's book *Istorichskie aforismy Mikhaila Pogodina* (Moscow: Universitetskaia Tipografiia, 1836), where many aphorisms seem to be borrowed from Herder, Humboldt, and other German sources.
46 Eikhenbaum, *Lev Tolstoj*, 2:323–41.
47 On the festive reception of A. v. Humboldt in Moscow by Pogodin, see Barsukov, *Zhizn' i trudy M.P. Pogodina*, 21 vols. (St Petersburg: Tipografiia Stasiulevicha, 1888–1907), 2:407–8.
48 This moment in Grigor'ev's and Pogodin's biographies is described in Robert Whittaker, *Russia's Last Romantic: Apollon Grigor'ev 1822–1864* (Lewiston, NY: Edwin Mellen Press, 1999), 95–176; see also Wayne Dowler, *An Unnecessary Man: The Life of Apollon Grigor'ev* (Toronto: University of Toronto Press, 1995), 90–163; and B.F. Egorov, *Apollon Grigor'ev. Zhizn' zamechatel'nykh liudei* (Moscow: Molodaia gvardiia, 2000), 90–119.
49 There is considerable critical literature on Tolstoy's relationship with Herzen and the latter's influence on Tolstoy. See, for example, S. Rozanova's

study *Tolstoy i Gertsen* (Moscow: Khudozhestvennaia literatura, 1974). See also Nicholas Rzhevsky, 'The Shape of Chaos: Herzen and *War and Peace*,' *Russian Review* 34, no. 4 (1975): 367–81.
50 Tolstoy, *PSS*, 60:373. My translation.
51 Tolstoy, *PSS*, 28:69.
52 See Richard Gustafson, 'The Three Stages of Man,' *Canadian-American Slavic Studies* 12, no. 4 (Winter 1978): 481–518. In his book *Tolstoy, Resident and Stranger; a Study in Fiction and Theology* (Princeton, NJ: Princeton University Press, 1986), Gustafson expands upon this idea. He reads Tolstoy's entire body of work as a systematic oeuvre based upon a set of unified theological principles, chief among which is the idea of development from the animal to the divine stage.
53 *PSS*, 60:373–4. My translation.
54 *PSS*, 60:374. My translation.
55 Quoted from Peter Brooks, *The Melodramatic Imagination: Balzac, Henry James, Melodrama, and the Mode of Excess* (New Haven, CT: Yale University Press, 1995), 154.
56 Orwin, *Tolstoy's Art and Thought*, 100.
57 Patricia Carden, 'The Expressive Self in War and Peace,' *Canadian-American Slavic Studies* 12, no. 4 (Winter 1978): 519–34.
58 Tolstoy, *PSS*, 13:367.
59 Tolstoy, *PSS*, 13:454–6.
60 Tolstoy, *War and Peace*, trans. A. Briggs (London: Penguin, 2005), 419–20. All translations of *War and Peace* are quoted from this edition and will be cited parenthetically in the text.
61 My translation.
62 *Sochineniia Karamzina*, 239–82.
63 See M.P. Pogodin, *Nikolai Mikhailovich Karamzin: po ego sochineniiam pis'mam i otzyvam sovremennikov* (Moscow: tip. Mamontova, 1866), 2 vols.
64 Tolstoy, *PSS*, 16:143.
65 Psyche is the name of Agathon's beloved in Wieland's novel.
66 Eikhenbaum, *Lev Tolstoj*, 2: 11.
67 See Apollon Grigor'ev, 'Graf L.Tolstoy i ego sochineniia,' in Apollon Grigor'ev, *Sochineniia v dvukh tomakh*, ed. B.F. Egorov (Moscow: Khudozhestvennaia literatura, 1990), 2:344–374, 348. First published in *Time*, 1862, no. 9, 1–27. This was the only positive review of *Family Happiness* and one of the few positive reviews of 'Luzerne.'
68 See Grigor'ev, *Sochineniia*, 2:344–74. Tolstoy himself, however, was so dissatisfied with *Family Happiness* that he called it a 'stain on his reputation as an artist and a man.' Eikhenbaum, *Lev Tolstoj*, 1:344–5.

69 See the essay 'Lermontov i ego napravlenie (krainiiaa gran' razvitiia otritsatel'nogo vzgliada),' in *Sobranie sochinenii Apollona Grigor'eva*, ed. V.F. Savodnik (Moscow: Kushner, 1915), 58–9. It is Gogol who represents, according to Grigor'ev, the 'comical' line in the literature of the 1840s. The hero who does not manage to reach the point when he can retire honourably from service ['*ne dosluzhivshikhsia do priazhki*'] is Herzen's Bel'tov from *Who Is to Blame?*

70 Grivor'ev, *Sochinenia*, ed. B.F. Egorov, 2 vols. (Moscow: Khudozhestvennaia literatura, 1990) 2:358–9. Herzen's Bel'tov (the protagonist of *Who Is to Blame?*) quit service after spending only six months on his assignment. Hence the joke about not reaching the term (fifteen years) after which one could reach a certain rank that allowed one to wear a special buckle ['*priazhka*'] and retire honourably. For a detailed not see A.I. Gerzen, *Sobranie sochinenii v tridtsati tomakh* (Moscow: Iz-vo Akademii Nauk SSSR, 1954–65), 4:103.

71 Rousseau's Savoyard Vicar says: 'When I abandon myself to temptations, I act according to the impulsion of external objects. When I reproach myself for this weakness I listen only to my will. I am enslaved because of my vices and free because of my remorse.' *Emile, or on Education*, trans. and intro. Allan Bloom (New York: Basic Books, 1979), 280.

72 Herder's popularity among the Russian Masons of the 1810s may be due to his membership in the Illuminati movement. When the persecutions of the Illuminati began, Herder gradually withdrew from the order. However, his works, along with Lessing's *Conversations of Masons*, were part of the Russian Masonic canon alongside the works of such mystics as Ekkartshausen, Baader, and Jung-Stilling. On Herder's place in the history of Russian Masonic thought, see A.N. Pypin, *Russkoe masonstvo XVIII i pervaia chast' XIX v.* (Petrograd: OGNI, 1916), and A.I. Serkov, *Istoriia russkogo masonstva XIX veka* (St Petersburg: Izdatelstvo imeni N.I. Novikova, 2000).

73 Pypin, *Masonstvo v Rossii: XVIII i pervaia cchetvert' XIX v*, 198–9.

74 On the Bildungsroman as a genre rooted in Pietist autobiography, see Todd Kontje, *Private Lives in Public Sphere: The German Bildungsroman as Metafiction* (University Park: Pennsylvania State University Press, 1992), esp. chaps. 1–3.

75 F. Schiller, *Ueber naïve und sentimentalische Dichtung* (*On the naïve and sentimental in literature*), trans. Helen Watanabe-O'Kelly (Manchester: Carcanet New Press, 1981).

76 See James Hardin, introduction to *Reflection and Action: Essays on the Bildungsroman* (Columbia: University of South Carolina Press, 1991), ix–xxvii.

77 Chaps. 33 and 34, part 3, vol. 3.
78 Chap. 34, part 2, vol. 2.
79 Tolstoy, *PSS*, 29:3–46.
80 The essays that are particularly pertinent in this connection are: 'O narodnom obrazovanii' ['On Popular Education'], 'O metodakh obucheniia gramote' ['On Methods of Teaching the Rudiments'], 'Vospitanie i obrazovaniie' ['Education and Culture'], 'Progress i opredelenie obrazovaniia' ['Progress and the Definition of Education'], 'Iasnopolianskaia shkola za noiabr' i dekabr' mesiatsy' ['The School at Iasnaia Poliana'], and 'Komu u kogo uchit'sia pisat', krest'ianskim rebiatam u nas ili nam u krest'ianskikh rebiat' ['Are the Peasant Children to Learn to Write from Us?']. All these essays are published in vol. 8 of *PSS* (Jubilee edition). The English translations of Tolstoy's essays' titles are cited from Tolstoy, *On Education*.
81 Tolstoy's very positive reaction to Dostoevsky's *Notes from the House of the Dead* is described in Gusev, *Lev Tolstoy: Materialy k biografii*, 787.
82 As is well known, Tolstoy admired Dostoevsky's *House of the Dead*. Dostoevsky found out about this when Strakhov gave him as a gift Tolstoy's letter, in which Tolstoy praised it highly and even ranked it above Pushkin. See A.S. Dolinin, ed., *F.M. Dostoevsky v vospominaniiakh sovremennikov* (Moscow: Khudozhestvennaia literatura, 1964), 2:311.
83 'Muzhik Marei' is a semi-fictional, semi-autobiographical novella published in the 1876 *Diary of the Writer*. For a detailed discussion of this chapter, see Joseph Frank, *Dostoevsky: The Stir of Liberation, 1860–1865* (Princeton, NJ: Princeton University Press, 1986), 213–323. See also Harriet Murav, 'Dostoevsky in Siberia: Remembering the Past,' *Slavic Review* 50, no. 4 (1991): 858–66.
84 See Rousseau, *Emile*, 42, 61, 270. See also Orwin, *Tolstoy's Art and Thought*, 39–44, 50–1, 135.
85 Giorgio Agamben, *Homo Sacer: Sovereign Power and Bare Life*, trans. Daniel Heller-Roazen (Stanford, CA: Stanford University Press, 1998).
86 Ginzburg, for example, claimed that 'Tolstoy remembered how he was bathed in a tub at the age of one or two.' See Lidiia Ginzburg, *Chelovek za pis'mennym stolom* (Leningrad: Sovetskii pisatel', 1989), 319.
87 Inessa Medzhibovskaya offers an insightful interpretation of Tolstoy's dream about Schiller in *Tolstoy and the Religious Culture of His Time: A Biography of a Long Conversion, 1845–1887* (Lanham, MD: Lexington Books, 2008), 74.
88 This is one of the main ideas of Tolstoy's essay 'Progress i opredelenie obrazovaniia,' in *PSS*, 8:325–55. In English: 'Progress and the Definition of Education,' in Tolstoy, *On Education*, ed. Leo Wiener 152–90.

89 *PSS*, 62:243–4.
90 Edward Wasiolek, in *Tolstoy's Major Fiction* (Chicago: University of Chicago Press, 1978), was one of the first critics to contest Percy Lubbock's view of *War and Peace* as an aesthetically flawed work. Wasiolek argued, to the contrary, that *War and Peace* constituted an organic unity. See Wasiolek, *Tolstoy's Major Fiction*, 65–128.
91 There is a growing body of criticism on the connection between political and novelistic representation, especially in the nineteenth-century British novel. See, for example, James Chandler, *England in 1819: The Politics of Literary Culture and the Case of Romantic Historicism* (Chicago: University of Chicago Press, 1998), 174–85.
92 Tolstoy's reflections on his role as a member of the aristocracy pervade his fiction, non-fiction, and diaries from the 1850s and 1860s. The unrealized plan of the '*Roman russkogo pomeshchika*' is one piece of the evidence for Tolstoy's intense preoccupation with the theme of the Russian gentry's social function. Another crucial work in this connection is, of course, *The Cossacks*, in *PSS*, 6:3–152.
93 See Gary Saul Morson, 'War and Peace,' in *The Cambridge Companion to Tolstoy*, ed. Donna Tussing Orwin (Cambridge: Cambridge University Press, 2002), 76.
94 See Victor Shklovskii, *Lev Tolstoy* (Moscow: Molodaia gvardiia, 1973), 296–7.
95 See Mikhail Bakhtin, 'The *Bildungsroman* and Its Significance in the History of Realism,' in *Speech Genres and Other Late Essays*, trans. Vern W. McGee, ed. Caryl Emerson and Michael Holquist (Austin: University of Texas Press, 1986), 10–59.
96 A letter to Princess L.I. Volkonskaia dated 3 May 1865 is cited from Gusev, *Letopis'*, 309–10.
97 As Eikhenbaum points out (referencing Tolstoy's letter to Bartenev from 1 November 1867), Natasha's infatuation with Anatole and her simultaneous friendship with Pierre is the most difficult place in the text and the 'knot' of the entire novel. See *Lev Tolstoj*, book 2, part 3:280.
98 *PSS*, 48/49:127.
99 See, for example, Herder's 1778 essay 'On Cognition and Sensation of the Human Soul,' which stops short of making the conjectural leap toward assuming the afterlife. In J.G. Herder, *Philosophical Writings*, trans. and ed. Michael N. Forster (Cambridge: Cambridge University Press, 2003), 187–246. However, some of the more mystically inclined Russian readers of Herder interpreted him as a proponent of a ladder-like structure of the universe, in which human life is followed by afterlife.

7. Dostoevsky on Individual Reform and National Reconciliation: *The Adolescent*

1 This journal was closed down in 1863 after it published Strakhov's article on Russian-Polish relations, which the government deemed politically dangerous.
2 Dostoevsky, *Biografiia, pis'ma i zametki iz zapisnoi knizhki F. M. Dostoevskogo* (St Petersburg: tip. A.S. Suvorina, 1883), 180–1. My translation.
3 Secondary literature on this topic is voluminous. For a concise overview of this issue see Jesse V. Claroy, *The Superfluous Man in Russian Letters* (Washington, DC: University Press of America, 1980); and Ellen Chances, *Conformity's Children: An Approach to the Superfluous Man in Russian Literature* (Columbus, OH: Slavica, 1978).
4 See Anonymous (N.N. Strakhov), 'Iasnaia Poliana,' *Time* (March 1862): 65–8.
5 Apollon Grigor'ev, '*Obozreniie otnoshenii literatury nashei k narodnosti*,' in *Polnoe sobranie sochinenii Apollona Grigor'eva v dvenadtsati tomakh* (Petrograd: Izdanie P.P. Ivanova, 1918), 1:216–25.
6 See Chenxi Tang, *The Geographic Imagination of Modernity: Geography, Literature, and Philosophy in German Romanticism* (Palo Alto, CA: Stanford University Press, 2008), see esp. chap. 5, 'Dwelling in Space,' 157–201.
7 In *Poslednii god Dostoevskogo: istoricheskie zapiski* (Moscow: Sovetskii pisatel', 1986), Igor' Volgin, through very intricate argumentation, strives to prove that Dostoevsky, especially in the last few months of his life, tried to serve as the medium of a rapprochement between the state and the radical intelligentsia, including those who participated in and sympathized with the terrorist group *Land and Freedom* (*Zemlia i Volia*).
8 The British reception of the German conception of *Bildung* as 'culture' is discussed by Raymond Williams, among others. See his works *Keywords: A Vocabulary of Culture and Society*, 2nd ed. (New York: Oxford University Press, 1983) and *The Long Revolution* (New York: Broadview Press, 2001). See also Catherine Gallagher, *The Industrial Reformation of English Fiction: Social Discourse and Narrative Form, 1832–1867* (Chicago: University of Chicago Press, 1985). Gallagher sheds a lot of light on the special significance of the trope of 'reconciliation' for mid-nineteenth-century British political debates and novels.
9 M. Dostoevsky, '*Dva lageria teoretikov*' ('Two camps of theoreticians') in *PSS*, 20:5–22.
10 Ibid.

11 F.M. Dostoevskii, 'Knizhnost' i gramotnost' ("Bookishness and literacy'), in *PSS*, 19: 5–56.
12 Dowler, *Dostoevsky, Grivor'ev, and Native Soil Conservatism* (Toronto: University of Toronto Press, 1982), 101.
13 For more on this debate, see Allen Sinel, *The Classroom and the Chancellery: State Educational Reforms in Russia under Count Dmitrii Tolstoy* (Cambridge, MA: Harvard University Press, 1973), 1–33.
14 This episode is carefully described in Joseph Frank, *Dostoevsky: The Stir of Liberation, 1860–1865* (Princeton, NJ: Princeton University Press, 1986), 133–59.
15 Sinel, *The Classroom and the Chancellery*, 95.
16 Orwin, *Consequences of Consciousness* (Stanford, CA: Stanford University Press, 2007), 141.
17 Mochul'skii, *Dostoevsky: His Life and Work*, trans. and intro. Michael A. Minihan (Princeton, NJ: Princeton University Press, 1967), 182.
18 A.L. Bem, 'Evoliutsiia obraza Stavrogina: k sporu ob "Ispovedi Stavrogina,"' in *Issledovaniia. Pis'ma o literature* (Moscow: Iazyki slavianskoi kul'tury, 2001), 111–57.
19 One obvious sign that these four novels are indeed closely interconnected is the fact that several pivotal characters from these novels stem from the same archetype, which is outlined in *The Life of a Great Sinner*. Upon a closer examination, the archetype of the sinner who undergoes a moral reform can be traced back to the drafts for *The Humiliated and the Wronged*, Dostoevsky's first large-scale post-Siberian novel. In one of his letters, Dostoevsky's brother Mikhail compares the plan, which was later partially realized in *The Humiliated and the Wronged*, to Goethe's *Wilhelm Meisters Lehrjahre*. See Mochul'skii, *Dostoevsky*, 182. There are a number of interesting studies that offer convincing speculations as to why Dostoevsky never wrote *The Life of a Great Sinner*. See, e.g., P.M. Bitsilli, '*Pochemu Dostoevsky ne napisal "Zhitiia velikogo greshnika,"*' in *O Dostoevskom*, ed. A.L. Bem, 3 vols. (Prague: F. Svoboda, 1929–36), 2:25–30.
20 B.M. Engel'gardt, '*Ideologicheskii roman Dostoevskogo*,' in *Izbrannye trudy*, ed. M. Muratov (St Petersburg: Izdatelstvo St Peterburgskogo universiteta, 1995), 270–308.
21 M.M. Bakhtin, *Problems of Dostoevsky's Poetics*, 28–9.
22 As I suggest in chapter 1 of part one, according to Franco Moretti (and, implicitly, to Lukács), the Bildungsroman is the dominant narrative genre of the nineteenth century. In his own essay on Goethe (the fragment of his book on the Bildungsroman), Bakhtin also argues that Goethe creates one of the main novelistic paradigms. Perhaps, had Dostoevsky's entire

manuscript survived, we would find in it a juxtaposition of Goethe and Dostoevsky as creators of two rather different paradigms. As I show, however, Dostoevsky, especially in his two last novels, actually leans on the tradition created by Goethe.

23 B.M. Engel'gardt, *Izbrannye trudy*, 270–308.
24 Ibid.
25 The relationship between epic and dramatic modes in Dostoevsky (introduced by George Steiner's book *Tolstoy, or Dostoevsky*) is one of the dominants of Jacques Catteau's study of Dostoevsky's composition. As Catteau maintains, Dostoevsky's predilection for the dramatic representation of events is due to his preoccupation with the hero's inner dialectic aimed at the attainment of freedom, expressed as a free act. However, argues Catteau (against Bakhtin), Dostoevsky does not annihilate time, but 'concentrates and accelerates it to give back to it the fertility of action. He saturates time with what matters in the past and what matters in the immediate future: choice.' See Jacques Catteau, *Dostoevsky and the Process of Literary Creation* (Cambridge: Cambridge University Press, 1989), 366. With regard to *The Adolescent*, Catteau suggests that Dostoevsky found a way of reconciling his focus on freedom with his historical idea to depict the coming of age of a young Russian, son of a man of the 1840s, by introducing a temporal split between the time of action, where the adolescent functions as the agent, and the recollection and rationalization of action, where the same person acts as a narrator. Although Catteau does not use these terms, his analysis of *The Adolescent* suggests that this particular novel represents a sort of compromise between traditional monologic memoirs/autobiography and a polyphonic novel in the Bakhtinian sense. See Catteau, *Dostoevsky*, 366–71.
26 Dostoevsky, *Pis'ma*, 2:258.
27 Joseph Frank, 'The Genesis of *Crime and Punishment*,' in *Russianness: In Honor of Rufus Mathewson*, ed. Robert L. Belknap (Ann Arbor: Ardis, 1990), 124–43.
28 In a well-known passage from *The Brothers Karamazov*, chapter 3 of book 3, titled 'The Confession of an Ardent Heart,' Dmitrii suggests that a human being is too broad and has too many contradictory sides to his character. See Dostoevsky, *PSS*, 14:100. Anticipating Dmitrii Karamazov, Arkadii Dolgorukii wonders whether human 'breadth' is an advantage or a curse, whether it can serve as a stepping stone to greatness or just keeps one from making a moral choice. See Dostoevsky, *PSS*, 13: 307. The precocious 'breadth' of Arkadii Dolgorukii's soul – a breadth that bespeaks early misery and acquaintance with sin – is also mentioned in '*Buduschii roman.*

Opiat' "Sluchainoie semesistvo"' ('The Future Novel. The "accidental family" once again'), from the 1876 *Diary of a Writer*, See F.M. Dostoevsky *PSS*, 22: 7–8.

29 Strakhov writes: 'Kogda ia vspominaiu ego [Dostoevskogo], to menia porazhaiet imenno neistoschimaiia podvizhnost' ego uma, neissiakaiuschaia plodovitost' ego dushi. V nem kak-budto ne bylo nichego slozhivshegosia, tak obil'no narostali mysli i chuvstva, stol'ko tailos' neizvestnogo i neproiavivshegosia pod tem, chto uspelo skazat'sia. [. . .] S cherzvychainoi iasnost'iu v nëm obnaruzhivalos' osobennogo roda razdvoenie, sostoiaschee v tom, chto chelovek predaiet'sia ochen' zhivo izvestnym mysliam i chuvstvam, no sokhraniaet v dushe nepoddaiuschuiusia i nekolebliuiuschuisia tochku, s kotoroi smotrit na samogo sebia, na svoi mysli i chuvstva. On sam inogda govoril ob etom svoistve nazyval ego refleksieiiu. Sledstviem takogo dushevnogo stroiia byvaet to, chto chelovek vsegda sokhraniiaet vozmozhnost' sudit' o tom, chto napolniiaet ego dushu, chto razlichnye chuvstva i nastroieniia mogut prokhodit' v ego dushe ne ovladevaia eiu do kontsa, i chto iz etogo gluboko dushevnogo tsentra iskhodit energiia, ochivliaiuschaia i preobrazuiuschaia vsiu deiatel'nost' i vse soderzhanie uma i tvorchestva. Kak-by to ni bylo, Fyodor Mikhailovich vsegda porazhal menia shirokost'iu svoikh sochuvstvii, umeniem ponimat' razlichnye i protivopolozhnye vzgliady.' ['When I remember him [Dostoevsky], I am amazed at the inexhaustible mobility of his intellect and the unremitting productivity of his soul. It is as if he was not completely formed. The ideas and feelings grew in him so abundantly, and there was so much unknown and hidden behind what was already expressed. [. . .] One could clearly perceive in him a special kind of internal division, which suggests that while he was intensely preoccupied by certain ideas or feelings, he nonetheless preserved within his soul an immutable point of observation, from which he looked at himself, examined his own ideas and feelings. He talked about this peculiarity of his character sometimes, calling it reflection. As a consequence of this spiritual predisposition, one can always judge what his soul was feeling, and that it can partake of different moods and feelings, none of which completely take hold of it. This deep spiritual center generates energy which illumines and transfigures the writer's entire intellectual and creative activity. Whatever was the cause, Fyodor Mikhailovich always amazed me by the breadth of his sympathy and his ability to understand different, even opposite points of view.'] N.N. Strakhov, *Vospominaniia o Fyodore Mikhailoviche Dostoievskom. Biografiia, pis'ma i zametki is zapisnoi knizhki F.M. Dostoevskogo* (St Petersburg: tipografiia Suvorina, 1883), 169–329. My translation.

30 A.S. Dolinin, 'Dostoevsky i Strakhov,' in *Dostoevsky i drugie: stat'i i issledovaniia o russkoi klassicheskoi literature* (Leningrad: Khudozhestvennaia literatura, 1989), 234–69.
31 See especially Strakhov's book *Mir kak tseloe: cherty iz nauki o prirode* (St Petersburg: tip. Zamyslovskogo, 1872). See also N.N. Strakhov's essays 'Darvin' and 'Polnoe oproverzhenie darvinizma,' in *Bor'ba s Zapadom v nashei literature* 2:250–70; 271–420. See also V.V. Rozanov, 'N.N. Strakhov, ego lichnost' i deiatel'nost',' in *Literaturnye izgnanniki* (Moscow: Agraf, 2000), 9–85; Linda Gerstein, *Nikolai Strakhov* (Cambridge, MA: Harvard University Press, 1971).
32 Strakhov, *Mir kak tseloe*, 71–134.
33 See William C. Brumford, 'The West and Russia: Concepts of Inferiority in Dostoevsky's Adolescent,' in Belknap, *Russianness*, 144–52.
34 In this connection it is appropriate to recall Dostoevsky's famous diary entry made after the death of his first wife. Dostoevsky writes: 'and thus man strives on earth toward an ideal opposed to his nature. When a man has not fulfilled the law of striving toward the ideal, that is, has not through love sacrificed his ego to people or another person (Masha and myself), he suffers and calls this condition a sin. And so, man must unceasingly feel striving, which is compensated for by heavenly joy of fulfilling the law, that is, by sacrifice.' F.M. Dostoevsky, *PSS* 20:172. Commenting on this passage, Joseph Frank points out that in Eastern Orthodoxy, as opposed to the Augustinian tradition, man is regarded not as having fallen into sin from a state of perfection, but rather as having emerged into earthly existence still imperfect and unformed. As Frank very appropriately points out, St Ireneus compares man on earth to a child required to grow and develop. 'For Dostoevsky too,' concludes Frank, 'human life was the anvil on which souls were being forged by the hammer blows of fate, and it was only in eternity that this endless process would come to halt.' Joseph Frank, *The Stir of Liberation*, 308.
35 This idea can be traced back to Schiller. On Schiller's presence and Dostoevsky, see N. N. Vil'mont, *Dostoevsky i Schiller; zametki russkogo germanista* (Moscow: Sovetskii pisatel', 1984).
36 Strakhov's later works, in which he attacks Darwin and Darwinism are revealing of his enduring loyalty to right Hegelianism. See 'Spor iz-za knig N.Ia Danilevskogo,' in *Bo'rba z Zapadom*, 445–65. When in the mid-1870s the young Vladimir Solov'ev enters the Russian intellectual scene with his own highly original appropriation of Spinoza and German idealism, he becomes Dostoevsky's main ally in his battle for the restoration of universal harmony through the divinization of nature and humanity.

37 As Strakhov argued in his essays on nihilism (later collected in the book *Bor'ba s Zapadom v nashei literature*), ideals are an essential power that propels our life on earth, helping to convert the energy generated by physical organisms into the energy of spiritual and cultural growth.

38 *PSS*, 11:182–4. My translation. A similar dialogue between 'He' (the future Versilov) and 'the adolescent' is found in the notebooks to *The Adolescent*. Interestingly, this particular dialogue contains a reference to Strakhov's discussion about the possibility of extraterrestrial life. Strakhov rejects the idea of aliens as creatures incomparable to human beings, suggesting that any other rational beings existing in the cosmos would in all essential ways resemble human beings. Dostoevsky's characters, however, pose this question without giving it a definite answer. See Strakhov, *Mir kak tseloe*, 242–8; Dostoevsky, *PSS*, 16:70.

39 It is important to bear in mind that, unlike Tolstoy, who admired the Decembrists and saw them as the best and the brightest of his father's generation, Dostoevsky's attitude toward the Decembrists (whom he saw as forerunners of contemporary radicalism) was much more critical. Likewise, Dostoevsky's attitude toward Herzen, the self-appointed heir to the Decembrists, was highly problematic. At the same time, it could be argued that Dostoevsky's efforts to redeem Versilov through his son bespeak the author's desire to redeem the Decembrists through his own work. For a detailed discussion of this issue, see Sophia Gurvich-Lishchiner, 'Chaadaev – Herzen – Dostoevsky: Individual and Reason in the Creative Mind,' in *Russian Studies in Literature* 43, no. 3 (Summer 2007): 6–54.

40 That the idea of social 'dissociation' is one of the integral ideas of *The Adolescent* is one of the key claims of A.S. Dolinin in *Poslednie romany Dostoevskogo: kak sozdavalis' Podrostok i Brat'ia Karamazovy* (Leningrad: Sovetskii pisatel', 1963).

41 Strakhov, *Kriticheskiia stat'ii ob I.S. Turgeneve i L.N. Tolstom (1865–1885)* (Kiev: tipografiia Chokolova, 1908), 145–387.

42 Strakhov first mentions his essays (which were then still an unpublished manuscript) in a letter to Dostoevsky in connection with the conflicts Strakhov experienced in trying to place his essays with the journal *Otechestvennye Zapiski (Notes of the Fatherland)*. Eventually the essays were published by a new journal *Zaria (Dawn)*. Evidently, Dostoevsky received *Zaria* after a significant delay. His polemics with Strakhov regarding Tolstoy's *War and Peace* and Strakhov's take on Tolstoy did not break out until May 1871. See Strakhov, 'Pis'ma N.N. Strakhova F.M. Dostoevskomu,' pub. A.S. Dolinin, *Shestidesiatye gody: materially po istorii literatury i obschestvennogo dviheniiu* ed. N.K. Piksanov (Moscow and Leningrad: Akademiia Nauk SSSR, 1940), 255–80.

43 Ibid.
44 In the notebooks to *The Adolescent* Dostoevsky writes: 'The Idea of "Fathers and Sons" – sons and fathers. The son who intends to become a Rothschild is essentially an idealist – a new phenomenon which, surprisingly, follows from nihilism.' *PSS*, 16:45. Importantly, in Turgenev's novel, nihilism also fails to sustain itself. However, all forms of idealism are also shattered. One of Strakhov's key philosophical ideas is that the survival and further development of mankind (humanity) depends upon the revival of some kind of idealism (as faith and historical optimism). Dostoevsky wholeheartedly concurred with this idea.
45 *PSS*, 29:111–12.
46 Joseph Frank, *The Stir of Liberation*, 413–98.
47 The fact that Dostoevsky was familiar with the law of double negation and sometimes applied it to his fictional narrative of personal *Bildung* can be proved with recourse to *Netochka Nezvanova* (1849), one of Dostoevsky's earliest attempts to write a Bildungsroman. The heroine's first and last names signify a double negation, which is also reflected in her life story. Before she reaches the age of maturity, she negates her infancy (symbolized by her father) and her childhood (symbolized by her attachment to her stepfather, a crazy musician named Efimov). See my essay '*Netochka Nezvanova* on the Path of *Bildung*,' *Die Welt der Slaven* 51 (2006): 233–52. See also E. Kransnoschekova, *Roman vospitaniia: Bildungsroman na russkoi pochve: Karamzin, Pushkin, Tolstoi, Dostoevskii* (St Petersburg: Izdatel'stvo Pushkinskogo fonda, 2008), 383–97.
48 *PSS*, 9:11–12.
49 See *PSS*, 16:30; 17:259, 278.
50 See Donna Orwin, 'The Return to Nature: Tolstoyan Echoes in *The Idiot*,' *Russian Review* 58 (January 1999): 87–102.
51 Boris Tikhomirov, 'Dostoevsky and Children in the *New Testament*,' *Dostoevsky on the Threshold of Other Worlds: Essays in Honor of Malcom V. Jones*, ed. Sarah Young and Lesley Milne (Ilkeston, UK: Bramcote Press, 2006), 189–206.
52 Hannah Arendt, *Love and Saint Augustine*, ed. Johanna Vecchiarelli, Scott and Judith Chelius Stark (Chicago: University of Chicago Press, 1996), 146–8.
53 Joseph Frank analyzes the significance of this well-known diary entry for the correct understanding of *Notes from the Underground* in *The Stir of Liberation 1860–1865*, 298–9.
54 On the significance of this motif in the notebooks and in the final text of *The Adolescent*, see the commentary to *The Adolescent* in *PSS*, 17:256–362.

266–8. See also Dostoevsky's discussion of Kairova's case and his visit to the orphanage (*Vospitate'nyi Dom*) in the 1876 *Diary of a Writer*, *PSS*, 23:20–7.

55 B.I. Bursov stresses the significance of the novel's title, which points to the young hero's transitional identity and developmental potential, in '*Podrostok*' – *roman vospitaniia*,' *Avrora* 11 (1971): 64–71.

56 This notion was coined by N.G. Chernyshevskii in his novel *What Is to Be Done?* (1863), to which Dostoevsky responded with his *Notes from the Underground*.

57 *PSS*, 13:452–5. Dostoevsky also discusses his attempt to transcend the mentality of 'landowner authors' in the 1877 *Diary of a Writer*, *PSS*, 25:32–5.

58 See the commentary to *The Adolescent* in *PSS*, 17:251–92.

59 See Strakhov, 'L.N. Tolstoy,' in *Bor'ba s Zapadom v nashei literature*, 1:145–387. Ten essays collected in this edition were originally published in 1869 in *Zaria*. When sending his essays to F.M. Dostoevsky, Strakhov accompanied them with a letter, which was published and commented on by A.S. Dolinin. See 'Pis'ma N.N. Strakhova Dostoevskomu,' in 255–80. See especially letter 4 (March 1868), 17–18.

60 It was the publication of *The Adolescent* (first published in *The Contemporary*) that escalated the tensions between Dostoevsky and Strakhov leading to their rupture. See A.S. Dolinin, 'Dostoevsky i Strakhov,' 137.

61 See A.S. Dolinin, *Poslednie romany Dostoevskogo*, 93.

62 This issue was aroused by the military reform, which allowed a greater mobility through the ranks; this in turn threatened to destroy the still-existing boundaries between the estates. Alarmed by this reform, the conservative members of the nobility mounted an anti-democratic campaign. See Ye. I. Semionov, *Roman Dostoevskogo 'Podrostok,'*: *problematika i zhanr* (Leningrad: Nauka, 1979), 2–23.

63 *PSS*, 8:449–55. In this connection Kirpotin's hypothesis that Evgenii Pavlovich Radomskii, the novel's most explicit spokesman for the nobility, is modelled on Strakhov appears illuminating. While Dostoevsky's (and Myshkin's) sympathies are ultimately on the side of self-made men or an intellectual aristocracy, Radomsky-Strakhov insists on the preservation of traditional estate boundaries. A conservative liberal, Strakhov believed that aristocracy was indispensable for the preservation of aesthetic and moral ideals in society. For more on this subject, see V. Kirpotin, 'Dostoevsky, Strakhov – i Evgenii Pavlovich Radomskii,' in *Mir Dostoevskogo*, 2nd ed. (Moscow: Sovetskii pisatel', 1983), 113–59. See also R.L. Jackson, 'A View from the Underground: On Nikolai Nikolevich Strakhov's Letter About His Good Friend Fyodor Mikhailovich Dostoevsky and on Leo

Nikolaievich Tolstoy's Cautious Response to It,' in *Dialogues with Dostoevsky: The Overwhelming Questions* (Stanford, CA: Stanford University Press, 1993), 104–20.

64 Dostoevsky's readiness to contribute to Nekrasov's journal may be due to the fact that several months earlier it published L.N. Tolstoy's article '*O narodnom obrazovanii*' ('On public education'), which was considered too controversial by other journals. In this article, Tolstoy argued against imposing European educational methods and standards on the Russian peasant schools. See also Strakhov's reviews of Tolstoy's essay in *Grazhdanin* (1874): 48–50 (republished under the title 'Obuchenie naroda' in *Bor'ba z Zapadom*, 315–31).

65 The name 'Makar,' usually linked to one of the monks from Optina Pustyn', the Monk Makarii, may have another intertextual origin: Goethe's saintly Makarie from Goethe's *Wilhelm Meisters Wanderjahre*.

66 For an illuminating discussion of the semantic cluster based on *obraz*, see Ye.I. Semionov's study. The image of the sinner cutting down the icon (*rubit obraza*) appears in the notebooks (16:65). It has been traced to Nekrasov's poem 'Vlas' (1854).

67 *PSS*, 18:80.

68 In his notebooks to the novel, Dostoevsky writes: '*Most important*. The idea of disintegration [*razlozhenie*] is present everywhere, for everything is falling apart, and there are no remaining ties not just in the Russian family, but even simply between people in general . . . *(Disintegration is the principal visible idea of the novel . . .)* Here we are, for example, a Russian family. We speak different languages and cannot understand one another. Society is decomposing [разлагается] chemically.' *PSS*, 16:16; italics are Dostoevsky's.

69 For a detailed discussion of Dostoevsky's treatment of the semantic cluster centred on *obraz* and its semantic correlates, see Semionov's study.

70 Dolinin, *Poslednie romany Dostoevskogo*, 73. See also Dostoevsky's discussion of Nekrasov's funeral in the *Diary of a Writer, PSS*, 26:111–25.

71 To the best of my knowledge, this connection has so far been overlooked by the critics. However, Vladimir Tunimanov has noted the parallels between Dostoevsky's *Notes from the Underground* and Grigor'ev's autobiographical works. See Vladimir Tunimanov, '"Podpol'ie" i "zhivaia zhizn,"' in *XXI vek glazami Dostoevskogo – perspektivy chelovechestva: materialy Mezhdunarodnoi konferentsii sostoiavsheisia v Universitete Tiba*, ed. Karen Stepanian (Moscow: Graal', 2002), 11–22. 18.

72 Apollon Grigor'ev, *Moi literaturnye i nravstvennye skital'chestva*, in *Vospominaniia*, ed. B.F. Egorov (Leningrad: Nauka, 1980), 4–144. 26–7.

73 Dostoevsky, *PSS*, 13: 307. Dostoevsky, *The Adolescent*, trans. Richard Pevear and Larissa Volokhonskii (New York: Vintage, 2003), 380. All references are to this edition and will appear in the body of the text.
74 Konstantin Mochul'skii believes that these subplots run parallel to each other without mixing and forming a coherent whole. He compares the dynamic composition of *The Adolescent* to the ocean's tide: 'Dostoevsky's dynamic composition can be compared with a series of waves, racing toward the shore. The mightiest wave begins to swell earlier than the others, breaks later and with more force: coming in, the smaller waves anticipate the roar of its fall. So, the partial catastrophes prepare the main one and are joined with it in dynamic unity' (*Dostoevsky*, 508). I believe, however, that on the ideological level we are invited to think of Arkadii's experiences not as separate 'waves' that never intermix, but rather as different tributaries to one big stream.
75 Strakhov, *Mir kak tseloe*, 164–5.
76 See Gurvich-Lischiner, 'Chaadaev – Herzen – Dostoevsky, 6–54.
77 See 'Author and Hero in Aesthetic Activity,' in *Art and Answerability: Early Philosophical Essays*, ed. Michael Holquist and Vadim Liapunov, trans. Vadim Liapunov (Austin: University of Texas Press, 1990), 4–256.
78 Mochul'skii maintains that Versilov emerges as the true hero of the novel, whereas Arkadii is a mere witness. However, I intend to show that Arkadii is a co-protagonist who in the end wrests complete freedom from Versilov's overbearing presence and even comes to finalize Versilov in Bakhtin's sense. See Mochul'skii, *Dostoevsky*, 492.
79 Alex Woloch, *The One vs. the Many: Minor Characters and the Space of the Protagonist in the Novel* (Princeton, NJ: Princeton University Press, 2003), 244–6.
80 Ibid., 243–318.
81 The notebooks to *The Adolescent* suggest that it took Dostoevsky some time to devise the narrative structure of this novel, where both father and son are of crucial importance. See *PSS*, 16: 98; see also pp. 47, 56, 86.
82 Michael Holquist, *Dostoevsky and the Novel*, 2nd ed. (Evanston, IL: Northwestern University Press, 1986), 165–91.
83 See also Alex Woloch, *The One vs. the Many*, 317–35.
84 Mochul'skii suggests that 'the main theme of the novel is the problem of communality' (*Dostoevsky*, 511).
85 As I have pointed out in note 24 above (with reference to Catteau's reading of *The Adolescent*), only at the end of his dialectical development does the adolescent absorb Versilov's legacy.

86 As noted above, both the drafts to the unwritten *Life* and the notebooks to the novels that stem from this project, *The Devils* and *The Adolescent*, contain passages that an be interpreted in light of the *Naturphilosophical* discussion of human life as a middle link between the animal and spiritual realms.
87 As Olga Meerson argues, the liaison between Arkadii's parents is one of the novel's chief taboos. See Olga Meerson, *Dostoevsky's Taboos* (Dresden: Dresden University Press, 1998), 165.
88 N.A. Nekrasov, *Moroz, Krasnyi nos* in *Sochineniia v trekh tomakh*, (Moscow: Gosudarstvennoe izdatel'stvo Khudozhestvenaia literatura, 1959), 1:323–53.
89 For an illuminating analysis of the melodramatic mode in Dostoevsky's fiction, see Robin Feuer Miller, 'The Metaphysical Novel and the Evocation of Anxiety: Melmoth the Wanderer and *The Brothers Karamazov*, A Case Study,' in *Russianness*, ed. Belknap, 94–112. See also chapter 7, 'Evocations and Revocations of Anxiety in the Metaphysical Novel: Reading *The Brothers Karamazov* through the Lens of *Melmoth the Wanderer*,' in Miller, *Dostoevsky's Unfinished Journey* (New Haven, CT: Yale University Press, 2007), 128–47.
90 In this connection, we are reminded of a similar but not fully worked-out (and therefore ultimately not entirely convincing) attempt to represent Raskol'nikov's conversion by transforming the style of his interior monologue into something corresponding to the biblical style. See the references to patriarchal times in the epilogue to *Crime and Punishment*, which functions as one of the vectors of this change in style and world view.
91 Schiller's strong presence in Dostoevsky has been well researched and described by the Russian scholar N. Vil'mont. See his *Dostoevskii i Schiller* (Moscow: Sovetskii pisatel', 1984).
92 Jacques Catteau, *Dostoevsky and the Process of Literary Creation*, 428–33; Liza Knapp, *The Annihilation of Inertia: Dostoevsky and Metaphysics* (Evanston, IL: Northwestern University Press, 1996), 131–71. In one of the parables recounted by Makar, a painter tries to represent the redemption of a young boy who has committed suicide as a sunray falling onto the surface of the sea, where the youth had drowned himself. This sunray, like the onion from Grushen'ka's famous parable, represents a single chance for redemption and forgiveness to which all sinners are entitled. Makar's appearance in the lives of Versilov and Arkadii can be compared to this beam of light: he illuminates the souls of father and son, giving them both a chance to regenerate.

93 Knapp, *Annihilation of Inertia*, 131–71.
94 We could describe Makar's mysterious influence on the souls of those around him in terms of a genuine psychological miracle, comparable to the miracle of Job's suffering transforming into quiet joy. In this sense, Makar's role is to represent in a nutshell the message contained in the chapter 'The Russian Monk' in *The Brothers Karamazov*. For an illuminating discussion of Zosima's teachings as both an exposé and an exemplar of the Christian psychological miracle, see Nathan Rosen, 'Style and Structure in *The Brothers Karamazov*: The Grand Inquisitor and the Russian Monk,' *Russian Literature Triquarterly* 1 (1971): 352–65. Rosen draws attention to the role of the rhetorical and stylistic devices that set Zosima's words apart from the rest of the narrative. Zosima's highly stylized, psychologically charged language manifests on the linguistic level the kind of spiritual conversion that he describes in his stories about his brother Markel (who underwent a deathbed conversion at Easter), Job, and others. According to Rosen, in making recourse to this special style, Dostoevsky seeks, as it were, to re-enact spiritual and psychological regeneration by affecting his readers. As I try to show, the same ambition underlies the representation of Makar Dolgorukii in *The Adolescent*. However, as I argue throughout the chapter, while Makar serves as a catalyst for Arkadii's regeneration, a complete conversion along the lines of Markel's bedside conversion does not occur within the boundaries of the novelistic narrative.
95 See Gurvich-Lishchiner, 'Chaadaev – Herzen – Dostoevsky, 6–54.
96 As Strakhov has argued apropos Herzen, Herzen's pessimism was not at bottom nihilistic, but rather stemmed from his (arguably quintessentially Russian) thirst for an ideal. See Strakhov, 'Gertsen,' in *Bor'ba s Zapadom*, 1:1–136.
97 It is noteworthy that genuine polyphony between father and son no longer holds after Versilov breaks the icon and cuts short his redemption.
98 As Catteau points out, there are three types of saints venerated by the Russian people: 'the martyr, not a glorious martyr who dies for his faith, but a spiritual imitator of the Passion of Christ, someone who yields to the exhortations of the Gospel in the terror of his flesh and gives up his life, endangered often for reasons outside religion; the simpleton (*iurodivyi*), a holy fool who chooses folly, derision, physical and social humiliation and inverts worldly values to recall the truth of Christ to men; or third, like Tikhon, he is a *starets* (the elder).' *Dostoevsky and Process of Literary Creation*, 241. Makar Dolgorukii clearly belongs to the third type of Russian saint. The adolescent's mother, like her namesakes in *Crime and Punishment* and *The Brothers Karamazov*, also tends toward saintliness, but of the first type, the martyr.

99 As Irene Zohrab reminds us, during his tenure as managing editor of *Grazhdanin*, Dostoevsky was keenly interested in Matthew Arnold's educational activities and in the British system of public education. See Irene Zohrab, 'Public Education in England in the Pages of The Citizen (1873–1874) during Dostoevsky's Editorship,' in *Dostoevsky on the Threshold of Other Worlds: Essays in Honor of Malcom V. Jones*, ed. Sarah Young and Lesley Milne (Ilkeston, UK: Bramcote Press, 2006), 98–109.

Conclusion

1 Robin Feuer Miller, *Dostoevsky's Unfinished Journey* (New Haven, CT: Yale University Press, 2007), 17.
2 I cannot miss this occasion to point out that the theme of memory and its significance for the poetics of *The Brothers Karamazov* and of Dostoevsky's oeuvre as a whole has been analysed by a number of scholars, most notably by Robert Belknap in *The Genesis of* The Brothers Karamazov*: The Aesthetics, Ideology and Psychology of the Text-Making* (Evanston, IL: Northwestern University Press, 1991) and by Diane Oening Thompson, The Brothers Karamazov *and the Poetics of Memory* (Cambridge: Cambridge University Press, 1991).
3 In this connection, it is worthwhile to cite Anna Grigor'evna Dostoevskaia, who mentions in her memoirs that Dostoevsky himself had very early memories and that he believed that positive impressions were extremely important for their children's education, because they would remain imprinted in their souls. See A.G. Dostoevskaia, *Vospominaniia* (Moscow: Khudozhestvennaia literatura, 1971), 89, 312.
4 Igor' Volgin, *Posldenii god Dostoevskogo: istoricheskie zapiski* (Moscow: Sovetskii pisatel', 1991), 356–370.
5 F.M. Dostoevsky, 'Pushkin (Ocherk),' *Dnevnik pisatelia na 1880 god, PSS* (Leningrad: Nauka, 1984), 26: 136–48.
6 See F.M. Dostoevsky, *Novye materialy i issledovaniia. Literaturnoe Nasledstvo* 86 (Moscow: Nauka: 1973), 106. My translation.
7 See Thomas Mann, 'Goethe and Tolstoy,' in *Leo Tolstoy: Modern Critical Views*, ed. Harold Bloom (New York: Chelsea House Press, 1986), 15–52. 16. Tolstoy and Dostoevsky were once physically present in the same room at Vladimir Solov'ev's lecture in Solianyi Gorodok on 10 March 1878. Strakhov, who accompanied Tolstoy, did not introduce them. There are endless speculations as to why Strakhov decided not to introduce Dostoevsky to Tolstoy. See also B.I. Bursov, 'U svezhei mogily Dostoevskogo (Perepiska L.N. Tolstogo s N.N. Strakhovym),' in *Problemy zhanra v istorii russkoi*

literatury, ed. N.N. Skatov (Leningrad: [n.p.], 1969); R.L. Jackson, 'A View from the Underground: On Nikolai Nikolaevich Strakhov's Letter About His Good Friend Fyodor Mikhailovich Dostoevsky and on Leo Nikolaevich Tolstoy's Cautious Response to It,' in *Dialogues with Dostoevsky: The Overwhelming Questions* (Stanford, CA: Stanford University Press, 1993), 104–20; and L. Rosenblum, 'Tolstoy and Dostoevsky (Closing the Distance) at the Turn of the 1870s–1880s,' *Russian Studies in Literature* 45, no. 4 (Fall 2009): 62–97. 64.

8 Vogüé, *Le roman russe* (Paris: Plon, 1892), 341–3.
9 Hegel, *Aesthetics: Lectures in Fine Art*, trans. T.M. Knox (Oxford: Clarendon, 1975), 1:592–5.
10 Ibid., 593.
11 Vogüé, *Le roman russe*, 343.

Appendix

1 *Apollon Aleksandrovich Grigor'ev: Materialy dlia biografii* (Petrograd: Izdanie Pushkinskogo Doma pri Akademii Nauk, 1917), 227–28. The italics are in the original.
2 A.A. Grigor'ev, 'Graf L. Tolstoy i ego sochineniia: stat'ia vtoraia,' in *Sochineniia v dvukh tomakh*, ed. B.F. Egorov (Moscow: Khudozhestvennaia literatura, 1990), 2:344–72. 364–5.
3 Yu.M. Lotman, *Kul'tura i vzryv* (Moscow: Gnozis, 1992), 236–7.
4 Yu.M. Lotman, 'O dvukh modeliakh kommunikatsii v sisteme kul'tury,' in *Izbrannye stat'i*, 1:76–89. 77.
5 Ibid., 90.
6 Yu.M. Lotman, *Struktura khudozhestvennogo teksta* (Providence, RI: Brown University Press, 1971), 333.
7 Lotman, *Kul'tura i vzryv*, 182.
8 A.A. Grigor'ev, 'Vzgliad na russkuiu literaturu so smerti Pushkina,' in *Sochineniia v dvukh tomakh*, 2:48–124. 71.
9 Ibid., 355.
10 Ibid., 66.
11 Lotman, 'Ideinaia struktura Kapitanskoi Dochki,' in *Izbrannye stat'i*, 2: 416–29. 422.
12 L.N. Tolstoy, *PSS*, 8: 212.
13 Tolstoy, *PSS*, 60:373.
14 Ibid., 373–4.
15 A.N. Pypin, *Masonstvo v Rossii: XVIII i pervaia chetvert' XIX v*.198–9.
16 Tolstoy, *PSS*, 48/49: 127.

17 N. Strakhov, 'Vospominaniia o Fyodore Mikhailoviche Dostoevskom,' in *Materialy dlia zhizneopisaniia F.M. Dostoevskogo* (St Petersburg: tipografiia A.S. Suvorina, 1883), 169–332. 180. (Italics are in the original.)
18 F.M. Dostoevsky, 'Dva lageria teoretikov,' in *PSS* 20: 5–22.
19 F.M. Dostoevsky, '*Besy*: podgotovitel'nye materialy,' in *PSS*, 11:58–308. 183–4.
20 Apollon Grigor'ev, *Moi literaturnye i nravstvennye skital'chestva*, in *Vospominaniia*, 4–144. 26–7.
21 N.N. Strakhov, *Mir kak tseloe: cherty iz nauki o prirode* (St Petersburg: tip. Zamyslovskogo, 1872), 164–5.
22 See F.M. Dostoevsky, *Novye materially i issledovaniia. Literaturnoe Nasledstvo* 86 (Moscow: Nauka, 1973), 106.

Bibliography

Agamben, Giorgio. *Homo Sacer: Sovereign Power and Bare Life*. Translated by Daniel Heller-Roazen. Stanford, CA: Stanford University Press, 1998.

Akhsharumov, Nikolai. *Voina i mir: sochinenie grafa L.N. Tolstogo: 1–4 chasti*. St Petersburg: M. Khan, 1868.

Aldanov, Mark. *Zagadka Tolstogo*. Providence, RI: Brown University Press, 1969.

Alekseev, M.P. 'Epigraph iz E. Berka v Evgenii Onegine' and 'K stat'e Pushkina *Dzhon Tenner*.' In *Pushkin i mirovaia literatura*, edited by G.P. Makogonenko, 560–71; 542–8. Leningrad: Nauka, 1987.

Alexandrov, Vladimir. 'Biology, Semiosis, and Cultural Difference in Lotman's Semiosphere.' *Comparative Literature* 52, no. 4 (2001): 341–62.

Alston, Patrick. *Education and the State in Tsarist Russia*. Stanford, CA: Stanford University Press, 1969.

Al'tshuller, M.G. *Beseda liubitelei russkogo slova: u istokov slavianofil'stva*. Moscow: Novoe literaturnoe obozrenie, 2007.

– *Epokha Val'tera Skotta v Rossii: istoricheskii roman 1830–kh godov*. St Petersburg: Akademicheskii proekt, 1996.

– 'Mistifikatsiia semeinogo predaniia ('A ded moi v krepost', v karantin . . .'). In *Mezhdu dvukh tsarei: Pushkin 1824–1836*, 186–200. St Petersburg: Akademicheskii proekt, 2003.

Anderson, Benedict. *Imagined Communities: Reflections on the Origins and Spread of Nationalism*. London: Verso, 1983.

Andrews, Edna. *Conversations with Lotman: Cultural Semiotics in Language, Literature, and Cognition*. Toronto: University of Toronto Press, 2003.

Annenkov, P.V. *Literaturnye vospominaniia*. Moscow: Pravda, 1989.

– *Materialy dlia biografii A.S. Pushkina*. St Petersburg: Tovarischestvo Obschchestvennaia pol'za, 1873.

Ardens, N.N. *Dostoevsky i Tolstoy*. Moscow: Pedagogicheskii Institut imeni Lenina, 1970.

Arendt, Hannah. *Love and Saint Augustine*. Edited by Johanna Vecchiarelli: Scott and Judith Chelius Stark. Chicago: University of Chicago Press, 1996.

– *Reflections on Literature and Culture*. Edited with an introduction by Susannah Young-Ah Gottlieb. Stanford, CA: Stanford University Press, 2007.

Arnold, Matthew. *Culture and Anarchy and Other Writings*. Edited by Stefan Collini. New York: Cambridge University Press, 1993.

– *Democratic Education*. Edited by R.H. Super. Ann Arbor: University of Michigan Press, 1962.

Auerbach, Erich. *Mimesis: The Representation of Reality in Western Literature*. Translated by Williard R. Trask. Princeton, NJ: Princeton University Press, 1953.

– 'Philology and *Weltliteratur*.' Translated by Maire and Edward Said. *Centennial Review* 13, no. 1 (Winter 1969): 1–17.

Avetisian, V.A. *Poslednie literaturnye sobesedniki Pushkina: eshche raz o probleme 'Pushkin-Gete.'* Moscow and Izhevsk: R and C Dynamics, 2009.

Avrich, Paul. *Russian Rebels, 1600–1800*. New York: Schoken Books, 1976.

Baguley, David. 'Pushkin and Mérimée, the French Connection: On Hoaxes and Impostors.' In *Two Hundred Years of Pushkin*. Vol. 3, *Pushkin's Legacy*, edited by Joe Andrew and Robert Reid, 177–92. New York and Amsterdam: Rodopi, 2003.

Balibar, Étienne. 'Citizen Subject.' Translated by James B. Swenson, Jr. In *Who Comes after Subject?*, edited by Eduardo Cadava, Peter Connor, and Jean-Luc Nancy, 177–92. New York: Routledge, 1991.

Bakhtin, M.M. 'Author and Hero in Aesthetic Activity.' In *Art and Answerability: Early Philosophical Essays*. Edited by Michael Holquist and Vadim Liapunov. Translated by Vadim Liapunov. Austin: University of Texas Press, 1990.

– *The Bildungsroman and Its Significance in the History of Realism (Toward a Historical Typology of the Novel)*. In M.M. Bakhtin, *Speech Genres and Other Late Essays*, translated by Vern W. McGee, edited by Caryl Emerson and Michael Holquist, 10–59. Austin: University of Texas Press, 1986.

– *Problems of Dostoevsky's Poetics*. Edited by Carol Emerson. Translated by Willaim Booth. Minneapolis: University of Minnesota Press, 1984.

Barran, Thomas. *Russia Reads Rousseau, 1762–1825*. Evanston, IL: Northwestern University Press, 2002.

Barsukov, Nikolai. *Zhizn' i trudy M.P. Pogodina*. St Petersburg: Tipografiia Stasiulevicha, 1888–1907. 21 vols.

Bayley, John. *Pushkin: A Comparative Commentary*. Cambridge: Cambridge University Press, 1971.
– *Tolstoy and the Novel*. Chicago: University of Chicago Press, 1966.
Beiser, Frederick. *The Fate of Reason*. Cambridge, MA: Harvard University Press, 1986.
– *German Idealism: The Struggle Against Subjectivism, 1781–1801*. Cambridge, MA: Harvard University Press, 2002.
– *The Romantic Imperative: The Concept of Early German Romanticism*. Cambridge, MA: Harvard University Press, 2003.
Belinskii, V.G. *Sobranie sochinenii v deviati tomakh*. Moscow: Khudozhestvennaia literatura, 1981.
Belknap, Robert. *The Genesis of* The Brothers Karamazov*: The Aesthetics, Ideology and Psychology of the Text-Making*. Evanston, IL: Northwestern University Press, 1991.
– *The Structure of* The Brothers Karamazov. The Hague: Mouton, 1967.
Belknap, Robert, ed. *Russianness: In Honor of Rufus Mathewson*. Ann Arbor, MI: Ardis, 1990.
Bem, A.L. 'Evoliutsiia obraza Stavrogina: k sporu ob "Ispovedi Stavrogina."' In *Issledovaniia. Pis'ma o literature*, 111–57. Moscow: Iazyki slavianskoi kul'tury, 2001.
Benjamin, Walter. *Selected Writings*, Edited by Marcus Bullock and Michael W. Jennings, Cambridge, MA: The Belknap Press at Harvard University Press, 1996. 2 vols.
– 'The Storyteller.' In *Illuminations*, edited with an introduction by Hannah Arendt, 83–110. New York: Schoken Books, 1968.
Berlin, Isaiah. *The Hedgehog and the Fox: An Essay on Tolstoy's View of History*. New York: Simon & Schuster, 1953.
– *Russian Thinkers*. London: Penguin, 1994.
– 'Tolstoy and Enlightenment.' *Encounter* 16, no. 2 (1961): 29–40.
– 'Vico and Herder.' In *Three Critics of the Enlightenment: Vico, Hamann, Herder*, edited by Henry Hardy, 1–242. Princeton, NJ: Princeton University Press, 2000.
Bethea, David M. 'Bakhtinian Prosaics versus Lotmanian "Poetic Thinking": The Code and Its Relation to Literary Biography.' *Slavic and Eastern European Journal* 41, no. 1 (Spring 1997): 1–15.
– 'Iurii Lotman in the 1980s: the Code and Its Relation to Literary Biography.' In *Reconstructing the Canon: Russian Writing in the 1980s*, edited by Arnold B. McMillin, 9–32. London: Harwood Academic Publishers, 2000.

- *Realizing Metaphors: Alexander Pushkin and the Life of the Poet*. Madison: University of Wisconsin Press, 1998.
Bethea, David M., ed. *The Pushkin Handbook*. Madison: University of Wisconsin Press, 2005.
- *Pushkin Today*. Bloomington: Indiana University Press, 1993.
Berezina, V.G. 'Iz Istorii "Sovremennika" Pushkina.' In *Pushkin: issledovaniia i materialy*, vol. 1., edited by M.P. Alekseev, 278–312. Moscow: Izdatel'stvo Akademii Nauk SSSR, 1956.
Bitsilli, P.M. 'Pochemu Dostoevskii ne napisal "Zhitiia velikogo greshnika."' In *O Dostoevskom*, vol. 2, edited by A.L. Bem, 25–30. Prague: F. Svoboda, 1929–36.
Black, J.L. *Nicholas Karamzin and Russian Society in the Ninteenth Century: A Study in Russian Political and Historical Thought*. Toronto: University of Toronto Press, 1975.
Black, J.L., ed. *Essays on Karamzin: Russian man of letters, political thinker, historian, 1766–1826*. The Hague: Mouton, 1975.
Blagoi, D.I. 'Blok i Apollon Grigor'ev.' In *Tri veka: iz istorii russkoi poezii XVIII, XIX i XX vv.*, 29–30. Moscow: Sovetskaia literatura, 1933.
- *Tvorcheskii put' Pushkina (1826–1830)*. Moscow: Sovetskii pisatel', 1967.
Bloom, Harold, ed. *Leo Tolstoy: Modern Critical Views*. NY: Chelsea, 1986.
Bollenbeck, Georg. *Bildung und Kultur: Glanz und Elend eines deutschen Deutungsmusters*. Frankfurt am Main: Insel, 1994.
Boyle, Nicholas. *Goethe: The Poet and the Age*. Oxford: Oxford University Press, 1992.
Brodskii, N.L., ed. *Literaturnye salony i kruzhki: pervaia polovina XIX veka*. Moscow: Agraf, 2001.
Brooks, Peter. *Henry James Goes to Paris*. Princeton, NJ: Princeton University Press, 2007.
- *The Melodramatic Imagination: Balzac, Henry James, Melodrama, and the Mode of Excess*. New Haven, CT: Yale University Press, 1995.
Bruford, W.H. *The German Tradition of Self-Cultivation: 'Bildung' from Humboldt to Thomas Mann*. New York: Cambridge University Press, 1975.
Brumfield, William C. 'The West and Russia: Concepts of Inferiority in Dostoevsky's Adolescent.' In *Russianness: In Honor of Rufus Mathewson*, edited by Robert L. Belknap, 144–152. Ann Arbor: Ardis, 1990.
Bunin, Ivan. *Liberation of Tolstoy: A Tale of Two Writers*. Edited and translated by Thomas Gaiton Marullo and Vladimir T. Khmelkov. Evanston, IL: Northwestern University Press, 2001.
Bursov, B.I. '*Podrostok*– roman vospitaniia.' *Avrora* 11 (1971): 64–71.

– 'U svezhei mogily Dostoevskogo (Perepiska L.N. Tolstogo s N.N. Strakhovym).' In *Problemy zhanra v istorii russkoi literatury*, edited by N.N. Skatov, 254–70. Leningrad: [n.p.], 1969.
Cain, Tom. 'Tolstoy's Use of David Copperfield.' In *Tolstoi and Britain,'* edited by W. Gareth Jones, 67–78. Oxford: Berg, 1995.
Carden, Patricia. 'The Expressive Self in *War and Peace.' Canadian-American Slavic Studies* 12 no. 4 (1978): 519–34.
Casanova, Pascale. *La république mondiale des lettres*. Paris: Éditions du Seuil, 1999.
Cassedy, Steven. *Dostoevsky's Religion*. Stanford, CA: Stanford University Press, 2005.
Catteau, Jacques. *Dostoevsky and the Process of Literary Creation*. Cambridge: Cambridge University Press, 1989.
Chaadaev, P.Ia. *Philosophical Works by Peter Chaadaev*. Edited by Raymond T. McNally and Richard Tempest. Dordrecht and Boston: Kluwer Academic Publishers, 1991.
– *Polnoe sobranie sochinenii i izbrannye pis'ma*. 2 vols. Edited with an introduction by Z.A. Kamenskii. Moscow: Nauka, 1991.
Chances, Ellen B. *Conformity's Children: An Approach to the Superfluous Man in Russian Literature*. Columbus, OH: Slavica, 1978.
Chandler, James. *England in 1819: The Politics of Literary Culture and the Case of Romantic Historicism*. Chicago: University of Chicago Press, 1998.
Chernyshevskii, N.G. *Polnoe sobranie sochinenii v piatnadtsati tomakh*. Moscow: OGIZ, 1947.
Clardy, Jesse V. *The Superfluous Man in Russian Letters*. Washington, DC: University Press of America, 1980.
Coetzee, J.M. 'Confession and Double Thoughts: Tolstoy, Rousseau, Dostoevsky.' In *Doubling the Point: Essays and Interview*, edited by David Atwell, 251–93. Cambridge, MA: Harvard University Press, 1992.
Cohen, Margaret. *The Sentimental Education of the Novel*. Princeton, NJ: Princeton University Press, 1999.
Cornwell, Neil. 'Pushkin and Henry James: Secrets, Papers and Figures (*The Queen of Spades, The Aspern Papers* and *The Figure in the Carpet*).' In *Two Hundred Years of Pushkin*, vol. 3, *Pushkin's Legacy*, edited by Joe Andrew and Robert Reid, 193–208. New York and Amsterdam: Rodopi, 2003.
Cracaft, James, ed. *Peter the Great Transforms Russia*. 3rd ed. Lexington, MA: Heath, 1991.
Cross, A.G. *N.M. Karamzin: A Study of His Literary Career, 1783–1803*. Carbondale and Edwardsville: Southern Illinois University Press, 1971.

Custine, Astolphe de. *La Russie en 1839*. Paris: Librairie d'Amyot, 1843.
Damrosch, David. *What Is World Literature*. Princeton, NJ: Princeton Univesity Press, 1993.
Davydov. Sergei .'The Evolution of Pushkin's Political Thought.' In *The Pushkin Handbook*. Edited by David M. Bethea, 193–208. Madison: University of Wisconsin Press, 2005.
Dilthey, Wilhelm. *Poetry and Experience. Selected Works*. Vol. 5. Edited by Rudolf Makkreel and Frithjof Rodi. Princeton, NJ: Princeton University Press, 1985.
Diment, Galya. 'Tolstoy and Bloomsbury.' *Tolstoy Studies Journal* vol. 5 (1992): 39–54.
Dolinin, Alexander. 'Historicism or Provindentialism? Pushkin's *History of Pugachev* in the Context of French Romantic Historiography.' *Slavic Review* 58, no. 2 (Summer 1999): 291–309.
– *Istoriia odetaia v roman: Val'ter Skott i ego chitateli*. Moscow: Kniga, 1988.
– *Pushkin i Angliia*. Moscow: Novoe literaturnoe obozrenie, 2007.
– 'Swerving from Walter Scott: *The Captain's Daughter* as a Metahistorical Novel.' *Elementa*, 4 (2000): 313–29.
Dolinin, A.S. *Dostoevsky i drugie*. Leningrad: Khudozhestvennaia literatura, 1989.
– 'Dostoevsky i Strakhov.' In *Dostoevsky i drugie: stat'i i issledovaniia o russkoi klassicheskoi literature*, 234–69. Leningrad: Khudozhestvennaia literatura, 1989.
– 'F.M. Dostoevsky and N.N. Strakhov.' In *Shestidesiatye gody: materialy po istorii literatury i obshchestvennomu dvizheniiu*, edited by N.K. Piksanov, 238–54. Moscow and Leningrad: Akademiia Nauk SSSR, 1940.
Dolinin, A.S., ed. *F.M. Dostoevsky v vospominaniiakh sovremennikov*. Moscow: Khudozhestvennaia literatura, 1964. 2 vols.
– *Poslednie romany Dostoevskogo: kak sozdavalis' Podrostok i Brat'ia Karamazovy*. Leningrad: Sovetskii pisatel', 1963.
Donskov, A., G. Galagan, and L. Gromova. *Edinenie liudei v tvorchestve L.N. Tolstogo: fragmenty rukopisei*. Ottawa: University of Ottawa, 2002.
Dostoevsky, F.M. *The Adolescent*. Translated by Richard Pevear and Larissa Volokhonsky. New York: Vintage, 2003.
– *F.M. Dostoevsky v rabote nad romanom 'Podrostok.' Tvorcheskie rukopisi. Literaturnoe Nasledstvo* 77. Moscow: Nauka, 1965.
– *Novye materially i issledovaniia. Literaturnoe Nasledstvo* 86. Moscow: Nauka: 1973.
– *Polnoe sobranie sochinenii v tridsati tomakh*. Edited and annoted by G.M. Fridlender et al. Leningrad: Nauka, 1972–90.

Dostoevskaia, A.G. *Vospominaniia*. Moscow: Khudozhestvennaia literatura, 1981.
Dowler, Wayne. *Dostoevsky, Grigor'ev, and Native Soil Conservatism*. Toronto: University of Toronto Press, 1982.
– *An Unnecessary Man: The Life of Apollon Grigor'ev*. Toronto: University of Toronto Press, 1995.
Druzhinin, A.V. *Sobranie sochinenii*. St Petersburg: Imperatorskaia akademiia nauk, 1865. 7 vols.
Druzhnikov, Yurii. *Prisoner of Russia: Alexander Pushkin and The Political Uses of Nationalism*. Translated by Thomas Moore and Iulia Druzhnikov. New Brunswick, NJ: Transaction Publishers, 1999.
Durylin, S. 'G-zha de Stal' i ee russkie otnosheniia.' *Literaturnoe nasledie* 32–4 (1939): 215–30.
– 'Russkie pisateli u Gëte v Veimare.' *Literaturnoe nasledstvo* 4/6 (1932): 83–504.
Echevarria, Roberto G and Pupo-Walker, Enrique. *The Cambridge History of Latin American Literature: Discovery to Modernism*. Cambridge, UK: Cambridge, University Press, 1996.
Egan, David R., and Egan, Melinda A. *Leo Tolstoy: An Annotated Bibliography of English-Language Sources to 1978*. Metuchen, NJ: Scarecrow Press, 1979.
Egorov, B.F. 'Apollon Grigor'ev – kritik. Stat'ia 1,' 'Apollon Grigor'ev – kritik. Stat'ia 2,' 'Materialy ob Apollone Grigor'eve iz arkhiva N.N. Strakhova,' and 'Pis'ma A. Grigor'eva M.P. Pogodinu (1855–1858).' In *Uchenye zapiski Tartuskogo gosudarstvennogo universiteta*. Vols. 3, 4, 6, 21. Tartu, Estonia: Tartuskii gosudarstvennyi universitet, 1960–73.
– *Apollon Grigor'ev*. (*Zhizn' zamechatel'nykh liudei*.) Moscow: Molodaia gvardiia, 2000.
– 'Khudozhestvennaia proza Ap. Grigor'eva.' In Apollon Grigor'ev. *Vospominaniia*, edited by B.F. Egorov, 355–7. Leningrad: Nauka, 1980.
– 'Lotman kak chelovek i iavelenie.' In *Yurii Mikhailovich Lotman*, edited by V.K. Kantor, 13–81. Moscow: Rasspen, 2009.
– *Zhizn' i tvorchestvo Yu.M. Lotmana*. Moscow: Novoe literaturnoe obozrenie, 1999.
Eikhenbaum, Boris. *Lev Tolstoj*. Her. D. Tschizewskij. 2 vols. in 1. Muenchen: Wilhelm Fink Verlag, 1968.
– *O proze*. Leningrad: Khudozhestvennaia literatura, 1969.
Emerson, Caryl. 'Bakhtin, Lotman, Vygotskii, and Lydiia Ginzbug on Types of Selves: A Tribute.' In *Self and Story in Russian History*, edited by Laura Engelstein and Stephanie Sandler, 20–45. Ithaca, NY: Cornell University Press, 2000.

- *Boris Godunov: Transpositions of a Russian Theme*. Bloomington: Indiana University Press, 1986.
- 'Grinev's Dream: *The Captain's Daughter* and a Father's Blessing.' *Slavic Review* 40, no. 1 (Spring 1981): 60–76.
- 'Jurii Lotman's Last Book and Filiations with Bakhtin.' *Die Welt der Slaven* 48 (2003): 201–16.
- 'The Tolstoy Connection in Bakhtin.' In *Rethinking Bakhtin: Extensions and Challenges*, edited by Gary Saul Morson and Caryl Emerson, 149–72. Evanston, IL: Northwestern University Press, 1989.
- 'Tolstoy's Aesthetics.' In *The Cambridge Companion to Tolstoy*, edited by Donna Tussing Orwin, 237–51. Cambridge: Cambridge University Press, 2002.

Emerson, Caryl, and Inessa Medzhibovskaya. 'Dostoevsky, Tolstoy, Bakhtin on Art and Immortality.' In *Critical Theory in Russia and the West*, edited by Alastair Renfrew and Galin Tihanov, 26–43. BASEES: Routledge, 2010.

Engel'gardt, B.M. 'Ideologicheskii roman Dostoevskogo.' In *Izbrannye trudy*, edited by M. Muratov, 270–308. St Petersburg: Izdatelstvo St Peterburgskogo universiteta, 1995.

Engelstein, Laura, and Stephanie Sandler, eds. *Self and Story in Russian History*. Ithaca, NY: Cornell University Press, 2000.

Evdokimova, Svetlana. *Pushkin's Historical Imagination*. New Haven, CT: Yale University Press, 1999.

Fanger, Donald. *Dostoevsky and Romantic Realism A Study of Dostoevsky in Relation to Balzac, Dickens, and Gogol*. Cambridge, MA: Harvard University Press, 1965.

Feuer, Kathryn B. *Tolstoy and the Genesis of War and Peace*. Edited by Robin Feuer Miller and Donna Tussing Orwin. Ithaca, NY: Cornell University Press, 1996.

Figes, Orlando. *Natasha's Dance: A Cultural History of Russia*. New York: Picador, 2002.

Forster, Michael. *After Herder: Philosophy of Language in the German Tradition*. Oxford: Oxford University Press, 2010.

- Introduction to Herder, *Philosophical Works*, translated and edited by Michael N. Forster, vii–xxxv. Cambridge: Cambridge University Press, 2002.

Frank, Joseph. *The Seeds of Revolt, 1821–1849*. Princeton, N.J.: Princeton University Press, 1976.

- *Dostoevsky: The Years of Ordeal, 1850–59*. Princeton, NJ: Princeton University Press, 1983.

- *Dostoevsky: The Stir of Liberation, 1860–1865*. Princeton, NJ: Princeton University Press, 1986.
- *Dostoevsky: The Mantle of Prophet, 1871–1881*. Princeton, NJ: Princeton University Press, 2002.

Frank, Semen. 'Pushkin kak politicheskii myslitel'.' In *Pushkin v russkoi filosofskoi kritike*, edited by R.A. Gal'tseva, 396–422. Moscow: Kniga, 1990.

Froebel, Friedrich. *Autobiography of Friedrich Froebel*. Translated and annotated by Emilie Michaelis and H. Keatley Moore. Syracuse, NY: C. W. Barden, 1889.

Gadamer, Hans-Georg. *Truth and Method*. Translated by Joel Weinsheimer and Donald G. Marshall. New York: Crossroad, 1975.

Gallagher, Catherine. *The Industrial Reformation of English Fiction: Social Discourse and Narrative Form, 1832–1867*. Chicago: University of Chicago Press, 1985.

Gasparov, Boris. *Poeticheskii iazyk Pushkina kak fakt istorii russkogo literaturnogo iazyka*. Vienna: Wiener Slawistischer Almanach, 1992.

Gerder, I.G. *Izbrannye prozivedeniia*. Moscow and Leningrad: Akademiia Nauk SSSR, 1959.

Gershenzon, M.O. *Istoriia molodoi Rossii*. In *Izbrannoe*, 2:7–179. Moscow and Jerusalem: Universitetskaia kniga, Gershsarim, 2000.
- 'P. Ia. Chaadaev. Zhizn' i myshlenie.' In *Izbrannoe*, 1:381–562.

Gershenzon, Michael. *A History of Young Russia*. Translated by James P. Scanlan. Irvine, CA: Charles Schlacks, 1986.

Gerstein, Linda. *Nikolai Strakhov*. Cambridge, MA: Harvard University Press, 1971.

Gerzen, A.I. *Pis'ma ob izuchenii prirody*. Moscow: OGIZ, 1946.
- *Sobranie sochinenii v tridtsati tomakh*. Moscow: Izdatel'stvo Akademii Nauk SSSR, 1954–65.

Gettmann, Royal A. *Turgenev in England and America*. Urbana: University of Illinois Press, 1941.

Geyer, Deitrich. *Russian Imperialism: the interaction of domestic and foreign policy, 1860–1914*. Translated by Bruce Little. New Haven, CT: Yale University Press, 1987.

Ginzburg, Lydiia. *Chelovek za pis'mennym stolom*. Leningrad: Sovetskii pisatel', 1989.
- 'O probleme narodnosti i lichnosti v poezii dekabristov.' In *O russkom realizme XIX veka i voprosakh narodnosti literatury; sbornik statei*, edited by Pavel Gromov et al., 52–93. Moscow-Leningrad: Khudozhestvennoi literatura, 1960.
- *O psikhologicheskoi proze*. Leningrad: Sovetskii pisatel', 1971.

Girard, René. *Deceit, Desire, and the Novel: Self and Other in Literary Structure.* Translated by Y. Freccero. Baltimore: Johns Hopkins University Press, 1965.

Glinka, Sergei. *Zapiski o 1812 gode Sergeia Glinki, pervogo ratnika moskovskogo opolcheniia.* St Petersburg: tipografiia Imperatorskoi' Rossii'skoi' Akademii Nauk, 1836.

Goncharov, I.A. 'Mil'on terzanii.' In *A.S. Griboedov v russkoi kritike*, edited by A.M. Gordin, 243–78. Moscow: Khudozhestvennaia literatura, 1958.

Gor'kii, M. *Sobranie sochinenii v tridtsati tomakh.* Vol. 14. Moscow: Khudozhestvennaia literatura, 1951.

Greenleaf, Monica Frenkel. *Pushkin and Romantic Fashion: Fragment, Elegy, Orient, Irony.* Stanford, CA: Stanford University Press, 1994.

– 'Pushkin's "Journey to Arzrum": The Poet at the Border.' *Slavic Review* 50, no. 4 (Winter 1991): 940–53.

Grigor'ev, A.A. *Apollon Grigor'ev: materially dlia biografii*, edited by V. Kniazhnin, 1–97. Petrograd: Izdanie Pushkinskogo Doma pri Akademii Nauk, 1917.

– *Estetika i kritika.* With and introduction and notes by A.I. Zhuravleva. Moscow: Iskusstvo, 1980.

– *Polnoe sobranie sochinenii Apollona Grigor'eva v dvenadtsati tomakh.* Petrograd: Izdanie P.P. Ivanova, 1918.

– *Sobranie sochinenii Apollona Grigor'eva.* Edited by V.F. Savodnik. Moscow: Kushner, 1915.

– *Sochineniia v dvukh tomakh.* Edited by B.F. Egorov. Moscow: Khudozhestvennaia literatura, 1990. 2 vols.

– *Vospominaniia.* Edited by B.F. Egorov. Leningrad: Nauka, 1980.

Gromova-Opul'skaia, L.D. *Izbrannyie trudy.* Moscow: Nauka, 2005.

– *Lev Nikolaevich Tolstoy: materially k biografii s 1892 po 1899.* Moscow: Rossiskaia Akademiia Nauk, 1998.

Gulyga, A.V. *Gerder.* Moscow: Mysl', 1975.

Gurvich-Lischiner, Sophia. 'Chaadaev – Herzen – Dostoevsky: Individual and Reason in the Creative Mind.' *Russian Studies in Literature* 43, no. 3 (Summer 2007): 6–54.

Gusev, N.N. *Lev Nikolaevich Tolstoy: Materialy k biografii s 1855 po 1869 god.* Moscow: Izdatel'stvo Akademii Nauk SSSR, 1957.

– *Letopis' zhizni i tvorchestva L.N Tolstogo.* Moscow: Academia, 1936.

Gustafson, Richard F. *Leo Tolstoy: Resident and Stranger; a Study in Fiction and Theology.* Princeton, NJ: Princeton University Press, 1986.

– 'The Three Stages of Man'. *Canadian-American Slavic Studies* 12, no. 4 (Winter 1978): 481–518.

Hammarberg, Gitta. *From the Idyll to the Novel: Karamzin's Sentimental Prose.* Cambridge: Cambridge University Press, 1991.
– Hardin, James. *Reflection and Action: Essays on the Bildungsroman.* Columbia: University of South Carolina Press, 1991.
Hartman, Geoffrey. *The Fateful Question of Culture.* New York: Columbia University Press, 1997.
Hegel, G.W.F. *Aesthetics: Lectures in Fine Art.* Translated by T.M. Knox. Oxford: Clarendon, 1975.
– *The Philosophy of History.* Translated by J. Sibree. Mineola, NY: Dover Philosophical Classics, 2004.
Herder, J.G. *Briefe zur Befoerderung der Humanitaet.* Riga, 1793–1797. Brief 26; translated in *Vestnik Evropy,* 22, no. 6 (1802): 116–129.
– 'Critical Forests' and 'Shakespeare.' In *Selected Writings on Aesthetics,* translated and edited by Gregory Moore, 100–1; 291–307. Princeton, NJ: Princeton University Press, 2006.
– 'Letters for the Advancement of Humanity (1793–7) (excerpts),' 'On Cognition and Sensation of the Human Soul,' and 'This, Too, Is a Philosophy of History for the Formation of Humanity.' In *Philosophical Writings,* translated and edited by Michael N. Forster, 370–73; 187–246; 268–358. Cambridge: Cambridge University Press, 2003.
– *On World History: An Anthology.* Edited by Hans Adler and Ernest A. Menze. Translated by Ernest A. Menze with Michael Palma. New York: M.E. Sharpe, 1997.
– 'Razgovor o nevidimo-vidimom obshchestve.' Translated by N. Karamzin. *Vestnik Evropy* 19 (1802): 116–28
– *Werke in zehn Bänden.* Vols. 4 and 6. Edited by Martin Bollacher. Frankfurt am Main: Deutscher Klassiker Verlag, 1995–2000.
Hoffmann, David L., and Yanni Kotsonis, eds. *Russian Modernity: Politics, Knowledge, Practices.* New York: St Martin's Press, 2000.
Hokanson, Katya. *Writing at Russia's Borders.* Toronto: University of Toronto Press, 2008.
Holland, Kate Rowan. *The Novel in the Age of Disintegration: Dostoevsky and the Problem of Genre in the 1870s.* Forthcoming.
Holquist, Michael. *Dostoevsky and the Novel.* 2nd edition. Evanston, IL: Northwestern University Press, 1986.
Holquist, Peter. *Making War and Forging Revolution: Russia's Continuum of Crisis, 1914–1921.* Cambridge, MA: Harvard University Press, 2002.
Hosking, Geoffrey. *Russia: People and Empire, 1552–1917.* Cambridge, MA.: Harvard University Press, 1997.
Humboldt, Wilhelm von. *The Limits of State Action.* Edited by J.W. Burrow. Indianapolis, IN: Liberty Fund, 1969.

– *Linguistic variability and intellectual development*. Trans. George C. Buck and Frithjof A. Raven. Philadelphia: University of Pennsylvania Press, 1971.

Jackson, Robert L. *The Art of Dostoevsky: Deliriums and Nocturns*. Princeton, NJ: Princeton University Press, 1981.

– *Dialogues with Dostoevsky: The Overwhelming Questions*. Stanford, CA: Stanford University Press, 1993.

Jackson, Robert L., ed. *Dostoevsky: New Perspectives*. Englewood Cliffs, N.J.: Prentice-Hall, 1984.

James, Henry. 'The Art of Fiction,' 'The Future of the Novel,' 'The New Novel,' and 'The Present Literary Situation in France.' In *Literary Criticism*, 44–65; 100–23; 26–33; 124–59. New York: Literary Classics, 1984.

– 'The Preface.' In *The Tragic Muse*, 9–26. Whitefish, MT: Kessinger Publisher, LLC, 2010.

James, William. *Varieties of Religious Experience*. Cambridge, MA: Harvard University Press, 1985.

Jay, Martin. *Songs of Experience: Modern American and European Variations on a Universal Theme*. Los Angeles: University of California Press, 2005.

Jeffers, Thomas L. *Apprenticeships: The Bildungsroman from Goethe to Santayana*. New York: Palgrave Macmillan, 2005.

Jones, Malcolm V. *Dostoevsky after Bakhtin: Readings in Dostoevsky's Fantastic Realism*. Cambridge: Cambridge University Press, 1990.

Jones, Paul. *Raymond Williams's Sociology of Culture: A Critical Reconstruction*. New York: Palgrave Macmillan, 2004.

Kahn, Andrew, ed. *The Cambridge Companion to Pushkin*. Cambridge: Cambridge University Press, 2006.

– *Pushkin's Lyric Intelligence*. Oxford: Oxford University Press, 2008.

Kant, Immanuel. 'Reviews of Herder's Ideas on the Philosophy of History of Mankind.' In *Political Writings*, edited by H.S. Reiss, 201–20. Cambridge: Cambridge University Press, 1991.

Kantor, V.K. ed. *Yurii Mikhailovich Lotman*. Moscow: Rasspen, 2009.

Karamzin, N.M. *Istoriia gosudarstva Rossiskogo*. St Petersburg: Zolotoi Vek, 1997. 3 vols.

– *Karamzin's Memoir on Ancient and Modern Russia*. Translation and analysis by Richard Pipes. Cambridge, MA: Harvard University Press, 1959.

– *Karamzin: pro et contra: lichnost' i tvorchestvo Karamzina v otsenke russkikh pisatelei, kritikov, issledovatelei*. St Petersburg: Iz-vo Russkoi Khristianskoi gumanitarnoi akademii, 2006.

– *Sochineniia Karamzina*. St Petersburg: Karl Krai, 1848. 4 vols.

Khomiakov, A.S. *Izbrannye sochineniia*. New York: Izdatel'stvo imeni Chekhova, 1955.

- 'O starom i novom.' In A.S. Khomiakov, *Sochineniia v dvukh tomakh*, 1456–70. Moscow: Medium, 1994.
- *Polnoe sobranie sochinenii A.S. Khomiakova*. Vol. 3. Moscow: Universitetskaia tipografiia, 1900.
Kireevskii, I.V. *Polnoe sobranie sochinenii*. Moscow: Tipografiia I. Moskovskago universiteta, 1911.
Kirpotin, V. 'Dostoevskii, Strakhov – i Evgenii Pavlovich Radomskii.' In *Mir Dostoevskogo*, 113–59. 2nd edition. Moscow: Sovetskii pisatel', 1983.
Kiseleva, L.N. 'Pushkin i Zhukovskii v 1830-e gody (tochki ideologicheskogo sopriazheniia).' In *Pushkinskaia konferentsia v Stenforde*, edited by L. Fleishman et al., 171–85. Moscow: OGI, 2001.
Kliger, Ilya. 'Genre and Actuality in Belinsky, Herzen and Goncharov: Toward a Genealogy of the Tragic Pattern in Russian Realism.' *Slavic Review* 66, no. 1 (Spring 2011): 45–66.
Knapp, Liza. *The Annihilation of Inertia: Dostoevsky and Metaphysics*. Evanston, IL: Northwestern University Press, 1996.
Knauft, Bruce. *Geneologies of the Present in Cultural Anthropology*. New York: Routledge, 1996.
Kochetkova, Natalia. *Nikolay Karamzin*. New York: Twayne, 1975.
Kochetkova, Tatiana. 'Stendhal, Viazemskii et les décembristes.' *Stendhal Club* 8 (1960): 311–19.
Kontje, Todd. *The German Bildungsroman: History of a National Genre*. Columbia, SC: Camden House, 1993.
- *Private Lives in Public Sphere: The German Bildungsroman as Metafiction*. University Park: Pennsylvania State University Press, 1992.
Koselleck, Reinhart et al. *Bildung*. In *Geschichtliche Grundbegriffe: Historisches Lexikon zur politisch-sozialen Sprache in Deutschland*. Stuttgart: E. Clett, 1994.
Kotrelev, V.N., ed. *Biblioteka L'va Nikolaevicha Tolstogo v Iasnoi Poliane: bibliograficheskoe opisanie*. 3 vols. Moscow: Kniga, 1972–99.
Koyré, Alexandre. *La Philosophie et le problème national en Russie au début du XIX siècle*. Paris: Librarie Ancienne Honoré Champion, 1929.
Krasnoschekova, Elena. *Roman vospitaniia: Bildungsroman na russkoi pochve: Karamzin, Pushkin, Tolstoi, Dostoevskii*. St Petersburg: Izdatelstvo Pushkinskogo fonda, 2008.
Krasnov, G. *Geroi i narod v romane L'va Tolstogo 'Voina i Mir*. Moscow: Sovetskii pisatel', 1964.
- 'Herder und Lev Tolstoj.' *Zeitschrift fuer Slawistik* 6, no. 3 (1961): 415–33.
Kupreianova, Ye. N. *Estetika L.N. Tolstogo*. Moscow, Leningrad: Nauka, 1966.
Lachmann, Renate. 'Value Aspects in Jurij Lotman's *Semiotics of Culture/Semiotics of Text*.' *Disapositio* 12, no. 30–2 (1987): 13–33.

Layton, Susan. *Russian Literature and Empire: Conquest of the Caucasus from Pushkin to Tolstoy*. Cambridge: Cambridge University Press, 1994.

Levin, Harry. *The Gates of Horn: A Study of Five French Realists*. New York: Oxford University Press, 1966.

Levitt, Marcus. *Russian Literary Politics and the Pushkin Celebration of 1880*. Ithaca, NY: Cornell University Press, 1989.

Lichtenstein, Ernst. *Zur Entwicklung des Bildungsbegriffs von Meister Eckhart bis Hegel*. Heidelberg: Quelle & Meyer, 1966.

Lloyd, David, and Paul Thomas. *Culture and the State*. New York: Routledge, 1998.

Lotman, Yu.M. 'Blok i narodnaia kul'tura goroda.' *Blokovskii sbornik*. Vol. 4. Tartu, Estonia: Tartusskii gosudarstvennyi universitet, 1981.

– *Culture and Explosion*. Translated by Wilma Clark. Edited by Marina Grishakova. New York and Berlin: Mouton de Gruyter, 2009.

– 'Ideinaia struktura "Kapitanskoi Dochki."' In *Izbrannye stat'i v trekh tomakh*, 2:419–29. Tallinn, Estonia: Alexandra, 1992.

– *Izbrannye stat'i v trekh tomakh*. Tallinn, Estonia: Alexandra, 1992.

– *Karamzin*. St Petersburg: Iskusstvo-SPb, 1997.

– *Kul'tura i vzryv*. Moscow: Gnozis, 1992.

– *O poetakh i poezii*. St Petersburg: Iskusstvo Spb, 2001.

– 'Poeziia 1790–1810kh godov' (predislovie).' In *Poety 1790–1810kh godov*, edited by Mark Alt'shuller, 5–62. Leningrad: Sovetskii pisatel', 1971.

– 'Problema narodnosti i puti razvitiia literatury preddekabristskogo perioda.' In *O russkom realizme XIX veka i voprosakh narodnosti literatury*, edited by Pavel Gromov, 3–49. Leningrad: Gosudarstvennoe izdatel'stvo khudozhestvennaia literatura, 1960.

– *Pushkin: Biografiia pisatelia; stat'i i zametki, 1960–1990; 'Evgenii Onegin' kommentarii*. Introduction by B.F. Egorov. St Petersburg: Iskusstvo-SPb, 1995.

– *Roman v stikhakh Pushkina 'Evgenii Onegin.'* Tartu, Estonia: Tartusskii gosudarstvennyi universitet, 1975.

– *Struktura khudozhestvennogo teksta*. Providence, RI: Brown University Press, 1971.

– *The Structure of the Artistic Text*. Translated by Ronald Vroon. Ann Arbor: Michigan Slavic Contributions 1977.

– *Vospitanie dushi: vospominaniia, interviu, besedy; v mire pushkinskoi poezii; besedy o russkoi kul'ture (televizionnye lektsii)*. St Petersburg: Iskusstvo SPb, 2003.

Love, Jeff. *The Overcoming of History in Tolstoy's* War and Peace. Amsterdam: Rodopi, 2004.

Lounsbery, Anne. *Thin Culture, High Art: Gogol, Hawthorne, and Authorship in Nineteenth-Century Russia and America.* Cambridge, MA: Harvard University Press, 2007.
Lubbock, Percy. *The Craft of Fiction.* London: J. Cape, 1921.
Luhmann, Niklas. *Social Systems.* Translated by John Berdnarz Jr with Dirk Baecker. Stanford, CA: Stanford University Press, 1995.
Lukács, Georg. *The Theory of the Novel.* Translated by Anna Bostock. Cambridge, MA: MIT Press, 1972.
Lyotard, Jean-François. *Le différend.* Paris: Editions de Minuit, 1983.
Madariaga, Isabel de. *Russia in the Age of Catherine the Great.* New Haven, CT: Yale University Press, 1981.
Mandelker, Amy. 'Semiotizing the Sphere: Organicist Theory in Lotman, Bakhtin and Vernadsky.' *PMLA* 109, no. 3 (May 1994): 385–96.
Mann, Thomas. 'Goethe and Tolstoy.' In *Three Essays,* translated by H.T. Lowe-Porter, 3–142. New York: Alfred Knopf, 1929.
– *Thomas Mann's 'Goethe and Tolstoy': Notes and Source.* Edited by Clayton Koelb. Translated by Alcyone Scott and Clayton Koelb. Tuscaloosa: University of Alabama Press, 1984.
Martin, Alexander. *Romantics, Reformers, Reactionaries: Russian Conservative Thought and Politics in the Reign of Alexander I.* DeKalb: Northern Illinois University Press, 1997.
Matlow, Ralph, ed. *'The Brothers Karamazov': Novelistic Technique.* The Hague: Mouton, 1957.
– *Tolstoy: A Collection of Critical Essays.* Englewood Cliffs, NJ: Prentice-Hall, Inc., 1967.
Maude, Aylmer. *Tolstoy on Art and Its Critics.* London: Oxford University Press, 1925.
May, Rachel. *Translator in the Text: On Reading Russian Literature in English.* Evanston, IL: Northwestern University Press, 1994.
Mazur, Natalia. 'Pushkin i "Moskovskie iunoshi" vokrug problemy geniia.' In *Pushkinskaia konferentsia v Stenforde,* edited by L. Fleishman et al., 54–105. Moscow: OGI, 2001.
McNally, Raymond T. 'Chaadaev's Evaluation of Peter the Great' *Slavic Review* 23, no. 1 (March 1964): 31–44.
Medzhibovskaya, Inessa. *Tolstoy and the Religious Culture of His Time: A Biography of a Long Conversion, 1845–1887.* Lanham, MD: Lexington Books, 2008.
Meerson, Ol'ga. *Dostoevsky's Taboos.* Dresden: Dresden University Press, 1998.
Mendelssohn, Moses. 'Rhapsody or additions to the Letters on sentiments,' 'On the ability to know, the ability to feel, and the ability to desire,'

and 'On the question: what does "to enlighten" mean?' In *Philosophical Writings*, translated and edited by Daniel O. Dahlstrom, 131–68; 307–10; 311–17. Cambridge: Cambridge University Press, 1997.

Merezhkovskii, Dmitrii. *L. Tolstoi i Dostoevskii: vechnye sputniki*. Moscow: Respublika, 1995.

Mérimée, Prosper. *Stat'ii o russkoi literature*. Moscow: IMLI RAN, 2003.

Meyer, Priscilla. *How Russians Read the French: Lermontov, Dostoevsky, Tolstoy*. Madison: University of Wisconsin Press, 2008.

Mikhailovskii, N.K. 'Desnitsa i shuitsa L'va Tolstogo.' In *Literaturno-kriticheskie stat'I*, edited by V. Vorovskii, 59–180. Moscow: Gosudarstvennoe izdatel'stvo khudozhestvennaia literatura, 1957.

– *Dostoevsky: A Cruel Talent*. Translated by Spencer Cadmus. Ann Arbor, MI: Ardis, 1978.

Mill, J.S. 'Civilization,' 'Coleridge,' and 'On Genius.' *Mill's Essays on Literature and Society*, edited with an introduction by J.B. Scheneewind, 148–82, 290–347, 87–101. New York: Collier, 1965.

Miller, Alexei. '*Natsiia, Narod, Narodnost'* in Russia in the 19th Century: Some Introductory Remarks to the History of Concepts.' *Jahrbuecher fuer Geschichte Osteuropas* 56, no. 3 (2008): 379–90.

Miller, Robin Feuer. The Brothers Karamazov: *Worlds of the Novel*. Rev. 2nd ed. New Haven, CT: Yale University Press, 2008.

– *Dostoevsky's Unfinished Journey*. New Haven, CT: Yale University Press, 2007.

– *Dostoevsky and* The Idiot: *Author, Narrator, and Reader*. Cambridge, MA: Harvard University Press, 1981.

Miller, Robin Feuer, ed. *Critical Essays on Dostoevsky*. Boston: G.K. Hall, 1986.

Mints, Z.G. *Lirika Aleksandra Bloka*, reprinted in *Poetika Aleksandra Bloka*, 11–332. St Petersburg: Iskusstvo SPb, 1999.

Mochul'skii, Konstantin. *Dostoevsky: His Life and Work*. Translated with an introduction by Michael A. Minihan. Princeton, NJ: Princeton University Press, 1967.

Modzalevskii, B.L. *Biblioteka A.S. Pushkina: bibliograficheskoe opisanie*. St Petersburg, Tipografiia Imperatorskoi Akademii nauk, 1910.

Mohrenshildt, Dmitri von. *Russia in the Intellectual Life of Eighteenth-Century France*. New York: Columbia University Press, 1936.

Montesquieu, Charles de Secondat. *The Spirit of the Laws*. Edited by Anne M. Cohler, Basia C. Miller, and Harold S. Stone. Cambridge: Cambridge University Press, 1989.

Moretti, Franco. *Atlas of the European Novel, 1800–1900*. London and New York: Verso, 1998.

– 'Serious Century.' In *The Novel, Vol. 1: History, Geography, and Culture*, edited by Franco Moretti, 364–400. Princeton, NJ: Princeton University Press, 2006.
– *The Way of the World: The Bildungsroman in European Culture*. Translated by Albert Sbragia. London and New York: Verso, 2000.
Morgan, Peter. *The Critical Idyll: Traditional Values and the French Revolution in Goethe's* Hermann und Dorothea. Columbia, SC: Camden House, 1990.
Morgenstern, Karl. 'On the Nature of the *Bildungsroman*.' Translation and with an introduction by Tobias Boes. *PMLA* 124, no. 2 (March 2009): 647–59.
Morson, Gary Saul. *The Boundaries of Genre: Dostoevsky's 'Diary of a Writer' and the Traditions of Literary Utopia*. Austin: University of Texas Press, 1981.
– *Hidden in Plain View: Narrative and Creative Potentials in War and Peace*. Stanford, CA: Stanford University Press, 1987.
– 'The Tolstoy Questions: Reflections on the Silbarjoris Theses,' *Tolstoy Studies Journal*, 4 (1991): 115–141.
– 'War and Peace.' In *The Cambridge Companion to Tolstoy*, edited by Donna Tussing Orwin, 76. Cambridge: Cambridge University Press, 2002.
Murav, Harriet. 'Dostoevsky in Siberia: Remembering the Past,' *Slavic Review* 50, no. 4 (Winter, 1991): 858–66.
Nechaeva, V S. *Zhurnal M.M. i F.M. Dostoevskikh 'Vremia' 1861–1863*. Moscow: Nauka, 1972.
– *Zhurnal M.M. i F.M. Dostoevskikh 'Epokha' 1864–1865*. Moscow: Nauka, 1975.
Nekrasov, N.A. *Sochineniia v trekh tomakh*. Edited by N. Skatov. Moscow: Gosudarstvennoe izdatelstvo khudozhestvennoi literatury, 1959.
Neuhauser, Rudolf. *Toward the Romantic Age*. The Hague: Martinus Nijhoff, 1974.
Ng, Mau-sang. *The Russian Hero in Modern Chinese Fiction*. Hong Kong: Chinese University Press; New York: State University of New York Press, 1988.
Nickell, William. *The Death of Tolstoy: Russia on the Eve, Astapovo Station, 1910*. Ithaca, NY, and London: Cornell University Press, 2010.
– 'Tolstoy in 1828: in the Mirror of the Revolution.' In *Epic Revisionism: Russian Literature and History as Stalinist Propaganda*, edited by Kevin M.F. Platt and David Brandenberger, 17–38. Madison: University of Wisconsin Press, 2006.
O'Bell, Leslie. 'Pushkin's Novel *The Captain's Daughter* as a Fictional Family Memoir.' *Pushkin Review* 10 (2007): 47–57.

Oksman, Yu.G. Commentary. In A.S. Pushhin, *Kapitanskaia dochka*, 149–244. Moscow: Nauka, 1964.
– 'Pushkin i dekabristy.' *Osvoboditel'noe dvizhenie v Rossii* 1 (1971): 70–88.
Orwin, Donna Tussing, ed. *Anniversary Essays on Tolstoy*. Cambridge: Cambridge University Press, 2010.
– *Consequences of Consciousness*. Stanford, CA: Stanford University Press, 2007.
– 'Did Tolstoy or Dostoevsky believe in Miracles?' In *A New Word on* The Brothers Karamazov, edited by Robert Louis Jackson, 105–41. Evanston, IL: Northwestern University Press, 2004.
– 'The Return to Nature: Tolstoyan Echoes in *The Idiot*.' *Russian Review* 58 (January 1999): 87–102.
– 'Strakhov's *World as a Whole*: A Missing Link between Dostoevsky and Tolstoy.' In *Poetics, Self, Place: Essays in Honor of Anna Lisa Crone*, edited by Catherine O'Neil, Nicole Boudreau, and Sarah Krive, 473–93. Bloomington, IN: Slavica, 2007.
– *Tolstoy's Art and Thought: 1847–1880*. Princeton, NJ: Princeton University Press, 1993.
Ospovat, A.L. 'Imenovanie geroia *Kapitanskoi dochki*.' In *Lotmanovskii sbornik*, edited by E. Permiakov, 261–7. Moscow: ITS Garant, 2004.
Owen, Robert. *New Lanark*. London, 20 February 1849. Electronic reproduction. Reproduction of original from Goldsmiths' Library, University of London. Farmington Hills, MI: Thomson Gale, 2005.
Paperno, Irina. *Chernyshevsky and the Age of Realism*. Stanford, CA: Stanford University Press, 1988.
– 'Leo Tolstoy's Correspondence with Nikolai Strakhov: A Dialogue on Faith.' In *Anniversary Essays on Tolstoy*, edited by Donna Tussing Orwin, 96–119. New York: Cambridge University Press, 2010.
Pavel, Thomas. *La pensée du roman*. Paris: Gallimard, 2003.
Pavlenko, N.I. *Mikhail Pogodin*. Moscow: Pamiatniki istoricheskoi mysli, 2003.
Perlina, Nina. *Varieties of Poetic Utterance: Quotation in* The Brothers Karamazov. Lanham, NY: University Press of America, 1985.
– 'Vico's Concept of Knowledge as an Underpinning of Dostoevsky's Aesthetic Historicism.' *Slavic and East European Journal* 45, no. 2 (Summer 2001): 323–42.
Petrunina, N. *Proza Pushkina: puti evoliutsii*. Leningrad: Nauka, 1987.
Piksanov, N., and A. Tzekhnovitser, eds. *Shestidesiatye gody. Materialy po istorii literatury i obshchestvennomu dvizheniiu*. Moscow: Akademiia Nauk SSSR, 1940.

Pipes, Richard. 'Karamzin's Conception of Monarchy.' *Harvard Slavic Studies* 4 (1957): 35–58.
– *Karamzin's Memoir on Ancient and Modern Russia: A Translation and Analysis.* Cambridge, MA: Harvard University Press, 1959.
– *Russian Conservatism and Its Critics: A Study in Political Culture.* New Haven, CT: Yale University Press, 2005.
Pogodin, M. 'Detstvo, vospitanie i pervye literaturnye opyty Karamzina.' In *Utro*, 1–58. Moscow: tipografiia Stepanovoi, 1866
– *Istoricheskie aforizmy Mikhaila Pogodina.* Moscow: Universitetskaia Tipografiia, 1836.
– ' "Moe predstavlenie istoriografu." ' *Russkii arkhiv* (1866) 3: lines 1766–70.
– *Nikolai Mikhailovich Karamzin po ego sochineniiam, pis'mam i otzyvam sovremennikov: materialy dlia bigrafii.* 2 vols. Moscow: tipografiia A. I Mamontova, 1866.
Proskurin, Oleg. *Poeziia Pushkina, ili podvizhnyi palimpsest.* Moscow: Novoe Literaturnoe Obozrenie, 1999.
– 'Pushkin and Politics.' In *The Cambridge Companion to Pushkin*, edited by Andrew Kahn, 105–17. Cambidge: Cambridge University Press, 2006.
Pushkin, Aleksandr Sergeevich. *Complete Prose Fiction.* Translated with an introduction by Paul Debreczeny. Stanford, CA: Stanford University Press, 1983.
– *Polnoe sobranie sochinenii.* Moscow and Leningrad: Nauka, 1937–59.
Pustarnakov, V.F., ed. *Filosofiia Shellinga v Rossii.* St Petersburg: Izdatelstvo Russkogo khristianskogo gumanitarnogo instituta, 1998.
Pypin, A.N. *Masonstvo v Rossii: XVIII i pervaia chetvert' XIX v.* Petrograd: OGNI, 1916.
Raeff, Marc. *Origins of the Russian Intelligentsia: the Eighteenth-Century Nobility.* New York: Harcourt and Brace, 1966.
Ram, Harsha. *The Imperial Sublime: A Russian Poetics of Empire.* Madison: University of Wisconsin Press, 2003.
Redfield, Marc. 'Imagi-nation: The Imagined Community and the Aesthetics of Mourning.' *Diacritics* 29, no. 4 (Winter, 1999): 58–83.
– *Phantom Formations: Aesthetic Ideology and the Bildungsroman.* Ithaca, NY: Cornell University Press, 1996.
Reitblat, A.I. *Kak Pushkin vyshel v genii: istoriko-sotsiologicheskie ocherki o knizhnoi kul'ture Pushkinskoi epokhi.* Moscow: Novoe literaturnoe obozrenie, 2001.
Reyfman, Irina. 'Poetic Justice and Injustice: Autobiographical Echoes in Pushkin's *The Captain's Daughter.*' *Slavic and East European Journal* 38, no. 3 (1994): 463–78.

Riasanovsky, Nicholas. *The Image of Peter the Great in Russian History and Thought*. New York: Oxford University Press, 1985.
– 'Nationality in the State Ideology During the Reign of Nicholas I,' 'Pogodin and Shevyrëv in Russsian Intellectual History,' and 'Some Comments on the Role of the Intelligentsia in the Reign of Nicholas I of Russia, 1812–1855.' In *Collected Writings, 1947–1994*, 96–101, 72–85, 86–95. Los Angeles: Charles Schlacks, 1993.
– *Nicholas I and Official Nationality in Russia, 1825–1855*. Berkeley and Los Angeles: University of California Press, 1961.
– *Russian Identities: A Historical Survey*. Oxford: Oxford University Press, 2005.
Riehl, W.H. *The Natural History of the German People*. Translated with an introduction by David J. Diephouse. Lewiston, NY: Edwin Mellen Press, 1990.
Rimer, J. Thomas. *A Hidden Fire: Russian and Japanese Cultural Encounters, 1868–1926*. Stanford, CA: Stanford University Press, 1995.
Rogov, K.Iu. 'Iz istorii uchrezhdeniia *Moskovskogo Vestnika*,' *Pushkinskaia konferentsia v Stenforde*, edited by L. Fleishman et al., 106–32. Moscow: OGI, 2001.
– 'K istorii Moskovskogo romantizma: kruzhok i obshchestvo S. E. Raicha.' *Lotmanovskii sbornik*, edited by E. Permiakov, 523–676. Moscow: Garant, 1995.
Rosen, Nathan. 'Notes on War and Peace.' *Tolstoy Studies Journal* 3 (1990): 111–19.
– 'Style and Structure in *The Brothers Karamazov*: The Grand Inquisitor and the Russian Monk.' *Russian Literature Triquarterly* 1 (1971): 352–65.
Rousseau, J.J. *Emile, or on Education*. Translated with an introduction by Allan Bloom. New York: Basic Books, 1979.
– *On the Social Contract with Geneva Manuscript and Political Economy*. Edited by Roger D. Masters. Translated by Judith R. Masters. New York, Boston: St Martin's Press, 1978.
Rosenblum, L. 'Tolstoy and Dostoevsky (Closing the Distance) At the Turn of the 1870s–1880s.' *Russian Studies in Literature* 45, no. 4 (Fall 2009): 62–97.
– 'Tvorcheskie dnevniki Dostoevskogo,' *Literaturnoe nasledstvo* 83 (1971): 17–23.
Rozanov, V.V. 'N.N. Strakhov, ego lichnost' i deiatel'nost.' In *Literaturnye izgnanniki*, 9–85. Moscow: Agraf, 2000.
Rozanova, S.A. *Tolstoi i Gertsen*. Moscow: Khudozhestvennaia literatura, 1974.

Ruttenburg, Nancy. *Dostoevsky's Democracy*. Princeton, NJ: Princeton University Press, 2008.
Rzhevsky, Nicholas. 'The Shape of Chaos: Herzen and *War and Peace.*' *Russian Review* 34, no. 4 (October 1975): 367–81.
Sapchenko, L.A., ed. *N. M. Karamzin: Pro et Contra*. St Petersburg: Izdatel-stvo russkoi khristianskoi gumanitarnoi akademii, 2006.
Scanlan, James P. 'Tolstoy Among the Philosophers: His Book On Life and Its Critical Reception.' *Tolstoy Studies Journal* 18 (2006): 52–69.
Schaarschmidt, Ilse. 'Der Bedeutungswandel der Begriffe *Bildung* und *bilden* in der Literaturepoche von Gottsched bis Herder.' In *Beiträge zur Geschichte des Bildungsbegriffs*, edited by Franz Rauhut and Ilse Schaarschmidt, 24–87. Weinheim: Verlag Julius Belz, 1965.
Schiller, Friedrich. *On the Aesthetic Education of Man*. Edited by Elizabeth M. Wilkinson and L.A. Willoughby. Oxford: Clarendon Press, 1982.
– *Ueber naïve und sentimentalische Dichtung. (On the naïve and sentimental in literature.)* Translated by Helen Watanabe-O'Kelly. Manchester: Carcanet New Press, 1981.
Schlegel, Friedrich. 'Ueber Goethes *Meister.*' *Aesthetische und politische Schriften*, vol. 2, 126–47. Munchen, Padeborn, Wien, Zuerich: Kritische Neueausgabe, 1967.
Schmid, Ulrich. 'The Family Drama as an Interpretive Pattern in Aleksandr Gercen's *Byloe i Dumy.*' *Russian Literature* 61 (January 2007): 67–102.
Schmidt, James, ed. *What Is Enlightenment? Eighteenth-Century Answers and Twentieth-Century Questions*. Los Angeles: University of California Press, 1996.
Schoenle, Andreas. *Lotman and Cultural Studies: Encounters and Extensions*. Madison: University of Wisconsin Press, 2006.
– '"Modernity as a Destroyed Anthill": Tolstoy on History and the Aesthetics of Ruins.' In *Ruins of Modernity*, edited by J. Hell and Andreas Schoenle, 89–103. Durham, NC: Duke University Press, 2010.
Shklovskii, Viktor. *Lev Tolstoy*. Moscow: Molodaia gvardiia, 1973.
Shchhukin, V.G. 'Dukh karnavala i dukh prosvescheniia.' In Yurii Mikhailovich Lotman, edited by V.K. Kantor, 132–90. Moscow: Rasspen, 2009.
Semionov, E.I. *Roman Dostoevskogo 'Podrostok': problematika i zhanr*. Leningrad: Nauka, 1979.
Serkov, A.I. *Istoriia russkogo masonstva XIX veka*. St Petersburg: Izdatelstvo imeni N.I. Novikova, 2000.
Silbarjoris, Rimvydas. *Tolstoy's Aesthetics and His Art*. Columbus, OH: Slavica, 1991.

Sinel, Allen. *The Classroom and the Chancellery: State Educational Reforms in Russia under Count Dmitrii Tolstoy.* Cambridge, MA: Harvard University Press, 1973.

Skaftymov, A. 'Obraz Kutuzova i filosofiia istorii v romane L. Tolstogo *Voina i mir.*' In *Nravstvennye iskaniia russkikh pisatelei*, 182–217. Moscow: Khudozhestvennaia literatura, 1972.

Skatov, N. 'N.N. Strakhov (1828–1896).' In N.N. Strakhov, *Literaturnaia kritika*, edited by N. Skatov, 40–1. Moscow: Sovremennik, 1984.

Slaughter, Joseph R. 'Enabling Fictions and Novel Subjects: The *Bildungsroman* and International Human Rights Law.' *PMLA* 121, no. 5 (May 2006): 1405–23.

Sprache und Bildung: Beitraege zum 150. Todestag Wilhelm von Humboldts. Her. Rudolf Hoberg. Darmstadt: Techniche Schule Darmstadt, 1987.

Spence, G.W. *Tolstoy the Ascetic.* Edinburgh and London: Oliver and Boyd, 1967.

Staël, Germaine de. *Ten Years of Exile.* Translated by Avriel H. Goldberger. De Kalb: Northern Illinois University Press, 2000.

Stahl, Ernst L. *Die religiöse und die humanitätsphilosophische Bildungsidee und die Entstehung des deutschen Bildungsromans im 18. Jahrhundert.* Bern: Paul Haupt, 1934.

Starygina N.N. *Russkii roman v situatsii filosofsko-religioznoi polemiki 1860–1870-kh godov.* Moscow: Iazyki slavianskoi kul'tury, 2003.

Steedman, Marek. 'State Power, Hegemony, and Memory: Lotman and Gramsci.' *Lotman and Cultural Studies: Encounters and Extensions*, edited by Andreas Schoenle, 136–58. Madison: University of Wisconsin Press, 2006.

Steiner, George. *Tolstoy, or Dostoevsky: An Essay in the Old Criticism.* New York: Knopf, 1959.

Steiner, Lina. 'Gertsen's Tragic *Bildungsroman*: Love, Autonomy and Maturity in Aleksandr Gertsen's *Byloe i dumy.*' *Russian Literature* 61 (2007): 139–74.

– 'My most mature poèma:' Pushkin's *Poltava* and the Irony of Russian National Culture.' *Comparative Literature* 61, no.1 (Spring 2009): 1–45.

– '*Netochka Nezvanova* on the Path of *Bildung*,' *Die Welt der Slaven* 51 (2006): 233–52.

– 'Pushkin's Vision of the Enlightened Self: Individualism, Authority and Tradition beyond Karamzin.' *Pushkin Review* 6 (2003): 1–23.

– 'Toward Ideal Universal Community: Iurii Lotman's Revisiting the Enlightenment and Romanticism.' *Comparative Literature Studies* 40, no. 1 (2003): 37–53.

Strakhov, Nikolai. *Bor'ba s Zapadom v nashei literature.* Kiev: tipografiia Chokolova, 1897. 3 vols.

- 'Iasnaia Poliana,' *Vremia* (March 1862): 65–8.
- *Kriticheskie stat'ii ob I.S. Turgeneve i L.N. Tolstom*. Kiev: tipografiia Chokolova, 1908.
- *Mir kak tseloe: Cherty iz nauki o prirode*. St Petersburg: tipografiia K. Zamyslovskogo, 1872.
- 'Pis'ma N.N. Strakhova F.M. Dostoevskomu.' Published by A.S. Dolinin. In *Shestidesiatye gody: materially po istorii literatury i obshchestvennomu dvizheniiu*, edited by N.K. Piksanov, 255–80. Moscow and Leningrad: Akademiia Nauk SSSR, 1940.
- *Vospominaniia o Fyodore Mikhailoviche Dostoevskom*. In F.M. Dostoevsky, *Biografiia, pis'ma i zametki iz zapisnoi knizhki*, 169–329. St Petersburg: tipografiia Suvorina, 1883.

Strakhov, N.N., and L.N. Tolstoy. *Polnoe sobranie perepiski; Complete Correspondence*. Edited by A.A. Donskov. Moscow and Ottawa: Slavic Research Group at the University of Ottawa and the State L.N. Tolstoy Museum, 2003.
- *Perepiska L.N. Tolstogo s N.N. Strakhovym*. St Petersburg: Tolstovskii muzei, 1914.

Strich, Fritz. *Goethe und die Weltliteratur*. Bern: A. Francke, 1946.

Tang Chenxi. *The Geographic Imagination of Modernity: Geography, Literature and Philosophy in German Romanticism*. Palo Alto, CA: Stanford University Press, 2008.

Tartakovskii, A.G. 'Pokazaniia russkikh ochevidtsev o prebyvanii frantsuzov v Moskve v 1812 g. (K metodike istochnikovedcheskogo analiza).' *Istochnikovedenie otechestvennoi istorii*, no.1 (1973): 232–73.

Terras, Victor. *Belinskii and Russian Literary Criticism*. Madison: University of Wisconsin Press, 1974.

Thompson, Diane O. The Brothers Karamazov *and the Poetics of Memory*. Cambridge: Cambridge University Press, 1991.
- 'Poetic Transformations of Scientific Facts in *Brat'ia Karamazovy*.' *Dostoevsky Studies* 8 (1987): 73–91.

Tikhomirov, Boris. 'Dostoevsky and Children in the *New Testament*.' In *Dostoevsky on the Threshold of Other Worlds: Essays in Honor of Malcom V. Jones*, edited by Sarah Young and Lesley Milne, 189–206. Ilkeston, UK: Bramcote Press, 2006.

Tolz, Vera. *Inventing the Nation: Russia*. London: Arnold, 2001.

Tomashevskii, B.I. 'Pervonachal'naia redaktsiia XI glavy *Kapitanskoi dochki*' and 'Pushkin i Iul'skaia revoliutsiia 1830–1831 gg.' In *Pushkin*, 2:281–344. Moscow: Akademiia nauk SSSR, 1956–61.
- *Pushkin*. Moscow: Khudozhestvennaia literatura, 1990. 2 vols.

Todd, William Mills, III. 'The Brothers Karamazov and the Poetics of Serial Publication.' Dostoevsky Studies 7 (1986): 87–97.
– *Fiction and Society in the Age of Pushkin: Ideology, Institutions, and Narrative.* Cambridge, MA: Harvard University Press, 1986.
– 'The Ruse of the Russian Novel.' In *The Novel, Volume 2: Forms and Themes,* edited by Franco Moretti, 401–23. Princeton, NJ: Princeton University Press, 2006.
Todd, William Mills, III, ed. *Literature and Society in Imperial Russia, 1800–1914.* Stanford, CA: Stanford University Press, 1978.
Toennies, Ferdinand. *Community and Society.* Translated by Charles P. Loomis. East Lansing: Michigan State University Press, 1957.
Tolstoy, L.N. *On Education.* Translated by Leo Wiener. Chicago: University of Chicago Press, 1967.
– *Polnoe sobranie sochinenii.* 90 vols. Jubilee edition. Moscow: Khudozhestvennaia literatura, 1928–58.
– *War and Peace.* Translated by Anthony Briggs. London: Penguin, 2005.
Tunimanov, Vladimir. ' "Podpol'e" i "zhivaia zhizn".' In *XXI vek glazami Dostoevskogo – perspektivy chelovechestva: materialy Mezhdunarodnoi konferentsii sostoiavsheisia v Universitete Tiba,* edited by Karen Stepanian, 11–22. Moscow: Graal', 2002.
Turgenev, I.S. 'Hamlet and Don Quixote.' In *The Essential Turgenev,* edited by Elizabeth Cheresh Allen, 547–64. Evanston, IL: Northwestern University Press, 1994.
Tynianov, Yu.N. 'Pushkin.' In *Istoriia literatury. Kritika,* 133–87. St Petersburg: Akademicheskii proekt, 2001.
Universalismus und Wissenschaft im Werk und Wirken der Bruder Humboldt. Her. Klaus Hammacher. Frankfurt am Main: Vittorio Klostermann, 1974.
Urban, Michael .'Post-Soviet Political Discourse and the Creation of Political Communities.' In *Lotman and Cultural Studies: Encounters and Extensions,* edited by Andreas Schoenle, 115–35. Madison: University of Wisconsin Press, 2006.
Uspenskii, B.A. *Poetika kompozitsii: Struktura khudozhestvennogo teksta i tipologiia kompozitsionnoi formy.* Moscow: Iskusstvo. 1970.
Vatsuro, Vadim. 'Povesti pokoinogo Ivana Petrovicha Belkina.' In *Zapiski kommentatora,* 29–47. St Petersburg: Akademicheskii proekt, 1994.
Vernadskii, V.I. *Biosfera: izbrannye trudy po biogeokhimii.* Edited by V.V. Dobrovol'skii. Moscow: Nauka, 1992.
– *The Biosphere.* Translated by Mark A.S. McMenamin. New York: Copernicus, 1998.

Vinitsky, Ilya. 'The worm of doubt: Prince Andrei's death and Russian spiritual awakening of the 1860s.' In *Anniversary Essays on Tolstoy*, edited by Donna Tussing Orwin, 120–37. New York: Cambridge University Press, 2010.
Vinogradov, V.V. *Istoriia slov*. Moscow: Akademiia Nauk Rossiiskoi Federatsii, 1999.
Vil'mont, N. *Dostoevskii i Shiller: zametki russkogo germanista*. Moscow: Sovetskii pisatel', 1984.
Vogüé, Eugene-Melchior de. *Le roman russe*. Paris: Plon, 1892.
Volgin, Igor'. *Polsednii god Dostoevskogo: istoricheskie zapiski*. Moscow: Sovetskii pisatel', 1986.
Wachtel, Andrew. *An Obsession with History: Russian Writers Confront the Past*. Stanford, CA: Stanford University Press, 1994.
Walicki, Andrzej. *A History of Russian Thought from the Enlightenment to Marxism*. Translated by Hilda Andrews-Rusiecka. Stanford, CA: Stanford University Press, 1979.
– *The Slavophile Controversy: A History of a Conservative Utopia in Nineteenth-Century Russian Thought*. Translated by Hilda Andrews-Rusiecka. Notre Dame, IN: University of Notre Dame Press, 1989.
Wasiolek, Edward. *Tolstoy's Major Fiction*. Chicago: University of Chicago Press, 1978.
Wasiolek, Edward, ed. Fyodor Dostoevsky, *The Notebooks for the 'Possessed.'* Translated by Victor Terras. Chicago: University of Chicago Press, 1968.
– Fyodor Dostoevsky, *The Notebooks for the 'Brothers Karamazov.'* Translated by Victor Terras. Chicago: University of Chicago Press, 1976.
Wellek, René, ed. *Dostoevsky: A Collection of Critical Essays*. Englewood Cliffs, NJ: Prentice-Hall, 1962.
Whittaker, Robert. '"My Literary and Moral Wanderings": Apollon Grigor'ev and the Changing Cultural Topography of Moscow.' *Slavic Review* 42, no. 3 (Autumn 1983): 390–407.
– *Russia's Last Romantic: Apollon Grigor'ev, 1822–1864*. Lewiston, NY: Edwin Mellen Press, 1999.
Wiener, Norbert. *The Human Use of Human Beings: Cybernetics and Society*. Boston: Houghton Mifflin, 1950.
Wilberger, Carolyn H. *Voltaire's Russia: Widow on the East*. Studies in Voltaire and the Eighteenth Century 164. Edited by Theodore Besterman. Oxford: Voltaire Foundation at the Taylor Institution, 1976.
Williams, Raymond. *Culture and Society*. New York: Columbia University Press, 1958.

- *Keywords: A Vocabulary of Culture and Society*. 2nd edition. New York: Oxford University Press, 1983.
- *The Long Revolution*. New York: Broadview Press, 2001.

Wolff, Larry. *Inventing Eastern Europe: The Map of Civilization on the Mind of the Enlightenment*. Stanford, CA: Stanford University Press, 1994.

Woloch, Alex. *The One vs. the Many: Minor Characters and the Space of the Protagonist in the Novel*. Princeton, NJ: Princeton University Press, 2003.

Woolf, Virginia. *The Essays of Virginia Woolf*. Edited by Andrew McNeillie. London: Harcourt Brace, 1987.

Wortman, Richard. *Scenarios of Power: Myth and Ceremony in Russian Monarchy*. Princeton, NJ: Princeton University Press, 2006.

Zaidenshnur, E.E. 'Istoriia napisaniia i pechataniia *Voiny i mira*.' In L.N. Tolstoy, *Polnoe sobranie sochinenii*, 15/16:19–140. Moscow: Khudozhestvennaia literature, 1928–58.

- 'Kak sozdavalas' pervaia redaktsiia romana *Voina i mir*.' *Literaturnoe nasledstvo* 94 (1983): 9–66.

Zhirmunskii, V. M. *Bairon i Pushkin*. Leningrad: Nauka, 1968.
- *Gëte v russkoi literature*. Leningrad: Nauka, 1981.
- Introduction. In I.G. Gerder, *Izbrannye proizvedeniia*. Moscow and Leningrad: Akademiia Nauk SSSR, 1959.

Zhivov, Victor. 'Chuvstvitel'nyi natsionalizm: Karamzin, Rastopchin, natsional'nyi suverenitet i poiski natsional'noi identichnosti.' *Novoe literaturnoe obozrenie* 91 (2008): 114–40.

Zhukova, E.P. *Gerder i filosofsko-kul'turologicheskaia mysl' v Rossii*. Moscow: Universitetskaia kniga, 2007.
- *Gerder v Rossii: Bibliograficheskii ukazatel'*. Moscow: Universitetskaia kniga, 2007.

Zohrab, Irene. 'Public Education in England in the Pages of The Citizen (1873–1874) during Dostoevsky's Editorship.' In *Dostoevsky on the Threshold of Other Worlds: Essays in Honor of Malcom V. Jones*, edited by Sarah Young and Lesley Milne, 120–37. Ilkeston, UK: Bramcote Press, 2006.

Zorin, Andrei. *Kormia dvuglavogo orla: literatura i gosudarstvennaia ideologia v Rossii v poslednei treti XVIII-pervoi treti XIX veka*. Moscow: Novoe literaturnoe obozrenie, 2001.

Index

accidental upbringing, 159–60
Adolescence (Tolstoy), 92, 95, 111
The Adolescent (Dostoevsky): and *bezobrazie*, 157–8; and *Bildung*, 160–1; and Bildungsroman, 12, 147–8; and *blagoobrazie*, 157–8, 168; and breadth, 168; and *The Brothers Karamazov*, 174–5; and *The Captain's Daughter*, 72; and Catteau, 225n25; and causality, 143; and characters, 12–13, 71, 118, 161–73, 232n74; and disintegration, 231n68; and educational debates, 157, 158; and family, 164, 171, 229n44, 233n87; and Grigor'ev, 159; history of creation of, 149–52; influences on, 143; and *The Life of a Great Sinner*, 141, 153; and morality, 74; narration of, 157, 162–3, 232n81; and *Naturphilosophie*, 145, 170, 233n86; and *Notes from the Underground*, 154; plot lines of, 148–9; predatory type characters, 71; recognition of, 13; and religion, 234–5n98; and Russian society, 176; and social dissociation, 228n40; and societal change, 158; spiritual adolescence, 172–3; and spiritual transformation, 168–71; and Strakhov, 155, 228n37, 230n60; structure of, 232n74; and suicide, 147, 233n92; theme of, 232n84; title of, 163, 230n55; and *War and Peace*, 155
The Aesthetic Relations of Art to Reality (Chernyshevskii), 91–2
afterlife, 222n99
Agathon (Wieland), 109
Aksakov, K.S., 24, 92
Aksakov, S.T., 24, 92
'Al'bert' (Tolstoy), 98, 111–12
Alexander I: and *Boris Godunov*, 62; cultural policies of, 17; and Imperial Lyceum, 59; and nationalism, 19; and Pushkin, 60, 83
Alexander II, 97, 140, 156
aliens, 228n37
Annenkov, P.V., 25, 91, 92, 93
Antonovich, M.A., 137
'The Apology of a Madman' (Chaadaev), 24
Arakcheev, A.A., 60
archival youths, 27, 209n37
Arendt, Hannah, 152

aristocracy, 61–2, 68, 85, 156–7, 214–15n79, 222n90, 230–1n63
Arnold, Matthew, 4, 137, 235n99
art: 'Art for Art's Sake' movement, 93, 96; and Bakhtin, 52; as modelling system, 201n20; practice of, 43–4, 91
Artsybashev, N.S., 210–11n43
Arzamas, 61
Atheism (Dostoevsky), 141
Austin, Jane, 77
author, 68
authorship, 51–2
auto-communication, 45–6, 78–9, 215n86
autocracy, 63
autopoesis, 44, 45–6, 213n69. See also *Bildung*

'Bakhtinian Prosaics Versus Lotmanian "Poetic Thinking,"' 201–2n25
Bakhtin, Mikhail Mikhailovich: and art, 52; and Catteau, 225n25; and characters, 13, 164; and dialogism, 40, 41, 46; and distinction between author and hero, 68; and Dostoevsky, 141–2, 153; and Goethe, 224–5n22; and humanism, 200–1n18; and Lotman, 201–2n25; and polyphonic discourse, 40, 41, 45–6; theory of the novel, 9, 53
Balzac, Honoré de, 108
Barsukov, Nikolai, 26
Barthes, Roland, 44, 201n23
Beiser, Fredric, 101
Belinskii, Vissarion Grigor'evich: death of, 91; and Dostoevsky, 135; and George Sand, 33; and Grigor'ev, 31, 32, 36, 50; and Hegel, 94; and Pushkin, 33, 93;
and realism, 49, 50; reverence of, 93; 'Sochineniia Aleksandra Pushkina,' 33; and Westernizers, 25. See also *The Contemporary* (journal)
Bem, A.I., 141
Benjamin, Walter, 3–4, 90, 215n85
Beseda liubitelei russkogo slova, 18
besporiadok, 158, 163
Bethea, David, 40, 82–3, 201n23, 201–2n25, 213n66
bezobrazie, 157–8
Bezukhov, Pierre, 192n2
Biblioteka dlia chteniia. See *Library for Reading* (journal)
Bild, 157. See also *obraz*
Bildung: and *The Adolescent*, 160–1; and auto-communication, 46; and Dostoevsky, 165; and Grigor'ev, 49; and Herder, 4, 35, 106; and Lotman, 52, 77–8; and Morgenstern, 38; and *obrazovanie*, 100–1, 117; and Tolstoy, 12; use of term, 191n20; and *War and Peace*, 107–8; and Williams, 202n35. See also autopoesis; culture; *obrazovanie*
Bildungsroman: and *The Adolescent*, 12, 147–8; and communication, 52; criticism of, 203n5; and culture, 53; as dominant narrative genre, 224–5n22; and Dostoevsky, 141–3, 144–7, 153, 229n47; and Hegel, 177; *The Knight of Our Time*, 11, 108, 109; and Lotman, 39; and modernity, 8; and Morgenstern, 38, 52; in Russia, 178–9; and socialization, 109–10; and Tolstoy, 95, 141; use of term, 191n20; and *War and Peace*, 11–12. See also novels; *War and Peace* (Tolstoy)
blagoobrazie, 157–8, 168

Blok, Alexander, 34, 46
Boas, Franz, 200n16
Boris Godunov (Pushkin), 62, 63, 65, 68, 194n28, 207n26, 208n31
Botkin, V.P., 25, 91, 92, 93, 94, 96
breadth, 33, 70, 144, 159–60, 168, 225–6n28
The Brothers Karamazov (Dostoevsky): and characters, 143–5, 173; and closure, 174; 'The Confession of an Ardent Heart,' 225–6n28; and family, 159–60, 164, 171; and *The Life of a Great Sinner*, 141; and memory, 235n2; and redemption, 117; 'The Russian Monk,' 234n94; and saints, 169–70, 234–5n98; and suicide, 147; and *The Adolescent*, 174–5. *See also* Dostoevsky, Fyodor (works of)
Bulich, N.N., 218n41
Burke, Edmund, 207nn24–5
Bursov, B.I., 230n55
Byronic hero, 71, 143, 172

Cain, Tom, 216n8
The Captain's Daughter (Pushkin): and aristocracy, 85, 214–15n79; and auto-communication, 79; and characters, 10–11; compared to Pushkin's earlier works, 69, 212n50; completion of, 87–8; and dreams, 83–5, 86–7; and elemental and demonic powers, 82; and ethnography and ethnology, 66; and Evdokimova, 211n45; goals of, 64–5; and Grigor'ev, 33, 64–5, 69, 72–4, 81–2; and history, 10, 58, 59, 79–80; and *The History of Pugachev*, 66–8; and humanity, 89; Kalmyk tales in, 86; and Lotman,
34, 40, 50, 51; narration of, 67–8, 78, 88, 157; and paternal blessing, 83–5, 131; plot of, 75–7, 80–2, 83–8, 214n73; and poetry, 75; and power, 87; protagonist of, 72–4, 77–8, 81–2, 83–7; publication of, 58; and realism, 82; recognition of, 10, 13; and Strakhov, 149, 155; and Walter Scott, 10, 81, 83, 88. *See also* Pushkin, Alexander (works of)
Carden, Patricia, 105–6, 128
Catherine II, 5, 58
Catteau, Jacques, 225n25, 234–5n98
causality, 142–3, 225n25
Chaadaev, Pyotr (Petr) Iakovlevich: attitude of, 195n35; and Dostoevsky, 161; influence of, 26; and Pushkin, 60; and Russia, 22–3, 24; sources of, 23
Chaadaev, Pyotr (Petr) Iakovlevich (works of): 'The Apology of a Madman,' 24; *First Philosophical Letter*, 22, 24, 194n30; *Philosophical Letters*, 23, 24
chaos, 158, 163
characters: and *The Adolescent*, 12–13, 118, 161–73, 232n74; and Bakhtin, 13, 164; and *The Brothers Karamazov*, 143–5, 173; Byronic hero, 71, 143, 172; and *The Captain's Daughter*, 10–11; character types, 71; comparison of Dostoevsky and Tolstoy's characters, 118; and Dostoevsky, 142–3; and Herzen, 220n69–70; and *The Idiot*, 175; predatory type, 71, 143, 166; and Pushkin, 112, 213n66; and Tolstoy, 107–8, 111–13; and *War and Peace*, 11–12, 104–7, 108, 109–10, 112–16, 117–18, 127–9, 222n97

Chernyshevskii, N.G.: and Belinskii, 94; and *The Contemporary*, 91–2; and Dostoevsky, 139; and Nekrasov, 216n6; and Tolstoy, 92–3

Chernyshevskii, N.G. (works of): *The Aesthetic Relations of Art to Reality*, 91–2; *Sketches of the Gogolian Period of Russian Literature*, 93; *What Is to Be Done?*, 230n56

childhood, 151–4, 221n86

Childhood (Tolstoy), 92, 94–5, 111

The Citizen. See *Grazhdanin* (journal)

class: and cultural gaps, 19–20; and education, 61; and empathy, 118; and Grigor'ev, 29, 34; and Lotman, 34; and military reform, 230n62; and novels, 77; and Tolstoy, 150; and *War and Peace*, 113, 115, 118–21

codes, 44–5, 78–9, 201n23, 201–2n25, 211n45

coexistence, 142

Coleridge, Samuel Taylor, 59

communication: auto-communication, 45–6, 78–9, 215n86; and Bildungsroman, 52; dialogue, 40; double contingency, 44–5; first type of, 202n26; and Tiutchev, 202n30

Confession (Tolstoy), 96

'The Confession of an Ardent Heart' (Dostoevsky), 225–6n28

Confessions (Rousseau), 154

consciousness: autopoesis of, 44; and Dostoevsky, 141–2; rational consciousness, 103, 129; romanticism vs. realism, 49–51; self-consciousness, 32–3, 133

Constant, Benjamin, 206–7n23

The Contemporary (journal): and *Adolescence*, 141; and *The Captain's Daughter*, 58; dispute over, 135; editor of, 25; and educational debates, 156–7; and *First Philosophical Letter*, 194n30; leadership of, 91; and native soil movement, 137; prestige of, 31; suspension of, 139; and Tolstoy, 92; and *Youth*, 95, 216n6. See also Belinskii, Vissarion Grigor'evich; *Sovremennik* (journal)

Conversations of Masons (Lessing), 220n72

The Cossacks (Tolstoy), 95, 97, 110, 120, 127, 222n90

The Countess of Rudolstadt (Sand), 30

creativity, 201n23, 213n69

Crime and Punishment (Dostoevsky): and conversion, 233n90; and moral regeneration, 145; publication of, 140; and saints, 234–5n98; and Turgenev, 143. See also Dostoevsky, Fyodor (works of)

Crimean War, 92, 107

Critique of Judgment (Kant), 101

cultivation (theory of), 100

culture: and Bildungsroman, 53; class and cultural gaps, 19–20, 122, 165–7; cultural evolution, 77–9; cultural nationalism, 17–18; development of, 35–6; *différend*, 51; European standards of, 137–8; and freemasonry, 114; and geography, 7, 22–3, 36–7; and Grigor'ev, 33–4, 41, 50, 70; and Herder, 4–6, 35, 50; and Karamzin, 6, 63, 193n11; and Lotman, 9, 34–5, 38–9, 40, 52, 191n22; Moscow intellectual circles, 22; and nationalism, 59;

and the novel, 40–1; organic school of criticism, 42, 102; and Pushkin, 58–9; role of cultural critic, 47–8; role of cultural elite, 59, 64; Russian-German connections, 35, 38, 66; Russianness, 4; Russian thick journals, 58; and salon society, 58–9; self-consciousness, 32–3; semiosphere, 42–7; and Strakhov, 144; and sympathy, 72, 73; and Tolstoy, 95; and translation, 39–40; and Williams, 202n35. See also *Bildung*

Culture and Explosion (Lotman), 43–4, 46, 52–3

Culture and Society (Williams), 47–8, 64

current, 35

Custine, Astolphe de, 3, 21

David Copperfield (Dickens), 216n8

Dawn. See *Zaria*

death: and Tolstoy, 100, 134; and *War and Peace*, 12, 115–16, 123–5, 128, 131–4

The Death of Ivan Il'ich (Tolstoy), 134

Decembrists: aftermath of uprising, 20–1; and Dostoevsky, 228n37; and Herzen, 228n37; and Nicholas I, 60–1; and Pushkin, 205–6n16, 206n22; and Tolstoy, 127–8, 228n37; and *War and Peace*, 104–5, 126, 128. *See also* political unrest

Del'vig, Anton, 209–10n40

de Man, Paul, 203n5

Derzhavin, Gavriil, 60, 213n66

'Detstvo, vospitanie i pervye literaturnye opyty Karamzina' (Pogodin), 195–6n44

The Devils (Dostoevsky): character development in, 143; character types in, 71; and family, 148, 150–1; and *The Life of a Great Sinner*, 141, 146, 147, 153; and *Naturphilosophie*, 233n86. *See also* Dostoevsky, Fyodor (works of)

dialogue, 40, 49, 52

Diary of the Writer (Dostoevsky), 118

Dichtung und Wahrheit (Goethe), 50

Dickens, Charles, 216n8

Dilthey, Wilhelm, 191n20

disintegration, 231n68

Disorder (Besporiadok) (Dostoevsky), 163

Dmitriev, M.A., 210–11n43

Dmitriev-Mamonov, Matvei, 192n2

Dobroliubov, N.A., 92

Dolinin, Alexander, 64

Dolinin, A.S., 144, 155, 159, 228n40, 230n 59; *Poslednie romany Dostoevskogo*, 228n40

Dostoevskaia, Anna Grigor'evna, 149, 235n3

Dostoevskaia, Maria Dmitrievna, 139, 153, 227n34

Dostoevsky, Fyodor Mikahilovich: and aliens, 228n37; and aristocracy, 230–1n63; and *Bildung*, 165; and Bildungsroman, 144–7, 153, 229n47; and childhood, 151–4; and consciousness, 141–2; and conversion, 143, 145; and cultural nationalism, 19; and Decembrists, 228n37; and disintegration, 231n68; and double negative, 229n47; and education, 137–8, 155, 157–8, 174, 235n99, 235n3; and first wife (Maria Dmitrievna), 139, 153, 227n34; and Goethe,

224–5n22; and Grigor'ev, 7–8, 29, 32, 50, 139; and Hegel, 164; and Herzen, 228n37; and history, 146; influences on, 143; and nationalism, 143–4, 152; and native soil movement, 25; personal life of, 139–40, 153; and politics, 138–9, 223n7; and Pushkin, 36, 49, 149; and redemption, 153, 224n19; and regeneration, 234n94; relationship between epic and dramatic modes, 225n25; and religion, 144–7; return to Russia, 135; and second wife (Anna Grigor'evna), 149; and Solov'ev, 227n36; and Strakhov, 149–50, 226n29, 228n42, 230n59; and Tolstoy, 117–18, 140–1, 148, 149, 169, 177, 221n82, 235–6n7; and Turgenev, 150. See also *Epoch* (journal); *Time* (journal)

Dostoevsky, Fyodor Mikhailovich (works of): *Atheism*, 141; *Diary of the Writer*, 118; *Disorder* (*Besporiadok*), 163; essays on education, 157; *The Gambler*, 168; *The Humiliated and the Wronged*, 139, 141, 224n19; *The Life of a Great Sinner*, 141, 144–7, 153, 162, 165, 224n19, 233n86; *Netochka Nezvanova*, 229n47; *The Notes from the House of the Dead*, 117–18, 121, 139, 153, 221n82; *Notes from the Underground*, 139, 153–4, 230n56, 231n71; 'Peasant Marei,' 118; 'Pedantry and Literacy,' 138; *The Possessed*, 135; 'Pushkin speech,' 7, 175–7; 'Two theoretical camps,' 137–8; *Winter Notes on Summer Impressions*, 19, 139. See also *The Adolescent*; *The Brothers Karamazov*; *Crime and Punishment*; *The Devils*; *The Idiot*

Dostoevsky, Mikhail, 25, 32, 135, 139, 224n19. See also *Epoch* (journal); *Time* (journal)

Dostoevsky's Unfinished Journey (Miller), 174

double contingency, 44–5

dreams: and *The Captain's Daughter*, 83–5, 86–7; and *War and Peace*, 105, 119–21, 124–5

Druzheskoe literaturnoe obschestvo, 193–4n20

Druzhinin, Alexander, 33, 92, 93, 96; *The Sketches of the Gogolian Period of Russian Literature and Our Attitudes to It*, 93–4

Dukh Karamzina (Ivanchin-Pisarev), 212n49

education: and class, 61; debates on, 155–7; and Dostoevsky, 137–8, 155, 157–8, 174, 235n99, 235n3; educational reform, 17, 20; and Germany, 99–100; and the Imperial Lyceum, 59–60; and Lotman, 39; and native soil movement, 135–8; and Nicholas I, 21–2; and pedagogy, 217n28; and Pushkin, 21–2, 57, 59, 61, 64, 204n5; restrictions on students, 140; and Strakhov, 155; student revolts, 138; and theory of cultivation, 100; and Tolstoy, 97–100, 152, 231n64; utilitarian tradition, 100

Egorov, Boris, 34, 39, 41, 191n25, 197n17, 200n12

Eikhenbaum, Boris, 94, 98, 101, 102, 216n8, 216–17n17, 222n97

elders, 234–5n98

Elizabeth (empress), 21
Emerson, Caryl, 52, 76, 82, 83–4, 200–1n18
empathy, 118
Engel'gardt, V.M., 142, 164
England, 100
enlightenment: and novels, 4; and Pushkin, 57–8, 64, 67; and Russia, 177; and Tolstoy, 113–14
epic. *See* Bildungsroman
Epoch (journal), 29, 139. *See also* Dostoevsky, Fyodor; Dostoevsky, Mikhail
Epokha. See *Epoch* (journal)
Erziehung, 99
ethnology, 66
ethnography, 66
Eugene Onegin (Pushkin), 34, 41, 58, 76, 199n4
Evdokimova, Svetlana, 67, 211n45
evolution, 42, 144–5, 146
executions, 121–2, 124–5

Fadeev, Roştislav, 156
family: accidental upbringing, 159–60; and *The Adolescent*, 164, 171, 229n44, 233n87; and *The Brothers Karamazov*, 159–60, 164, 171; and *The Devils*, 148, 150–1; and Dostoevsky, 229n44; family novels, 93, 110, 164; and Russian epics, 149; and *War and Peace*, 123, 126
Family Happiness (Tolstoy), 96, 98, 110–12, 127, 219nn67–8
Fathers and Sons (Turgenev), 143, 229n44
Fet, Afanasii Afanas'ievich, 96
Feuerbach, Ludwig, 151
Feuer, Kathryn, 96

First Philosophical Letter (Chaadaev), 22, 24, 194n30
force, 35
foreign ideals, 71–2, 111
Four Epochs of Development (Tolstoy), 94–5, 104, 110
Fourier, Charles, 151
France, 96, 100, 110, 115
Frank, Joseph, 139, 143, 151, 227n34
freemasonry. *See* Masons
Freud, Sigmund, 24
Frost-the Red Nose (Nekrasov), 168

The Gambler (Dostoevsky), 168
'The Gentleman's Morning' (Tolstoy), 127
geography: and boundaries, 215n82; and culture, 7, 36–7; geographic separation, 22–3
Germany: cultural connections with, 35, 38, 66; educational system, 99–100; German metaphysics and Pushkin, 209–10n40; German national project, 39; novelistic tradition of, 191n20; organicism, 101; poetry, 205n14
'Geroi' (Pushkin), 211n45
Gershenzon, Mikhail, 23
Gide, André, 4
Ginzburg, Lydia, 124, 200–1n18, 221n86
Le Globe (journal), 212n51
Goethe, Johann Wolfgang von, 27, 59, 77, 99, 196–7n12, 198n19, 212n51, 224–5n22
Goethe, Johann Wolfgang von (works of): *Dichtung und Wahrheit*, 50; *Hermann und Dorothea*, 109, 177; *Wilhelm Meister's Apprenticeship*, 11, 50, 126, 141; *Wilhelm Meisters*

Lehrjahre, 109; *Wilhelm Meisters Wanderjahre*, 196–7n12, 224n19, 231n65
Gogol, Nikolai, 91, 204n6, 213n58, 220n69
Golovnin, A.V., 140
Goncharov, I.A., 92
Göttingen University, 193n16
Granovskii, Timofei Nikolaevich, 25, 151
Grazhdanin (journal), 156, 235n99
The Green Lamp, 206n22
Greenleaf, Monika, 205n14
Griboiedov, Alexander, 163
Grigor'ev, Alexander Ivanovich, 29
Grigor'ev, Apollon: and *The Adolescent*, 159; background of, 29–30; and Belinskii, 31, 32, 36, 50; and *Bildung*, 49; career of, 30–2; and characters, 166; contemporary opinions on, 29; and culture, 33–4, 41, 50, 70, 78–9; death of, 139; and Dostoevsky, 7–8, 143, 175–6; and Egorov, 197n17; and *Family Happiness*, 110–12, 219n67; and global humanistic dialogue, 175–6; and Goethe, 196–7n12, 198n19; and Gogol, 220n69; and Hegel, 30, 42, 50; and Herder, 35–6; and history, 143–4; influences on, 30; and Lotman, 34, 41, 201–2n25; and native soil movement, 25–6, 32, 136–7; and organicism, 101; organic school of criticism, 32–3, 42, 102; personal life of, 30, 31; and poetry, 34; and Pogodin, 30, 31; and Pushkin, 33, 36, 49, 64–5, 69–74, 81–2, 200n10; recognition of, 29, 31–2; and romanticism, 50; spiritual crisis of, 30; and Strakhov, 144; and Tolstoy, 110–12; use of A. Trismegistov pseudonym, 30
Grigor'ev, Apollon (works of): *Moi literaturnye i nravstvennye skital'chestva*, 50; *My Literary and Moral Wanderings*, 29, 139, 159, 196–7n12, 231n71; 'Ob organicheskoi kritike,' 112; 'Stat'ia Lorda Jeffrey o *Vil'gel'me Meistere*,' 196–7n12
Grigor'eva, Tat'iana Andreevna, 29
Gukovskii, G.A., 42
Gustafson, Richard, 104

Hammarberg, Gitta, 211n46
La Harpe, Frédéric César, 59
Hegel, G.W.F.: and Belinskii, 94; and Bildungsroman, 177; and Dostoevsky, 164; and Goethe, 50; and Grigor'ev, 30, 42, 50; influence of, 25, 30, 91
Hegel, G.W.F. (works of): *Philosophy of History*, 71
Herder, Johann Gottfried von: and afterlife, 222n99; and *Bildung*, 4, 35, 106; and culture, 4–6, 35, 50; and Goethe, 198n19; and Grigor'ev, 35–6; and history, 5–6; influence of, 18–19; and Karamzin, 211–12n47; and Lotman, 9, 35, 43, 44; and Masons, 220n72; and philosophy of history, 6, 106; and poetry, 35; scholarly study of, 198n19; and Slavophiles, 24–5; and Tolstoy, 101, 105–6, 128; and Uvarov, 20; and Voltaire, 191n23; and *War and Peace*, 106–7
Herder, Johann Gottfried von (works of): *Ideen zur Philosophie der Geschichte der Menschheit*, 6, 106;

Journal of 1769, 5, 7; *Letters on the Advancement of Humanity*, 6, 36; 'On Cognition and Sensation of the Human Soul,' 222n99
hereditary aristocracy, 61–2, 68, 85, 156–7, 222n90, 230–1n63
Hermann und Dorothea (Goethe), 109, 177
Herzen, A.I.: and characters, 220nn69–70; and Dostoevsky, 161, 228n37; emigration of, 91; and Grigor'ev, 111; and history, 104, 105; on Nicholas I, 21; and organicism, 101; political philosophies of, 170; and Tolstoy, 102–3, 105, 127; and Westernizers, 25
Herzen, A.I. (works of): *My Past and Thoughts*, 21, 29, 103; 'Robert Owen,' 102–3, 118; *Who Is to Blame?*, 220nn69–70
Historical Aphorisms (Pogodin), 102
The Historical Novel (Lukács), 10
history: and *The Captain's Daughter*, 10, 58, 59; debate over meaning and direction of, 24; and Dostoevsky, 146; and Grigor'ev, 143; and Hegel, 91; and Herder, 5–6; and Herzen, 104, 105; and humanity, 89; and Karamzin, 62–3; and nationalism, 18–19; and organic historicity, 79–80; and Pushkin, 58, 62–3, 66–8, 211n45; and Strakhov, 144; and Tolstoy, 102, 104; and *War and Peace*, 105
History of Peter (*Istoriia Petra*) (Pushkin), 66, 205n11
The History of Pugachev's Rebellion (*The History of Pugachev*) (Pushkin), 58, 66–8, 73–4, 211n45

The History of the Russian State (Karamzin), 63, 207n25, 207–8n30, 210–11n43
The History of the Village of Goriukhino (Pushkin), 70
Holquist, Michael, 164
human goodness, 117
humanity, 9–10, 36, 89, 145, 175–6, 200–1n18
Humboldt, Wilhelm von, 4, 59
The Humiliated and the Wronged (Dostoevsky), 139, 141, 224n19

Iasnaia Poliana (journal), 98, 152
Ideen zur Philosophie der Geschicte der Menschheit (Herder), 6, 106
'The Ideological Structure of *The Captain's Daughter*' (Lotman): and auto-communication, 89–90; as career milestone for Lotman, 191n25; dialectical structure of *The Captain's Daughter*, 10; and history, 80; multiple perspectives approach, 40, 50, 51, 199n4. *See also* Lotman, Yurii (works of)
The Idiot (Dostoevsky): and *Atheism*, 141; and characters, 71, 143, 175; children's conspiracy in, 152, 153; and *The Life of a Great Sinner*, 141, 153; and redemption, 171. *See also* Dostoevsky, Fyodor (works of)
I-I communication, 45–6, 78–9, 202n26
The Iliad, 177
Illuminati movement, 220n72
Imperial Lyceum, 59–60, 87, 205n12
influence, 35
intellectual circles: archival youths, 27, 209n37; and Goethe, 212n51;

Lovers of Wisdom, 22, 27, 65, 194n26, 209n37; native soil movement, 25–6, 136; and Pogodin, 27; polarization of, 24; and Pushkin, 22, 65; role of, 59; Slavophiles, 24–5, 31, 59, 92, 136; Westernizers, 25–6, 136. *See also* literary societies
interaction, 142
Isaev, Pavel, 140
Ivanchin-Pisarev, Nikolai, 212n49

Jakobson, Roman, 201n23
James, Henry, 104–5
Journal of 1769 (Herder), 5, 7
Journal of the Ministry of Public Enlightenment (journal), 32
Journey to Arzrum (Pushkin), 66
Julie, or the New Heloïse (Rousseau), 97, 131
Jung-Stilling, Johann Heinrich, 23, 220n72

Kant, Immanuel, 46, 101
Karakozov, Dmitrii, 140, 143–4
Karamzin, Nikolai: and culture, 6, 63, 193n11; democratic sympathies of, 213n64; and enlightenment, 67; and government, 20, 63; and Hammarberg, 211n46; and Herder, 19, 106; and history, 62–3; legacy of, 47; and liberal public sphere, 17; and Lotman, 38, 80; and Myth of 1812, 18–19; and nationalism, 6, 63, 193n11; and Pogodin, 26, 195–6n44, 210–11n43, 212n49; and purpose of literature, 76; and Pushkin, 10–11, 62–3, 74, 208n31, 210–11n43, 212n49; and sensibility, 68; study of, 208n31

Karamzin, Nikolai (works of): *The History of the Russian State*, 63, 207n25, 207–8n30, 210–11n43; *The Knight of Our Time*, 11, 108, 109, 211–12n47; *Letters of a Russian Traveller*, 6, 98–9, 108; 'Poor Liza,' 77, 213n64
Karamzin, Nikolai, See also *Messenger of Europe* (journal)
Katkov, Mikhail, 97
Khomiakov, A.S., 24, 25
'Khudozhnik' (Blok), 46
Kierkegaard, Søren, 41
The Kingdom of God Is Within You (Tolstoy), 103–4, 133–4
Kireevskii, I.V., 24, 209n37
Kirpotin, V., 230–1n63
Kiseleva, L.N., 21, 206n19, 209n39
The Knight of Our Time (Karamzin), 11, 108, 109, 211–12n47
Komissarov, Osip, 140
Korsh, Antonina, 30
Korsh, Lidiia, 31
Krasnoshchekova, Elena, 216–17n17

land reform, 97
language. *See* translation
law, 89
legitimacy (ideology of), 77
Leont'ev, Konstantin, 33
Lermontov, Mikhail Yur'evich, 111
Lessing, Gotthold Ephraim, 220n72
Letters of a Russian Traveller (Karamzin), 6, 98–9, 108
Letters on the Advancement of Humanity (Herder), 6, 36
Levi-Strauss, Claude, 40
liberalism, 60
'Liberty' (Pushkin), 60, 89
Library for Reading (journal), 31, 93

The Life of a Great Sinner (Dostoevsky), 141, 144–7, 153, 157–8, 162, 165, 224n19, 233n86
literacy, 138
literary gatherings, 31–2
literary societies: Arzamas, 61; Beseda liubitelei russkogo slova, 18; *Druzheskoe literaturnoe obschestvo*, 193–4n20; Society of the Lovers of Russian Literature, 93. *See also* intellectual circles
Liubomudry. *See* Lovers of Wisdom
Lotman, Yurii Mikhailovich: and authorship, 51–2; auto-communication, 215n86; and *Bildung*, 52, 77–8; and Blok, 34, 46; career of, 38; and communication, 44, 78–9; and creativity, 201n23, 213n69; as cultural historian, 47–8; and culture, 9, 34–5, 38–9, 40, 52; and Egorov, 200n12; and geography, 215n82; and Grigor'ev, 34, 41; and Herder, 9, 35, 43, 44; and humanism, 200–1n18; influences on, 39, 40; and Karamzin, 80; and *narodnost'*, 20, 193–4n20; and nationalism, 40; and the novel, 39–42, 79; and poetry, 46; and public education, 39; and Pushkin, 9, 34, 41, 47, 49, 51, 75, 89, 191n21, 202n3; and reading, 179; and realistic irony, 41, 50–1; and semiosphere, 42–7, 51, 53, 199n4, 201n23, 201–2n25, 211n45; and *Uchenye Zapiski Tartusskogo Gosudarstvennogo Universiteta*, 197n17; and University of Tartu, 8–9
Lotman, Yurii Mikhailovich (works of): biography of Pushkin, 191n21, 199n4; *Culture and Explosion*, 43–4, 46, 52–3; 'On the Two Models of Communication,' 44, 78; 'The Phenomenon of Art,' 43–4; 'Problema tochki zreniia v romane,' 199n4; *Roman v stikhakh A.S. Pushkina 'Evgenii Onegin,'* 199n4, 200n10; *The Structure of the Artistic Text*, 40–1, 50. *See also* 'The Ideological Structure of *The Captain's Daughter*' (Lotman)
Lounsbery, Anne, 213n58
Lovers of Wisdom, 22, 27, 65, 194n26, 209n37
Lubbock, Percy, 222n90
Luhmann, Niklas, 43–7, 202n26
Lukács, Georg, 79, 224–5n22
'Luzerne' (Tolstoy), 96–7, 98, 111–12, 219n67
the Lyceum, 59–60, 87, 205n12
Lyotard, Jean-François, 51

Mandelker, Amy, 40
Martin, Alexander, 18–19
martyrs, 234–5n98
Masons, 17, 113–15, 120, 220n72
Master and Man (Tolstoy), 116
Maturana, Humberto, 44
maturation, 103–4
McNally, Raymond, 195n35
Mead, Margaret, 200n16
Medzhibovskaya, Inessa, 125, 221n87
Meerson, Olga, 233n87
'The Memorandum on National Education' (Pushkin), 61, 68
memory, 235nn2–3
Mérimée, Prosper, 3
Messenger of Europe (journal): creation of, 17; and Herder, 6, 106, 211–12n47; and Tolstoy, 109. *See also* Karamzin, Nikolai

metanoia, 116–17
Mikhailovskii, Nikolai Konstaninovich, 156–7
military reform, 230n62
Miliukov, A.P., 31–2
Miller, Robin Feuer, 174
Miller, V.F., 26
Mill, J.S., 4, 99
Mints, Zara Grigor'evna, 34, 197n17
Mochul'skii, Konstantin, 141, 232nn74, 78, 84
modernity, 4, 8
Moi literaturnye i nravstvennye skital'chestva (Grigor'ev), 50
Montesquieu, Charles de Secondat, 62, 207n26
Mordovchenko, N.I., 42
Moretti, Franco, 8, 77, 141, 191n22, 224–5n22
Morgenstern, Karl, 38, 39, 52, 191n20
Morskoi sbornik (journal), 217n28
Morson, Gary Saul, 127
Moscow, 22, 30–1
Moscow Messenger (journal): editor of, 26; and Lovers of Wisdom, 209n37; and Pushkin, 28, 65–6, 209–10n40; rationale for creation of, 27–8, 66. See also *Moskovskii Vestnik* (journal); Pogodin, Mikhail
Moscow-Tartu School, 201–2n25
Moscow University, 29–30, 201–2n25
Moskovskii Vestnik (journal): and *Boris Godunov*, 194n28; and Karamzin, 210–11n43. See also *Moscow Messenger* (journal)
Moskvitianin. See *The Muscovite* (journal)
Murav, Harriet, 118

The Muscovite (journal), 26, 30–1. See also Pogodin, Mikhail
'My Genealogy' (Pushkin), 204–5n9
My Literary and Moral Wanderings (Grigor'ev), 29, 159, 196–7n12, 231n71
My Past and Thoughts (Herzen), 21, 29, 103
mysticism. See Masons
Myth of 1812, 18–19
Mythologies (Barthes), 201n23
My Uncle's Library (Toepffer), 95

Nabokov, Vladimir, 177
narodnost', 20–1, 32–3, 193n19
narration: of *The Adolescent*, 157, 162–3, 232n81; of *The Captain's Daughter*, 67–8, 78, 88, 157; dominant narrative genre, 224–5n22; narrative principles, 40
national education. See education
nationalism: and culture, 17–18, 59; and Dostoevsky, 143, 152; educational reforms, 20; German national project, 39; and history, 18–19; and Karamzin, 6, 63, 193n11; and Lotman, 40; and Myth of 1812, 18–19; and *narodnost'*, 20–1, 32–3, 193n19; and novels, 53; official nationality doctrine, 6, 19–20, 61, 100; Pan-Slavist movement, 27; and Pogodin, 27; rise of, 17; and Strakhov, 155; and Tolstoy, 112–13, 177
native soil movement: and Dostoevsky, 25; and education, 135–8; and Grigor'ev, 25–6, 32, 136–7; and nationalism, 33–4; and reconciliation, 137; and Tolstoy, 111, 112, 152

natsional'nost', 193n19
nature, 105
Naturphilosophie, 101, 145, 170, 233n86
Nekrasov, N.A., 25, 91, 92, 137, 159, 216n6; *Frost-the Red Nose*, 168
Netochka Nezvanova (Dostoevsky), 229n47
Nicholas I: and Decembrists, 60–1; and education, 21–2; educational reform, 20; and Pushkin, 61–2, 83, 206nn19–20, 209n39, 214n77; reign of, 21; and Uvarov, 214n77
Nikolai Mikhailovich Karamzin po ego sochineniiam (Pogodin), 195–6n44
Notes for the Fatherland (journal), 137, 140
The Notes from the House of the Dead (Dostoevsky), 117–18, 121, 139, 153, 221n82
Notes from the Underground (Dostoevsky), 139, 153–4, 230n56, 231n71
'The Notes of a Billiard-Marker' (Tolstoy), 112
novels: and Bakhtin, 9, 53, 224–5n22; British novels, 216n8; and class, 77; and culture, 40–1; as dialogue, 52; and the enlightenment, 4; and *Eugene Onegin*, 199n4; family novels, 93, 110, 164; and Goethe, 224–5n22; and Lotman, 9, 39–42, 79, 202n3; and nationalism, 53; and Pushkin, 41, 202n3. *See also* Bildungsroman

'Ob organicheskoi kritike' (Grigor'ev), 112
obraz, 157, 158, 171. *See also Bild*

obrazovanie: creation of term, 4; and Dostoevsky, 156; etymology of, 158; and *Moscow Messenger*, 28, 66; and Tolstoy, 98–101, 109, 117, 127, 134; use of term, 190n7. *See also Bildung*; *obrazovannost'*
obrazovannost', 114, 156, 190n7. *See also obrazovanie*
An Obsession with History (Wachtel), 211n45
Odoevskii, V.F. (prince), 194n26, 209n37
official nationality doctrine, 6, 19–20, 61, 100
Oksman, Yu.G., 73, 206n22
'On Cognition and Sensation of the Human Soul' (Herder), 222n99
On Life (Tolstoy), 103, 133
'On Popular Education' (Tolstoy), 99, 231n64
'On the Origins of Rus'' (Pogodin), 26–7
On the Social Contract (Rousseau), 5
'On the Two Models of Communication' (Lotman), 44, 78
The Order of the Russian Knights, 192n2
organic theories: organic historicity, 79–80; organicism, 101–2, 104; organic school of criticism, 32–3, 42, 102, 201–2n25; organisms (metaphysics of), 161
Orlov, Mikhail, 192n2
Orwin, Donna, 92, 105, 141, 216–17n17
Ostrovskii, Aleksandr Nikolaevich, 7, 32
Otechestvennye Zapiski (journal), 228n42
Owen, Robert, 103

278 Index

Panaev, I.F., 25, 91, 92
Pan-Slavist movement, 27
Paris, 96, 100
paternal blessings, 83–5, 130–1
Paul I, 17
'Peasant Marei' (Dostoevsky), 118
pedagogy, 217n28
Pestalozzi, Johann Heinrich, 95
Peter the Great: and class system, 19–20; and Grigor'ev, 32; and Pushkin, 204–5n9, 205n11, 207n27; and Rousseau, 5
Petrashevskii circle, 30
'The Phenomenon of Art' (Lotman), 43–4
Philosophical Letters (Chaadaev), 23, 24
Philosophy of History (Hegel), 71
Pirogov, N.I., 98, 217n28
Pisarev, D.I., 92
Pletnev, P.Ia., 62
Pobedonodtsev, Konstantin, 34
pochvennichestvo movement. *See* native soil movement
poetry: and Blok, 34, 46; and Grigor'ev, 34; and Herder, 35; and Lotman, 34, 46; and *narodnost'*, 193–4n20; and Ostrovsky, 7; and Pushkin, 60, 75, 203n2, 205n14, 211n45; and Vassilii Zhukovskii, 21
Pogodin, Mikhail: career of, 26–8; and Goethe, 212n51; and Grigor'ev, 30, 31; and intellectual circles, 209n37; and Karamzin, 212n49; and nationalism, 27; and organicism, 101, 102; and Pushkin, 22, 27, 65; and Tolstoy, 101. *See also Moscow Messenger* (journal); *The Muscovite* (journal)
Pogodin, Mikhail (works of): biography of Karamzin, 108–9, 195–6n44; '*Detstvo, vospitanie i pervye literaturnye opyty Karamzina*,' 195–6n44; *Historical Aphorisms*, 102; *Nikolai Mikhailovich Karamzin po ego sochineniiam*, 195–6n44; 'On the Origins of Rus,' 26–7, 210–11n43; *Utro*, 195–6n44
point of view, 41, 52, 191n21
polite society, 58–9, 74, 76–7, 110, 120, 130, 204n6
political unrest: disruption of political systems, 207n25; and Dostoevsky, 138–9, 223n7, 231n68; July Revolution, 206–7n23; and Petrashevskii circle, 30; political societies, 192n2; Pugachev uprising, 203–4n4; student revolts, 138; 'Young Russia,' 138. *See also* Decembrists
polyphonic discourse, 13, 40
'Poor Liza' (Karamzin), 77, 213n64
Poslednie romany Dostoevskogo (Dolinin), 228n40
The Possessed (Dostoevsky), 135
power, 87
predatory type, 71, 143, 166
priceless triumvirate, 93
pride, 129–30
prisoner of war camps, 118–19, 121
'Problema tochki zreniia v romane' (Lotman), 199n4
Propp, Vladimir, 40
Proskurin, Oleg, 60, 207n24
public education. *See* education
public executions, 121–2, 124–5
Pugachev, Emel'ian, 21
Pugachev uprising, 203–4n4
Pushkin, Alexander: and Alexander I, 83; and aristocracy, 68; and Belinskii, 93; and Chaadaev, 60;

and characters, 112, 213n66; and culture, 58–9, 64; and the Decembrists, 205–6n16, 206n22; and disruption of political systems, 207n25; and Dostoevsky, 49, 149, 175–7; and education, 21–2, 57, 59–60, 61, 64, 204n5; energy in writings of, 82–3; and enlightenment, 57–8, 64, 67; exile of, 60–1, 206nn19–20, 209n39; and foreign ideals, 71–2; Germanophile phase of, 66; goals of, 63–4; and Goethe, 212n51; and Grigor'ev, 33, 36, 41, 49, 69–74, 200n10; heroines of, 76; and history, 58, 62–3, 66–8, 211n45; and ideology of legitimacy, 77; importance of, 49; and intellectual circles, 65; journalistic career of, 204n5; and the July Revolution, 206–7n23; and Karamzin, 62–3, 74, 207n25, 207–8n30, 208n31, 210–11n43, 212n49; and liberalism, 60; and Lotman, 9, 40, 41, 47, 49, 51, 75, 89, 191n21, 199n4, 200n10, 202n3; and *Moscow Messenger* (journal), 28, 65–6, 194n28; and Nicholas I, 83; and the novel, 41; plans to open journal, 210n41; and poetry, 60, 75, 203n2, 205n14, 211n45; and Pogodin, 27, 65, 209–10n40; role of national genius, 209n39; and romanticism, 60; and salon society, 74, 76–7; and sensibility, 211n46; and social anxiety, 204–5n9; and Tolstoy, 112
Pushkin, Alexander (works of): *Boris Godunov*, 62, 63, 65, 68, 194n28, 207n26, 208n31; *Eugene Onegin*, 13, 34, 41, 58, 76, 199n4; 'Geroi,' 211n45; *History of Peter (Istoriia Petra)*, 66, 205n11; *The History of Pugachev's Rebellion (The History of Pugachev)*, 58, 66–8, 73–4, 211n45; *The History of the Village of Goriukhino*, 70; *Journey to Arzrum*, 66; 'Liberty,' 60, 89; 'The Memorandum on National Education,' 61, 68; 'My Genealogy,' 204–5n9; *The Queen of Spades*, 69, 212n50; 'Recollections,' 60; *The Tales of the Late Ivan Petrovich Belkin*, 33, 64–5, 69–71, 112, 149; *Tazit*, 72. See also *The Captain's Daughter* (Pushkin)
'Pushkin and Politics' (Proskurin), 207n24
Pushkin and Romantic Fashion (Greenleaf), 205n14
Pushkin's Historical Imagination, 211n45
Pypin, A.N., 21, 114

The Queen of Spades (Pushkin), 69, 212n50
Quine, Willard Van Orman, 40

Radischev, Aleksandr Nikolaevich, 38
rational consciousness, 103
realism: literary theory of, 49–51, 82, 178; and Lotman, 199n4; realistic irony, 41, 50–1, 200n10
'Recollections' (Pushkin), 60
Recollections (Tolstoy), 95
reconciliation, 137, 223n8
religion: and conversion, 145; and Dostoevsky, 144–7; and Eastern Orthodoxy, 227n34; and moral regeneration, 145; saints, 234–5n98; spiritual development, 113,

116–17, 129–34; theology, 103–4; and *War and Peace*, 124–5
Renan, Ernest, 159
'Robert Owen' (Herzen), 102–3, 118
Rob Roy (Scott), 81
romanticism, 49–51, 60, 71, 111, 145, 200n10, 205n14
Roman v stikhakh A.S. Pushkina 'Evgenii Onegin' (Lotman), 199n4, 200n10
Rorty, Richard, 200n16
Rosen, Nathan, 234n94
Rousseau, Jean-Jacques, 5, 95, 97, 105, 121, 216–17n17
Rousseau, Jean-Jacques (works of): *Confessions*, 154; *Emile, or On Education*, 220n71; *Julie, or the New Heloïse*, 97, 131; *On the Social Contract*, 5
Rozhalin, Nikolai, 209n37
Russian-German intellectual connections, 35, 38, 66
Russian Messenger (journal), 97
'The Russian Monk' (Dostoevsky), 234n94
Russianness, 4
Russkii Vestnik. See *Russian Messenger* (journal)

salon society, 58–9, 74, 76–7, 110, 120, 130
Saltykov-Schedrin, Mikhail, 30
Sand, George, 30, 33, 159; *The Countess of Rudolstadt*, 30
Schelling, Friedrich Wilhelm Joseph, 101, 170, 194n26
Schiller, Johann Christoph Friedrich von, 125, 170, 221n87
Schlegel, Friedrich, 41, 200n10

Scott, Walter, 10, 77, 81, 83, 88; *Rob Roy*, 81; *Waverley*, 11, 81
self-accounting, 115
self-analysis, 121
self-consciousness, 32–3, 133
self-development, 100–1
self-sufficiency, 125–6
semiosphere, 42–7, 51, 53, 199n4, 201n23, 211n45
sensibility, 68, 89, 208n31, 211n46
Sevastopol Sketches (Tolstoy), 92, 111
Shakespeare, William, 208n31
Shevyrev, Stepan, 209n37
Shishkov, Alexander, 18, 19
Shklovskii, Viktor, 40, 127–8, 216–17n17
simpletons, 234–5n98
Sketches of the Gogolian Period of Russian Literature (Chernyshevskii), 93
The Sketches of the Gogolian Period of Russian Literature and Our Attitudes to It (Druzhinin), 93–4
Slavophiles, 31, 59, 92, 136
'*Sochineniia Aleksandra Pushkina*' (Belinskii), 33
social dissociation, 228n40
socialization, 109–10, 191n22
societal change, 158
soldiers, 119–22
Solov'ev, Vladimir, 227n36, 235–6n7
Somov, O.M., 210–11n43
Sovremennik (journal), 155–6, 157, 159, 231n64. See also *The Contemporary*
Speranskii, M.M., 59
Spinoza, Baruch (Benedict de), 218n41
spiritual development, 113, 116–17, 129–34
spiritual transformation, 168–71

Staël, Madame de, 17, 189n1, 193n16
Stankevich, N.V., 25
'Stat'ia Lorda Jeffrey o *Vil'gel'me Meistere*,' 196–7n12
Steiner, George, 225n25
Sterne, Laurence, 95, 216–17n17
St Petersburg, 30–1
Strakhov, Nikolai: and aliens, 228n37; and aristocracy, 230–1n63; context of, 214n72; and Dostoevsky, 31–2, 143, 144, 149–50, 221n82, 226n29, 228n42, 230n59, 230n60, 235–6n7; and Grigor'ev, 31–2, 37; and ideals, 228n37, 229n44; and native soil movement, 136; and organicism, 101; and romanticism, 145; and *Time*, 32, 139; and Tolstoy, 98, 126, 221n82, 235–6n7
Strakhov, Nikolai (works of): essays on nihilism, 228n37; essays on Tolstoy's *War and Peace*, 149, 155, 228n42; *The World as a Whole*, 161
Stritter, Yu.G., 26
The Structure of the Artistic Text (Lotman), 40–1, 50
suicide, 147, 233n92
Suslova, Apolinariia, 140
sympathy, 49, 72, 73
systems theory, 43–7

The Tales of the Late Ivan Petrovich Belkin (Pushkin), 33, 64–5, 69–71, 112, 149
Tartu University, 34, 197n17, 201–2n25
Tazit (Pushkin), 72
theology, 103–4
'The Storyteller' (Benjamin), 215n85
'The Three Deaths' (Tolstoy), 111, 112

Thunmann, Johann, 26
Time (journal): creation of, 135–6; Dostoevesky's essays on education, 157; *My Literary and Moral Wanderings*, 29; success of, 139; suspension of, 139; and Tolstoy, 98, 111. See also Dostoevsky, Fyodor; Dostoevsky, Mikhail
Tiutchev, Fyodor, 124, 202n30
Todd, William Mills, III, 58, 76, 192n2
Toennies, Ferdinand, 25
Toepffer, Rudolf, 95, 216–17n17
Tolstaya, A.A. (countess), 97
Tolstoy, A.K., 92
Tolstoy, D.I., 140
'Tolstoyevsky,' 177
Tolstoy, Lev: and aristocracy, 222n90; 'Art for Art's Sake' movement, 93, 96; and *Bildung*, 12; and Bildungsroman, 95, 141; and British novels, 216n8; and characters, 111–13; and Chernyshevskii, 92–3, 216n6; and childhood, 153, 221n86; and class, 150; and *The Contemporary*, 92; and culture, 95; and death, 100, 134; and Decembrists, 127–8, 228n37; and Dostoevsky, 117–18, 140–1, 148, 149, 169, 177, 221n82, 235–6n7; and dreams, 221n87; and Druzhinin, 93; and education, 97–100, 152, 231n64; European trips of, 96–7, 98–100; and family novels, 110; and France, 96, 110, 115; and Herder, 105–6, 128; and Herzen, 102–3, 105, 127; and history, 102, 104; *Iasnaia Poliana* (journal), 98; intellectual development of, 94, 216–17n17, 218n41; and land reform, 97; and maturation,

103–4; and nationalism, 112–13, 177; and native soil movement, 111, 112, 136; and *obrazovanie,* 100–1, 117; and organicism, 101, 104; and 'priceless triumvirate,' 93; protagonists of works, 107–8; and public execution, 96, 100; and Pushkin, 112; and rational consciousness, 129; and Rousseau, 97, 105, 216–17n17; and salon society, 74, 110; and theology, 219n52; translators of, 40

Tolstoy, Lev (works of): *Adolescence,* 92, 95, 111; 'Al'bert,' 98, 111–12; autobiographical trilogy, 92; *Childhood,* 92, 94–5, 111; *Confession,* 96; *The Cossacks,* 95, 97, 110, 120, 127, 222n90; *The Death of Ivan Il'ich,* 134; *Family Happiness,* 96, 98, 110–12, 127, 219nn67–8; *Four Epochs of Development,* 94–5, 104, 110; 'The Gentleman's Morning,' 127; *The Kingdom of God Is Within You,* 103–4, 133–4; list of pedagogical works, 217–18n37, 221n80; 'Luzerne,' 96–7, 98, 111–12, 219n67; *Master and Man,* 116; 'The Notes of a Billiard-Marker,' 112; *On Life,* 103, 133; 'On Popular Education,' 99, 231n64; *Recollections,* 95; *Sevastopol Sketches,* 92, 111; 'The Three Deaths,' 111, 112; '*Vospitanie i obrazovanie,*' 100; *Youth,* 92, 94–5, 110, 111. See also *War and Peace* (Tolstoy)

Tolstoy, Nikolai, 100, 107

Tolstoy, or Dostoevsky (Steiner), 225n25

Tolstoy's Art and Thought, 216–17n17

Tomashevskii, Boris, 206–7n23, 214n73

translation: and authorship, 51–2; and creativity, 201n23; and culture, 39–40; and Dostoevsky, 231n68; of Russian literature, 3; and *War and Peace,* 122–3

Trismegistov, A., 30

Trubetskoi (prince), 31

Tsvetaeva, Marina, 82, 85

Tunimanov, V.N., 231n71

Turgenev, Andrei, 20, 193–4n20

Turgenev, I.S.: and Belinskii, 25; and *The Contemporary,* 91, 92; and Dostoevsky, 143; *Fathers and Sons,* 143, 150, 229n44; and Grigor'ev, 31; and Tolstoy, 92, 97

'Two theoretical camps' (Dostoevsky), 137–8

Tynianov, Yurii, 40

Uchenye Zapiski Tartusskogo Gosudarstvennogo Universiteta, 197n17

University of Dorpat, 191n20. *See also* University of Tartu

University of Kazan, 140, 218n41

University of Tartu, 8–9, 38. *See also* University of Dorpat

Urusov (prince), 102

Ushinskii, K.D., 98

utilitarian tradition, 100

Utro (Pogodin), 195–6n44

Uvarov, Sergei (count): educational background of, 193n16; and Nicholas I, 214n77; and official nationality doctrine, 19–20, 21; Uvarov formula, 61

Vatsuro, Vadim, 64

Venevitinov, D.V., 27, 65, 209n37

Vernadskii, V.I., 42

Vestnik Evropy. See *Messenger of Europe* (journal)
Viazemskii, P.A., 210–11n43
Vinogradov, V.V., 4
'Vital Questions' (Pirogov), 217n28
Vogüé, Melchior de, 178, 179
Volgin, Igor', 223n7
Volkonskaia, Zinaida (princess), 27
Voltaire, 5, 191n23
'Vospitanie i obrazovanie' (Tolstoy), 100
Vygotskii, Lev Semyonovich, 200–1n18

Wachtel, Andrew, 211n45
Walicki, Andrzej, 24–5
War and Peace (Tolstoy): and *The Adolescent*, 155; and *Bildung*, 107–8; and Bildungsroman, 11–12; and characters, 11–12, 104–10, 112–18, 129, 222n97; and class, 113, 115, 118–21; controversy over, 149–50, 222n90; and correspondence, 104; and *David Copperfield*, 216n8; and death, 12, 115–16, 123–5, 128, 131–4; and Decembrists, 104–5, 126, 128; and dreams, 105, 119–21, 124–5; and executions, 121–2, 124–5; and family, 123, 126; female characters, 127; and freemasonry, 120; and Herder, 106–7; history and nature in, 105; and ideology, 177; influence of Pogodin on, 26, 101; intentions for, 126–7, 177; and language, 122–3; life as development, 104; main character of, 127–8; motivation for writing of, 102; and Myth of 1812, 18; and paternal blessing, 130–1; and pride, 129–30; prisoner of war camp, 118–19, 121; and religion, 124–5; and salon society, 120, 130; and self-analysis, 121; and self-sufficiency, 125–6; and soldiers, 119–22; and spiritual development, 113, 116–17, 129–34; and Strakhov, 149, 155, 228n42; Tolstoyan alter egos in, 107. *See also* Bildungsroman; Tolstoy, Lev (works of)
War of 1812, 17–19
Wasiolek, Edward, 222n90
Waverley (Scott), 11, 81
Westernizers, 25–6, 136
What Is to Be Done? (Chernyshevskii), 230n56
Who Is to Blame? (Herzen), 220n69–70
Wieland, Christopher Martin, 109
Wiener, Leo, 40
Wiener, Norbert, 40
Wilhelm Meister's Apprenticeship (Goethe), 11, 50, 126, 141
Wilhelm Meisters Lehrjahre (Goethe), 109
Wilhelm Meisters Wanderjahre (Goethe), 29, 196–7n12, 224n19, 231n65
Williams, Raymond, 4, 47–8, 64, 202n35
Winter Notes on Summer Impressions (Dostoevsky), 19
Woe from Wit (Griboiedov), 163
Woloch, Alex, 162
Woolf, Virginia, 3
The World as a Whole (Strakhov), 161

'Young Russia,' 138
Youth (Tolstoy), 92, 94–5, 110, 111

Zaria (journal), 150, 228n42

Zaychnevskii (student), 138
Zhirmunskii, V.M., 198n19, 209n37
Zhukova, E.P., 193n11, 198n19
Zhukovskii, Vassilii Andreevich, 21, 27, 209n39

Zhurnal Ministrerstva narodnogo prosveschemia. See *Journal of the Ministry of Public Enlightenment* (journal)
Zohrab, Irene, 235n99
Zorin, Andrei, 20

www.ingramcontent.com/pod-product-compliance
Lightning Source LLC
Chambersburg PA
CBHW020358080526
44584CB00014B/1067